Linux® For Dummies, 3rd Edition

S0-AHK-541

vi quick reference

Command	Description
A	Enter insert mode directly after the cursor's position
P	Copy buffered text into the document at cursor's position
U	Undo the last command
#CC	Cut the entire selected line(s)
#d->	Delete the specified characters
#dd	Delete the entire selected line(s)
#o	Add a blank line below the cursor and enter insert mode
#x	Delete the specified characters into the buffer
#yy	Copy the specified line(s) into the buffer
:WQ	Save a file without closing it
Esc	Return to command mode
Shift+ZZ	In command mode, save and close a file

mtools

Command	Description
mcat	Write raw data to a diskette
mcopy [options] sourcefile targetfile	Copy files on an MS-DOS formatted disk to and from Linux without manually mounting the floppy device
mdel [-v] msdosfile [msdosfiles]	Delete a file on an MS-DOS formatted diskette
mdeltree [-v] msdosdirectory [msdosdirectories]	Delete entire MS-DOS tree structure
mdir [options] msdosdirectory	Display the contents of an MS-DOS directory on diskette
mformat [options] drive:	Add an MS-DOS file system to a floppy diskette
mmount msdosdrive [mountargs]	Mount an MS-DOS formatted device
mmove [options] sourcefile targetfile	Move or rename an MS-DOS file on a formatted diskette

For Dummies®: Bestselling Book Series for Beginners

Linux® For Dummies® 3rd Edition

Cheat Sheet

Common Commands

Command	Description
cat [filename]	Display the contents of a file to the standard output device
cd /directorypath	(bash built-in) Change the current working directory
chgrp [options] group filename	Change the primary group ownership of a file
chmod [options] mode filename	Change the permissions of a file
chown [options] filename	Change file and/or group ownership of a file
cp [options] source destination	Copy files and directories
date [options]	Display or set the system date and time
df [options]	Display used and available disk space for all currently mounted file system volumes
du [options]	Report the number of disk blocks each file is consuming
file [options] filename	Perform several tests to verify that a file is ASCII
find [pathname] [expression]	Search all branches of a given point in the file system hierarchy for files matching a provided regular expression
grep [options] pattern [filename]	Search files for lines containing a given regular expression or pattern
kill [options] pid	Send a signal to a process (default is TERM)
less [options] [filename]	View the contents of a file (more features than the more command)
ln [options] source [destination]	Create a link to a specified target
lpr [options]	Spool print job for device queueing by the printer daemon
ls [options]	List information about the files in a directory
mkdir [options] directory	Create a new directory
more [options] [filename]	View the contents of text files and standard output one page at a time
mv [options] source destination	Rename or move file(s) or directories
passwd [name [password]]	Change the password or allow the System Administrator to change any password
ps [options]	Display a snapshot of currently running processes
pwd	Display the pathname of the current directory
rm [options] directory	Remove (delete) file(s) and/or directories
rmdir [options] directory	Delete empty directories
su [options] [user [arguments]]	Switch user (note: not superuser)
tail [options] [filename]	Display the last *n* lines of a file (default is 10)
tar [options] filename	Store and extract files from a tarfile or tarball (archive file)
who [options]	Display who is logged on

IDG BOOKS WORLDWIDE

For Dummies®: Bestselling Book Series for Beginners

TM

References for the Rest of Us!®

BESTSELLING BOOK SERIES

Are you intimidated and confused by computers? Do you find that traditional manuals are overloaded with technical details you'll never use? Do your friends and family always call you to fix simple problems on their PCs? Then the *...For Dummies*® computer book series from IDG Books Worldwide is for you.

...For Dummies books are written for those frustrated computer users who know they aren't really dumb but find that PC hardware, software, and indeed the unique vocabulary of computing make them feel helpless. *...For Dummies* books use a lighthearted approach, a down-to-earth style, and even cartoons and humorous icons to dispel computer novices' fears and build their confidence. Lighthearted but not lightweight, these books are a perfect survival guide for anyone forced to use a computer.

> *"I like my copy so much I told friends; now they bought copies."*
>
> — Irene C., Orwell, Ohio

> *"Quick, concise, nontechnical, and humorous."*
>
> — Jay A., Elburn, Illinois

> *"Thanks, I needed this book. Now I can sleep at night."*
>
> — Robin F., British Columbia, Canada

Already, millions of satisfied readers agree. They have made *...For Dummies* books the #1 introductory level computer book series and have written asking for more. So, if you're looking for the most fun and easy way to learn about computers, look to *...For Dummies* books to give you a helping hand.

IDG BOOKS WORLDWIDE ®

Linux®

FOR

DUMMIES®

3RD EDITION

Linux®

FOR

DUMMIES®

3RD EDITION

by Dee-Ann LeBlanc, Melanie Hoag,
and Evan Blomquist

**IDG
BOOKS**
WORLDWIDE

IDG Books Worldwide, Inc.
An International Data Group Company

Foster City, CA ◆ Chicago, IL ◆ Indianapolis, IN ◆ New York, NY

Linux® For Dummies® 3rd Edition

Published by
IDG Books Worldwide, Inc.
An International Data Group Company
919 E. Hillsdale Blvd.
Suite 300
Foster City, CA 94404
www.idgbooks.com (IDG Books Worldwide Web site)
www.dummies.com (Dummies Press Web site)

Library of Congress Control Number: 00-103656

ISBN: 0-7645-0744-3

Printed in the United States of America

10 9 8 7 6 5 4 3 2 1

3B/RU/RS/QQ/IN

Distributed in the United States by IDG Books Worldwide, Inc.

Distributed by CDG Books Canada Inc. for Canada; by Transworld Publishers Limited in the United Kingdom; by IDG Norge Books for Norway; by IDG Sweden Books for Sweden; by IDG Books Australia Publishing Corporation Pty. Ltd. for Australia and New Zealand; by TransQuest Publishers Pte Ltd. for Singapore, Malaysia, Thailand, Indonesia, and Hong Kong; by Gotop Information Inc. for Taiwan; by ICG Muse, Inc. for Japan; by Intersoft for South Africa; by Eyrolles for France; by International Thomson Publishing for Germany, Austria and Switzerland; by Distribuidora Cuspide for Argentina; by LR International for Brazil; by Galileo Libros for Chile; by Ediciones ZETA S.C.R. Ltda. for Peru; by WS Computer Publishing Corporation, Inc., for the Philippines; by Contemporanea de Ediciones for Venezuela; by Express Computer Distributors for the Caribbean and West Indies; by Micronesia Media Distributor, Inc. for Micronesia; by Chips Computadoras S.A. de C.V. for Mexico; by Editorial Norma de Panama S.A. for Panama; by American Bookshops for Finland.

For general information on IDG Books Worldwide's books in the U.S., please call our Consumer Customer Service department at 800-762-2974. For reseller information, including discounts and premium sales, please call our Reseller Customer Service department at 800-434-3422.

For information on where to purchase IDG Books Worldwide's books outside the U.S., please contact our International Sales department at 317-572-3993 or fax 317-572-4002.

For consumer information on foreign language translations, please contact our Customer Service department at 1-800-434-3422, fax 317-572-4002, or e-mail rights@idgbooks.com.

For information on licensing foreign or domestic rights, please phone +1-650-653-7098.

For sales inquiries and special prices for bulk quantities, please contact our Order Services department at 800-434-3422 or write to the address above.

For information on using IDG Books Worldwide's books in the classroom or for ordering examination copies, please contact our Educational Sales department at 800-434-2086 or fax 317-572-4005.

For press review copies, author interviews, or other publicity information, please contact our Public Relations department at 650-653-7000 or fax 650-653-7500.

For authorization to photocopy items for corporate, personal, or educational use, please contact Copyright Clearance Center, 222 Rosewood Drive, Danvers, MA 01923, or fax 978-750-4470.

About the Authors

Dee-Ann LeBlanc, RHCE, is a writer, course developer, and trainer who specializes in Linux topics. She is the author of numerous books on Linux and other computer topics, including most recently *Linux System Administration Black Book* (Coriolis, 2000), *General Linux I Exam Prep* (Coriolis, 2000), and *Linux Install and Configuration Little Black Book* (Coriolis, 1999). When she's not teaching, developing course materials, writing, or chatting about Linux topics online or at conferences, Dee-Ann hikes with her dog Zorro and experiments on her husband Rob with new recipes. See the latest that Dee-Ann's up to at www.Dee-AnnLeBlanc.com/.

Contact Dee-Ann at dee@renaissoft.com

Melanie Hoag, PhD, MCNI, MCNE, MCT, MCSE, CTT, is a full-time trainer for Productivity Point International in Austin, Texas, where she teaches a variety of network-related subjects that include Linux. She's currently prepping for Sair's LCA (Linux Certified Administrator) exams and LCI (Linux Certified Instructor) certification. Melanie is the author of two books on NetWare: *Exam Cram for Advanced NetWare 5 Administration* and *Exam Cram for Service and Support* (both by The Coriolis Group). When she's not busy with teaching, writing, or researching, Melanie and her family raise and show Texas Longhorns and try to keep up with a few Black Angus cattle, chickens, and two golden retrievers outside Hutto, Texas.

Contact Melanie at MelHoag@aol.com

Evan Blomquist is CEO and Director of Training for Viking Systems, Inc. (www.vikingsystems.com), which develops courseware and provides corporate technical training services exclusively on open source software topics. He has authored three instructor-led Linux courses for Viking Systems and is an advocate for the use of free software in the corporate enterprise. Evan's professional computing career began in the mid-1980s and he hasn't left the trenches since. Holding positions from Computer Operator to CEO, he has seen how the information revolution has affected people and business from many angles. In those rare days away from the free software crusade, Evan enjoys spending time with his family, preferably exploring the back roads of the desert southwest.

Contact Evan at evan@vikingsystems.com

ABOUT IDG BOOKS WORLDWIDE

Welcome to the world of IDG Books Worldwide.

IDG Books Worldwide, Inc., is a subsidiary of International Data Group, the world's largest publisher of computer-related information and the leading global provider of information services on information technology. IDG was founded more than 30 years ago by Patrick J. McGovern and now employs more than 9,000 people worldwide. IDG publishes more than 290 computer publications in over 75 countries. More than 90 million people read one or more IDG publications each month.

Launched in 1990, IDG Books Worldwide is today the #1 publisher of best-selling computer books in the United States. We are proud to have received eight awards from the Computer Press Association in recognition of editorial excellence and three from Computer Currents' First Annual Readers' Choice Awards. Our best-selling ...For Dummies® series has more than 50 million copies in print with translations in 31 languages. IDG Books Worldwide, through a joint venture with IDG's Hi-Tech Beijing, became the first U.S. publisher to publish a computer book in the People's Republic of China. In record time, IDG Books Worldwide has become the first choice for millions of readers around the world who want to learn how to better manage their businesses.

Our mission is simple: Every one of our books is designed to bring extra value and skill-building instructions to the reader. Our books are written by experts who understand and care about our readers. The knowledge base of our editorial staff comes from years of experience in publishing, education, and journalism — experience we use to produce books to carry us into the new millennium. In short, we care about books, so we attract the best people. We devote special attention to details such as audience, interior design, use of icons, and illustrations. And because we use an efficient process of authoring, editing, and desktop publishing our books electronically, we can spend more time ensuring superior content and less time on the technicalities of making books.

You can count on our commitment to deliver high-quality books at competitive prices on topics you want to read about. At IDG Books Worldwide, we continue in the IDG tradition of delivering quality for more than 30 years. You'll find no better book on a subject than one from IDG Books Worldwide.

John Kilcullen
Chairman and CEO
IDG Books Worldwide, Inc.

Eighth Annual Computer Press Awards ≥1992

Ninth Annual Computer Press Awards ≥1993

Tenth Annual Computer Press Awards ≥1994

Eleventh Annual Computer Press Awards ≥1995

Authors' Acknowledgments

As a team, the authors and editors on this project would like to thank IDG Books for inviting LANWrights for putting a team together to take over for Jon "Maddog" Hall on this book. He is too busy leading Compaq's UNIX Software Group, acting as Executive Director for Linux International, and sitting on the Board of Advisors for Sair Linux/GNU certification to take on a third edition, and we're glad to have been asked to take over this time around.

Next, we'd like to thank the great teams at LANWrights and IDG Books for their efforts on this title. At LANWrights, our fervent thanks go to Kim Lindros, who nearly tied herself in knots making some pretty challenging deadlines on this project. We'd also like to thank Dawn Rader for her outstanding leadership and planning skills. At IDG Books, we must thank our project editor, James Russell, for his extraordinary efforts, and copy editor Nicole Laux for her marvelous way with our words. Other folks we need to thank include production coordinator Dale White and his fabulous PLTs for their artful page layouts, Marianne Santy for her painstaking trials, and Laura Carpenter and her team for their CD production panache. IDG Books' Joe Wikert and Judy Brief demonstrated extraordinary insight and taste by hiring us for this project.

Finally, we want to thank our gifted, talented — and above all, quick-witted — team of writers for their work on this book. Dee-Ann: thanks for taking the first chair, and helping to shape the content and coverage for this book, as well as for your excellent work. Melanie: an outstanding job on some tricky and time-consuming subjects. Evan: thanks not only for your great work, but also for your great ideas on some useful chapters and appendixes.
—*Ed Tittel, for LANWrights, Inc.*

Rather than making this a huge mutual back-patting session, I'll just thank the folks at IDG Books, LANWrights, and my co-authors for all working so hard to pull this together! I'd also like to thank Zorro for his great patience when I kept telling him "in a minute" to all of his requests to go play or go hiking.
—*Dee-Ann LeBlanc*

I would like to thank LANWrights and IDG Books for the opportunity to work on this project and for their wonderful teamwork. My gratitude also goes to my fellow authors, Dee-Ann and Evan, whose suggestions and pointers were very helpful and educational. I would also like to say a big thank you to Kim Lindros who coordinated, edited, and performed tasks I probably don't know about for this project and made sure I didn't wander too far off base. I want to also thank my family for giving me time, support, and encouragement on this book. Bob, thanks for your help, guidance, and love. And Lee Ann, thanks for your laughs and hugs and helping Mama "do her computer work."
—*Melanie Hoag*

My appreciation to Kim Lindros, who is always full of good cheer and encouragement, a true professional who miraculously formatted my ranting into something meaningful. Deepest thanks to the Viking crew: Dennis Blomquist, Ken Bowley, Joy Bowley, Marty Fenn, Leon Hauck, Robby Moeckel, and Adelina Musina who continued to row the ship while I worked on this project. My special gratitude to Melanie Hoag, a brilliant teacher and kind human being with whom I'm honored to share an author line with . . . thank you for the opportunity. As always, my heartfelt thanks to my wife Mala and my daughters, Mylan and Solvay . . . you light my way! Thanks.
—*Evan Blomquist, for Viking Systems, Inc.*

Publisher's Acknowledgments

We're proud of this book; please send us your comments through our IDG Books Worldwide Online Registration Form located at www.dummies.com.

Some of the people who helped bring this book to market include the following:

Acquisitions, Editorial, and Media Development

Associate Project Editor: James H. Russell

Acquisitions Manager: Gregory S. Croy

Copy Editor: Nicole Laux

Proof Editor: Sarah Shupert

Technical Editor: Drew Michaels

Permissions Editor: Laura Moss

Media Development Specialist: Gregory Stephens

Media Development Coordinator: Marisa E. Pearman

Editorial Manager: Kyle Looper

Media Development Manager: Laura Carpenter

Media Development Supervisor: Richard Graves

Editorial Assistant: Jean Rogers

Production

Project Coordinator: Dale White

Layout and Graphics: LeAndra Johnson, Kristin Pickett, Jill Piscitelli, Jacque Schneider, Jeremey Unger

Proofreaders: Laura Albert, Marianne Santy, York Production Services, Inc.

Indexer: York Production Services, Inc.

Special Help
Kim Lindros, Red Hat Software, Inc.

General and Administrative

IDG Books Worldwide, Inc.: John Kilcullen, CEO; Bill Barry, President and COO; John Ball, Executive VP, Operations & Administration; John Harris, CFO

IDG Books Technology Publishing Group: Richard Swadley, Senior Vice President and Publisher; Mary Bednarek, Vice President and Publisher; Walter R. Bruce III, Vice President and Publisher; Joseph Wikert, Vice President and Publisher; Mary C. Corder, Editorial Director; Andy Cummings, Publishing Director, General User Group; Barry Pruett, Publishing Director

IDG Books Manufacturing: Ivor Parker, Vice President, Manufacturing

IDG Books Marketing: John Helmus, Assistant Vice President, Director of Marketing

IDG Books Online Management: Brenda McLaughlin, Executive Vice President, Chief Internet Officer; Gary Millrood, Executive Vice President of Business Development, Sales and Marketing

IDG Books Packaging: Marc J. Mikulich, Vice President, Brand Strategy and Research

IDG Books Production for Branded Press: Debbie Stailey, Production Director

IDG Books Sales: Roland Elgey, Senior Vice President, Sales and Marketing; Michael Violano, Vice President, International Sales and Sub Rights

◆

The publisher would like to give special thanks to Patrick J. McGovern, without whom this book would not have been possible.

◆

Contents at a Glance

Cartoons at a Glance

By Rich Tennant

page 295

page 203

page 101

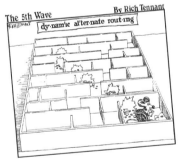

page 9

page 323

page 135

Fax: 978-546-7747
E-mail: richtennant@the5thwave.com
World Wide Web: www.the5thwave.com

Table of Contents

Introduction

● ●

*W*elcome to the fascinating world of open source software that is Linux. In this book, we introduce you to the wonders of the Linux operating system originally created by Linus Torvalds in the early 1990s as a labor of love. Our goal is to initiate you into the rapidly growing gang of Linux users and enthusiasts who are so busily rewriting the rules for the operating system marketplace.

If you've contemplated switching to Linux but find the prospect too forbidding, you can relax. If you can boil water or set your alarm clock, you too can become a Linux user. (No kidding!)

When this book appeared in its first edition, Linux was an emerging phenomenon that was neither terribly well known nor understood. In this edition for a new generation of Linux users, we went after the best of today's broad understanding of what Linux is and what it does, along with the most usable of the many online resources, tips, and tricks that have gathered around this subject.

We've kept the amount of techno-babble to a minimum and stuck with plain English as much as possible. Besides plain talk about Linux installation, boot-up, configuration, and tuning, we include lots of examples, plus lots of detailed instructions to help you build and manage your very own Linux machine with a minimum of stress or confusion.

We also include with this book three peachy CDs that contain a copy of the latest Red Hat Linux distribution — plus a number of interesting widgets that you can use to embellish your installation with the best that the Open Source movement has to offer for your delectation. For this edition, we've added discussions of important topics that have come increasingly to the fore (though not yet to the putting green) in the last few years. And we carry on a time-honored tradition upheld by the computer industry generally and IDG Books Worldwide in particular:

Anything silly you may read in this book is *a feature, not a bug*!

About This Book

Think of this book as a friendly, approachable guide to tackling terminology and taking up the Linux operating system and its retinue of tools, utilities, and widgets to build yourself a capable and powerful Linux system. Although Linux isn't terribly hard to figure out, it does pack a boatload of details, parameters, and administrivia (administrative trivia, in Unix-speak). You need to wrestle them into shape while you install, configure, manage, and troubleshoot a Linux-based computer. Some sample topics you find in this book include:

- ✔ Understanding where Linux comes from and what it can do for you
- ✔ Installing and configuring the Linux operating system
- ✔ Working with a Linux system to manage files, add devices, or add and configure software
- ✔ Networking a Linux system for LAN use and Internet access
- ✔ Customizing, tuning, and optimizing your Linux system
- ✔ Managing Linux system security and resources

Although at first glance it may seem that working with Linux requires years of arduous training, advanced computer science training, and intense dedication, take heart: It's not true! If you can tell somebody how to find your office, you can certainly build a Linux system that does what you want it to. The purpose of this book isn't to turn you into a full-blown Linux geek (this being the ultimate state of Linux enlightenment, of course); it's to show you all the ins and outs you need to master to build a smoothly functioning Linux system and give you the know-how and confidence to do a great job!

How to Use This Book

This book tells you how to install, configure, customize, and tune a Linux system. We tell you what's involved in using this powerful and capable operating system after it's up and running — assuming, of course, that's why you bought this book in the first place — and maybe have some high-tech high jinks along the way.

Because much of the input needed to make Linux do its thing happens at the command prompt — where you type detailed instructions to load or configure software, access files, and so forth — input appears in monospace type like this:

```
rmdir /etc/bin/devone
```

When you type Linux commands or other related information, be sure to copy the information exactly as you see it in the book, because that's part of the magic that makes Linux behave properly.

Failure to follow instructions exactly can have all kinds of unfortunate, unseemly, or unexpected side effects. If you don't know exactly what you're doing at the command prompt, don't experiment for the sake of exploration — you may come to regret your carefree departure from our instructions!

Other than that, you find out how to marshal and manage the many commands, utilities, and programs that help to make Linux the powerful and all-encompassing computing environment that it is today.

The margins of a book don't give you the same room as does your computer screen. Therefore, some lengthy command at the command prompt, or designations for World Wide Web sites (called *URLs,* for *Uniform Resource Locators*), may wrap to the next line when we present them. Remember that your computer sees such wrapped lines as a *single set of instructions,* or as a single URL — so if you're typing in a hunk of text, keep it on a single line. Don't insert a hard return if you see one of these wrapped lines. We'll clue you in that it's supposed to be all one line by breaking the line at a slash (to imply "but wait, there's more!") and slightly indenting the overage, as in the following silly example:

```
http://www.infocadabra.transylvania.com/nexus/plexus/lexus/
          praxis/okay/this/is/a/make-
          believe/URL/but/some/real/ones/
          are/SERIOUSLY/long.html
```

In some cases, Linux or its attendant software wants you to match all input text as to uppercase, lowercase, or both. Do yourself a favor: please, enter all input text as it appears in the book, unless we tell you explicitly that you can take liberties with upper- and lowercase characters. This is especially true for account names, passwords, and filenames where case matters a lot!

Three Presumptuous Assumptions

They say that making assumptions makes a fool out of the person who makes them and the person about whom those assumptions are made (and just who are *They,* anyway? We *assume* we know, but . . . never mind). Even so, practicality demands that we make a few assumptions about you, our gentle reader:

✔ You can turn your computer on and off.

✔ You know how to use a mouse and a keyboard.

✔ You want to install, configure, and use a Linux system because you're curious, interested, or it's your job to do so.

You don't need to be a master logician or a wizard in the arcane art of programming to use this book, nor do you need a Ph.D. in computer science. You don't even need a complete or perfect understanding of what's going on in the innards of your computer to deal with the material in this book.

If you can boot a PC, or install an application on your machine, then you're better off than nine out of ten playground bullies — *and* you can install, configure, and manage a basic Linux system. If you have an active imagination and the ability to solve rudimentary problems, even better — you've already mastered the key ingredients necessary to making Linux work for you. The rest is details, and we help you with those!

How This Book Is Organized

This book contains six major parts, arranged in an order to take you from Linux installation and configuration through the activities and issues involved in keeping a Linux system up and running, if not humming like a (happy) top! Most parts contain three or more chapters or appendixes, and each chapter or appendix contains modular sections. Any time you need help or information, pick up the book and start anywhere you like, or use the Table of Contents and Index to locate specific topics or key words.

Following is a breakdown of the book's six parts and what you find in each one.

Part 1: Getting Your Feet Wet

This part sets the stage and includes an overview of and introduction to the terms, techniques, and software components that make Linux the raging software tiger that's so ready, willing, and able do its operating system thing. Of course, we also introduce you to the Open Source movement that made Linux possible and popular, along with its many and various software components, and lots of step-by-step instructions that help you take a hunk of inert metal and turn it into a functioning Linux system (assuming that the hunk of inert metal you start with is a properly-configured PC and not a lawn mower, anyway).

To be a little more specific, you start out with a Linux overview that explains what Linux is, where it came from, and how it works. Next, you tackle the various tasks and activities involved in preparing for and installing Linux on a PC. After that, you go through the motions necessary to configure your Linux system to do what you want and need it to do. The experience culminates by giving Linux the boot — not to get rid of it by any means — but rather, to fire off your brand-new system to take you to higher heights of computing ecstasy (at least, we hope it's as good for you as it usually is for us)! You also learn how to add devices and software to a basic Linux installation and how to edit and manipulate the all-important text files that govern so much of Linux's behavior.

Part II: Internet NOW

In this part, you explore the issues involved in connecting a Linux system to the Internet, including selecting and configuring a modem, managing dial-up to an Internet Service Provider (or ISP), and configuring the various Internet protocols involved to make your Internet connection work. You also go through the details involved in downloading, installing, and configuring a Web browser for your system, and setting up and using an e-mail client and newsreader.

Part III: Getting Up to Speed with Linux

Linux includes a great many facilities and capabilities, so once you get past initial installation and configuration, you'll probably want to use your system to *do* something. Here's where the doing begins! This is the part of the book where you can read about the Linux file system and how to work with files, directories, and related access rights — called permissions in Linux-speak. You discover how to move in, out, and around GNOME, our preferred GUI, and go through a short introduction to another GUI — KDE.

In addition, we include an in-depth exploration of Linux's command prompt-environments, also known as shells. Part III concludes with an overview of text editors available in Linux, with enough commands and examples of the vi text editor in particular to get you well on your way.

Part IV: Sinking Your Teeth into Linux

Just as no man or woman should be an island, no Linux machine can be fully utilized unless it's part of a network. That's not only because of the many services a Linux system can offer to other users but also because so much of what makes Linux powerful and popular has to do with its networking abilities. In this part of the book, you start with the mechanics of hooking up to a network and managing a network interface. Then, you explore the accounts and services that make Linux able to push packets around on networks, and provide file and print services for network users. After that you delve into the

Linux file system, meeting the root (/) directory and its subdirectories, and we show you how to keep them all in order. You also find out how to use removable media on your system and add a hard drive, painlessly. In addition, you go a little beyond the basic, built-in capabilities that Linux delivers to its users, to examine some interesting facilities that sometimes show up in more highly evolved — or perhaps, more highly *customized* — Linux environments.

You can also read about tuning and optimizing your Linux installation, from monitoring and enhancing your system's basic performance, to some of the ins and outs and keeping busy servers happy and healthy. Finally, security issues are important on any system that makes itself available to a network, and Linux is no exception to this rule; that's why you can also read about what's involved in keeping tabs on who's messing with your machine's files and resources, and how to plug holes and fix potential leaks as well.

Part V: The Part of Tens

In the penultimate part of this book, we sum up and distill the very essence of what you now know about Linux and its inner workings. Here, you have a chance to review answers to the most frequently asked questions about Linux, to revisit some key troubleshooting tips and tricks for Linux systems, and to identify and locate some cool Linux information, resources, and tools online and in print.

Part VI: Appendixes

This book ends with a set of appendixes designed to sum up and further expand on the book's contents. Appendix A delivers a comprehensive list of Linux commands, complete with syntax, and explanations, arranged in alphabetical order for easy access and reference. Appendix B includes a glossary of the various technical terms that we just couldn't help using in this book, given the requirements to expose at least some of the details that make Linux do its thing. Finally, Appendix C lists the details about what's on the *Linux For Dummies, 3rd Edition* CD-ROMs. As we note in this appendix, the materials on the CD-ROM include the Red Hat Linux 7 distribution and all the tools and utilities that pertain thereto.

In addition, CD3 contains four bonus appendixes (these latter files are in the top (/) directory of the CD and are named "BonusAppA.doc" through "BonusAppD.doc") that are referenced throughout the book. Check them out! By the time you make it through all the materials in the book and on the CDs, you should be pretty well equipped to install, configure, and manage a Linux system of your very own!

Icons Used in This Book

The Tip icon flags useful information that makes living with your Linux system even less complicated than you feared it might be.

We sometimes use this icon to point out information that you just shouldn't pass by — don't overlook these gentle reminders (the life, sanity, or page you save could be your own).

Be cautious when you see this icon — it warns you of things you shouldn't do; the bomb is meant to emphasize that the consequences of ignoring these bits of wisdom can be severe.

This icon signals technical details that are informative and interesting, but not critical, to understanding and using Linux. Skip these if you want (but please, come back and read them later).

This icon flags information or steps that are specific to Red Hat Linux. So, if you're running a Linux distribution other than Red Hat but using this book as the ultimate reference tool that it is, take note that this particular information may not apply directly to your system — but it's probably going to be close.

Wherever you see this icon, you know that the accompanying text contains information about what's on the three CD-ROMs conveniently packaged with this book.

Where to Go from Here

This is where you pick a direction and hit the road! *Linux For Dummies,* 3rd Edition is a lot like the *1001 Nights* because it almost doesn't matter where you start out. You'll look at lots of different scenes and stories as you prepare yourself to build your own Linux system. While each story has its own distinctive characters and plot, the whole is surely something to marvel at. Don't worry — you can handle it. Who cares if anybody else thinks you're just goofing around? We know you're getting ready to have the time of your life.

Enjoy!

Part I
Getting Your Feet Wet

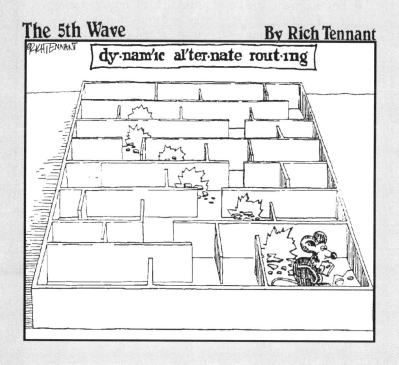

The 5th Wave   By Rich Tennant

dy·nam′ic al′ter·nate rout·ing

In this part . . .

This part includes an introduction to the history, development, and capabilities of the Linux operating system. We also cover the terms and tools that make Linux what it is, along with detailed step-by-step instructions (two chapters' worth, in fact) of what it takes to prepare your computer for and install Linux on your very own PC. We even explain how to configure this marvelous operating system to do what you want it to do and how to boot your brand-spanking-new system into a powerful and productive computing colossus. After that, you find out what's involved in adding new hardware and software to an already running Linux system and what to do if things just don't work.

Chapter 1

Getting Acquainted with Linux

• •

In This Chapter

▶ Describing Linux

▶ Telling Linux apart from the rest of the operating system pack

▶ Depending on GNU and the GPL

▶ Marveling at the Linux company (or lack thereof)

▶ Checking out popular Linux distributions

• •

"Ford, you're turning into a penguin, Stop it."

— Arthur Dent

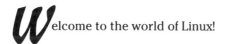elcome to the world of Linux!

Understanding Linux requires a radical shift of thought regarding the way that you acquire and use computer software. (***Note:*** By *radical* we mean *getting to the root of the matter,* rather than, *growing your body hair and camping out in the administration building.*) Your first step to shifting your mind-set is to alter your general connotation of the word *free* to represent *freedom*, rather than *free lunch*. That's right, you can sell free software for a fee . . . and you're encouraged to do so, as long as you relay the same freedom to any other recipient of the software.

Don't scratch your head too hard, these concepts are tough to grasp initially, especially when you consider the conditioning you've received by the marketing departments of the commercial software industry. Perhaps you didn't know that when you purchase most proprietary, shrink-wrapped software, you don't actually *own* the software, rather you're granted permission to *use* the software within the bounds dictated by the licensor. As a citizen of the planet Earth, however, you already own Linux and can use it for anything you like!

Linux: Revolution or Just Another Operating System?

"Contrary to popular belief, penguins are not the salvation of modern technology. Neither do they throw parties for the urban proletariat."

— Anonymous

Author note: Cute quote…obviously Anonymous has never been to a Linux convention!

Before going any further, we need to get some terminology out of the way. . . .

Tux is the formal name of the mascot penguin that represents Linux. Rumor has it that Linux's creator is rather fond of these well-dressed inhabitants of the Antarctic.

An *operating system* is the *software* (instruction) that makes the *hardware* (computer) do something. Whether you're writing a letter, calculating a budget, or managing your recipes on your computer, the operating system provides the essential *air* that your computer breathes.

Who's behind all this hype? You can't open a computer trade rag these days without at least one article or announcement mentioning Linux in the heading. When you stop to consider that Linux has no marketing budget behind it, you see that this is an interesting phenomenon. No company owns Linux and no formal organization earns profit directly from the installed user base! We can determine only one answer that seems to account for the popularity of Linux: *It stands on its own merits*. In other words, it works and it works well. People are discovering that fact in droves.

Linux has been accused of being *just another operating system*. On the surface, it may appears so, but if you look deeper you can see that this isn't so. The Linux project is a flagship leading the current apocalypse within the software industry. A rock-solid operating system because of the model under which it was, and continues to be, developed, Linux represents all that is good and pure in software development.

Two fundamental distinctions separate Linux from the rest of the operating system pack:

1. Linux is licensed under the unique and ingenuous *General Public License* (which we discuss in the next section).
2. Linux is developed and maintained by a worldwide team of volunteer programmers working together over the Internet.

Linux is great for many reasons. Linux was built from the ground up with the following features in mind:

- ✔ **Multi-user:** More than one user can be logged into a single computer at one time. This is a nice feature for the currently popular thin-client computing model that relies heavily on a central computer host to perform the heavy lifting.

- ✔ **Multi-process:** True preemptive multi-tasking enables the operating system core to efficiently juggle several running programs at once. This is important for providing multiple services on one computer.

- ✔ **Multi-platform:** Linux currently runs on Intel-based PCs, Digital/Compaq Alpha, PowerPC-based (Apple Macintosh), Sun Sparc, Amiga, and StrongARM-based computers.

- ✔ **Interoperable:** Linux plays nice with most network protocols and operating systems including Microsoft Windows, Unix, Novell, and Apple's Mac OS.

- ✔ **Scalable:** As your computing needs grow, you can rely on Linux to grow with you. The Linux kernel is currently scalable to four processors, with a flurry of current development activity to increase this number.

- ✔ **Portable:** Linux is mostly written in the C programming language. C is a mid-level language, created specifically for writing system-level software that can be readily ported to new computer hardware.

- ✔ **Flexible:** You can configure the Linux operating system as a network host, router, graphical workstation, office productivity PC, home entertainment computer, file server, Web server, cluster, or just about any other computing appliance that you can think of.

- ✔ **Stable:** The Linux kernel has achieved a level of maturity to make most software developers envious. It's not uncommon to hear reports of Linux servers running for years without any downtime.

- ✔ **Efficient:** The modular design of Linux enables you to configure in just those components that you need to run your desired services. Even older 486 computers can utilize Linux to become useful again.

- ✔ *Free!:* The most intriguing aspect of Linux to most people is the fact that it's free. How (the capitalists murmur) can a better mousetrap be built with no incentive of direct monetary return?

In this chapter, we intend to answer that last question for you. We also hope to paint a picture of the *open source* software development model that created Linux.

So, where did Linux come from?

To understand Linux requires a peek at its rich heritage. Even though programming of the Linux core started in 1991, the design concepts were based on the academic and time-proven Unix operating system.

Unix was developed at Bell Laboratories in the early 1970s *by* programmers *for* programmers. The original architects of Unix created it out of a need for a special layer of software known as the operating system. This system would provide tools for abstracting common computing tasks to a human level, and also provide portability that would simplify the installation of it on new computer hardware as it emerged. In other words, some engineers needed a tool that wasn't available at the time, so they built it.

In 1991, Linus Torvalds was a computer science student at the University of Helsinki in Finland. He wanted an operating system for his 386 personal computer that was like the Unix he'd grown fond of at the University. As a computer science student, he also wanted to look inside the software to see how it worked. This was impossible to do with the proprietary, and closed source, system that came with his PC.

Torvalds set out to write an operating system himself. Six months later he posted his work to the Internet for anyone else who was interested in the work he was doing. Writing an operating system is no small task. Even after six months of hard work, Torvalds had made very little progress toward the general utility of the system. Still, there were enough people on the Internet who shared his interest and curiosity. Before long, some of the brightest minds around the world were contributing to Linus' project, adding enhancements or fixing bugs.

Torvalds originally referred to his project as Freax but later changed it to Linux. Can you imagine convincing your company that an operating system known as *freaks* would be good for them?

Anatomy of an Open Source Software Project

"Linux isn't a product. Linux is an organic part of a software ecosystem."

— Michael Robinson, Netrinsics

To the casual observer (and most corporate IT decision makers), Linux appears to be a freak mutation, a rogue creature randomly generated by anarchy. How, after all, can something so complex and discipline-dependent as a computer operating system be developed by a loose knit web of computer geeks from around the world on a volunteer basis?

Just as science forever attempts to classify and identify the world, technology commentators are currently trying to understand just how this open source model creates superior software. We're sure the reasons have much to do with our innate desire to fill a need with a correct solution. Although the essence of *why* open source works perhaps is yet to be identified, the framework has indeed been recognized.

GNU who?

Imagine, software created out of need rather than projected profit. Even though Unix ultimately became expensive proprietary software, the ideas and motives for its creation were intrinsic. What we usually refer to in singular as the Linux operating system is actually a collection of software tools that were created with the express purpose of solving specific computing problems.

Linux wouldn't be possible without the vision of a man whom Steven Levy (author of the book *Hackers*) refers to as, *The last of the great MIT AI-LAB hackers*. This pioneer and advocate of *freedom* software, who made Linux even possible, is Richard Stallman.

The Massachusetts Institute of Technology (MIT) has long held a reputation for nourishing the greatest minds in the technological disciplines. In 1984, a gifted student and brilliant programmer at MIT was faced with a dilemma — sell his talent to a company for a tidy sum of money or donate his gifts to the world. He did what we'd all do . . . right?

Richard Stallman set out on a journey to create a completely free operating system that he would donate to the world. He understands and continues to live the hacker ethic, which declares that information should be freely exchanged and made available to anyone. This wasn't a new concept.

The early days of the computing industry made advancements by freely sharing ideas and programming code. Manufacturer-sponsored user groups brought the best minds together for solving complicated problems. This ethic, Mr. Stallman felt, was lost when companies begin to hoard software as their own intellectual property with the single purpose of profit.

As you may or may not have gathered by this point, widespread and accessible source code is paramount to successful software development. *Source code* is the term for the human-readable text that we type to communicate instructions to the computer.

A computer stores information in 1s and 0s, or *binary.* Writing computer programs in binary is an extremely arduous task. Modern computer software is usually written in a human language and then *compiled,* or translated, into the native instruction set of the computer. To make changes to this software, a programmer needs access to a program's source code. Most proprietary software comes only as pre-compiled and the source code for those programs is kept under lock and key by the software developer.

Stallman had to devise a name to refer to his free software project. He chose a recursive acronym, *GNU* (pronounced Ga-New), which means Gnu's Not Unix. Having determined that his operating system would be built around the conceptual framework of Unix, Stallman wanted the actual project name to distinguish the fact that his wasn't Unix.

To manage the GNU project, Stallman organized the Free Software Foundation (FSF), which actually sold free software to help feed the programmers who worked the on-going development of the GNU project. Although this organization and goal setting was necessary and important, a much more important piece of the puzzle had to be put into place to protect this new software from the pirates of big business.

The *General Public License* (GPL) is a unique and creative software license that uses copyright law to protect the freedom of the software user. This is opposite of how we usually think of copyright as an enforceable designation of ownership and restriction from duplication by anyone but the copyright holder. When software is licensed under the GPL, recipients are bound by copyright law to respect the freedom of anyone else to use the software in any way they choose. Software licensed with the GPL is also known as copy-*left* software. Another way to remember the GPL is that it means Guaranteed Public for Life.

Who's in charge of Linux anyway?

As an open source project evolves, various people emerge as leaders. The leader has become known as the *benevolent dictator*. People who become the benevolent dictator have probably spent more time on a particular problem and perhaps have some unique insight. A leader becomes recognized as someone who can make prudent decisions with regard to the project. Normally, we don't pair the word *democratic* with *dictator* in the same sentence. However, the open source model is a very democratic process that endorses the reign of a benevolent dictator.

Linus Torvalds is still considered the benevolent dictator of the Linux kernel. He ultimately determines what features are added to the kernel and what features aren't. The community trusts his vision and discretion. In the event that he loses interest in the project, or the community decides that he has gone senile in his decision-making ability, a new leader will emerge.

An open source project has no politics; climbing the success ladder is truly based on your merits. The ultimate goal is to get a job done and get it done in the most correct manner possible. It's a natural selection process at work. Linux only fails after the last person stops using it.

Einstein was a volunteer

Someone who is a volunteer or donates their time to a project isn't necessarily providing a second-rate effort or only working on weekends and holidays. In fact, any human resource expert will probably tell you that people choosing to do so of their own free will perform the best work.

The volunteers who contribute to open source projects are often leaders in their field who depend on community collaboration to get useful work done. The open source concept is no stranger to the scientific community. The impartial peer review process that the open source project fosters is critical in validating something as being technically correct.

Packaging Linux: The Distribution

What we call a *Linux distribution* is actually the culmination of the GNU project, Linux kernel, and a number of other open source software development projects that have sprung up along the way.

Robert Young, CEO of Red Hat, has coined the analogy comparing Linux to catsup. Essentially, the operating system we call Linux, with the GNU tools, Linux kernel, and other software, is a freely available commodity that, like catsup, different distributors can package and label in different containers. Anyone is encouraged to package and market the stuff, even though the ingredients are fundamentally the same.

Because Linux is a very complex, malleable operating system, it can take on many appearances. The greatest advancement with Linux in recent years has been creating an easier installation. The tools and methods haven't traditionally been available to enable the casual PC user to install Linux. Companies such as Red Hat saw this as an opportunity to add value to an existing product.

Rest assured that any of the following distributions have the same Linux/GNU heart and soul running your computer. To draw on the catsup analogy, your distribution preference may be spicy, mild, thick and gooey, or runny.

Following, in alphabetical order, are a few of the major Linux distributions along with a short commentary on each:

✔ **Corel Linux:** This relative newcomer to the Linux distribution list has made an impressive entrance. The installation process is very simple and does a great job of detecting and automatically configuring many sound and video adapters. Corel also comes bundled with Corel's famous WordPerfect word processing package which has been ported to run on Linux.

```
www.corellinux.com
```

✔ **Debian GNU/Linux:** This distribution is one of the oldest and recognized favorites among advanced technical circles. Historically, it's relatively difficult to install; perhaps this can be correlated to the very high granularity of installation options. The Debian team works closely with the GNU project and is considered the most *open* of the Linux distributions.

```
www.debian.org
```

✔ **OpenLinux** (Caldera): The Caldera folks led the way in consumer-izing Linux by marketing shrink-wrapped software packages that include the first graphical Linux installation. OpenLinux also makes good use of your time . . . you get to play a game in the foreground while your computer loads software in the background during installation!

```
www.caldera.com
```

✔ **Red Hat:** Red Hat claims the prize for the first company to mass market (relatively speaking) the Linux operating system. They have validated Linux by packaging the GNU/Linux tools in a familiar method of distribution (shrink wrapped) and have included value-added features to their product such as telephone support, training, and consulting services.

```
www.redhat.com
```

Red Hat Linux 7 was chosen as the standard Linux distribution on which to base the examples in this book and is also included on CD with this book. We show you how to install Red Hat Linux in Chapters 2 and 3, and Bonus Appendix B (found only on CD3). In this book we try to cover Linux in general, so we help you out by including the Red Hat Only icon so that you know when we're talking specifically about Red Hat Linux.

✔ **Slackware:** Of all the more recognized surviving Linux distributions, Slackware has been around the longest. Until about a year ago, the installation interface had remained the same since the beginning. Slackware has a very loyal following yet isn't well known. Like Debian in terms of spirit, the Slackware crowd is respected in Linux circles as the weathered old-timers who share stories of carrying around a shoebox full of diskettes.

```
www.slackware.com
```

✔ **SuSE:** (Pronounced Soo-Za) This distribution hails from Germany where it has a very loyal following. SuSE works closely with the XFree86 project (the free X graphical server component of all Linux distributions). Consequently, they have a terrific graphical configuration tool called SaX.

```
www.suse.com
```

✔ **TurboLinux:** TurboLinux provides a terrific graphical desktop environment along with a few great tools for configuring your system. TurboLinux has also led the way in turnkey installations by providing CD installations exclusive to Server, Workstation, and Clusters.

```
www.turbolinux.com
```

Chapter 2

Prepping Your Computer for Linux

. . . .

. . . .

*M*ost current Linux distributions include the ability to automatically detect your hardware and guide you through the installation process. On most relatively modern systems, installing Linux is painless and trouble-free. But whatever your system is, it's very important that you know your computer's hardware before you begin installation. A little bit of time documenting your system may help prevent a problem either at installation time or later. Plus, if you ever need to replace any hardware, upgrade, or add new hardware, you have a record of your system's hardware.

Your Linux pre-installation preparation steps are like Chinese food preparation, which involves no time to prepare ingredients in the middle of the cooking process unless you want overcooked and/or burnt food. Before you begin, you must have all ingredients assembled and within reach so that while you're cooking, all you need to do is grab the next ingredient, add it to the wok, and keep flipping and stirring. Likewise, before you install Linux, you need all the necessary information and components on hand — assembled and within reach — so that you don't have to (hopefully) hunt around and find the next component as the install screens wait impatiently for you to continue.

In this chapter we address some suggested preparation tasks before you start installing Linux. In addition, we show you how to set up your system to install Linux directly from the CD or with an installation floppy disk.

Knowing What You Need to Do

You got to be careful if you don't know where you are going, because you might not get there.

— Yogi Berra

Before you begin your first attempt at installing Linux, you need to do the following:

✔ **Determine your computer's hardware and networking information (if any).** Most distributions' documentation contain detailed lists of Linux-supported hardware. This is sometimes available in the printed documentation and/or in the information contained on the CDs. If your hardware is very new, the printed or CD-based documentation may not reflect your hardware. In that case, check out the distribution's Web site for up-to-date hardware information. Likewise, if you have older hardware that isn't included in the list of supported hardware, do some sleuthing on the Internet. Linux supports a tremendous range of hardware from the very old to the very new and chances are your hardware will do just fine.

✔ **Make sure that you have access to all the necessary software components to install Linux.** Most distributions place all the necessary software files on the CD or CDs. In addition, these CDs often contain lots of additional useful utilities and software you can install at a later time. If your system contains any hardware not supported or provided for by your Linux distribution, make sure that you have access to the necessary Linux hardware drivers *before* installing Linux. Also, if your system contains old hardware, make sure that the distribution includes a compatible driver or try to find a Linux driver on the Internet.

✔ **Figure out which method you'll use to install Linux.** You can choose from three methods:

  • **CD:** If your computer can boot from a CD and your Linux distribution installation CD is bootable, you can start the installation directly from the CD.

  • **Floppy:** You can also start the installation from a floppy disk. This method gets the process started from a floppy disk and uses the contents of the CD to install the system.

  • **Network source:** This method enables you to install Linux from a network source. In this procedure, you start your computer, establish a network connection to the location where the Linux installation files reside, and then complete the installation by accessing the files across the network. Information about installing Linux from a network source can be found in the README file contained on CD1 that came with this book.

In this chapter, we concentrate on preparing to install Linux from the CD or with the installation floppy disk.

✔ **Determine where on your target hard drive you want Linux to reside.**
If your computer already has an existing operating system, you can choose to retain that operating system and have the option to boot to Linux or the other operating system. You can also choose to remove any existing operating systems and install just Linux. Furthermore, you can install another operating system or another Linux system later. All of this depends, of course, upon how much hard drive space you have available. In this case, you may want to make sure that you leave some disk space for any future operating systems. In Chapter 3, we address the different installation options that can affect your disk architecture.

You must complete some basic tasks prior to beginning any Linux installation. The first of these is to locate the documentation. If you encounter a required configuration setting or problem during installation, the documentation may help you get over the roadblock. In addition, the Linux documentation can help you get the most out of your system after installation. Depending on your Linux distribution and how you obtained it, the documentation may exist in different forms. Some come with printed documentation and most include the documentation on the CD or CDs. In addition, most distributions have the documentation available on their Web sites. If you come across a situation that the documentation doesn't cover, refer to your distribution's Web site or check out one of the many Linux reference Web sites.

Knowing Your Hardware

Before you begin installing Linux, document your computer's hardware. The critical items that you need to note are the processor, memory, hard drive(s), CD-ROM drive, mouse, video card, monitor, network card, modem, and printer. We explain this in detail in the following list:

✔ **CPU (central processing unit):** Linux can run on a wide range of processor brands, speeds, and models. In general, the faster the processor, the better your performance. Other than maybe some really, really old processors and architectures, your system should do just fine.

✔ **RAM (random access memory):** Linux doesn't require a lot of memory to run when compared to other popular current commercial operating systems. But you should still have at least 8MB of physical memory and you'll do better with a minimum of 32MB. Of course, Linux supports a huge amount of memory if your system has more than 32MB of RAM.

- **Hard drive:** Document the number and type of hard drives you have (IDE or SCSI).

    - **For IDE systems, note the channels the drives are attached to and whether they're a master or slave.**

    - **For SCSI systems, document the SCSI ID numbers.**

    In addition to the disk hardware, if you already have an existing operating system that you want to retain, note what drive or drives it's on and the space allocated. Linux recognizes most other operating systems' file architectures, but it's a good idea to know what's already present to verify what Linux detects.

    Besides your disk and file system architecture, you need to make sure that you have sufficient disk space to install Linux. In Chapter 3, we cover installing the Workstation mode of the Red Hat Linux 7 distribution, which requires about 1GB of disk space. If you choose to install all the packages on the Red Hat distribution, the total amount of disk space that you need is about 2.1GB. Some distributions' complete install run around 3GB. Each distribution's documentation tell you the amount of disk space that you need.

- **CD-ROM drive:** The type of CD drive in your system (IDE or SCSI) should be documented. If you're using an IDE CD drive, it's most likely using the *ATAPI* (*AT A*ttachment *P*acket *I*nterface) standard. ATAPI CD-ROM drives are supported by many operating systems and system architecture. If your IDE CD-ROM does not support the ATAPI standard, make a note of the CD-ROM's architecture.

- **Mouse:** If you're planning on using a mouse, note the brand and model number if specified on the mouse. If it's a serial mouse, indicate which serial port it's attached to. For both serial and PS/2 mice, note the number of buttons (2 or 3) and whether or not it has a wheel. If you aren't sure of the type of mouse you have, look at its connector where it's plugged into your machine. If the connector is round with pins sticking out, you've got a PS/2 mouse. If the connector is rectangular with holes, it's a serial mouse.

- **Video card:** Documenting your video hardware is very important. You need to know the brand and model number of your video card or interface and the amount of video memory and supported resolutions. Also document the make and model of your video monitor and its capabilities.

Setting up the video parameters is the most likely place that the hardware probe may fail or return incorrect information. Unfortunately, many types and versions of video cards are available in addition to onboard video. Some onboard video, which is built into the computer's main circuitry, isn't exactly the same as its comparable external video card. You must establish the details of your video hardware before beginning any Linux installation.

✔ **Network card:** If you have a network card, document its manufacturer and model number. Note whether it's ISA (*I*ndustry *S*tandard *A*rchitecture) or PCI (*P*eripheral *C*omponent *I*nterconnect) architecture and jot down the interrupt, I/O port, base memory, and DMA (Direct Memory Access) channel parameters. If you are *not* using DHCP (Dynamic Host Configuration Protocol), note the IP (Internet Protocol) address, network mask, default gateway, and DNS (Domain Name System) server values you're using.

✔ **Modem:** If you have a modem that you plan on using with Linux, document its make and model number. If it's an external modem, indicate which serial port it's attached to. If it's an internal modem, make note whether it's PCI or ISA, the interrupt, I/O port, base memory, and DMA channel details. Also, document the maximum communication rate and whether or not it supports the ability to send and/or receive fax documents. If you have a Winmodem, or software modem, you probably can't make it work in Linux. See Chapter 7 for more information.

✔ **Printer:** You need to document the printer attachment point. If it's connected to a computer, note the parallel port it's attached to. If the printer is directly connected to the network, document its IP information. Also document the manufacturer, model number, memory, and language capabilities of the printer.

Finding Out What Hardware You Have

> *Not everything that can be counted counts, and not everything that counts can be counted.*
>
> — Albert Einstein (1879-1955)

Now that you have an idea of the information you need to gather, how do you find what you've got? Do you have to rip out all the hardware and hope that you can put it back the same way you took it out? Probably not. You can determine your computer's hardware in many ways:

✔ **Refer to the documentation that came with your system.** If you purchased a complete, preassembled system within the last couple of years, you should have a nice pile of literature — assuming you know where you put it.

✔ **Check out your system provider's Web site.** If you've misplaced your original documentation, some complete system providers supply the details of your system on their Web sites. In some cases, all you need to do is enter your system's asset tag or unit/customer number and the details of your system appear in your browser.

✔ **Use an existing operating system to document the hardware.** For example, if your system has Windows 9*x*/ME, go to the System Control Panel and choose the Device Manager tab. You can either write down the information or use the Print button to send the information to a printer. If your system has Windows NT (Workstation or Server), use the Windows NT Diagnostics tool to gather the information. The NT diagnostic utility also enables you to print out the information.

✔ **Download PC hardware detect tools.** If you don't have any diagnostic tools and you have a relatively current version of DOS, you can download various PC hardware detect tools from the Internet.

PC-CONFIG is a tool that you can download from the Internet at www. holin.com. The PC-CONFIG tool contains several screens of information and menus to choose hardware areas and options. This tool is shareware and the usage and fee information is available from the Holin Datentechnik Web site.

✔ **Gather information by reading the screen when the computer starts.** If your system doesn't contain any operating systems and you don't have any of your system's documentation, you can resort to reading the screen as your computer starts. On some systems, the video information appears as the computer boots. You may have to reboot several times to read the information if it goes by too fast. Also, some systems display the PCI components and their settings as the system is starting up. Again, you may need to reboot several times to capture all the information.

✔ **Access the BIOS (Basic Input/Output System) information.** Stored in a small area of memory and retained by a battery, this is sometimes referred to as *CMOS* (which stands for *C*omplimentary *M*etal-*O*xide *S*emiconductor), which indicates the type of computer chip that can store and retain information. The type of information stored in the BIOS can be very little to quite a lot. Some newer systems may display several screens of information about the computer's hardware.

In order to access the BIOS, you need to get into the BIOS before any operating systems load. Most manufacturers indicate the keyboard key or key sequence to get into the BIOS, or Setup, on the screen when the system is starting up. If you can't find the keyboard sequence, check out the manufacturer's Web site. After you've entered the BIOS, you typically navigate around with the arrow keys, Tab key, or Enter key. In some BIOS environments, the function keys are also used.

One of the BIOS screens usually includes information about the computer's drives — floppy drive, hard drive, and CD-ROM drive — and the amount of memory contained in the computer.

BIOS screens usually includes settings for the type of mouse and other IDE settings. Your system may contain several other BIOS setting screens. Check these out to see if you can determine any more information about your system's hardware.

Trying to Boot from CD-ROM

A really nice installation option is the ability to install Linux from the CD-ROM. This means that you don't have to have any other operating system already installed on your hard drive to install Linux. Before you attempt to set up your system to boot from a CD, you must complete two steps:

1. **Determine if the Linux installation CD is bootable.** You see this information in the documentation or in the features listing of your Linux distribution.

   The version of Linux that comes on the CDs with this book — Red Hat Linux 7, to be exact — allows installation directly from CD.

2. **Determine if your system is capable of booting from a CD.** If you've ever booted your system from a CD, you'll have no problem booting from the Linux installation CD.

Whether or not you've booted from a CD before, your system must be configured to boot from the CD first. Most computers enable you to boot from the hard drive or floppy disk. Many others also enable you to boot from a CD or other removable media such as a Zip drive. Your system's BIOS configuration enables you to select the storage devices that are checked for an operating system at boot time.

An easy way to tell if your computer can boot from CD-ROM is to simply put CD1 that came with this book into your CD-ROM drive and boot (or reboot) your computer. If your computer boots from the CD, your computer is set up to boot from CD-ROM. If your computer ignores the CD-ROM, your computer isn't set up to boot from CD-ROM. In that case, you can either try to set up your computer to boot from CD-ROM or give up and create a boot disk, as we show you how to do in the following section.

When you start your computer, you should see a line of text indicating the keyboard sequence to enter your computer's setup or BIOS settings. If this information doesn't appear on-screen and you don't know the key sequence, check the documentation that came with your computer or check your computer manufacturer's Web site.

If your computer can't boot from a CD, you won't see an option to choose the CD as a bootable device in the BIOS settings.

Refer to the BIOS settings to see the order in which the system looks for an operating system. If your computer can boot from a CD and is set up that way, the first device searched is the CD drive. Many BIOSes allow you to specify the order of devices to boot from. For example, if your system's boot device order is as follows, the system first tries to boot from the CD-ROM.

Device Number	Device Type
1st	CD-ROM
2nd	Floppy disk
3rd	Hard drive
4th	Network

After booting from the CD-ROM fails (if there's not a bootable CD-ROM in the drive), the system then checks the floppy drive, then the hard drive, and finally a network boot configuration. In your system's BIOS, make sure the CD is listed first in the sequence. Make sure to save your changes before exiting the BIOS; otherwise, the items you set don't take effect.

Setting Up to Boot from the Floppy Installation Disk

If your system can't boot from a CD, the Linux installation CD isn't bootable, or you just don't want to boot from the CD, you can start the installation from a floppy disk. Some distributions include the installation boot floppy disk, but some don't (Red Hat Linux 7, which accompanies this book, does not). Whatever the situation is, you can make the installation floppy disk on another system that's running MS-DOS or Windows or Linux.

When you're creating a Linux installation boot disk, the original contents of the floppy disk are erased, so make sure the disk contains nothing that you want to keep.

Usually, a directory of DOS utilities is on the Linux installation CD — it's called dosutils on CD1 that came with this book. The name of the utility that creates the installation boot disk is called rawrite.exe. The documentation for rawrite is located in the same directory as the utility. You can use Windows Explorer or the DOS dir command to investigate the contents of the /dosutils directory. In addition, the CD1 also contains disk image files, which contain the information that's copied to the installation boot disk. With Red Hat Linux 7 on CD1 that comes with this book, image files are kept in the /images directory. The images directory contains images for English and other languages.

To make an English-language boot disk on a Windows 9x/ME system using Red Hat Linux 7 and the CDs that came with this book, follow these steps:

1. **Insert CD1 that came with this book into the CD drive and make a note of the drive letter that corresponds to your CD drive.**

2. **Open an MS-DOS window by choosing Start➪Programs➪MS-DOS Prompt.**

3. **Change over to the drive that corresponds to your CD drive by typing the drive letter followed by a colon at the command prompt and pressing Enter.**

   The prompt in the MS-DOS window changes to reflect the CD's drive letter.

4. **To change to the** dosutils **directory, type** cd dosutils **at the command prompt and press Enter.**

5. **To create a boot disk in floppy drive A, type** rawrite -f ..\images\ boot.img -d a.

   The -f parameter specifies the location and name of the image file. The -d option indicates the floppy drive letter.

   The following instruction phrase is echoed in the MS-DOS window:

   ```
   Please insert a formatted diskette into drive A and press
   -ENTER-  :
   ```

6. **Insert a blank, formatted, 1.44 MB floppy disk into the floppy drive and press Enter.**

   When the process is complete, the MS-DOS prompt returns to reflect the /dosutils directory and the flashing underscore cursor appears.

You can also create a boot floppy disk from another Linux system. To make an English-language boot disk using Red Hat Linux 7, follow these steps:

1. **Insert CD1 that came with this book into the CD drive and the floppy disk into the disk drive.**

2. **In a command or terminal window, mount CD1 with the following command:**

   ```
   mount /dev/cdrom /mnt/cdrom
   ```

   This command makes the CD accessible by the system.

3. **Navigate to the images directory by entering the** cd /mnt/cdrom/ images **command.**

4. **Copy the installation disk image onto the floppy disk by typing the following line at the prompt and pressing Enter:**

   ```
   dd if=boot.img of=/dev/fd0
   ```

   Your floppy disk drive light comes on while the image is copied to disk. The light goes out when the copy process is complete; the command prompt appears.

After you've created the installation boot disk, you need to configure, or verify, that your computer is set to boot from the floppy drive first. The easiest way to do this is to insert a floppy disk into your main floppy drive, make sure no other drives have media in them (such as a CD in your CD-ROM drive), and then reboot your computer. If your computer boots from the floppy, you're set.

If your computer doesn't boot from the floppy when you start your computer, remove the disk and reboot your computer. You should see a line of text indicating the keyboard sequence to enter your computer's setup or BIOS settings. If this information doesn't appear on-screen and you don't know the key sequence, find the documentation that came with your computer or check your computer manufacturer's Web site.

Refer to the BIOS settings to see the order in which the system looks for an operating system. If your computer is set up to boot from a floppy drive, the first device searched is the floppy drive. Many BIOSes allow you to specify the order of devices to boot from. For example, if your system's boot device order is in the same order as the following table represents, the system first tries to boot from the floppy disk.

Device Number	*Device Type*
1st	Floppy disk
2nd	Hard drive
3rd	CD-ROM
4th	Network

If that fails, the system then checks the hard drive, then the CD drive, and finally a network boot configuration. In your system's BIOS, make sure the floppy drive is listed first in the sequence. Save your changes before exiting the BIOS; otherwise, the items you set don't take effect.

Setting Up to Install Linux Using DOS

If your computer already contains a DOS operating system (Microsoft or other vendor's versions), you can start the installation without the installation floppy or booting from the CD.

To start the process at a DOS prompt using Red Hat Linux 7, follow these steps:

You *cannot* use this process at an MS-DOS prompt window inside of Windows 9*x*/ME or at a Command Prompt window in Windows NT/2000.

1. **Insert CD1 that came with this book into the CD drive and note the drive letter of the CD drive.**

2. **Change over to the drive letter that corresponds to your CD drive by typing the drive letter followed by a colon and pressing Enter.**

   The prompt changes to reflect the CD's drive letter.

3. **To change to the** /dosutils **directory, type** cd dosutils **at the command prompt and press Enter.**

4. **To begin installation, type** autoboot **at the command prompt and press Enter.**

   The installation process that uses the graphical interface begins.

Customizing Your Disk Partitions

Before you install Linux, you can modify and set up your disk partitions. If you already have an existing operating system on your drive(s) that you want to keep but all of the disk space is used, you need to resize your partitions before you begin installing Linux. Also, some people prefer setting up all the disk partitions for Linux before installation rather than during the installation process. See Chapter 3 for information about managing disk partitions.

Commercial programs are on the market, such as Partition Magic, that can resize, move, and add partitions for a wide range of operating systems. In addition, free programs (some are shareware) are available that you can also use to modify your disk architecture.

Partitioning safely with fips

Probably the most common free disk partition modification program is fips (*F*irst nondestructive *I*nteractive *P*artition *S*plitting program). Most Linux installation CDs contain this program. If not, you can download it from the Internet.

On the Red Hat Linux 7 CD1 that came with this book, it's contained in the /dosutils directory. In that directory, you find two subdirectories for fips — /fips15c and /fips20. The /fips20 directory contains the most recent version of fips and the documentation.

As its name implies, fips enables you to modify your disk partitions without destroying existing data or operating systems. However, because you'll be modifying your disks' file system architecture, make a backup of your existing files and important data before using fips.

We *highly* recommend that you read through the entire documentation before attempting to use fips. In addition to the documentation, we recommend also reading through the /dosutils/fipsdocs/fips.faq file located on CD1 that accompanies this book.

If possible, have the fips documentation in front of you before proceeding. To set up and use fips, follow these steps:

1. **Insert a DOS bootable floppy disk into the disk drive.**

2. **On a system running DOS or in a MS-DOS window in Windows 9***x***/ME, type** format a: /s **at the command prompt and press Enter.**

   The a: refers to the drive letter of your floppy drive — insert the appropriate drive letter on your system if it isn't a:. The /s copies the necessary files to the floppy to make it bootable.

3. **Copy the following files from the** /fips20 **directory to the floppy disk:**

   - restorrb.exe

   - fips.exe

   - errors.txt

   If you're using Windows 9*x*/ME, you can use Windows Explorer to copy the files to the floppy disk. For DOS or in a DOS window under Windows 9*x*/ME, you can use the xcopy or copy command.

   Before using fips, you must defragment your hard drive. Windows 9*x*/ME includes a defragmentation utility.

4. **Click the Start button and choose Run.**

5. **Type** defrag **in the Open field and click OK.**

   Defragmentation shuffles around your files so that they occupy the beginning of your disk's storage area. This frees up unused space at the end of the drive so that you can shrink your partition. If you don't defragment your hard drive, you may not be able to shrink your partition.

   The Defragmentation Utility dialog box opens.

6. **Select your drive or drives and click OK.**

   Depending on the size of your hard drive, the number of files, and how much the drive is already fragmented, defragmentation may take a *long time*. A long time may translate to *several hours*. We recommend that you start this task in the evening and allow defragmentation to occur overnight.

7. **Reboot your machine with the bootable `fips` disk you created.**

   Make sure you reboot and run from the floppy. Do NOT use `fips` within an MS-DOS window in Windows 9*x*/ME or within a DOS emulator. Bad things may happen. In Windows ME, you will have to reboot using the disk because there is no "Restart in MS-DOS Mode" option.

8. **After the system reboots to DOS, type `fips` at the command prompt and press Enter.**

   The initial screen that you see contains information about some `fips` cautions. After reading the information, press any key to continue.

   If your system has more than one drive, the utility presents the drives and asks you to select one.

9. **Type the number that corresponds to the drive you want to work with.**

   The screen displays the partition table for the drive that you selected, and `fips` asks for a partition number, as shown in Figure 2-1.

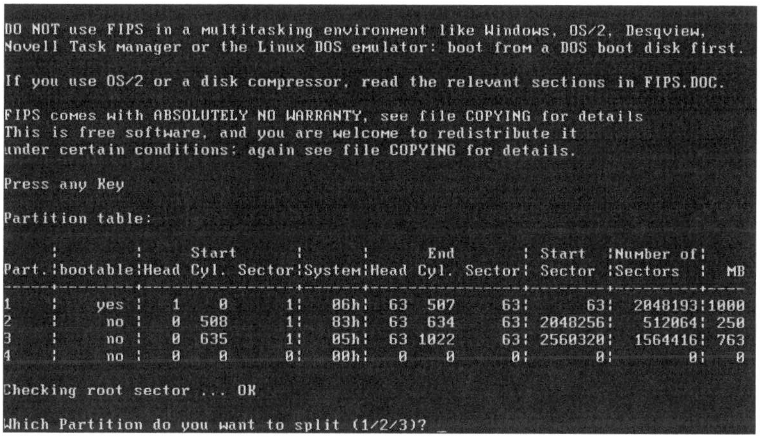

```
DO NOT use FIPS in a multitasking environment like Windows, OS/2, Desqview,
Novell Task manager or the Linux DOS emulator: boot from a DOS boot disk first.

If you use OS/2 or a disk compressor, read the relevant sections in FIPS.DOC.

FIPS comes with ABSOLUTELY NO WARRANTY, see file COPYING for details
This is free software, and you are welcome to redistribute it
under certain conditions: again see file COPYING for details.

Press any Key

Partition table:

     |        |      Start        |      |      End         | Start   |Number of|
Part.|bootable|Head Cyl. Sector|System|Head Cyl. Sector| Sector |Sectors  |  MB
-----+--------+----------------+------+----------------+--------+---------+----
1    |   yes  |  1    0       1|  06h|  63  507      63|      63|  2048193|1000
2    |    no  |  0  508       1|  83h|  63  634      63| 2048256|   512064| 250
3    |    no  |  0  635       1|  05h|  63 1022      63| 2560320|  1564416| 763
4    |    no  |  0    0       0|  00h|   0    0       0|       0|        0|   0

Checking root sector ... OK

Which Partition do you want to split (1/2/3)? _
```

Figure 2-1: Example of the `fips` utility.

10. **At the bottom of the screen, type the number that corresponds to the partition that you want to split.**

    The screen displays information about the partition you've selected. At the bottom of the screen, the application asks if you want to make a backup copy of your root and boot sector before proceeding. If you choose to make a backup, you're able to go back and undo the partition split. Having this backup also enables you to restore your partition architecture if you have a problem using `fips`.

11. **Insert a blank formatted disk into the disk drive and type** y.

12. **Use the arrow keys on the keyboard to adjust the size of the two partitions to the values that you want and press Enter.**

    fips asks if you want to continue or edit the partition table.

13. **If you're satisfied with your changes, type** c.

    At the bottom of the screen, the application asks if you want to write the new partition information to disk.

14. **To apply the changes and exit the application, type** y; **to ignore the changes and exit the application, type** n.

Partitioning not-so-safely with fdisk

If you don't want to retain any existing disk partitions on your hard drives, you can remove these prior to installing Linux. The DOS utility fdisk can remove any DOS partitions from any of your drives. Figure 2-2 shows the initial opening screen that you see when you run fdisk.

```
                          MS-DOS Version 6
                       Fixed Disk Setup Program
                (C)Copyright Microsoft Corp. 1983 - 1993

                           FDISK Options

        Current fixed disk drive: 1

        Choose one of the following:

        1. Create DOS partition or Logical DOS Drive
        2. Set active partition
        3. Delete partition or Logical DOS Drive
        4. Display partition information



        Enter choice: [1]




        Press Esc to exit FDISK
```

Figure 2-2:
Example of
the fdisk
utility.

We highly recommend that you learn about fdisk *before* you use it. This utility doesn't have an *undo* option — you can't go back to the partition architecture that existed before you made changes. All information in deleted partitions is gone *forever*.

After you've (thoughtfully and carefully) removed the partitions, you can create one primary and one extended partition per drive. Within the extended partition, you can create multiple logical drives.

To setup and use `fdisk` to delete existing partitions, follow these steps:

1. **Insert a DOS-bootable floppy disk into the disk drive.**

2. **On a system running DOS or in a MS-DOS window in Windows 9*x*/ME, type** format a: /s.

   The `a:` refers to the drive letter of your floppy drive — insert the appropriate drive letter on your system if it isn't `a:`. The `/s` copies the necessary files to the floppy to make it bootable.

3. **Copy the** `fdisk.exe` **utility to the floppy disk.**

   If you're using Windows 9*x*/ME you can use Windows Explorer to copy `fdisk` to the floppy disk. For DOS or in a DOS window under Windows 9*x*/ME you can use the `xcopy` or `copy` commands.

4. **Reboot your machine with the bootable** `fdisk` **floppy that you created.**

5. **After the system reboots to DOS, type** fdisk **at the command prompt and press Enter.**

   The initial screen displays a menu of options. If you have more than one drive in your system, the last menu item enables you to choose the hard drive on which you want to destroy or create partitions.

6. **To delete a primary partition, type** 3 **for the choice to** Delete partition or Logical DOS Drive **and press the Enter.**

   The Delete DOS Partition or Logical DOS Drive screen appears.

7. **In the Delete DOS Partition or Logical DOS Drive screen, type** 1 **for the** Delete Primary DOS Partition **option and press Enter.**

   The next screen displays the partitions on the disk and their corresponding numbers.

8. **Type the partition number of the partition that you want to delete and press Enter.**

9. **If the partition has a volume label, type the name of the label and press Enter; otherwise, leave the volume label empty and press Enter.**

10. **If you want to delete the partition, type** y **and press Enter; if you don't want to remove the partition, type** n **and press Enter.**

11. **When you're finished using** `fdisk`, **press Esc to exit.**

The DOS utility `fdisk` doesn't recognize some partitions used by Windows operating systems. If your disks contain FAT32 or NTFS partitions, `fdisk` doesn't *see* these and can't remove them. The `delpart` MS-DOS utility can remove many partition types including NTFS and FAT32. You can download `delpart` from Microsoft's Web site at `www.microsoft.com` and other Windows-related Web sites.

Chapter 3

Installing Red Hat Linux

- -

In This Chapter

▶ Installing Linux as a Workstation using the graphical interface

▶ Checking out some neat features and installation improvements

- -

*R*ecently many enhancements have been added to the Linux installation procedure, mostly designed to make installation easier. In the following list, we describe a few of the newer features increasingly used in many Linux distributions (including Red Hat Linux 7, the distribution that comes on the CD-ROMs packaged with this book):

- ✔ **Have Linux automatically detect your hardware.** Most Linux distributions now support the majority of current hardware peripherals and configurations.

- ✔ **Start the installation or boot your computer from a CD.** This makes it very easy to begin the installation without the need to first make the installation floppy disk. In Chapter 2, we cover the process of setting up your system to boot from the CD and creating the installation floppy disk if you just can't boot from CD.

- ✔ **Use a GUI (graphical user interface) to install Linux.** This installation option makes full use of your mouse while also supporting keyboard navigation.

In this chapter, we cover installing Red Hat Linux for a Workstation role using the graphical interface. If you aren't a GUI-type individual or your computer can't use the graphical installation, you can install Linux in text mode (without the mouse and without the graphical interface). We describe the text-mode installation in Bonus Appendix B, which you can find on CD3 that came with this book.

- ✔ **Define your disk partitions in any of the installation modes.** In the past, some of the installation choices automatically altered and/or erased your disks and partitions. If your system has an existing operating system and you want to keep it, the Workstation mode does this for you by default. However, you also have the choice to decide what partitions to remove. In addition, you can also specify the size and location of your disk partitions.

Getting Down and Installing Red Hat Linux

Do, or do not. There is no "try."

— Yoda ("The Empire Strikes Back")

You can install Red Hat Linux by booting with the Red Hat Installation CD or by booting with an installation floppy disk, and having the remainder of the installation files read from the CD.

The Red Hat Linux 7 distribution is included on the CD-ROMs that come with this book. The instructions in this chapter tell you how to follow the installation for only Red Hat Linux 7 (although the instructions are similar for Red Hat 6.1 and 6.2, as well).

To begin the installation from the CD, you must first change your system to start or boot from a CD. In Chapter 2, we cover an example of configuring a computer to boot from the CD.

If you want or need to make the installation floppy disk and have access to a DOS, Windows 9x/ME, or Linux system, perform the steps to create the installation floppy that we outline in Chapter 2.

In this chapter, we concentrate on Red Hat Linux and its installation for two main reasons: because covering the installation of every Linux distribution in existence would make this book a set of encyclopedias, and because we've included Red Hat Linux on the CDs with this book. We chose the Workstation installation to cover because it requires little or no hard drive preparation and doesn't use umpteen partitions like other installations do. In addition, if your computer already has an existing non-Linux operating system, the Workstation installation retains the other operating system by default and allows you to boot to either operating system. The Workstation installation option installs the X Window System and applications that are commonly used on workstations. Server or service type applications, such as the Apache Web server and FTP server, aren't installed with the Workstation option. You can always add these later to your Workstation installation or choose a different option at installation time.

Up until you reach the About To Install (GUI install) screen, you can back out of the installation without changing anything on your system. None of the configuration options you make before the About to Install screen are saved to your disks. After you continue beyond the About To Install screen, data is written to disk and your system is changed.

To install Red Hat Linux, follow these steps:

1. **If you would rather boot and install from the Red Hat installation CD, place CD1 that came with this book in your CD-ROM drive and reboot your system; if not, place the installation floppy disk in your floppy drive, put CD1 in your CD-ROM drive, and reboot your system.**

The default installation mode for Red Hat Linux is graphical. Other Linux distributions, such as Caldera and Corel, also have graphical installation options. Even though the installation screens in other distributions are different than Red Hat, the same basic steps are contained in other distributions.

If you don't choose any options or press Enter, the graphical installation process starts.

Whether you start the installation from the floppy disk or the CD, the first installation screen appears containing several options, as shown in Figure 3-1. We describe each option in the following list:

- The first option in the graphical interface is for installing Red Hat Linux for the first time or for upgrading an existing version of Linux. This installation uses probing to detect your system's hardware. The graphical interface is designed to work with a mouse to select options. If you don't have a mouse, you can use the keyboard to navigate around the screens. In most places, the Tab key and/or the arrow keys advance you to the next option, the space bar toggles options off and on, and the Enter key accepts the choices and moves to the next screen. In most screens, if you want to change a previous setting, a Back button is available to navigate to earlier selection screens. The graphical installation screens also include help in the left panel. The content changes to reflect information about the current configuration screen.

In this chapter, we follow the graphical installation. If you can't use the graphical installation for some reason (if Linux doesn't support your video card, for example), see Bonus Appendix B, which you can find on CD3 that comes with this book, to follow the text-based installation instead.

- The second option enables you to install or upgrade Red Hat Linux using a *text menu interface*. This interface presents the options in text menus and you use the arrow keys and/or Tab key to move the selection area. In some areas, the space bar is used to turn off and on options. To install using the text interface, type **text** at the boot: prompt and press Enter.

- The third option is *expert mode*. This method enables you to have complete control over the installation process and doesn't use autoprobing for hardware detection. In this mode, you need to know all of your hardware specifics. The expert mode also enables you to enter optional parameters for modules. To use this mode, type **expert** at the boot: prompt and press Enter.

- The fourth option is to enable *rescue mode*. You can use this when the Linux system doesn't start properly. This mode includes many useful utilities to restore your system to a functional state. To start rescue mode, type **linux rescue** at the `boot:` prompt and press Enter.

- The fifth option is if you have a disk drive whose driver isn't included with Linux. You need to have the Linux driver for your disk system on a floppy disk or CD. To invoke this option, type **linux dd** at the `boot:` prompt and press Enter.

- The last item listed points out the function keys displayed at the bottom of the screen. One function key, F4 for Kernel, enables you to enter parameters when you install Linux. For example, you may need to indicate how much memory is in your system or turn off auto-probing of the PCI hardware bus.

2. **Press Enter to start the graphical installation.**

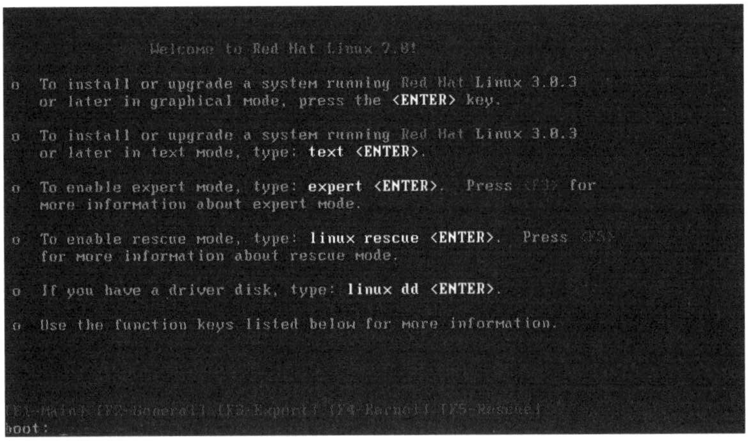

Figure 3-1: The initial Red Hat screen.

Many lines of information scroll down the screen as the installation begins. During this time, a *mini* version of Linux is loading. The last few lines load the graphic engine, a gray screen with a small X in the middle appears, and then a screen with a large Red Hat logo appears. The logo screen automatically disappears and is replaced by the Language Selection screen. Linux supports many different languages, some of which you can see in Figure 3-2.

3. **Use the mouse or up/down arrow keys to select your language and click Next.**

The Keyboard Configuration screen appears, as shown in Figure 3-3.

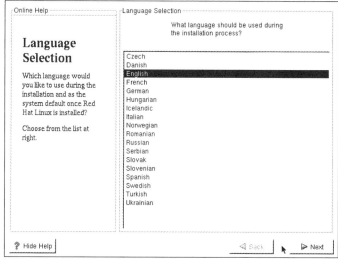

Figure 3-2:
The
Language
Selection
screen.

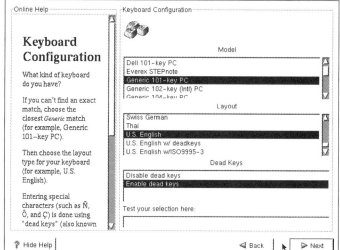

Figure 3-3:
The
Keyboard
Configura-
tion screen.

The Keyboard Configuration screen contains three options:

- **Model:** If you're using a standard U.S. English keyboard, the defaults work just fine. But some keyboards contain extra or special keys; if your model is available from the models listed, you can use the mouse to make your choice.

- **Layout:** This option enables you to choose the arrangement of keys. Different languages arrange the keys differently on keyboards; you may want to choose the matching language for your keyboard.

• **Dead Keys:** The third option is to enable or disable *Dead Keys*. Dead Keys aren't keys that don't work but key combinations that produce special characters. These are sometimes referred to as *compose key sequences.*

After you make your selections, you can test your settings in the Test your selection here: entry field.

4. **Choose your keyboard configuration and click Next.**

   Notice this screen also includes a Back button, which enables you to go back to the previous configuration installation screen if you need to make changes.

   Next you need to configure your mouse. By this stage of the installation, you're probably already using a mouse to make your selections. This configuration screen enables you to choose the model and features of your mouse, as shown in Figure 3-4.

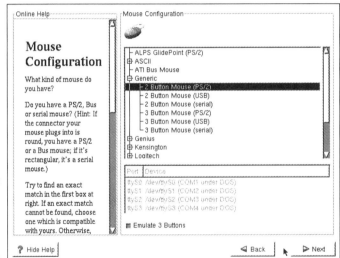

Figure 3-4:
The Mouse
Configura-
tion screen.

If you're using a two-button mouse, you also have the option to emulate three buttons; you can do so by depressing both mouse buttons at the same time.

5. **After making any corrections to your mouse settings, click Next.**

   The Welcome to Red Hat Linux screen appears, indicating where you can read or obtain the Red Hat manuals. The information recommends you read the installation documentation before you install Linux for the first time and so do we!

6. **Click Next after you've finished with the material on the Welcome to Red Hat Linux screen.**

   The Install Options selection screen appears, shown in Figure 3-5, displaying the following four options:

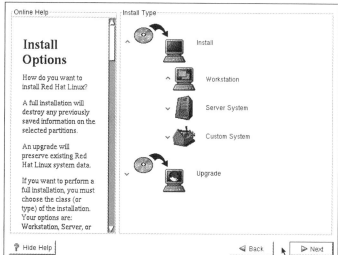

Figure 3-5:
The Install
Options
screen.

- **Workstation:** Installs the X Window System and the desktop manager(s) of your choice. If your system already contains a copy of Linux, the default for the Workstation installation is to remove any existing Linux-related partitions and use all the remaining free unpartitioned disk space. If you choose this default, any existing non-Linux partitions, such as DOS/Windows, remain untouched. After installation, you're able to boot to Linux and your other existing operating system or systems. If you decide not to enable Linux to automatically partition and delete existing Linux partitions, you can manually partition with Disk Druid or with fdisk. For more information, see the sidebar, "Defining partitions manually," elsewhere in this chapter.

- **Server System:** Designed for a basic Linux-based server without the X Window System and contains just the necessary server customization options. When you select this option, the default disk partitioning scheme is to remove *ALL* existing partitions on *ALL* your hard drives. This means all partitions and operating systems of any type, Linux and others, are removed and all drives are erased. If you decide not to enable Linux to automatically partition and delete existing partitions, you can manually partition with Disk Druid or with fdisk.

- **Custom System:** Enables the most flexibility to retain your existing operating systems and configuration options. This option enables you to choose the packages or applications/roles you want to install, the size of your disk partitions, and how you want the system to boot.

- **Upgrade:** Enables you to upgrade an existing Linux system to Red Hat Linux 7. This option retains the existing partitions, file systems, and data.

7. **Click the Workstation installation option to select it and then click Next.**

The Automatic Partitioning installation screen appears, as shown in Figure 3-6. Here you're given the option to accept the default partitioning strategy or you can define your own manually. Your hard drive must contain at least one Linux partition to continue with the installation.

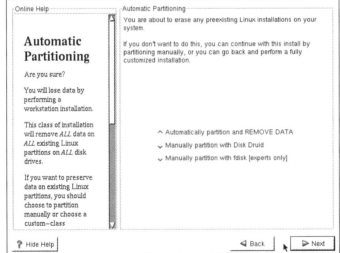

Figure 3-6:
The
Workstation
Automatic
Partitioning
screen.

If you choose automatic partitioning, the installation program partitions your disk without you having to make any decisions.

Be careful — you lose *all* data in *all* existing Linux partitions after choosing to define partitions automatically.

8. **Choose the Automatically partition and REMOVE DATA option and then click Next.**

If you really, really want to partition manually, see the nearby sidebar.

The Network Configuration options screen appears.

Defining partitions manually

If you choose to define partitions manually, you can choose between two main Linux tools that you can use: Disk Druid and fdisk. When the installation gets to the Automatic Partitioning screen (refer to Figure 3-6), you have the option to accept the default or to set your partitions with Disk Druid or fdisk.

To use Disk Druid, select Manually partition with Disk Druid and click Next. The Partitions installation screen appears, as shown in the following figure.

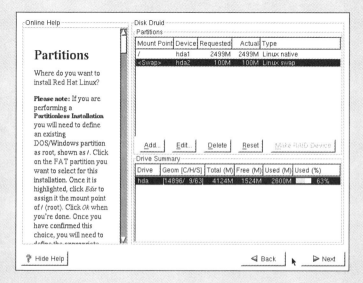

Disk Druid enables you to delete existing partitions and add new partitions. If you don't know how to use Disk Druid, we recommend that you *not* proceed any further. Click Back to return to the Automatic Partitioning screen.

The following figure shows an example of adding a 20MB Linux native partition to the hard drive with Disk Druid.

(continued)

(continued)

The mount point, or starting point in the Linux directory hierarchy, for this example is /boot. For Linux native partitions, you need to define the mount point, size, and hard drive. For a Linux swap partition, you need to define the size and hard drive. When you're finished making all your changes, click Next to continue the installation.

If you want to use fdisk instead of Disk Druid, select the Manually partition with fdisk [experts only] option in the Automatic Partitioning screen and click Next. The next option is to select the hard drive that you want to run fdisk on. At this point, you're in a command window inside the Partitioning With fdisk screen, as shown in the following figure.

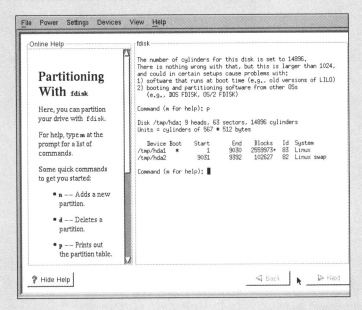

If you don't know how to use fdisk, we recommend that you *not* proceed any further. To exit fdisk, type **q** and press Enter. The Back button is now activated, so you can go back and use Disk Druid or accept the default partitioning strategy.

If you're installing Linux using the text interface, the Disk Druid text interface is similar to the graphical interface except that you use the Tab key and arrow keys to navigate to various portions of the screen. The interface for fdisk in both the graphical and text installation modes are identical. The fdisk utility is used from a command prompt. To find out more about both utilities before using them, consult the Linux distribution documentation or the vendor's Web site. In addition, most Linux reference Web sites contain information about the use of both utilities.

9. **If you're using DHCP on your network, choose the DHCP option; if you aren't using DHCP, make sure the Configure using DHCP option is not selected and enter values for the IP Address and Netmask settings.**

   If you aren't sure whether to use DHCP or not, ask your network administrator or IT department for the appropriate information for your network. In Chapter 7, we cover DHCP and other IP related information.

   Type a name for your machine in the Hostname field and, if your DHCP server doesn't provide the gateway or DNS information, enter values in the Gateway and DNS fields that are valid for your network. Figure 3-7 shows the Network Configuration screen.

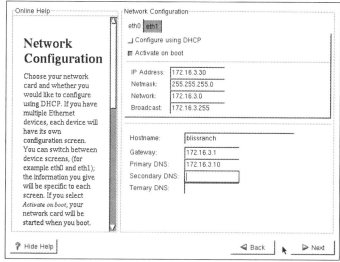

Figure 3-7:
The
Network
Configura-
tion screen.

After you enter these two values, the Network and Broadcast fields are populated with standard values for your network. You probably don't need to modify these settings unless your network is using nonstandard Network and Broadcast values. If your network has more than one DNS server, you can enter up to three DNS server addresses.

10. **After you've made all your selections and entered your data, click Next.**

    The Time Zone Selection installation screen appears, shown in Figure 3-8, where you choose the time zone in which your Linux system resides.

If you don't find the exact name of the city you're in, choose another city in your same time zone that supports the same options, such as Daylight Savings Time. You can also click the UTC Offset tab at the top of the screen and select your offset from UTC time and whether you use Daylight Saving Time or not. If your computer uses UTC (Universal Coordinated Time), you can also choose this option.

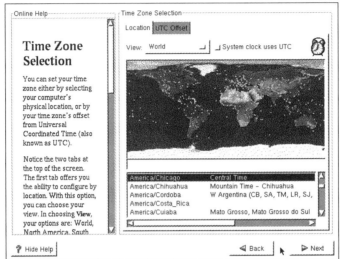

Figure 3-8:
The Time
Zone
Selection
screen.

11. **Choose your location and click Next.**

    The Red Hat Account Configuration screen appears, as shown in
    Figure 3-9. Here you need to set the root account password and add any
    accounts for yourself and other users of your system.

12. **In the Account Configuration screen, type the root account password
    into the Root Password field and then type the same password in the
    Confirm field.**

    You don't see the password when you type it — just an asterisk for
    each character. This prevents unauthorized individuals from seeing the
    password.

    After the values in the two fields agree, the phrase Root passwords do
    not match below the Confirm field is replaced with Root password
    accepted.

13. **Type a name for your regular account in the Account Name field.**

14. **Type the password for your regular account in both the Password and
    Password (confirm) fields.**

    If you want, type your full name in the Full Name field. This isn't
    required, but, if you create multiple user accounts, this documents
    which account is for which user. For example, the account name of
    rbliss isn't obvious if it is for Ruth or Rob or Richard or Rachael or . . .

15. **When you've entered all the data for your account, click Add.**

    If you want to add more accounts at this time, repeat Steps 14 and 15 as
    many times as you need to add users. You can add user accounts after
    installation is complete. For more information, see Chapter 5.

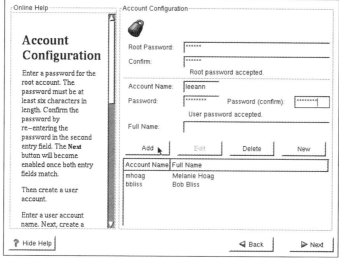

Figure 3-9:
The
Account
Configura-
tion screen.

16. When you've entered all your account information, click Next.

The installation system pauses and displays a progress dialog box for a few seconds while it reads in the package options. When this is complete, you can choose one or all of three package options or choose to select individual packages (see Figure 3-10).

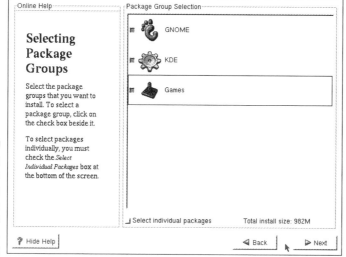

Figure 3-10:
The
Selecting
Package
Groups
screen.

If you choose Select Individual Packages, the screen changes to display the contents of the individual packages, as shown in Figure 3-11. Use the + and – boxes to the left of the categories to expand and collapse the selections. The components of a package to be installed are indicated with a large red check mark in the right pane. If you want to select additional components, click the package once — the details of the package are displayed at the bottom of the screen. To select the package, click the Select Package For Installation button. A large red check mark appears on top of the package. To skip installation of a component, click the component, deselect the Select Package For Installation button, and the red check mark disappears.

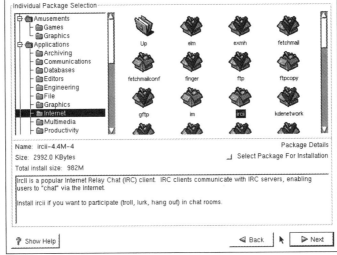

Figure 3-11:
The
Individual
Package
Selection
screen.

Choose the GNOME package if you want to use the default Red Hat graphical user interface (if you want games and KDE then select those, too). KDE is another graphical interface for the X Window System and includes some different applications and tools. If you want to switch between GNOME and KDE, then choose to install both desktops.

17. Select any packages that you want to install and click Next.

A dialog box appears indicating that package dependencies are being checked. Some packages depend on other components. If you selected any packages and not its needed components, the Unresolved Dependencies installation screen appears, shown in Figure 3-12, offering the option of automatically installing the dependency packages.

18. **If you do have any unresolved dependencies, choose the Install packages to satisfy dependencies button and click Next.**

We recommend installing these dependencies. If not, the package may not perform properly or may not work at all. Depending on the packages you selected to install, you may see several Unresolved Dependencies screens.

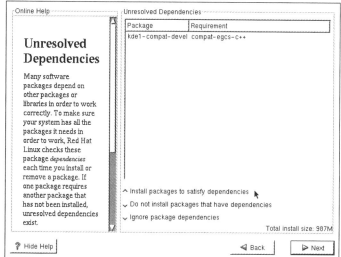

Figure 3-12: The Unresolved Dependencies screen.

After all unresolved dependencies (if any) are resolved, you see the Red Hat X Configuration Monitor Configuration installation screen, shown in Figure 3-13, as the Linux installation probes your hardware in an attempt to determine your monitor.

The information that Linux finds is highlighted in the list of monitors.

19. **If the monitor configuration information is correct for your hardware, click Next; if the information isn't correct, click + and – to expand and collapse the choices, choose the brand and model of your monitor (or the one that matches your hardware), and then click Next.**

Be sure to select the correct monitor. Selecting a monitor with resolution rates and scan frequencies that are higher than your monitor is built for, especially older models, can actually cause damage. An incorrect monitor selection, at the worst, can manifest itself in the way of sparks and/or smoke coming from your monitor. Should that happen, shut your monitor off immediately and disconnect it from your computer. Then proceed to the computer store for another one, if you don't have an extra monitor on hand.

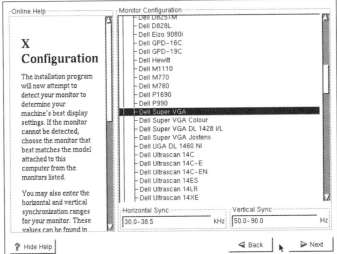

Figure 3-13:
The X
Configura-
tion Monitor
Configura-
tion screen.

The next X Configuration screen that appears, shown in Figure 3-14, enables you to select your video card or interface hardware.

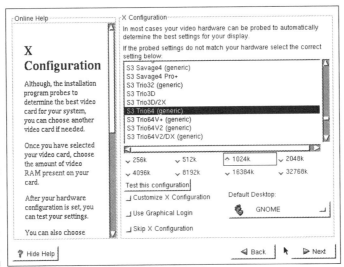

Figure 3-14:
The X
Configura-
tion video
card screen.

The installation program probes your video hardware. Whatever is detected is visible in the selection list at the top of the window. If the information isn't correct, scroll through the list and select the proper video card or interface for your computer. Verify that the amount of video memory selected below the hardware list is correct. If not, make the appropriate change. To make sure the information is correct, click the Test this configuration button.

You also have the option of choosing to use a graphical login when your system starts up (select this option if you want the graphical login). In addition, you can choose the default desktop used when X is started (the default for Red Hat Linux is GNOME).

If you're having trouble configuring your video hardware, select the Skip X Configuration button. You can always go back later after Linux is installed and configure the video settings. Xconfigurator is the utility you can use to configure your video settings. We cover how to access and use Xconfigurator in Chapter 4.

20. **After you've selected all the options you want, click Next.**

The About to Install window appears.

If you want to stop your installation of Linux, this is the *last* place that you can stop. If you would like to stop at this point, press the Ctrl+Alt+Del keys together and your system reboots. After you click Next to continue, your hard drive is modified.

If you gaze long into an abyss, the abyss will gaze back into you.

— Friedrich Nietzsche (1844-1900)

21. **When you're ready to commit to the installation, click Next.**

As the system is installing, you see several progress screens:

- The first is formatting and setting up the file system.

- Following that is setting up your Linux system's swap space. A Preparing to install progress bar appears after setting up the file systems.

- After preparation is complete, installation of the packages begins. An estimate of the amount of time remaining to complete the installation appears.

  Depending on the number of packages selected, and the memory and processor of your computer, this may take anywhere from 15 minutes to a few hours.

After the packages and software are installed, the Boot Disk Creation screen appears, as shown in Figure 3-15. This enables you to create a disk that you can use to start your system for troubleshooting booting problems.

22. **If you started the Linux installation from the floppy installation disk, remove the floppy disk from the drive and insert a blank, 1.44MB floppy disk into your drive and click Next to create the boot disk; If you *don't* want to create a boot disk, select the Skip boot disk creation button and click Next.**

Any existing data on the floppy disk is erased.

Your Linux installation is now finished! A Congratulations screen appears reminding you to remove the installation CD and any floppy disks from your computer as the system reboots.

Figure 3-15:
The Boot
Disk
Creation
screen.

23. **When you're ready, click Exit.**

The graphical environment shuts down and a screen full of text stating the system is shutting down and preparing to reboot appears.

Before the system begins to reboot, make sure that you remove the CD and any floppy disks, if you set your system to boot to the CD or floppy disk. If the system reboots and the first installation screen appears, just remove the boot media and restart your machine.

Chapter 4

Configuring Linux

• •

In This Chapter

▶ Defining and detangling Linux configuration

▶ Finding configuration files

▶ Configuring common subsystems

▶ Perusing LinuxConf and the Control Panel

▶ Configuration tools a la carte

▶ Troubleshooting configuration

• •

A bus station is where a bus stops.

A train station is where a train stops.

On my desk I have a work station. . . .

— Steven Wright

*H*arley-Davidson considers each motorcycle that rolls out of its assembly plant a blank canvas. Harley-Davidson expects owners to customize their bikes to be an extension of their personalities. All bikes share the same proven engineering, yet it's rare that you find two of these American-made beauties that are exactly alike.

Just as Harley-Davidson motorcycle owners thrive on individuality, so too does Linux. A base installation provides you with an elegant and capable machine that can certainly transport you where you want to go. But to have the true riding experience, you need to add some ape-hanger handlebars, drag pipes, painted flames, and all the chrome you can get your leather-gloved hands on. In addition to all these cosmetics, you may also choose to bore and stroke the engine to help you muscle around those crowding tractor-trailers in a pinch.

As with customizing your hog, you can divide Linux configuration into two broad categories: cosmetic and mechanical. In this chapter, we provide an overview of common configuration options, from the system level to customizing individual user environments. Modular design, one of the great strengths of Linux, enables you to customize your system in any way you want and for any computing need. Along the way, we point into the dark corners of the file system where the configuration files lurk. We also introduce you to helpful configuration tools so that you don't have to get messy with these often-cryptic files.

Zen and the Art of Linux Configuration

Anyone can use Linux but to become a true Linux master requires an intimate knowledge of your system's internal mechanics. This is a daunting task when you consider that Linux is the sum of many different software subsystems, each written by different programmers with different backgrounds and beliefs regarding problem solving. Fortunately, software developers try to comply with a few universal truths. One of these truths is that mere mortals must be able to configure the program.

You can define a computer program as a series of instructions that direct the computer to perform a specified task. You can't change any instructions that are hard coded into the program (unless, of course, you make the required changes to the source code and recompile the program.) As you can imagine, the slightest variance in program use requires the handiwork of a skilled programmer. What if you had to edit the kernel code to include the new username and password and then recompile your system every time that you created a new user for your system?

Most Linux subsystems are comprised of, at least, the following files:

✔ The *executable file:* most likely a binary file that only speaks the language of the computer. (You undoubtedly experience this firsthand at some point when you attempt to view one of these files and your screen pukes gibberish and noise at you.)

✔ The *configuration file:* a simple text file that you can view and alter with your favorite editor.

The executable file reads directives from the configuration file to know how to behave. Keep in mind that the executable must understand the directives in the configuration files. Any old command doesn't work. This is why it's imperative that you RTFM (*Read The Fine Manual*) prior to doing any heavy lifting in a configuration file. Configuration file formats are as different as snowflakes and often very complex. For example, the Sendmail configuration is one of the most notorious; if not forewarned, you may think that the `sendmail.cf` file is a message from a distant planet. This complexity is often directly correlated to the flexibility and power of the program.

It's beyond the scope of this book to provide details on any of these configuration files. We identify them and show you where to find them and let your curiosity take it from there.

Knowing Where the Good Stuff Lives

Even though the configuration file formats are very different from one another, they usually hang out in the same directory or at least in the same branch of the directory tree. The location of a configuration file depends on the intended purpose of the subsystem. Following are the most common locations of configuration files, in context with their use.

- ✔ /etc **(System or host specific):** The configuration files kept here are global to the functioning of the host. For example, the passwd file that contains all the system user information is kept here. Other important subdirectories are under /etc as well. For example, the /etc/X11 directory contains X configuration files and the /etc/rc.d files, and directories define how to perform system startup and shutdown procedures. We cover those in detail in the "Pop the Hood and Take a Look Inside" section later in this chapter.

- ✔ /usr/etc **(application-specific):** Just as the /etc directory contains the configuration files for a specific host, the /usr/etc directory houses configuration files for *nonsystem-specific* applications. The reason for this may not be clear until you apply it to a distributed system over a network. Consider the example of a shared host where many network users require the same application. Rather than install the same application on each workstation, duplicating effort and creating a maintenance nightmare for the system administrator, she can install it to one server and allow everyone on the network to access it. This simplifies upgrading and configuration as the system administrator now needs to meddle with only one machine for configuration and upgrading of the package.

- ✔ ~/ **(user specific):** The user's home directory also contains a number of configuration files. These files define the behavior of applications and system services that the user has control over.

There may be more than one configuration file for the same service. A service may require a different configuration for a system level versus a user level. One example is when a bash shell session begins with a user logging in to the system — two levels of configuration occur:

  - First, the /etc/profile file is read and interpreted.
  - Then, the ~/.bash_profile file is read to provide specific configuration options that the user may have included.

You may be asking yourself what the named directory /etc has to do with anything. After all, isn't /configuration more descriptive of what's kept there? Before you start writing your own Linux distribution with just this type of naming scheme, please read the "Everyone join hands" sidebar nearby for a brief explanation of the Filesystem Hierarchy Standard.

Everyone join hands

Linux is a variant of Unix, which has a legacy of criticism because of its feature fragmentation. As universities and private companies developed their own flavors of Unix, few standards were in place. Unix was without any apparent agreement on plumbing standards or determining the location of certain files. The result? Numerous, Unix-like systems of differing forms that only resemble each other in function.

In an effort to bring some conformity to the Unix world, several standards were developed. These recognized conventions provide a target for Linux and Unix variants. One of these standards is called the *Filesystem Hierarchy Standard (FHS)*. You can read all about this proposed standard at www.pathname.com/fhs/. The intention is to reach a consensus among all Unix variants about how to organize the directory structure and where to put files. A standards-compliant system ensures that when you're asked to work on your friend's Debian distribution, you're able to find all the files in the same place as your Slackware distribution, and so on. Although not 100 percent compliant yet with the FHS, most distributions have recognized this effort as a good thing worth working toward.

Popping the Hood and Taking a Look

Linux distributions have integrated a significant amount of system configuration into the installation process. Most of the information that is asked of you during installation is regarding how you want your system configured. In this section, we look at each major Linux subsystem and direct you to the tools and files that you need to use to reconfigure an existing system.

Note: These utilities are making changes to system files, so you need to edit these files with root user privileges.

LILO

LILO is an acronym for *LI*nux *LO*ader. The LILO program and configuration file is a system for creating and installing a system boot loader. You write instructions to the /etc/lilo.conf file that describe how you want your boot record to behave. After saving your directions in the lilo.conf file, you actually create the boot loader by running the program /sbin/lilo. Note that you need a running Linux system to load LILO. Don't forget that rescue disk!

Starting up and shutting down

Linux is anything but an idle system. Running the `top` command at the command prompt reveals that a couple dozen processes are running in the background at any time. These processes were spawned somewhere along the way, likely during the boot process. Understanding the startup and shutdown procedure is critical to configuring the behavior of your Linux system. By configuring the startup procedure, you can fine tune your Linux computer to start just the processes you want and need while leaving others out of system memory.

All processes have to be spawned by an existing process. A program called `init` is the first process started by the kernel at boot time. All subsequent processes can trace their lineage to the `init` process. The file that directs the behavior of `init` is called `/etc/inittab`. `init` performs a few base system operations and manages another program called `rc` that performs the details of the startup process.

First, `rc` runs a script called `/etc/rc.d/rc.sysinit`. This performs general, system-level operations and environment settings that are required regardless of runlevel. `rc` then executes the script links in the subsequent runlevel directory. Finally, `rc` runs the shell script called `/etc/rc.d/rc.local`, which provides any post startup functions required after loading runlevel-specific scripts.

You can think of each *runlevel* as a different boot configuration. When your system boots you can choose to only allow yourself in as a user, allow others to login to your system (multi-user), or allow multi-user access with networking. These are three common runlevel examples. The runlevel directory contains symbolic links to the `/etc/init.d` directory where all the startup scripts are located. You'll notice that each runlevel has a separate directory. Adding or removing a service from a particular runlevel is as simple as adding or deleting the symbolic link from the runlevel directory.

The seven runlevels, along with their intended purpose, are as follows:

Runlevel	What It Does
0	Perform an orderly shutdown of all processes and halt the CPU
1	Single-user mode; used primarily for maintenance and troubleshooting
2	Multi-user mode without networking
3	Multi-user mode with networking
4	User defined
5	Multi-user mode with networking and X display manager
6	Perform an orderly shutdown and subsequent reboot to default runlevel

To determine the default runlevel of your system, enter the following command at a command prompt:

```
grep :initdefault: /etc/inittab
```

You'll see something like this in response:

```
id:3:initdefault:
```

This indicates that runlevel 3 is the default. If you opted to log in with a graphical interface during installation, your results are likely as follows:

```
id:5:initdefault:
```

Although a simple change with a text editor can change your default runlevel, just hold on. You can also change your default runlevel in LinuxConf, a configuration utility that we tell you about in the "To LinuxConf or not to LinuxConf: That's the Question" section later in this chapter.

The startup scripts that are called depend on the runlevel your system is starting at. For example, if our system defaults to runlevel 3, all the scripts in the directory rc3.d execute. To see what scripts are started, create a listing of files in that directory:

```
ls /etc/rc.d/rc3.d
```

The first thing you may notice is that all the files are symbolic links, or *symlinks* for short. In other words, these files just point elsewhere rather than containing the script instructions themselves. If you consider that the same services may be started under different runlevels, you see that it makes sense to call the same script. Otherwise, we need to copy the same script to all runlevel directories that need to start the service . . . a maintenance nightmare best avoided.

Another interesting part of this directory listing is the filenaming convention. The rc program that actually executes the script uses the filename to determine the order and event in which a particular service is executed. rc calls each script with a command prompt argument depending on the event. A startup event is passed a start argument, while a shutdown event is passed a stop argument. rc knows which script to run by evaluating the symlink name. The S at the front of the filename tells rc that this script must be run during the startup of this runlevel. The K in the script name tells rc that the script is run with a stop argument when a runlevel *change* is requested from this runlevel.

The next two characters after the event type represent a two-digit integer, which provides the order in which a process is started. Some processes require others to be started first. This naming convention enables the system to call services in a particular order.

Finally, the rest of the filename just provides a reference so that we can see what service is being handled. So where do all the actual service programs reside and what do they look like?

The rc<runlevel>.d directories contain files that point to the /etc/rc.d/ init.d directory, where all the actual scripts live. You're welcome to view these files, as they're shell scripts. If you understand shell programming, you can walk the sequence of events that the system travels during startup.

Note that you rarely have any need to make changes to any of these files. Enabling and disabling services at start time is simply a matter of creating or deleting the symlink for a process in the required runlevel directory. Be patient; we provide some easy configuration tools in the "Configuration Tools a la carte" section later in this chapter, so that you don't have to mess with the command prompt.

Kernel modules

You probably wake up panicked in the middle of the night wondering how the system knows what kernel modules to load at boot time. *Kernel modules* provide a way for you to add hardware and special system drivers after you've loaded the kernel into memory. Each kernel module may also require specific parameters to be passed to it at load time. You can find the configuration file that contains these parameters, as well as determining what modules to load at boot time, in the /etc/modules.conf file (/etc/conf.modules in Red Hat Linux 7).

Users and groups

Of course your system only benefits users if they can get to it. A critical file that maintains a list of the system users, along with password information, home directory, and default shell of each user, is the /etc/passwd file. The /etc/group files contain information about the groups on the host and the members (users) of each group.

If you enabled shadow passwords during install, you also need to be aware of the /etc/shadow file, which is owned and marked exclusively *read-only* by root. This file keeps the encrypted passwords instead of the traditional location in the second field of the /etc/passwd file.

Although it's possible to simply edit these files to make additions, deletions, or changes to users, we don't advise it. The login program matches these files line for line, and a simple fat-finger mistake in your editor can cripple your entire system. Use the useradd or LinuxConf utilities for user and group maintenance — you'll be glad you did!

XDM or getty

The first greeting you see after the system boots is either a *display manager* or a *getty* program. A getty process is used for the user login process if your default runlevel is set to 3. A default runlevel of 5 utilizes a display manager for login. Essentially, either of these programs perform the same function of validating a username and password — the display manager does it in graphical style and the getty does it in character style.

You can't do a lot of customization with the getty program. However, you may want to know about a couple files for greeting your users. The /etc/issue file is the text that is printed as part of the login prompt of the getty program. The /etc/motd (*Message Of The Day*) contains text that displays after the user has successfully logged in. Any text editor enables you to change the information in these files.

The display manager, on the other hand, provides a plethora of customization options. The *X Display Manager (xdm)* locates all of its supporting files from one configuration file called /etc/X11/xdm/xdm-config.~/.xsession, which is the configuration file, located in the user home directory, that you can use to start programs upon the initialization of X Window System (or X). Note that ~./xsession is only read during X initialization when using the display manager. ~./.xinitrc is read when X is started from the command prompt (that is, startx).

Several display managers are available. Along with xdm, you may also choose gdm (GNOME display manager) or kdm (KDE Display Manager).

bash

The bash shell is a powerful and highly configurable user interface. The system administrator can determine the shell configuration to provide execution paths, environment variables, and shell characteristics for all users of the system. The individual user can also configure bash to customize personal settings, such as any aliases and the command prompt. See Chapter 11 for in-depth coverage of bash and Bonux Appendix D for aliases.

The configuration files bash uses can get confusing. Initialization differs depending on how the shell is invoked:

✔ bash as an interactive login shell:

   1. /etc/profile is a system-wide bash configuration file. Global bash settings common to all users of the system are set here.

2. ~/.bash_profile is located in each user's home directory. This bash configuration file enables users to customize their own shell environment in addition to the global settings made by the /etc/profile file.

✔ bash as an interactive *non*-login shell:

~/.bashrc, if it exists and is readable.

X Window System

Hopefully, your installation was able to detect your video hardware and provide you with a graphical desktop. Because most desktop computer users have become accustomed to the graphical desktop environment, the popular distributions have integrated X configuration right into the installation process.

X configuration is the process of identifying your video hardware for X and establishing the visual settings that provide you with a comfortable and pleasing workstation viewing environment. In this section, we introduce you to the critical components of X and point you to some useful X configuration tools.

The two main components you need to know about for configuring X are the server and the configuration file. /etc/X11/X is a symbolic link (symlink) that points to the actual X server, located in the /usr/X11R6/bin directory. You can think of the X server as a program, or kernel, that knows how to control your video adapter in graphical mode. The X program itself isn't configurable and is just required to handle low-level requests. However, you need to make sure that you're using a server that's compatible with your video hardware.

The /etc/X11/XF86Config file contains your X configuration. Although this is just a normal text file, the format is complicated and confusing.

Red Hat Linux 7 was released with version 4 of XFree86 (recently released). Most Linux distributions and installations still use version 3.3. Make note that the configuration file format has changed in version 4 and you can't use version 3 configuration tools to create version 4 files and vice versa.

Fortunately, you aren't left to hack your way through this file. A few helpful tools are available that step you through all the required questions to get your graphical desktop working in short order. One of these, *Xconfigurator,* is included with Red Hat Linux 7. Xconfigurator probes your system for video hardware and prompts you through a series of questions, eventually creating your XF86Config file for you.

If X is already running and perhaps you're just trying to milk a higher resolution or greater color depth from your video hardware, we suggest that you make a backup of your current X configuration file. The following command creates a backup of the current X configuration for you in a file called /etc/X11/XF86Config.good:

```
cp /etc/X11/XF86Config /etc/X11/XF86Config.good
```

It's always nice to know that you can get back to where you started! Also note that you can always re-run Xconfigurator at any time to alter your settings.

As much as you've been told that it's impossible to physically destroy your computer by trying new things, you *can* actually fry your monitor configuring X. If you drive your monitor at too high a refresh rate, you'll hear a high pitch whine, followed by a pop and perhaps a wisp or two of smoke seeping out of the monitor air vents. If this happens, grab your money clip and head to your computer store because you need a new monitor. Fortunately, newer monitors now have fail-safe mechanisms that simply shut it down when it's driven too wildly.

To create a new X configuration file, follow these steps:

1. **Type** Xconfigurator **at the command prompt to start Xconfigurator (note the upper-case "X").**

   Xconfigurator attempts to detect your video hardware. Chances are good that it detects a compatible video adapter. Next, you're asked about your monitor.

2. **Scroll through the list to find your monitor and choose it**.

   If your monitor isn't listed, select the first item labeled Custom. Choosing the custom monitor requires you to provide information about the following:

   Vertical refresh rate:

   Horizontal sync rate:

To understand what these settings refer to, you need to know a little about television . . . not dialogs from early sitcoms mind you, rather how the actual picture gets painted in the phospour for your viewing pleasure. In a nutshell, what you're viewing is a single beam of light that draws your screen umpteen thousand times per second. This pinpoint beam of light starts at the upper left corner of the screen and proceeds to draw each line of pixels until it hits the bottom right corner of the screen. The video adapter inside your computer needs to know how fast it can drive that little beam of light. Vertical refresh rate refers to how long it takes for the beam to return to the top left of the screen from the bottom right. Horizontal sync rate refers to how long it takes for the beam to travel from one side of the screen to the other.

Specifications (the rates we're talking about) for your monitor is contained in the manuals you received with your monitor. If you're like us, your monitor manuals have long since gone to the missing-sock-parallel-universe. Never fear, you're provided with a selection of ranges. Just select a conservative setting at first. Remember, you can always rerun Xconfigurator and slowly increase the rates until they're comfortable on the eyeballs.

3. **After determining your sync and refresh rates, choose the video memory.**

   Don't confuse this with system memory. *Video memory* is physically part of your video adapter and determines your resolution and color depth ability. Your system probably detected the amount of memory on your adapter when it did the initial detection.

4. **Select No Clockchip Setting.**

   This is an option left in the configuration for older video adapters. It's most likely not needed for your X configuration.

5. **Select Video Modes.**

   You can select several video modes. Feel free to select all of them if you want, as your X session only runs under those supported by your video adapter. A video mode is comprised of three settings: number of pixels on your screen from side to side, number of pixels from top to bottom, and the number of bits associated to each pixel, used for color depth. One example is 800x600x24, meaning the screen shows 800 pixels across, 600 pixels up and down, and each pixel is capable of displaying one of 16 million+ colors (24 bits can hold 16,777,216 different combinations.)

6. **Xconfigurator tests your X configuration.**

   If you get a dialog box asking if you can see this message, then you know that Xconfigurator was successful.

   Note that even if the resolution isn't exactly where you want it, you can always go back to change it. Just start over with Step 1.

7. **Answer** Yes **to the next question if you want X to automatically start when the system boots.**

   Essentially, you're setting the default runlevel to 5.

8. **Xconfigurator writes the** XF86Config **file with all the selections you've made.**

XFree86 version 4 searches for the XF86Config file in several places, reading the first one it finds. The filename XF86Config-4 takes precedence over XF86Config. Xconfigurator writes to the file XF86Config-4 by default.

✔ **XF86Setup:** This is a popular, graphical XFree86 setup tool that's part of the version 3.3 package. It uses a VGA16 server so it can run on any VGA adapter and has a nice graphical interface for configuring X. Note that a VGA adapter is just an older version and has less capabilities than the SVGA adapters that are common in most personal computers today.

✔ **xf86config:** Another character-based X configuration tool.

✔ **SaX:** Delivered with the SuSE Linux distribution and provides a terrific graphical-based X configuration tool.

The following are a couple other helpful tools for getting your X graphical workstation working just right:

✔ **xvidtune:** This tool reads your existing X settings and enables you to fine tune your video modes. Note that after you've determined your optimal settings, you need to manually edit the mode lines into your `XF86Config` file.

✔ **SuperProbe:** A command prompt utility that does a nice job of determining what video hardware is inside your machine.

Networking

Linux and networking go together like peas and carrots. It's a rare event when your Linux computer has no networking functions enabled. Even a simple installation likely has a local *loopback interface* enabled. The loopback device is a phantom network interface that enables your computer to listen to itself and use network programs without having a physical network device.

Configuring your network requires two primary steps:

1. **Identify and configure your network interface.**

   Support for your network adapter is either compiled into your kernel or added via a *loadable module*. (A loadable module enables you to add hardware support while your system is running.) If you have a common network adapter, you probably don't need to do anything to configure the hardware. When you installed Linux, the network adapter was likely detected and the correct kernel module was configured to load at boot time.

2. **Give your interface identity to the network.**

   During installation, you're provided an opportunity to configure your network interface by either selecting DHCP or entering static IP numbers. Your system administrator is able to provide you with this information, and it's simply a matter of entering the numbers in the labeled text boxes. If, for some reason, you entered the wrong information during installation or even completely bypassed the network configuration, you can use LinuxConf to modify any of that information. (See next section "To LinuxConf, or not to LinuxConf?: That's the Question.")

The network configuration files are no different than any other configuration files in that they have text that you can edit; however, *where* the information is kept varies wildly from distribution to distribution.

In Red Hat, you find the networking information in files such as /etc/sysconfig/network, the network startup scripts in the directory /etc/sysconfig/network-scripts, and the main networking script that calls these scripts and configuration files in /etc/rc.d/init.d/network.

Printing

The Linux printing system uses only one file for its configuration — /etc/printcap. You have some handy tools available to help you create and maintain this file. As with other configuration files, you can also edit it manually; however, you must create spool directories /var/spool/lpd and set these with the correct permissions, a task best left to a utility designed to do the job.

Now close the hood and look at a few point and click tools that enable mere mortals to make changes to the system configuration.

To LinuxConf or Not to LinuxConf?: That's the Question

LinuxConf is GPL (General Public License) software that provides one-stop-shopping for all your Linux configuration and administration needs. At least that's what the creators of this software proclaim as their mission. As you know by now, Linux is a complicated and powerful beast, comprised of varied software from thousands of programmers around the world. Attempting to create a tool that understands the configuration of these many systems is ambitious indeed.

Some users think of LinuxConf as a magic tool that enables novices to configure their Linux system, yet others consider it the pocketknife of the devil. Experienced Systems Administrators encourage you to work toward understanding how the underlying services work and learn the syntax of the related configuration file(s). Their argument is valid in that you never know exactly what the configuration tool is doing behind the scenes. This is fine advice for the long term, but often you don't have time to climb the learning curve. LinuxConf gives you a boost up so that you can get your system configured and useful *today*.

LinuxConf provides an all-in-one configuration and activation tool. To provide contrast, look at the steps you're traditionally required to perform for system configuration:

1. Find the configuration file responsible for directing the intended service.

2. Edit the file, conforming to the exact syntax required by the service.

3. Load or reload the service into memory. Even if the process is already running, you may be required to restart the service in order for the updated configuration file to be read.

LinuxConf was created to be a single portal for all things configurable in Linux. As you may know, the dynamic nature of Linux and the plethora of services and configuration formats required to run your system make this impossible. While a worthy goal, it often doesn't provide the details you need. You are, however, able to use it safely for the more general system services.

To accommodate the different types of user interfaces that may be available with a Linux computer, LinuxConf has been developed to provide several different interfaces. Regardless of which interface you use, the functionality is the same. The four modes that LinuxConf runs in are:

- ✔ **Graphical:** Nice point and click interface that runs on an X graphical desktop.

- ✔ **Terminal:** Character based for when X isn't available, use your arrow keys to make menu selections.

- ✔ **Command prompt:** Enter on command line to make a single configuration change. Handy for use within shell scripts.

- ✔ **Web browser-based:** Use your browser to make changes in a point and click environment. You can also make changes remotely, over a network with this method.

The graphical LinuxConf interface for X is the easiest to use. You can utilize your mouse to easily make selections with familiar graphical controls. We've based the examples in this section on the graphical LinuxConf.

To use LinuxConf, you need to log in as the root user, because many of the files that LinuxConf modifies can only be written by root. On the GNOME desktop, start LinuxConf by choosing Programs⇨System⇨LinuxConf. The LinuxConf main screen appears, as shown in Figure 4-1.

As you can see from the main menu of LinuxConf, you have many options, not all visible at this point. Notice the three tabs, labeled Config, Control, and Status, across the top of the dialog box. LinuxConf does more than just configuration; it strives to be a complete administration tool, providing not only configuration options but also the ability to control and view system status. We focus on the Config tab in this section, but we encourage you to explore the other options.

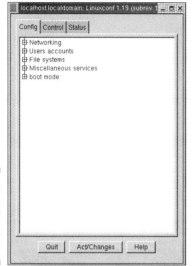

Figure 4-1:
The
LinuxConf
main
screen.

To the left of each listed item in the Config dialog is a plus (+) or minus (–) symbol. If you can see the plus sign, more listed options under the top level are available. This is just a nice way to categorize configuration options in a hierarchy. You can say that this first level is a birds-eye view of all the config-uration options available. We drill down through each top-level option and point out some important areas of consideration along the way.

Click the + next to Networking. It expands to show three more topics — Client tasks, Server tasks, and Misc. Next; click the + next to Client tasks. Once again, you see more options subordinate to that option. (For all the configuration options that you see under Client tasks in LinuxConf, see Figure 4-2.) Click the + next to Routing and gateways.

All options under Networking⇨Client tasks are now available for selection. By clicking the – next to an option, you can collapse each level.

Click the item labeled Basic host information. Notice that the window expands in width and a new dialog box appears, as shown in Figure 4-3. You can now see the specific options available under the selected item. The LinuxConf window is providing another level of depth, yet still allowing you to keep your perspective about where you are in the configuration scheme.

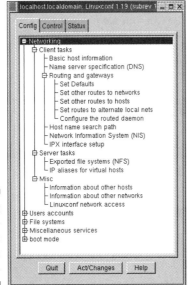

Figure 4-2:
Configuration options in LinuxConf.

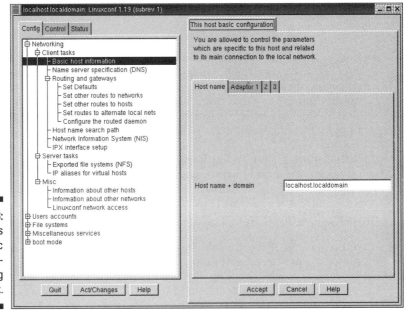

Figure 4-3:
The This host basic configuration dialog box.

Next, click the item labeled Name server specifications (DNS). On the right side of the window, notice that LinuxConf creates an additional tab with yet another dialog box (labeled Resolver configuration), as shown in Figure 4-4.

The host basic configuration tab is still available; its dialog box is just covered up. You can either hide these dialog boxes again by clicking the Cancel button on the active dialog tab, or simply leave them. Each new item that you open creates an additional tab. Click the Cancel button on both tabs to return the LinuxConf window to the original option listing.

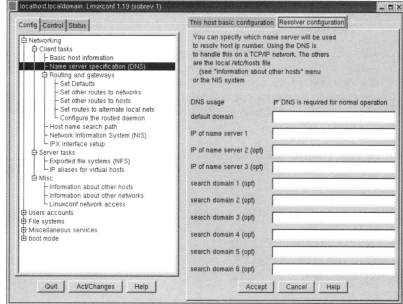

Figure 4-4:
The Name
server
specifica-
tion (DNS)
and
Resolver
configura-
tion dialog
box.

The information that you add to these fields doesn't instantly become active. LinuxConf maintains all this information in its own memory space until you give it the go-ahead to make the changes to the configuration files and activate the changes. Following is a list of some configuration options that LinuxConf provides:

⩗ **Config tab**

• **Network and host information:** Select how you want to configure your network interface and enter IP numbers.

• **Distributed services, NFS:** Determine how you want to share your system with other users on the network: Which directories you want to share, with whom, and what rights you want to allocate.

• **User accounts:** Add, modify, and delete users and groups in your system.

- **Default runlevel:** Determine what runlevel you want your system to start by default. Typically, you choose between runlevel 3 (text login) or runlevel 5 (graphical login).

- **Boot mode:** Configure LILO for booting Linux or another operating system, including arguments required to be passed to the kernel at boot time.

✔ **Control service activity (under the Control tab):** Determine which processes start at boot time and manually start and stop services.

After you make configuration changes, click the Quit or Activate the Changes button. Either button provides you with a Status of the system dialog box, as shown in Figure 4-5. From here you can choose to preview the changes that are about to be made, activate the changes, or exit without making any changes to the system by clicking the Quit button.

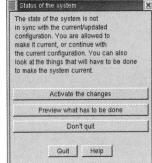

Figure 4-5:
The Status
of the
system
dialog box.

Control Panel

The Control Panel provides yet another configuration tool. You'll find plenty of overlap regarding the configuration options you have with the Control Panel versus LinuxConf. Remember, with Linux, new mousetraps are created all the time. Unlike commercial software, *free* software such as Linux enables anyone to create better ways to perform tasks, an inventor's paradise. Red Hat provides Control Panel as their portal to system configuration. To access the Control Panel, choose Programs⇨System⇨Control Panel (see Figure 4-6).

Figure 4-6:
The Control
Panel main
screen.

From left to right (or top to bottom), the buttons on the Control Panel are as follows:

✔ **Runlevel Editor:** Configure the services that start with each runlevel.

✔ **Time and Date:** Set the system time and date.

✔ **Printer Configuration:** Add/Modify/Delete printing devices and queues.

✔ **Network Configuration:** A nice graphical tool for configuring your network host name, /etc/hosts file, interface IP assignments, and routing.

✔ **Modem Configuration:** See Chapter 7 for details concerning Modem configuration.

✔ **Kernel Daemon Configuration:** Graphical interface for maintaining loadable kernel modules. Maintains the /etc/modules.conf file.

✔ **Search Help Systems:** A nice utility that provides yet another method for searching all available online help. You type a keyword and it searches specified document directories and info and man pages.

✔ **System Configuration** (LinuxConf): Provides another way to start the LinuxConf tool discussed earlier in this chapter.

Shooting Trouble, Configuration-wise

Unfortunately, no single, proven method for troubleshooting an errant configuration exists. As you probably know, Linux is an orchestra comprised of many different processes. The more understanding you have of the structure and process of Linux, the better your troubleshooting ability.

Becoming adept at Linux requires you to develop your own troubleshooting techniques. Here are a few pointers to help you along the way:

✔ **RTFM (Read The @#&! Manual):** We can't stress this enough (neither could whoever started the acronym!). Read through the documentation that came with the software in question. Read the man and info pages if they exist. Be sure that any configuration files have been formatted correctly.

✔ **Log files:** tail the log files for possible errors written to the kernel (located in /var/log/).

✔ **Command prompt options:** Set command prompt options for debugging. Often, commands have debugging, or *verbose*, options that perform more status reporting. Most commands just do their job and return you to the prompt, a verbose option provides more feedback to as to what the command is doing.

✔ **Dependent services:** Make sure that supporting services are running. Some processes may require that others are already running.

✔ **File permissions:** A common problem. Make sure that all the files and directories that are required by this service have the required permissions. Read the man page for the process to see what required files you may need.

✔ **Check returned error code:** Compiled programs often return an error code in the form of an integer. A zero (0) indicates that the process ran successfully; any other code indicates a problem. Usually the documentation lists the possible error codes and their meaning.

✔ **Use the Internet community:** If you're trying to configure a well-known and well-used program, chances are someone has gone before you and perhaps encountered a similar problem. You can probably find an instant solution after a quick search through the newsgroup archives at www.deja.com/usenet.

✔ **Learn** bash **shell programming:** Many processes are started by a shell script. If you understand the basics of shell scripting, you can follow through the code, trying each step manually to determine where the problem lies. See *Linux Programming For Dummies* by Jim Keogh (IDG Books Worldwide) to get up to speed on bash shell programming.

Chapter 5

Booting Linux and Setting Up a User Account

In This Chapter

▸ Turning on your Linux machine

▸ Fixing boot problems

▸ Shutting down safely

▸ Creating user accounts

▸ Understanding the GUI

> *I like work; it fascinates me. I can sit back and look at it for hours.*
>
> — Jerome K. Jerome

*I*f you came here from Chapter 4, you likely just survived the first two gauntlets of the Linux world: installing and configuring the operating system. No matter what operating system you're trying, computers don't always start up right after you install them, and Linux is no exception. After you install the operating system, you may find that the machine stops in the middle of a reboot. At that point, you may panic.

In this chapter, we strive to alleviate your panic by helping you properly boot a testy machine — whether it's failing during the initial part of the boot process or later. You also find out about adding user accounts and the many reasons why you want to do that.

Giving Linux the Boot

As with all operating systems, you start Linux by booting the machine that it's installed on. To get down to brass tacks and boot your Linux machine, follow these steps:

1. **Turn on your computer.**

   It's a good idea to start with turning on your monitor and any peripherals (printers and such) and then pressing your computer's power switch to turn it on last. This way, you don't miss any important messages.

   The `LILO boot:` prompt appears.

   RED HAT ONLY

   When you boot into Red Hat Linux 7 or later, you get a graphical boot menu, not the old straight-text `LILO boot:` prompt.

2. **Either press Enter to boot the default operating system or type the name of the non-default operating system that you want to boot and press Enter.**

   For example, type **linux** and press Enter to boot Linux.

   TIP

   If you press the Tab key, you get a list of the operating systems that LILO is configured to boot into. For example, if you set up a dual boot between Linux and Windows, you may see the following after pressing the Tab key:

   ```
   linux dos
   ```

   The first item listed is the default. If you do nothing for a few seconds, LILO boots whichever operating system is set as default (usually Linux).

   The computer finds Linux's kernel (we talk about the kernel in Chapter 4), which then boots Linux.

   After the boot process finishes, the login prompt appears, as shown in Figure 5-1. This default prompt is only different from other distributions in the version information it displays. The format and the prompt to enter your username are the same across the board.

Figure 5-1:
The default
Red Hat
Linux 7 login
prompt.

```
Red Hat Linux release 7.0 (Guinness)
Kernel 2.2.16-17 on an i586

blissranch login: _
```

Dealing with Initialization Woes

If at first you don't succeed, failure may be your style.

— Quentin Crisp

Fun with your BIOS and MBR

After you've switched the machine on and are listening to your obnoxiously loud fan, your computer looks for its *BIOS* (*B*asic *I*nput/*O*utput *S*ystem). The BIOS is a special chip on your machine's *motherboard* that stores information about your hardware and tests to make sure everything is there and working properly at boot time. This includes that memory test that most people find so annoying and press Esc to stop.

When the BIOS has finished doing its tests, the computer looks to the *MBR* (or Master Boot Record), which is always on the very first sector on your hard drive, for instructions on how to boot the operating system. The MBR looks and finds LILO and summons the initial LILO boot: prompt.

If you have multiple operating systems when you installed LILO, it put information into the MBR that ensures that when the system boots, you get a menu asking which operating system you want to boot from.

The MBR is the first *sector* on your hard drive — hard drives are usually divided into a bunch of different kinds of pieces, as shown in the following figure. Sectors are one of the measurements a PC uses to find data on a drive. Many versions of BIOS can't look past the 1024th sector (around the 8GB point) on the drive during the initial boot process. So, being familiar with sectors makes it easier to make sure that your /boot or / partition is somewhere where the BIOS can find it.

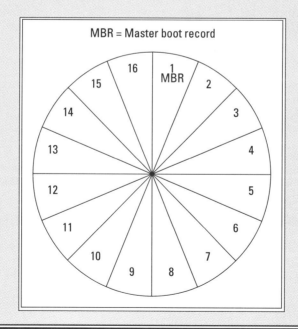

MBR = Master boot record

If you have problems with your machine as it boots up, you really need to be able to figure out where that problem is occurring before you can fix it. We cover some specific problems here and provide you with the tools that you need to diagnose other problems on your own.

Where's my boot prompt?

People typically cross their fingers the first time they boot their system after installing Linux. Booting the system properly means that the Linux installation went well! However, you don't always experience a trouble-free boot at first. Sometimes, you can't even get as far as the LILO boot: prompt. Don't worry, you have ways of dealing with this issue.

The first thing to look at is how much of the LILO boot: prompt you get. Each letter of LILO is printed at a specific stage of the loading process. If you don't get all four letters and the word boot, as shown in the following line of code, then something's wrong:

```
LILO boot:
```

Before you start worrying about how much of the prompt shows up in this situation, reboot the machine four more times to see if it eventually boots properly. Sometimes, the problem sorts itself out. Once, it magically started working for us after seven reboots!

If you reboot a few times and still can't get your machine to complete the boot process properly, your problem is more serious. (You didn't want to hear that — but it's true.) The solution for a partial LILO boot: prompt may be one of the following:

- ✔ Re-run LILO and reboot.
- ✔ Ensure that the root partition — or the /boot partition, if you made one and it's appropriate for your distribution — is active.
- ✔ Check the partition with the root or /boot partition for damage.

Each of these solutions probably sounds a bit overwhelming. Don't worry. Take a deep breath and relax. We tell you all you need to know about how to do these things. First, you have to find a way to boot into Linux even though your LILO doesn't work. Depending on what distribution you're using, you have a few different ways to handle this. In all Linux distributions, you have the capability to create a custom boot disk.

You shouldn't keep boot disks around just for Linux — things can go wrong with Windows and other operating systems, too. Each operating system has a method of creating boot disks. Be sure to make one and keep it handy, especially when you start dual- or triple-booting.

In fact, you have the chance to create a custom boot disk when you perform the installation process. If you've already created a custom boot disk, then you're set. Label it clearly and keep it somewhere convenient in case you have problems with the machine. If you're the really conservative type, you may also want to keep another version off-site, maybe at home.

If you haven't yet made a custom boot disk, refer to Chapter 2 for instructions.

Many distributions have special programs or tools available to make custom boot disks for you! Red Hat and TurboLinux have `mkbootdisk`, Mandrake has `mkbootdisk` and `drakfloppy` (graphical), Corel uses `mkboot`, and SuSE has `yast`.

Also, a lot of modern Linux distributions allow you to boot with the CD-ROM and choose `rescue` as your boot option without necessarily needing a custom disk.

My system never booted properly

With a custom book disk, you have the advantage of having the exact version of LILO you installed and the exact kernel you were using safely stored. However, if LILO never worked properly in the first place, then it's pretty hard to make a custom boot disk! Many distributions offer you a safety net: You can use the distribution's installation boot disk for an emergency boot.

Read the instructions for your particular distribution on how to accomplish this if you aren't using Red Hat Linux or one of its derivatives. The rescue process varies widely. For a lot of modern distributions, however, you can do a rescue by booting with the installation CD-ROM.

If you are having problems right now in Red Hat Linux 7, follow these steps:

1. **If your computer can boot from the CD-ROM, then put CD1 that came with this book in the CD-ROM drive; if not, put the original installation boot disk into the floppy drive and CD1 into the CD-ROM drive.**

   Don't have an installation floppy? You can make one by following the instructions in Chapter 2.

2. **Boot the machine.**

   It goes through the motions of getting the installation ready to start. Eventually, you end up at the installation boot screen.

3. **Type** linux rescue **and press Enter.**

   The first screen you see is from the text version of the Linux installation process. Don't panic! It simply asks you which language you want to use.

   If you're booting from the installation floppy, you may be asked at this point whether your Local CD-ROM (default) or Hard Drive contains the rescue image. If this happens, select Local CD-ROM.

4. **Select your language with the arrow keys.**

5. **Press the Tab key to move to the OK button and press Enter.**

   The next screen is also from the text version of the Linux installation process. It asks which keyboard you have.

6. **Select the keyboard you want to use. If you're in North America and predominantly work in English, then select** us.

7. **Press the Tab key to move to the OK button and press Enter.**

   You're now placed at the rescue shell prompt, which looks like this:

   ```
   sh-2.04#
   ```

Restoring LILO

After you manage to boot with the custom boot disk or the install boot disk, you need to fix the problem. The fastest thing you can try first is re-running LILO and rebooting. To run LILO in *verbose* mode (which means it tends to give you lots of information), type **lilo -v** at the command prompt and press Enter. You should get a result similar to the following:

```
LILO version 21, Copyright 1992-1998
Werner Almesberger

Reading boot sector from /dev/hda
Merging with /boot/boot.b
Boot image: /boot/vmlinuz-2.2.14-5.0
Added linux *
/boot/boot.0300 exists - no backup copy made.
Writing boot sector.
```

If you get something similar to this with no errors, then type **reboot** at the command prompt and press Enter to reboot the machine and see if it comes up right this time. Make sure to remove the floppy disk from the drive so it has to use the MBR on the hard drive.

If you do get errors, you may need to edit your LILO configuration file. To do so, you must be familiar with how it works. The file /etc/lilo.conf is broken into two parts: global and local. The global section contains the items that apply to everything. An example may be:

```
boot=/dev/hda
map=/boot/map
install=/boot/boot.b
prompt
timeout=50
message=/boot/message
linear
default=linux
```

We've listed the global settings that you may need to change, add, or remove in Table 5-1.

Table 5-1	Editing LILO
Option	*Purpose*
boot=*device*	The hard drive or other device that has the LILO boot information installed on it. For example, if LILO is on your first IDE hard drive, then this line is boot=hda.
default=*menu-item*	The menu choice from the local section that LILO should boot into if no one presses any keys at the LILO boot: prompt. If you want to use the first item listed, you don't need this option. For example, if you want to boot the Linux menu option and it's the third listed, then use default=linux.
delay=*secs*	How many seconds LILO should wait before giving up and booting into the first or specified menu item. You don't typically use this and timeout together. For example, if you wanted LILO to boot immediately because you don't have a multiboot system, then you would use delay=0.
linear	Many people find LILO works just as well with or without this setting. If you had it to begin with and LILO isn't working properly, remove it, or vice versa.
prompt	Enters the LILO prompt without expecting any intervention. If you're not there when the machine is booting or timeout isn't set, then it waits forever until someone tells it what operating system to boot into.
timeout=*tenthsecs*	How many tenths of a second LILO should wait at the boot prompt before booting the first or specified menu item. If you wanted LILO to wait at the boot prompt for twenty seconds, then you would use timeout=200.
verbose=*level*	Specifies how much information LILO should print on the screen as it loads (this is useful if you're having serious LILO problems but simply annoying if you aren't). The levels are 0 through 5, where 0 only shows warnings and errors, and 5 shows file information, directory information, sector information, and more.

The local section contains the individual boot menu items. For example, on a dual boot system with Linux on the first hard drive and Windows on the second, you may have:

Picking apart the kernel

A word that you hear a lot while reading about Linux is *kernel*. The kernel is the central core of your operating system. Everything else is a collection of applications, tools, trappings, and other such things to make it usable by people like you and us. A word of caution: Don't mess with your kernel! The Linux kernel is Linux itself. If you move or delete the kernel, you no longer have an operating system!

All operating systems have a kernel. Windows, Macintosh, and other such operating systems, however, keep the kernel under lock and key.

We're not saying this is right or wrong — it's just how it is. Linux allows a much closer relationship with the kernel, which can be both good and bad, depending on what happens when you try to develop this relationship.

The Linux kernel is kept in the boot section of your file system. In some distributions this is /boot, and in others, it's right there in the root (/). The file typically has a name starting with vmlinuz. Whenever you need to know what version of the kernel you're using, type **uname -r** either as the root user or as another user.

```
image=/boot/vmlinuz-2.2.16-12
       label=linux
       read-only
       root=/dev/hda1
other=/dev/hdb1
       table=/dev/hdb
       label=dos
```

The local section in LILO has as many boot menu items as you have operating systems. While the global section has a pretty freeform layout, the local section is more rigid. Each menu item for a Linux install looks similar to:

```
image=path_to_kernel
       label=linux
       root=partition
```

The image value points directly to the kernel. The path is usually either just the root directory (/) or /boot. The kernel itself typically starts with vmlinuz. You can find out more about how to follow partition structures in Chapter 14.

For an operating system such as Windows, the menu item entry looks different. Instead of using the structure shown in the preceding code example, use the following:

```
other=partition
       label=windows
       table=drive
```

Activating the root (/) or /boot partition

To boot from a partition (remember that partitioning is a way to divide a hard drive into a series of virtual drives), the partition must be marked *active*. An active partition has special meaning to your computer because it only boots from an active partition.

Various programs are available that can mark a partition as active. In both Linux and Windows (as an MS-DOS program), you have fdisk. Because this is a pretty complex program, we quickly explain here how to make a partition active in Linux — which you do after you've booted with the rescue methods that we discuss in the "My system never booted properly" section earlier in this chapter.

To make a partition active in Linux, follow these steps:

1. **Determine the designation for the partition you need to make active.**

   See Chapter 14 for info on how to do this.

   You need to activate the /boot or / partition for Linux.

   If you manually partitioned your hard drive(s), then you know what /boot or / was assigned to (something like /dev/hda1) during this process, regardless of what tool you used.

2. **Type** fdisk /dev/*hard_drive_designator* **to start** fdisk.

   For example, your hard drive designator may carry the ever popular hda designation.

3. **Tell** fdisk **to set a partition as active.**

4. **Type** a **and press Enter to tell** fdisk **that you want to set a partition as bootable.**

   The fdisk program asks for a partition number.

5. **Type in a number and press Enter to tell** fdisk **which partition to set active.**

6. **Type** q **and press Enter to exit the** fdisk **program.**

Checking a partition for damage

All operating systems tend to come with a way to check hard drives for damage. The program you use in Linux is e2fsck. If your system isn't booting properly, then check the root (/) or /boot partition for damage, depending on where your boot information is.

To check your partition for damage, follow these steps:

1. **Determine the designation for the partition that you need to check.**

   See Chapter 14 for info on how to do this.

2. **Make sure that the partition isn't mounted onto the file system.**

   This can be tricky with the `/boot` partition. If you booted using emergency methods, then you should be able to unmount this partition by using either the `umount /` or `umount /boot` commands.

3. **Check the partition.**

   Type **e2fsck /dev/*hard_drive_designator*** at the command prompt and press Enter to check the partition for damage (you discovered your *hard_drive_designator* in Step 1).

The `e2fsck` program asks you a lot of questions about whether it should fix things or not. If you want it to automatically fix problems, then use the `-y` flag, such as `e2fsck -y /dev/hda2`.

Where's my login prompt?

No operating system is immune from problems. The most frightening thing you may encounter as a Linux beginner is a machine that refuses to boot properly. It gets part way into the boot process and then just freezes up. Unfortunately, a machine can freeze up in a number of places throughout the boot process. In this section, we address the situation in which you enter your LILO choice and can't do anything else because the boot process froze after this point.

Why am I ending up here?

Basically, Linux machines end up in one of two places when you boot them: the command prompt or the GUI. If you're on one and want to be on the other, don't worry because you may find that this is one of the easier things to change in Linux! Follow these steps to do so:

1. **Determine the runlevel for the standard command prompt and the one for the standard GUI by typing** more /etc/inittab **at the command prompt and pressing Enter; then press Q to quit the program.**

2. **Open** /etc/inittab **with your favorite editing program.**

   If you're not familiar with any of the Linux text editors, see Chapter 12 where we discuss the `vi` editor.

3. **Locate the line that sets the boot runlevel.**

   This line looks similar to:

   ```
   id:3:initdefault:
   ```

4. **Edit the line such that the number reflects the runlevel you want to boot into.**

   In Red Hat Linux, if you were booting into the command prompt (3) and wanted to change this to the GUI (5), you need to change the line to:

```
id:5:initdefault:
```

5. **Save and exit** /etc/inittab.

The next time you reboot, the changes go into effect.

I could swear I saw an error while it was booting

Some boot problems appear as the kernel initializes the system. A booting Linux computer features a lot of information scrolling by, making it hard for you to catch specific pieces (especially if your machine is really fast). Fortunately, most distributions keep a *log* (a text file containing a record) of what happened during boot time. Table 5-2 lists where you can find this information in several popular Linux distributions.

Table 5-2	Log File Locations in Linux Distributions
Distribution	*Log File(s)*
Caldera	/var/log/messages
Corel	/var/log/messages
Mandrake	/var/log/boot.log, /var/log/dmesg, /var/log/messages
Red Hat	/var/log/boot.log, /var/log/dmesg, /var/log/messages
SuSE	/var/log/boot.msg, /var/log/messages

Type **dmesg** at a command prompt and press Enter to get your boot information to come back up at any time. You can also use **dmesg | more** to ensure that it doesn't just scroll past you again.

Don't Just Turn the Machine Off!

Linux is just like Windows, the Macintosh, and other modern operating systems when it comes to one important thing: shutting the machine off. At any time Linux may be doing several things, including holding information in memory that it hasn't written to disk yet. If you shut the machine off or reboot it without giving Linux any warning, you're just asking for trouble.

Two commands (type them at the command prompt) to shut down Linux properly that you'll grow to love over time are the following:

✔ halt: Linux shuts itself down and tells you when it's all right to turn off the machine.

✔ reboot: Linux goes through the motions of shutting itself down, and then immediately reboots the machine.

Accounts, Great and Small

Linux is a multi-user operating system. This allows everyone to have their own account and lets more than one user can log on at once. Even if you're the only user who is going to use this system, you need an account of your own that isn't the root user. Multiple accounts are especially fun for experimenting with different user setups.

Avoiding root

The *root user,* also known as the *superuser* or just as *root,* has access to anything and everything on the machine. No matter how you set things up, you can't keep the root account out of any area. The root user also has access to all commands and devices. Many Linux beginners figure they may as well always use the root account because it's so convenient.

For several reasons, however, the root account isn't for everyday use:

✔ You don't always need root-level access.

✔ Root-level access is as much a curse as it is a blessing. If you screw up as a user, you only mess up the stuff in your account. If you screw up as the root user, you can wipe out everything!

Don't think that can happen to you? Almost every experienced Linux administrator tells horror stories about the day they made a fatal typo or weren't paying attention to what they were doing when they were logged in as root.

✔ If you send e-mail or news posts as root for anything other than serious administrative business, people think you don't know what you're doing or are showing off.

✔ Root comes with too much temptation. The superuser can read people's e-mail and files, which introduces a few ethical issues.

Creating user accounts

Red Hat Linux 7 and most other modern Linux distributions enable you to create one or more users accounts during the installation process, so you may have already added some accounts. You can do this at any time, however, after the Linux machine is up and running. To create a user account in any distribution, utilize the useradd command while logged in as root. Although not all Linux distributions have the same useradd functionality, they all have the command. The generic version of useradd works very simply. To create an account, you type **useradd *accountname*** where *accountname* is the name of the new account. For example, to create an account for a user called test, you type **useradd test**.

The adduser command works too, depending on the distribution.

You then need to create a password for this account, otherwise you aren't able to log in to it! To do this, type **passwd *accountname*** where *accountname* is the name of the account that needs the new password. So, to create a password for a user called test, type **passwd test.** You then see the following text:

```
Changing password for user test
New UNIX password:
```

Enter the password for this user. If this isn't one of your own accounts, you probably want to use a set of random numbers and letters, such as 5A2g1AG, and tell the account user to change the password to something else when first logging in. When you press Enter, you see either both of the following lines or just the last one:

```
BAD PASSWORD: it is based on a dictionary word
Retype new UNIX password:
```

If you get warnings about the password, pay attention to them! A password is the first line of defense against people on the Internet snooping around in your files or, even worse, messing with your machine. If you only get that last line, then retype the password, press Enter, and you're done! If you get a warning, then we highly suggest that you heed it.

Good passwords consist of:

- ✔ A combination of numbers, letters, and even punctuation marks
- ✔ Uppercase and lowercase characters
- ✔ No dictionary words
- ✔ Six or more characters
- ✔ No family or pet names, friends' names, birthdays, anniversaries, or other items that someone can easily guess about you

You have to type in the password twice for confirmation. If you mistype one instance, you get:

```
Sorry, passwords do not match.
Enter new UNIX password:
```

Just try again until you get a working password and the new user account is ready to go!

Chapter 6

Adding Devices and Software to Linux

* *

* *

*M*ost Linux distributions contain a nice collection of software packages that range from productivity tools to fun and games. Although these may be sufficient and provide the features you need, you have many other software packages to consider. Some of these are similar to shrink-wrapped commercial products and often are capable of reading and writing to many file format types. At the other end of the software spectrum are applications that crash your environment, cause more harm than good, and get in the way. Between these two extremes sit hundreds of programs that range from productivity applications to utilities to games to you-name-it!

Undoubtedly, the time will come in your Linux experience when you need to add or change hardware. Depending on the type of change, you may have very little to do or may have a number of factors to think about. Typically, you simply have to go back in, add a new driver or two, and make the kernel aware of the changes.

In this section, we cover the basics of what to do when you add hardware and software. Covering all the different software and hardware options that you can stick in a Linux system is impossible. So we cover those topics that are most common to Linux systems.

Understanding Hardware and Software Basics

Before we start, we must first roll up our sleeves and delve into a little hardware and Linux kernel stuff. Before you add new hardware, you must know what the device's hardware settings are. You need to keep these straight so one device doesn't interfere with another device. Hardware conflicts can render your system completely inoperable or not fully functional. The following list describes the major points you need to grasp to understand hardware and software.

> *Those parts of the system that you can hit with a hammer (not advised) are called hardware; those program instructions that you can only curse at are called software.*
>
> — Anonymous

- **Controllers:** Each physical device on your system has some intelligence and its own hardware *controller*. The controller provides a mechanism for the CPU to interface with the hardware so that commands and data can pass between the two. Some devices, such as the keyboard and mouse ports, share the same controller. Others have their own controllers. For example, SCSI and IDE storage systems have their own types of controllers.

- **Interrupts:** When the hardware's controller needs something done, such as computations or data sent to another component, it *interrupts* the processor to get the CPU's attention. To keep straight which hardware device is which, each device is assigned an interrupt number. This number is commonly referred to as an IRQ (or Interrupt Request line) number. The IRQ is a direct line to the processor so when the doorbell rings on interrupt 5, the CPU knows who's at the door. The processor can then accept the request from the device and send the results back to the correct hardware. On most systems, common hardware devices use the same interrupt values. For example, the standard interrupt value assigned to a floppy drive is 6 and the first IDE controller is usually 14. You can see which interrupts your system is using by looking at the `/proc/interrupts` file (see Figure 6-1).

- **I/O port:** Hardware devices and the CPU pass data back and forth between them. If the CPU is busy performing one device's task, it can't just stop to accept data from another device. The system maintains a location in memory for each device to drop off data where the processor picks it up. The CPU uses this same location to place its data in for the device to use. You can think of this as an In/Out bin. On the system, it's known as the *I/O (Input/Output) port,* base address, or I/O address. Just like interrupts, one device's I/O port can't overlap or be the same as another device. Also, common hardware such as the hard drive uses the same addresses on different machines. You can find the I/O port values in use and the devices using them in the `/proc/ioports` file (see Figure 6-2).

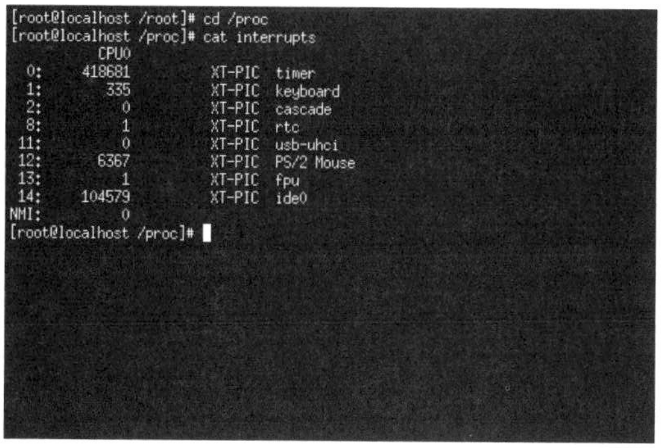

```
[root@localhost /root]# cd /proc
[root@localhost /proc]# cat interrupts
           CPU0
    0:    418681        XT-PIC  timer
    1:       335        XT-PIC  keyboard
    2:         0        XT-PIC  cascade
    8:         1        XT-PIC  rtc
   11:         0        XT-PIC  usb-uhci
   12:      6367        XT-PIC  PS/2 Mouse
   13:         1        XT-PIC  fpu
   14:    104579        XT-PIC  ide0
  NMI:         0
[root@localhost /proc]# ▮
```

Figure 6-1:
A sample
/proc/
inter-
rupts file.

➤ **DMA (Direct Memory Access):** Because the processor can only do one task, or thread, at a time, whenever a hardware device needs to interrupt the processor, it takes time away from another activity. Certain types of actions really don't need the processor's attention and can occur faster if time isn't used to interrupt the processor. The *DMA channel* (or Direct Memory Access channel) enables the device to move data in and out of memory without the processor intervening. As with interrupts, common devices use particular DMA channels. For example, the hard drive controller typically uses DMA channel 1, and the floppy disk controller typically uses DMA channel 2. In order for DMA to work properly, both the hardware device and the computer's hardware must support DMA. The /proc/dma file contains information about any DMA channels in use.

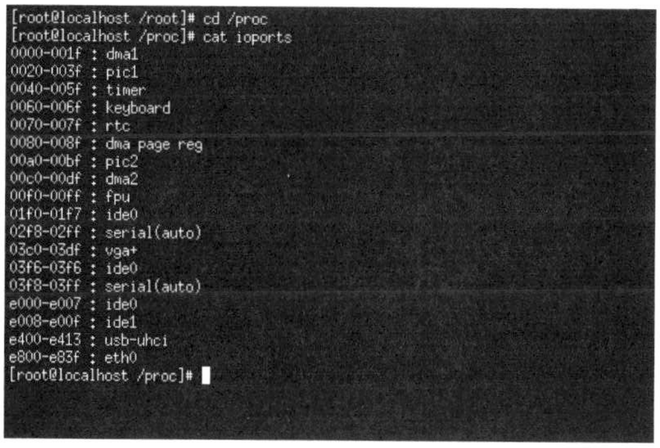

```
[root@localhost /root]# cd /proc
[root@localhost /proc]# cat ioports
0000-001f : dma1
0020-003f : pic1
0040-005f : timer
0060-006f : keyboard
0070-007f : rtc
0080-008f : dma page reg
00a0-00bf : pic2
00c0-00df : dma2
00f0-00ff : fpu
01f0-01f7 : ide0
02f8-02ff : serial(auto)
03c0-03df : vga+
03f6-03f6 : ide0
03f8-03ff : serial(auto)
e000-e007 : ide0
e008-e00f : ide1
e400-e413 : usb-uhci
e800-e83f : eth0
[root@localhost /proc]# ▮
```

Figure 6-2:
A sample
/proc/
ioports
file.

➤ **Base memory:** Each hardware device has some intelligence in the form of code embedded in the hardware's components. A copy of this code is placed in an assigned location in memory known as the *base memory* or shared memory address. Executing a device's code in memory is much faster than running the code from the device itself. As with the other hardware settings, common hardware devices use similar base memory addresses.

- **PCI (Peripheral Component Interconnect):** PCI is probably the most common interface today for your NIC (network interface card), video, SCSI, and sound cards. Devices placed on separate communication channels (buses) don't have to compete with each other for access to the bus. Each standard PCI bus can support up to ten devices. The PCI bus also supports *bus mastering,* which enables the devices to do some of their own processing without the need to bother the CPU. These features enable PCI to be faster than older architectures. Non-PCI and older devices are typically *ISA* devices. ISA (which stands for Industry Standard Architecture) devices operate more slowly than PCI because they depend on the CPU for processing and data exchange. You still find slots for ISA cards on newer computers. In general, if you have the choice between a PCI or an ISA device, choose the PCI device. You can view what PCI devices are in use by your system by examining the `/proc/pci` file (see Figure 6-3).

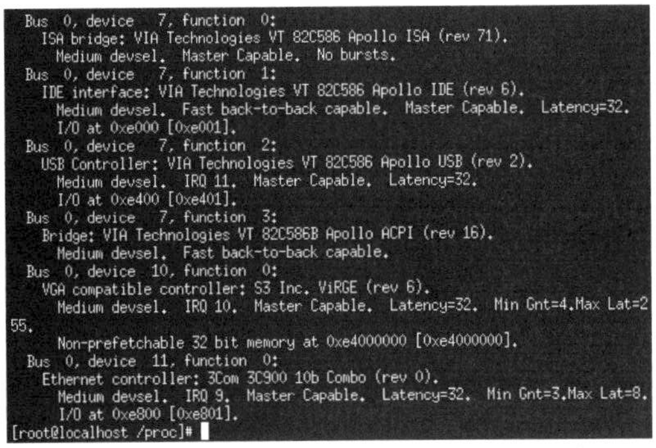

```
 Bus  0, device   7, function  0:
   ISA bridge: VIA Technologies VT 82C586 Apollo ISA (rev 71).
     Medium devsel.  Master Capable.  No bursts.
 Bus  0, device   7, function  1:
   IDE interface: VIA Technologies VT 82C586 Apollo IDE (rev 6).
     Medium devsel.  Fast back-to-back capable.  Master Capable.  Latency=32.
     I/O at 0xe000 [0xe001].
 Bus  0, device   7, function  2:
   USB Controller: VIA Technologies VT 82C586 Apollo USB (rev 2).
     Medium devsel.  IRQ 11.  Master Capable.  Latency=32.
     I/O at 0xe400 [0xe401].
 Bus  0, device   7, function  3:
   Bridge: VIA Technologies VT 82C586B Apollo ACPI (rev 16).
     Medium devsel.  Fast back-to-back capable.
 Bus  0, device  10, function  0:
   VGA compatible controller: S3 Inc. ViRGE (rev 6).
     Medium devsel.  IRQ 10.  Master Capable.  Latency=32.  Min Gnt=4.Max Lat=2
55.
     Non-prefetchable 32 bit memory at 0xe4000000 [0xe4000000].
 Bus  0, device  11, function  0:
   Ethernet controller: 3Com 3C900 10b Combo (rev 0).
     Medium devsel.  IRQ 9.  Master Capable.  Latency=32.  Min Gnt=3.Max Lat=8.
     I/O at 0xe800 [0xe801].
[root@localhost /proc]#
```

Figure 6-3: A sample `/proc/pci` file.

- **Device drivers:** The code containing commands directed to the controllers is commonly referred to as a *device driver.* You can think of it as software that talks to the device and makes it work. Many applications on your Linux system use device drivers. To make these commands readily available to applications, the Linux kernel contains the device driver code. Including the device driver code in the kernel also provides two other benefits: Keeping one copy of the code eliminates extra code baggage by reducing drive space use, and it provides one point where you can add new device drivers and device driver updates. Both PCI and ISA hardware components use device drivers.

Adding New Hardware to Linux

When Linux starts up, each device driver contained in the kernel or in the startup files is initialized. Each device driver then looks for the hardware device that it's controlling. If the hardware device isn't physically present, the system continues to load anyway. Any extra, unused device driver code hangs around but causes no harm. This unused code does take up a small amount of memory.

Ignoring missing hardware is great because it enables the system to continue loading instead of waiting for a non-present device to respond. You'll find this particularly useful when you're removing hardware for repair. After you replace hardware of the same type, the device driver recognizes the hardware and you're back up and rolling.

Those pesky drivers

When you add new hardware to Linux, you also need to add its device driver. A nice feature of most Linux drivers is that you can load and unload them dynamically. In short, you can add or remove device drivers at the command prompt or in X, which is especially useful for testing and adding updated device drivers. After you load a Linux device driver or module, it's as much a part of the kernel as any of the other kernel code.

An important item that you need to keep in mind is that some device drivers require supporting code to be present, either in the form of another device driver or as part of the kernel. If the device's supporting code isn't available, the device driver doesn't load and usually you get some type of error message. We cover methods you can use to determine what other component a device driver needs.

To illustrate some of these hardware and software concepts, we walk you through an example of adding a NIC device driver to the Linux system. For this example, we assume the hardware has already been properly installed.

A GUI way to add a device driver

Before we can begin adding a device driver, we need to document the type of NIC and its hardware settings. For an example, we use a common Ethernet card.

A very nice utility called LinuxConf enables you to configure many aspects of your Linux system. You can access it from within X or from the command prompt with LinuxConf. We use the X version of LinuxConf, but you use the same options and settings when executing it from the command prompt.

To access LinuxConf from X, follow these steps:

1. **Click the Main Menu button and choose Programs⇨System⇨LinuxConf.**

   The default display should be Config, but if it isn't, click the Config tab at the top of the LinuxConf window.

2. **Expand the Networking entry by clicking the + to the left of Networking.**

This displays a list of submenu.

3. **Expand the Client tasks submenu.**

More submenus appear.

4. **Select the Basic host information label. This creates a panel to the right that contains several tabs. Click the Adaptor 1 tab.**

Figure 6-4 shows the Adaptor 1 tab open in the Red Hat Linux 7 version of LinuxConf.

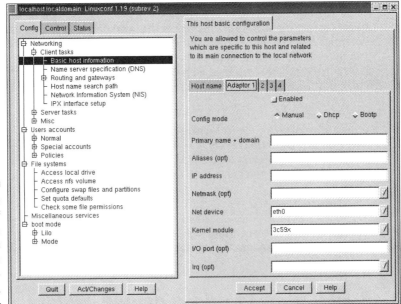

Figure 6-4: LinuxConf showing the This host basic configuration panel.

5. **Select the Enabled check box at the top of the Adaptor 1 panel.**

This enables the network card to use the settings that you specify.

6. **Select the DHCP radio button.**

This enables your Linux system to obtain the IP address and related information from a DHCP server. If you aren't using DHCP, select **Manual** and enter the IP address and subnet mask for your Linux system.

Next, you need to choose the type of network device — for example, Ethernet or Token Ring.

7. **Use the arrow to the right of the Net device field to display a drop-down list from which to select a network device.**

If your network card is an Ethernet device and the first one in your system, choose eth0 from the list (accessed by using the arrow to the right of the Net device field). The next item is the kernel module or device driver.

8. Choose a kernel module from the device driver drop-down list.

The kernel module varies depending on the type of device you have. For example, if your NIC is a 3Com 3C509, choose 3c509 in the device driver list (accessed by using the arrow to the right of the Kernel module field). If your NIC is a generic Ethernet card, you can probably choose ne as the driver.

9. Choose your NIC's I/O port from the I/O Port (opt) list and IRQ from the IRQ (opt) field drop-down list.

I/O port and IRQ (interrupt) fields are optional. Sometimes Linux detects these hardware settings. If not, you can enter the I/O port and IRQ values here. The I/O port value uses the syntax of 0 x address where address is the I/O port address. You can use the selection arrow to the right of the IRQ field for selecting the IRQ number as an alternative to typing in the value. The next step is to apply your new settings.

10. Click the Accept button at the bottom of the Adaptor 1 tab.

The Basic host information panel disappears.

11. Click the Quit button.

A dialog box appears indicating that the status of your system doesn't agree with the configuration files.

12. To apply your new changes, click the Activate the changes button.

13. To verify if your newly added NIC card and driver are enabled, open up a command window in X and type ifconfig **and press Enter.**

If everything worked out, the results indicate that your network card is in use and you can view the IP address information. If you don't see your network device listed, then the NIC driver did not load. When you see the network device, for example eth0, you also see the NIC hardware address after the label Hwaddr. You should also see an IP number following the inet addr label. See Figure 6-5 for an example.

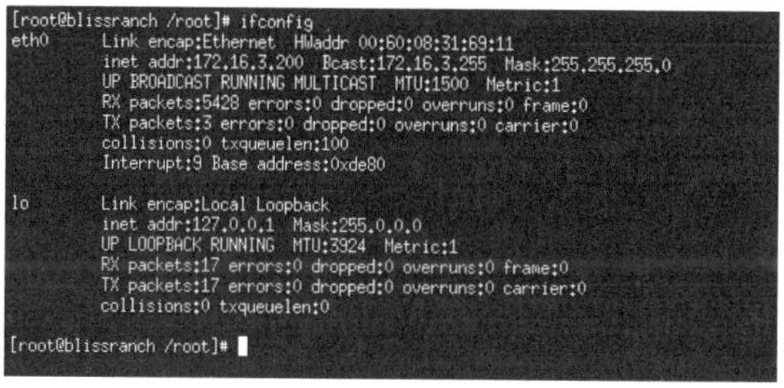

Figure 6-5:
Results
of the
ifconfig
command.

```
[root@blissranch /root]# ifconfig
eth0      Link encap:Ethernet  HWaddr 00:60:08:31:69:11
          inet addr:172.16.3.200  Bcast:172.16.3.255  Mask:255.255.255.0
          UP BROADCAST RUNNING MULTICAST  MTU:1500  Metric:1
          RX packets:5428 errors:0 dropped:0 overruns:0 frame:0
          TX packets:3 errors:0 dropped:0 overruns:0 carrier:0
          collisions:0 txqueuelen:100
          Interrupt:9 Base address:0xde80

lo        Link encap:Local Loopback
          inet addr:127.0.0.1  Mask:255.0.0.0
          UP LOOPBACK RUNNING  MTU:3924  Metric:1
          RX packets:17 errors:0 dropped:0 overruns:0 frame:0
          TX packets:17 errors:0 dropped:0 overruns:0 carrier:0
          collisions:0 txqueuelen:0

[root@blissranch /root]#
```

Adding a device driver from the command prompt

You can also add a device driver from the command prompt. This process uses several commands to test and add drivers to the Linux system.

To add a device driver from the command prompt, follow these steps:

1. **At the command prompt, use the** cd **command to change to the directory that stores the dynamically loadable device drivers.**

   Under the /lib/modules directory is another directory labeled with the version number of your Linux kernel (for example, 2.2.16-22). Below that directory is located the drivers themselves. Figure 6-6 shows several subdirectories listed for the different categories of drivers.

Figure 6-6:
The different categories of loadable Linux device drivers.

```
[root@localhost /root]# cd /lib/modules
[root@localhost modules]# ls
2.2.16-22
[root@localhost modules]# cd 2.2.16-22
[root@localhost 2.2.16-22]# ls -la
total 96
drwxr-xr-x  12 root    root     4096 Sep 26 09:57 .
drwxr-xr-x   3 root    root     4096 Sep 26 09:57 ..
-rw-r--r--   1 root    root      149 Aug 22 15:24 .rhkmvtag
drwxr-xr-x   2 root    root     4096 Sep 26 09:57 block
lrwxrwxrwx   1 root    root       21 Sep 26 09:57 build -> /usr/src/linux-
2.2.16
drwxr-xr-x   2 root    root     4096 Sep 26 09:57 cdrom
drwxr-xr-x   2 root    root     4096 Sep 26 09:57 fs
drwxr-xr-x   2 root    root     4096 Sep 26 09:57 ipv4
drwxr-xr-x   2 root    root     8192 Sep 26 09:57 misc
-rw-r--r--   1 root    root    36501 Sep 26 10:08 modules.dep
-rw-r--r--   1 root    root       99 Sep 26 10:08 modules.pcimap
drwxr-xr-x   2 root    root     4096 Sep 26 09:57 net
drwxr-xr-x   2 root    root     4096 Sep 26 09:57 pcmcia
drwxr-xr-x   2 root    root     4096 Sep 26 09:57 scsi
drwxr-xr-x   2 root    root     4096 Sep 26 09:57 usb
drwxr-xr-x   2 root    root     4096 Sep 26 09:57 video
[root@localhost 2.2.16-22]#
```

We use a driver in the /lib/modules/2.2.16-22/net directory.

2. **Type** ls /lib/modules/2.2.16-22/net **at the command prompt and press Enter to display the contents of that directory.**

   Several network card device drivers are available in the /lib/modules/2.2.16-22/net directory, as shown in Figure 6-7.

   The long number in the pathname above (2.2.16-22) refers to the Linux kernel. If you have a different version of Linux than the copy that comes with this book, the directory may vary depending on the kernel version included in the distribution. Change the directory path above if the directory you need differs from that in the preceding command.

```
drwxr-xr-x   2 root     root     4096 Sep 26 09:57 video
[root@localhost 2.2.16-22]# cd net
[root@localhost net]# ls
3c501.o      cs89x0.o    ewrk3.o        ne2k-pci.o   sk98lin.o
3c503.o      de4x5.o     fmv18x.o       ne3210.o     skfp.o
3c505.o      de600.o     hamachi.o      ni5010.o     sktr.o
3c507.o      de620.o     hdlc.o         ni52.o       slip.o
3c509.o      depca.o     hostess_sv11.o ni65.o       slhc.o
3c515.o      dgrs.o      hp-plus.o      old_tulip.o  smc-ultra.o
3c59x.o      dlci.o      hp.o           olympic.o    smc-ultra32.o
3c90x.o      dmfe.o      hp100.o        pcnet32.o    smc9194.o
82596.o      dummy.o     ibmtr.o        plip.o       strip.o
8390.o       e100.o      ipddp.o        ppp.o        syncppp.o
ac3200.o     e1000.o     ircomm.o       ppp_deflate.o tlan.o
acenic.o     e2100.o     irda.o         rcpci.o      tulip.o
arlan-proc.o eepro.o     irda_deflate.o rtl8139.o    via-rhine.o
arlan.o      eepro100.o  irlan.o        sb1000.o     wanpipe.o
at1700.o     eexpress.o  lance.o        sbni.o       wanxl.o
bonding.o    epic100.o   lanstreamer.o  sdla.o       wavelan.o
bsd_comp.o   eql.o       lne390.o       sdladrv.o    wd.o
cipcb.o      es3210.o    ltpc.o         sealevel.o   yellowfin.o
cops.o       eth16i.o    n2.o           shaper.o     z85230.o
cosa.o       ethertap.o  ne.o           sis900.o
[root@localhost net]#
```

Figure 6-7:
The
different
type of
network
card drivers
available.

3. Type lsmod **at the command prompt and press Enter to see what modules are already present in the system.**

Figure 6-8 shows the modules that are in our system. You can also see their size and whether or not another module is using the device. A value greater than 0 in the Used field indicates how many other components are dependent on that module.

```
s_mask driver_data
[root@localhost net]# depmod -e ne.o
depmod: *** Unresolved symbols in ne.o
depmod:          ei_open
depmod:          ethdev_init
depmod:          ei_interrupt
depmod:          NS8390_init
depmod:          ei_close
ne.o:

# module       vendor   device   subvendor subdevice class    clas
s_mask driver_data
[root@localhost net]# cd
[root@localhost /root]# cd /etc
[root@localhost /etc]# lsmod
Module          Size    Used by
ide-cd          23628   0   (autoclean)
lockd           31176   1   (autoclean)
sunrpc          52964   1   (autoclean) [lockd]
3c59x           19844   0   (autoclean) (unused)
agpgart         18600   0   (unused)
usb-uhci        19052   0   (unused)
usbcore         42088   1   [usb-uhci]
[root@localhost /etc]#
```

Figure 6-8:
Results of
the lsmod
command
before
adding a
NIC driver.

Another utility that comes with Linux is a module probe that you execute with the modprobe command. It enables you to detect whether the hardware is present at the settings you specify. A successful modprobe result sometimes echoes back that the device was found.

4. Type modprobe *device_driver* io=*io*# irq=*irq*# **to detect the specified hardware.**

For our network card example, we typed **modpobe ne** at a command prompt. If the modprobe command is successful, the module is loaded for you.

5. Type lsmod **at the command prompt and press Enter to verify whether or not the module loaded.**

6. **If the module isn't loaded, type** insmod **and press Enter to add the module with the command.**

   For our example, we typed **insmod ne.**

   Again, to verify that the appropriate module or modules are loaded, use the lsmod command. Figure 6-9 shows the ne.o module is loaded.

Figure 6-9:
Results of
the lsmod
command
showing
loaded
modules.

   You can't use your NIC until you've started network services.

7. **Navigate to the** /etc/rc.d/init.d **directory.**

8. **To start network services, type** ./network restart **at a command prompt.**

   The results appear on-screen and you see the eth0 interface activated. Figure 6-10 shows the result of a successful activation of the NIC driver that we've just added.

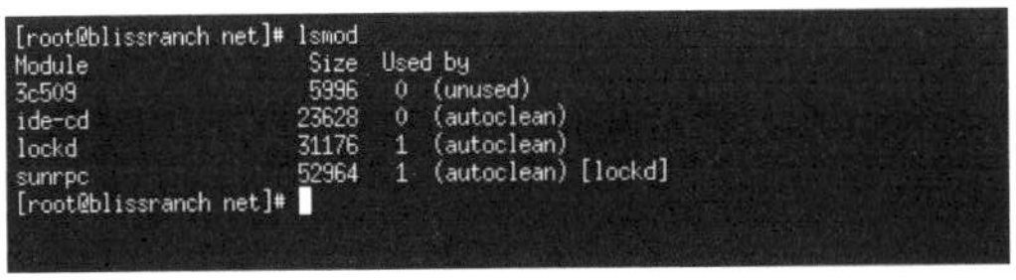

Figure 6-10:
Example of
a successful
result of
activating a
NIC card
with a newly
added
driver.

9. **To load the NIC module automatically when your Linux system starts up, use the** cd **command to change over to the** /etc **directory.**

10. **Open the** modules.conf **file with a text editor and add the appropriate information at the bottom for your module.**

You specifiy information for modules in the `modules.conf` file. The following contains the information for the `ne.o` module for our NIC example:

```
alias eth0 ne
```

If you are using a different Linux distribution than the copy that came with this book, the name of the modules configuration file maybe `/etc/conf.modules`.

No driver? Write one! (or find someone who has)

Linux contains many device drivers. If the one you need isn't in the packaged software, you can usually find one easily enough. Here are a few well-known places on the Web that have device drivers that you can use or that can point you to another location that has drivers:

```
www.rmpfind.net
www.linuxapps.com
www.freshmeat.net
```

You can also write your own driver if you have programming experience. Usually, you may find it easier to write a device driver as a run-time loadable kernel module. You can easily use these modules as loadable modules, or compile them and add them to the kernel. The Linux development environment provides routines for accessing interrupts, I/O ports, and DMA channels. In addition, Linux provides many software routines that device drivers commonly use.

Adding Software to Linux Manually

Linux provides tools to add software, such as productivity applications or games, from a GUI environment or the command prompt. You can make a pplications available to all users of the system by placing them in a common location such as under the `/usr` directory. If the application is only for your use or another single user, you can install the application in the home directory.

You typically find installation software as a package. You may also find it as a *tarball* — files in the tar (which stands for tape archive) format. The package form is more common now and, in some cases, has replaced the traditional tar format. Tools such as the Red Hat Package Manager (RPM), make it easier to work with packages. However, software is often first released as a tarball before it's packaged. A package may not be available for the software until several months later. In this section, we cover installing software from the command prompt using a tarball file.

After you download a tarball file, you need to compile it and install the application. Don't worry. You don't need to be a programmer to do this. For an example, we downloaded a little graphical application that you can run within X that generates special effects.

To go from a tarball file to a running application, follow these steps:

1. **Navigate to the** `tarball` **file directory using the** `cd` **command.**

2. **At the command prompt, expand a .tgz file with the** `gunzip` **utility by typing** gunzip *filename* **where** *filename* **is the name of the .tgz file you want to unzip.**

   The result of the `gunzip` command is to produce a `tar` file. In our example, the filename is `fxd.tar`. You must restore the tar file with the `tar` command.

3. **At the command prompt, type** tar xvf *filename* **and press Enter, where** *filename* **is the name of the .tar file you want to expand.**

   When you execute this, several lines of information appear on-screen. This is the name and locations of the files in the archive. The process places all the files in a subdirectory.

   In this directory, you may also find README, INSTALL, or HOWTO files. We recommend that you read these files. Sometimes, these files include information about how to compile the application or any software dependencies the application has.

   The next few steps compile the source into the application.

4. **Change to the subdirectory mentioned in Step 3 with the** `cd` **command, then enter** ./configure **at the command prompt and press Enter.**

   This process may take several seconds to minutes depending on the speed of your Linux system and the size of the software package. When the process has finished, the command prompt appears. If any errors occurred in this process, the problem areas appear on-screen.

   The next step uses the `make` command, which determines what portion of the programs to recompile and issues the necessary commands to perform the recompilations. This process usually takes longer than the previous process, possibly taking several minutes on some systems. While `make` is working, you see information on-screen.

5. **At the command prompt, type** make.

   Now you can run the application. Because our example is an X application, we make sure that we perform this step in a command window in X. Use the `cd` command to change to the `/src` directory. In here you find the application.

6. **To run the application, type** *./application_name* **at the command prompt and press Enter, where** *application_name* **is the name of the application you're dealing with.**

   Because the current location of the application may not be the most convenient, you can use the `make install` command to put the application in its location specified in the `Makefile` file.

7. **At the command prompt, type** make install.

   Most added software is placed under subdirectories of the `/usr` directory (like `/usr/local`) so that it's accessible to your users.

Troubleshooting New Additions to Your System

Adding hardware and its device drivers can create some interesting problems. If you're having trouble with your system immediately after adding a piece of hardware, suspect a hardware conflict. If the newly added device has the same interrupt or I/O address as an existing device, that can cause immediate problems. Remove the newly added hardware. Start up Linux and document the information contained in your `/proc/interrupts` and `/proc/ioports` files. If conflicts exist, you need to change the settings on the new hardware before adding it back into the system.

Another problem arises when adding modules with the `insmod` command and the module doesn't add. Try using the `modprobe` utility with the appropriate hardware settings to determine whether or not the device driver detects the hardware. If it isn't probed, you need to verify the hardware settings. Also, make sure that you're using the correct driver for the device.

If the `insmod` command produces messages about unresolved symbols, then a module dependency is missing. Here you may find the `depmod` command helpful. For example, the following command shows the dependencies of the `sb.o` module:

```
depmod -e sb.o
```

Figure 6-11 shows many dependencies. In fact, more dependencies exist than the command window can display at once. To determine what other modules are needed by the driver, refer to the driver's documentation.

Figure 6-11:
Results
of the
depmod-e
sb.o
command.

```
[root@blissranch init.d]# ./network restart
Setting network parameters:                          [  OK  ]
Bringing up interface lo:                            [  OK  ]
Bringing up interface eth0:                          [  OK  ]
[root@blissranch init.d]#
```

Some software you add to your system may also require the presence of other components. To determine any requirements when building or running the application, you must read the README, INSTALL, and/or HOWTO related files.

Finally, a common problem you may experience when adding device drivers or software is insufficient permissions. To add hardware device drivers and to install software, you need to make sure you're logged on as root.

Part II
Internet NOW

The 5th Wave   By Rich Tennant

"WELL, PERSONAL INFORMATION MANAGEMENT SOFTWARE HELPS SHOW YOU THE CONNECTION BETWEEN SEEMINGLY DISPARATE ITEMS, LIKE, OH SAY, THAT TIE YOU'RE WEARING, AND THIS BOWL OF GOAT VOMIT."

In this part . . .

In this part, you make the necessary mental and physical connections to hook up your Linux machine to the Internet, including selecting a modem for telephone dialup to an Internet Service Provider (ISP), not to mention setting up and configuring a working connection to the Internet. You go online and grab a Web browser, e-mail client, and newsreader software so that you can install and configure your Linux machine to surf the Web, send and receive e-mail, and access Usenet newsgroups. Armed with the facilities you install in this part, you enable yourself to extend and customize your Linux system to your heart's content!

Chapter 7

Connecting to the Internet

. . . .

In This Chapter

▶ Accessing the Internet

▶ Wrestling your modem into submission

▶ Connecting to your Internet Service Provider (ISP)

▶ Some TCP/IP tidbits

▶ Hacking your way around the Internet

. . . .

*M*ost folks simply assume that their personal computer is capable of connecting to the Internet. To become a Linux power user, you must become Internet savvy.

To get connected, Linux has traditionally required you to understand the mysterious details of dialup networking. Fortunately, Red Hat has developed graphical desktop tools to help grade the learning curve for you. In this chapter, we slash a trail through the dialup networking jungle and help you connect your Linux machine to the rest of the world. After you're connected, we show you how to mingle with the Linux community with the use of a few cool tools.

Bandwidth: I Want My OC-255

Okay, perhaps 13.21GB per second is overkill when you consider that your PC would seize while attempting to digest data at that speed. Regardless, every Internet surfer is on a quest: to find open lanes on the information superhighway. Telephone, cable, and satellite television companies are currently jockeying for a strategic location in your future Internet-connection budget. In the following list we briefly examine a few popular Linux-friendly options that may be available to you.

> ✔ **Cable modems:** Many cable television companies have expanded their product line to include Internet access over their cable infrastructure. When you subscribe to a cable Internet service, the install technician provides you with a special device called a cable modem along with a standard network adapter of some sort that they then install into your

computer. If available in your area, cable Internet connectivity provides the best cost to bandwidth ratio currently available. In other words, while the service will likely cost you more than a dialup connection, a cable connection can reach speeds 50 times faster than a 56 Kbps modem dialup account while typically costing only about two times as much.

You may be on your own to configure your Linux machine to work with cable Internet service. Most cable companies do not yet provide technical support for Linux. The following Web page provides a document that fills you in on all the details:

```
www.linuxdoc.org/HOWTO/Cable-Modem/index.html
```

As you've probably noticed by now, your computer is a conglomeration of micro-electronic components, each performing a unique function. A network adapter is a device that communicates digital (binary) information over a transport medium (cable, copper wire, fiber optic, infrared, or radio frequency) to another computer. A modem is an additional device that is required to convert the digital signal generated by the network adapter into the native signal of the carrier medium.

✔ **ISDN:** Just a couple of years ago, Integrated Services Digital Network (ISDN) provided the residential high-speed option when 28 Kbps was about all that you were able to milk from the copper strands that connected your telephone to the telephone company. Still available, ISDN promises a steady 128 Kbps — provided that you're within 3.4 miles of the telephone company's central office. You need a special device known as a *terminal adapter* (an ISDN modem) and a network adapter. The GNOME desktop includes the Red Hat ISDN `config` tool that you can use to configure your ISDN service (choose Programs⇨System⇨isdn-config).

✔ **DSL (Digital Subscriber Line):** DSL works much like ISDN in that it carries data to your telephone jack in a digital format. DSL is gaining popularity because it provides a faster connection with a lower cost of installation and service than ISDN and it utilizes your existing copper telephone wiring provided by your telephone company. A DSL connection requires additional communication hardware that should be provided by your ISP. Typical residential connection service ranges from 128 Kbps to 384 Kbps. For an overview of DSL, visit the following Web page:

```
www.linuxdoc.org/HOWTO/DSL-HOWTO/index.html
```

✔ **Dialup modems:** The modem, still the most widely used Internet connection device, translates the digital signal from the computer into an analog signal required for transmission from the wall jack to the telephone company. Because it utilizes existing voice telephone service, you need no special setup beyond subscribing to an Internet Service Provider (ISP). Throughout the following sections, we guide you through setting up a modem on your Linux workstation and connecting to the Internet.

Creating Your Internet-O-Matic

Sara, could you connect me with Goober down at the fillin' station?

— Andy Griffith

If only it were that simple. Fortunately, the good folks at Red Hat have provided us with a few tools that reduce the complexity of dial-up networking with Linux. Not long ago, configuring dialup networking on a Linux machine was nothing short of debugging a defective Rube Goldberg contraption.

Connecting to the Internet with your Linux PC is as easy as 1, 2, . . . er . . . um . . . 3–4–5.

1. **Determine if your modem is Linux-friendly.**

2. **Gather ISP service information.**

3. **Configure your modem.**

4. **Connect to the Internet.**

5. **Surf!**

Finding a modem

Please fasten your seat belts. No PC is immune to the turbulence encountered with modem installation. Historically, computer hardware manufacturers have considered modems luxury options that you must install yourself. Although you're led to believe that the Plug and Play concept is designed to harness those Fisher-Price skills you picked up as a child, you may ultimately have to become acquainted with the arcane ideas of IRQs and memory addresses to make the device work properly. You may even encounter problems with your factory-installed modem, as Linux doesn't currently provide support for many of these wannabe modems. (See the "Beware of devices posing as modems" sidebar later in this chapter.)

Hopefully, you're not sobbing into a pillow, cursing your misguided consumer instincts. Hang in there, we're here to help you through this! If you start by assuming the worst, you'll feel all that much better when it works. We refer to this frame-of-mind as

The sustenance of a positive attitude through the assumption of a negative result.

— Winning Through Intimidation, Robert Ringer

Excuse me modem, I'd like to see some ID

Two broad categories of desktop PC modems exist — *internal* and *external*. The external modem is characterized by the obvious presence of an additional chunk of hardware (secondarily, its use as a paperweight) that's independent of your computer case. You use a cable to plug it into one of the serial ports on the back of your computer. Also notice that you plug the telephone cord into this external unit rather than into the back of the computer. External modems also usually have an array of visible LEDs to let you know power and connection status.

Hopefully by now you have a good idea as to the integrity of your modem. If you're still unsure, continue with the preflight check and cross your fingers. Attempting to configure a software modem in Linux causes no harm to your system.

Connecting the hardware

Before you get too comfortable in your chair, you must physically check some items that may require you to do some low-level maneuvers (crawling under your desk):

- **External modem:** If you have an external modem, you need to verify that:
  - A cable is securely connected from the modem to the serial port on the computer.
  - The modem is powered on. (External modems have their own power supply.)
  - One end of a telephone cable is plugged into the wall jack, the opposite end is plugged into the modem.

- **Internal Modem:** If you have an internal modem, you need to verify that
  - The modem is *not* a software modem.
  - One end of a telephone cable is plugged into the wall jack, the opposite end is plugged into the phone plug on the back of your computer.

Okay, now you can climb back into your chair.

If you determine that your modem is, in fact, a software modem, we recommend the acquisition of an external modem. You don't have to touch your existing internal modem (Linux conveniently ignores it); just plug the external modem into an available serial port and step through the external modem checklist in this section.

Beware of devices posing as modems

We're going to try and save you some frustration . . . and ultimately your computer from the rounded end of a ball-peen hammer. Many a Linux newbie has become irritated by not being able to communicate with their internal modem. *"After all,"* the newbie reasons, *"the same hardware works with Microsoft Windows running on it."*

Well, the story is this: Several years ago, hardware manufacturers developed a device called a *software modem* in an effort to reduce hardware costs. The idea was to trim some responsibility from the modem and relegate these tasks to the CPU through the operating system. The result was an inexpensive interface card that routed signals to proprietary software that would only operate under Microsoft Windows. In short, these so-called modems, also known as *Winmodems,* aren't really modems at all, but rather a telephone cable interface to Windows.

The following lists methods you can use to determine whether or not you have a software modem:

✔ The model number has an "HCF-," "HSP-," or "HSF-" in front of it.

✔ The packaging refers to the device as a Winmodem, or designates that it only works with Windows.

✔ Your modem is recognized by Windows but not recognized by Linux.

In short, if you determine that you have a software modem, Linux simply doesn't work with it. For the adventurous out there, the LinModem project (`http://linmodems.org`) has successfully written Linux drivers to work with a few of these software modems. We encourage you to become involved in such a project if you're so moved. These groups of explorers drive the wonderful world of *freedom* software that Linux is a prominent part of.

The bummer in all this is that while you probably saved a few bucks buying a machine with a software modem, you probably need to acquire a real modem for use with Linux (unless you have a LinModem!).

We strongly advise searching the Linux modem compatibility list to determine whether your modem is a good buddy with Linux. You ultimately save money in headache medicine, which you can use to buy a real modem.

`www.o2.net/~gromitkc/winmodem. html`

Selecting an Internet Service Provider (ISP)

Due to the recent meteoric rise in popularity of Linux, many ISPs are training their support staff in the ways of Linux. If you already have a dialup service, give them a call to let them know of your Linux pursuits. Chances are they already have information pertinent to Linux subscribers and can provide you that information. If you're shopping for a new ISP, read on for some practical selection advice.

Some ISPs provide their own proprietary software that you must install on your PC to connect to the Internet. The software they provide is likely to run only on Windows. Several free dialup services now gaining in popularity don't work with Linux because of this. Their proprietary software meddles with the operating system to ensure that banner advertising isn't hidden, or that you only stay dialed in for a specified duration.

If you're shopping around for an ISP, consider the following:

- ✔ Can you get local dialup numbers across the country and around the world? If you travel a lot and need Internet access from different cities, this service is a handy money saver.

- ✔ Do they provide technical support for Linux?

- ✔ Ask a friend. An ISPs best friend is an endorsement from a satisfied customer.

- ✔ Although not entirely an accurate measure, a subscriber-to-line ratio of 7 to 1 (meaning that there will be on average 7 or less subscribers per line) or better should help you avoid frequent busy signals. Hey, it doesn't hurt to ask.

Information you need from your ISP

Most reputable ISPs provide you with a customer information sheet after signing up for their services. This sheet should include the following information at the minimum:

- ✔ Local telephone dial-in number(s)
- ✔ User login name
- ✔ User login password
- ✔ E-mail address
- ✔ E-mail host
- ✔ News host

With this information, you're able to establish an Internet connection using your Linux system.

Configuring your dialup service

If you haven't already done so, start up your computer and login to your GNOME desktop. You don't need to be logged in as the root user, but you *do* need to know the root password.

With your ISP information in hand and a glowing monitor in front of you, follow these steps to configure your dialup connection to the Internet:

1. **From the GNOME desktop, choose Programs⇨Internet⇨Dialup Configuration Tool**.

   If you're currently logged in as a regular user (not root), you're prompted to enter the root password.

   If this is the first time configuring a dialup connection for this machine, you're prompted through a series of dialog boxes (similar to a *setup wizard* that you may be familiar with using in Windows).

2. **To better illustrate the use of the Dialup Configuration Tool, bypass the Setup Help dialog box by clicking the Cancel button.**

   The Dialup Configuration Tool is shown in Figure 7-1.

3. **Click the Modems tab of the Internet Connections dialog box.**

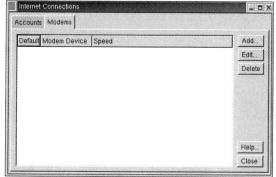

Figure 7-1:
The Dialup
Configura-
tion Tool
(Modems
tab).

4. **Click Add.**

5. **Click the Auto Configure button.**

   A dialog box appears as your system scans for modems. If it finds a modem, the Modem Properties dialog box is filled in with your device and baud rate information.

6. **Click to depress the button labeled** Make this modem the default modem **and click OK.**

7. **Click the Accounts tab of the Internet Connections dialog box.**

8. **Click Add.**

9. **Click Next.**

   Enter the account name. This label refers to the ISP you're dialing into. This becomes important if you have more than one account; for example,

"Behemoth Worldwide Telecartel" may be the label for the account you use when on the road, and "Fred's local IP-mart" may designate a local provider that provides you a cleaner local service when you're at home.

10. **Enter a prefix if you require a specific number to get an outside line.**

11. **Enter an area code, if required.**

12. **Enter the telephone number provided by your ISP and click Next.**

13. **Enter your username.**

    This is the username from your ISP, which is usually whatever is before the @ symbol in your e-mail address.

14. **Enter your password.**

    This is the password to log into your ISP.

15. **Select the type of Internet provider from the Account List. If your ISP isn't listed, select Normal ISP and click Next.**

    The final dialog box asks you to verify your information.

16. **If your information is correct, click the Finish button.**

    At this point, the Internet Connections dialog box displays the profile you just entered.

17. **Click Close.**

Whew, you made it . . . if all went well, you're ready to connect with the worldwide Linux party!

Activating your Internet connection with Red Hat Linux 7

To connect to the Internet in Red Hat Linux 7, you need to activate a program called the Red Hat PPP (Point-to-Point Protocol) Dialer. This tidy program utilizes the configuration that you need to perform the magic required to plug you into the Internet. To activate your Internet connection with Red Hat Linux 7, follow these steps:

1. **Choose Programs⇨Internet⇨RH PPP Dialer.**

   The Choose dialog box, shown in Figure 7-2, presents you with your interface options. If you've already created an ISP profile (see the previous section), the dialog box displays and highlights it at the top.

2. **Click OK.**

   The next dialog box queries you to start the interface.

Figure 7-2:
The Choose
dialog box
with ISP
profiles
displayed.

3. **Click Yes.**

   At this point, your modem springs to life while a Waiting dialog box displays, letting you know that it's attempting to make a connection with your ISP.

   After successful connection, a floating window with the title of your ISP showing current connection status replaces the Waiting dialog box (see Figure 7-3).

Figure 7-3:
The Red Hat
PPP Dialer
status.

   While you may notice a distinct absence of fanfare, your computer is now networked with the Internet. See the following section for information about a few tools for doing something useful on the Internet.

4. **To end your Internet connection, simply click the button with the green dot on the Dialer Status window.**

For quick access, you can place an applet for the RH PPP dialer on your menu bar to toggle dialup networking as required.

Turning to TCP/IP

It's a good thing.

— Martha Stewart

You can make it all the way to the Internet without one single mention of Internet Protocol (IP) numbers helping you get there! That demonstrates the progress that renders Linux easier to use. Rest assured, TCP/IP is still humming away in the background, doing its job of carrying information packets for you in all its complex and robust glory.

Transport Control Protocol/Internet Protocol (TCP/IP) is a set of rules for moving information from one point in a network to another. These TCP/IP rules of packet delivery are similar to the methods a parcel service like UPS uses to move packages. Each package contains a label with a destination and return address and also contains something important to the sender and/or receiver. Using this address, the package carrier can make a decision how to route the package. Each routing decision shuttles the package closer to its intended destination until it arrives. The network component that provides this routing information is known as, strangely enough, a *router.*

Every computer on a TCP/IP network requires a distinct *IP number.* You have two methods that you can use to assign this number to your computer — *static* and *dynamic.*

You assign a static IP number when you configure the machine; the number stays the way that you assign it until you change it. Servers and other computers that are required to service the network continually usually have static IP numbers. (Static IPs are generally administered by seasoned networking professionals.)

Typically, dialup Internet users or workstations that aren't continuously logged into the network use dynamic IP numbers. If your computer is configured to obtain an IP number dynamically, it requests an IP number from another network host computer configured as a *DHCP server.* The Dynamic Host Configuration Protocol (DHCP) server has authority for a range of IP numbers that it can assign as needed to trusted computers. The DHCP server also provides other handy services such as dishing out DNS, gateway, and routing information — that you're otherwise required to know — and stitching it into those cryptic and sometimes elusive configuration files.

You can be thankful that the dialup networking tools provided with your Red Hat distribution, along with services provided by your ISP, perform these geeky functions for you transparently.

The IP number looks like this to your computer (remember, the computer stores information in the form of *ones* and *zeroes*):

```
11010001100101001111010101100100
```

Ouch, do your eyes hurt?

```
11010001.10010100.11110101.01100100
```

Is that any better? . . . not hardly?

```
209.148.245.100
```

What about this?

The last example is a decimal representation of the first binary number example. Known as an IP number, every computer on the Internet requires a unique one.

IP numbers represent 32 bits of information. With 32 available address bits, only 4,294,967,295 possible IP numbers exist. When all six billion of the Earth's inhabitants connect to the Internet at the same time, we don't have enough IP numbers to go around. The current IP standard is known as IPv4. Experts are actively discussing the IPv6 standard, currently on the proverbial drawing board. Due to the explosive growth of the Internet, along with the problem of dwindling IP numbers, are other design considerations that the original TCP/IP architects never expected to encounter. IPv6 calls for a 128-bit IP address that provides enough addresses for our planet, along with a few hundred million more inhabited planets that we may connect with in the future. (We suspect that there was at least one AOL disk sent with *Voyager* into deep space.)

The IP number is the mailing address for your information packages. Granted, the casual cybestrian doesn't keep a list of IP numbers for friends; rather, he uses symbols that are more familiar to him. The Internet uses an ingenious method for resolving names into IP numbers: the *Domain Name System,* or DNS.

Dealing with DNS

DNS is a distributed database of information across the Internet that maps IP numbers to names more meaningful for humans. For example, when e-mail is sent to an address such as woodsman@mormonlake.az.us, our computer networking system wants an IP number and has no idea where, or what, mormonlake.az.us is. The DNS service resolves the domain mormonlake.az.us into an IP number that it stamps on the e-mail package and ships through the Internet. Note that the personal address of woodsman is of no concern to the routing address, it becomes part of the envelope that the recipient host uses for knowing where to place the message — in woodsman's P.O. box, of course!

Like an experienced librarian, a DNS server doesn't know everything, but simply knows where to look and who to ask for information. The Internet DNS system is comprised of network hosts that have the authority over a specified *domain* of computers. If you want information about a computer within a specific domain, you can query the DNS server that has authority for that domain. This method distributes responsibility to several computers instead of relying on a designated, single computer somewhere. DNS servers constantly maintain the Internet's who's who directory. You can visit the Network Solutions Web site at www.networksolutions.com.

Network Solutions is a company that provides the authority for the popular, top-level domains of .com, .org, and .net. By registering a unique domain with Network Solutions, you can become the authority for your own network domain. Linux also comes with a free software package called bind that provides the tools you need to become part of the Domain Name System.

To identify your TCP/IP setup and snoop around a bit, read on.

Checking out important IP utilities

Just to verify that you have a TCP/IP interface running in the background, run a command to show all the gory details of the network interface.

1. **Log in as root.**

   You need to be the root user because most of these network commands require some system administration authority.

2. **With your computer dialed into your favorite ISP, enter the** ifconfig **command.**

3. **Finally, enter the** route **command.**

   See Figure 7-4 for sample results.

```
[evan@localhost evan]$ /sbin/ifconfig
lo        Link encap:Local Loopback
          inet addr:127.0.0.1  Mask:255.0.0.0
          UP LOOPBACK RUNNING  MTU:3924  Metric:1
          RX packets:90 errors:0 dropped:0 overruns:0 frame:0
          TX packets:90 errors:0 dropped:0 overruns:0 carrier:0
          collisions:0 txqueuelen:0

ppp0      Link encap:Point-to-Point Protocol
          inet addr:209.250.14.153  P-t-P:209.250.14.150  Mask:255.255.255.255
          UP POINTOPOINT RUNNING NOARP MULTICAST  MTU:1500  Metric:1
          RX packets:16 errors:0 dropped:0 overruns:0 frame:0
          TX packets:16 errors:0 dropped:0 overruns:0 carrier:0
          collisions:0 txqueuelen:10

[evan@localhost evan]$ /sbin/route
Kernel IP routing table
Destination     Gateway         Genmask         Flags Metric Ref    Use Iface
209.250.14.150  *               255.255.255.255 UH    0      0        0 ppp0
127.0.0.0       *               255.0.0.0       U     0      0        0 lo
default         209.250.14.150  0.0.0.0         UG    0      0        0 ppp0
[evan@localhost evan]$ 
```

Figure 7-4:
Results of
ifconfig
and route.

These two commands provide a lot of information about your current network configuration.

ifconfig, with no command prompt options, displays the status of the currently active network interfaces. You're likely to notice two configured interfaces, as shown in Figure 7-4:

✔ **lo:** The local loopback interface that's always available and provides a doorway for programs that require a network interface. The 127.0.0.1 IP number is a special IP number that's reserved for this loopback interface. You may notice that every computer with an lo interface is likely to have this same number.

✔ **ppp0:** The RH Dialer creates this interface when it makes a connection with your ISP. ppp, known as *Point-to-Point Protocol,* provides the medium that TCP/IP packets can use to get from your machine to the telephone company through your modem. The 0 that trails the ppp interface just shows that it's the first ppp interface in your system. Yes! You can have more than one dialup interface operational at a time, but that's a topic for a future book possibly entitled *Advanced Linux For Rocket Scientists.*

The IP number listed adjacent to inet addr: in Figure 7-4 is the number that your ISP dynamically provided your system when you logged in. This number is likely to change each time you dial in. You may get the same number again, however, because your ISP is providing IPs from the same pool each time you connect.

If you care about how your information is traveling through the network, route provides you with some interesting reading. The most significant tidbit of data is the line labeled default. In that line under the Gateway column, the IP number listed is the machine acting as your drawbridge to the Internet at large. This number, likely handed to your machine by your ISP when you connected, is the first stop for the IP packets leaving your computer.

Putting IP to work on your network

The ping command is akin to a submarine using sonar to detect other objects in the ocean. Sonar sends out a ping signal, which reflects off a hard surface. By measuring the amount of time between sending the ping and the ping's return, the submarine's engineer can determine whether an object is out there and how far from the submarine that object is.

The ping command in Linux provides information similar to what sonar provides. If you consider the Internet to be your ocean, by pinging you can determine what other network computers exist and also how long it takes for your ping to return.

Latency, or the amount of time it takes for a signal to travel, on the Internet has little to do with physical distance. Rather, factors such as network traffic, bandwidth, and network hardware all contribute to a slow latency. These factors determine whether a ping to your neighbor's computer takes longer than pinging a host at the South Pole.

To use the `ping` command in Linux, you must have an object in mind that you want to ping, which is usually another host computer that's connected to the network. You can ping an IP number of another host, or a hostname if your DNS is working correctly.

For an example, ping the gateway IP number that you found from the `route` command issued in Figure 7-4, (remember, the gateway is the first intersection your network traffic crosses to get to the Internet at large) using the following command format:

```
ping 209.250.14.150
```

Press Ctrl+C to break the ping; otherwise, your machine continues to ping away at the target.

The `ping` line, shown in Figure 7-5, provides information about what the `ping` is doing. If the host is unreachable, a message indicates so. If the host is located, you receive a line that provides some useful data, namely the last item on the line: `time=`. This number is the time, in milliseconds that it takes for the signal from your computer to go out to the destination computer and return. Lower numbers are better. For an Ethernet, a ping time of 1–3ms is an acceptable response time from another machine on the same local net (that is, the gateway). For dialup connections, expect somewhere around 150ms (ms meaning milliseconds). When you start seeing ping times climbing to 900ms or better, some serious network traffic likely sits between you and your target host.

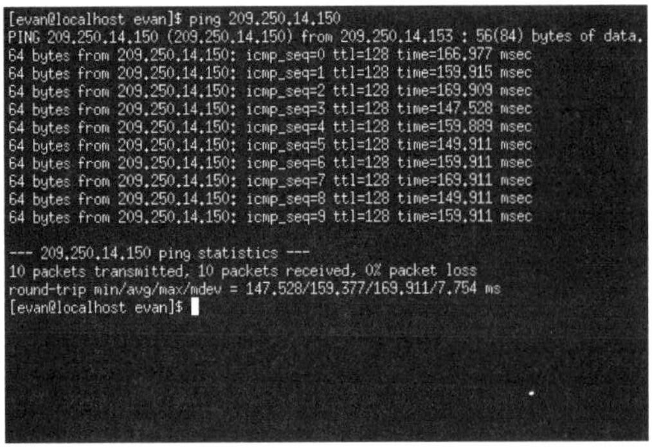

Figure 7-5:
Sample
results of
the `ping`
command.

Suppose you were attempting to visit `www.yahoo.com` and it didn't appear. You could jump out to a command prompt and type in the command:

```
ping www.yahoo.com
```

`ping` lets you know immediately whether or not a network problem sits between you and the host that manages the Yahoo.com Web site. Although this may indicate a network problem, `ping` doesn't provide much more information than that. To flush out more of the problem, you can use the `traceroute` command.

The `traceroute` command enables you to map the route your IP packets are taking from your computer to the intended destination. Just because you may not be able to visit your favorite Web site doesn't mean that the Web site is down, it may simply mean that a link along your route is down. Ever hear of traffic congestion on your morning commute due to a pile-up? The same thing happens on the Internet when a significant router or conduit *goes down*.

To use `traceroute`, you need to know of a destination. Try Yahoo.com!

```
traceroute yahoo.com
```

Notice that the first line, shown in Figure 7-6, indicates a warning simply noting that Yahoo.com uses multiple hosts (each of which needs its own unique IP number) to serve you its information. With the high volume of activity that Yahoo! gets, it can better service the community by dividing the load to various hosts around the Internet and having DNS direct traffic.

```
[root@localhost /root]# traceroute yahoo.com
traceroute: Warning: yahoo.com has multiple addresses; using 204.71.200.243
traceroute to yahoo.com (204.71.200.243), 30 hops max, 38 byte packets
 1  209.250.14.150 (209.250.14.150)  177.934 ms  166.626 ms  152.804 ms
 2  209.250.14.3 (209.250.14.3)  171.885 ms  178.143 ms  183.323 ms
 3  209.250.1.1 (209.250.1.1)  182.541 ms  182.986 ms  173.711 ms
 4  209.234.146.9 (209.234.146.9)  167.298 ms  168.132 ms  168.411 ms
 5  209.234.144.1 (209.234.144.1)  177.459 ms  173.201 ms  168.412 ms
 6  207.170.198.130 (207.170.198.130)  197.320 ms  188.181 ms  178.468 ms
 7  206.80.25.14 (206.80.25.14)  187.422 ms  178.120 ms  188.432 ms
 8  206.251.8.77 (206.251.8.77)  197.360 ms  198.243 ms  203.340 ms
 9  208.48.118.121 (208.48.118.121)  192.486 ms  188.221 ms  178.451 ms
10  206.132.254.213 (206.132.254.213)  187.313 ms  198.212 ms  178.443 ms
11  206.132.254.41 (206.132.254.41)  188.344 ms  188.176 ms  196.417 ms
12  208.178.103.62 (208.178.103.62)  197.368 ms  188.191 ms  198.340 ms
13  204.71.200.243 (204.71.200.243)  197.391 ms  203.181 ms  183.384 ms
[root@localhost /root]#
```

Figure 7-6: Results of the `traceroute` command.

Each line of your `traceroute` command result represents a *hop*. This command helps to illustrate the concept explained earlier of packets being routed, or handed off to carriers along the way to move your package closer to its destination. Each hop is a physical machine that reads your packet address and forwards it. You will also notice a latency time associated with each hop. You can identify heavy network congestion, or a weak router along the way, by identifying the relatively larger numbers in the list.

Sometimes, especially when you're troubleshooting why you can't access your intended Web site, you perform a `traceroute` that times out somewhere along the way. This usually indicates that a traffic accident has occurred somewhere along the information superhighway. Give it a few minutes and try again. TCP/IP is an amazingly robust networking protocol that was designed to reroute packets efficiently in the event of a failed network segment.

Chapter 8

Surfing the Web and Managing E-mail with Netscape Communicator

* *

In This Chapter

▶ Installing and configuring Netscape Communicator

▶ Surfing technique tips and tricks

▶ Test driving your e-mail

▶ Subscribing to newsgroups

* *

> *Give a man a fish and you feed him for a day; teach him to use the Net and he won't bother you for weeks.*
>
> — Anonymous

*A*ssuming you have your dialup networking configured (as we discuss in Chapter 7), you can now get on with doing something interesting with the Internet. In this section, we introduce you to a few useful communication utilities that provide you with the tools of the Internet trade.

Many hold the graphical Web browser personally responsible for the explosive growth of the Internet. The Internet has been around for much longer than the invention of the browser. It's just that most of the work done on the Internet was in plain old text, which held little attraction for us belonging to the more spatially oriented of the species (that is, we preferred picture books as young children).

Several graphical Web browsers are available for Linux. The most popular, and also the browser included with Red Hat Linux 7 on the CDs that come with this book, is Netscape Communicator, which does far more than just display Web pages. You can use Communicator to manage your e-mail and newsgroup subscriptions as well.

Finding and Downloading Netscape (If You Don't Already Have It)

Most Linux distributions, including Red Hat Linux 7, come with a copy of Netscape Communicator. If you select a standard workstation installation, Communicator installs for you automatically. If, for some strange reason, you don't have a Netscape icon, choose Programs⟹Internet⟹Netscape Communicator. If the icon doesn't work (which also may indicate why it's absent), you may want to download a fresh copy and install it.

Netscape Communicator is a *huge* download (somewhere in the vicinity of 15MB for the full package.) You can save yourself a lot of download time by installing Netscape Communicator 4.75 from your Red Hat CD-ROM.

Communicator installs by default with the Workstation install of Red Hat Linux 7, which we discuss in Chapters 2 and 3.

Netscape comes in many formats and versions. You can download the two primary formats, RPM and tarball, from several locations. For the sake of simplicity, we demonstrate the process of downloading the latest supported Netscape Communicator package (in RPM format) straight from the Red Hat FTP site.

By the time this book is out, so too will Netscape 6 be out. Unfortunately, Netscape 6 missed the Red Hat Linux 7 bandwagon and so it isn't included on the CDs that come with this book. If you want to check out the snazzy new Netscape 6 program, you can download it at the following URL, but bear in mind that the instructions in this chapter will differ significantly if you do, as these instructions are for Netscape Communicator 4.75:

```
http://home.netscape.com/browsers/6/index.html
```

If you're using a standard Red Hat installation, stick with RPMs for packages. They're simpler to manage and have been packaged to know where to find supporting system components.

To perform a complete download and installation of Netscape Communicator, follow these steps:

1. **Log in to your workstation and activate your dialup network connection.**

   If you aren't familiar with your dialup network connection, see Chapter 7.

2. **Click the Terminal program icon on the GNOME panel.**

   A terminal window appears.

3. **At the shell prompt, type** ftp ftp.redhat.com **and press Enter.**

   The FTP server login prompt appears. This means that you have made a successful connection with the Red Hat server.

4. **Type** anonymous **at the prompt and press Enter.**

   You're now prompted to enter a password.

5. **Type in your e-mail address.**

   A message appears welcoming you to the site. You may also see a message denying you access. The Red Hat FTP site gets a lot of traffic and only allows a limited number of users at one time. You can find a listing of mirror sites that also keep copies of the Red Hat distribution software at www.redhat.com/mirrors.html. A successful FTP login displays the last few lines of the FTP welcome:

6. **Type** cd redhat/current/i386/RedHat/RPMS **at the FTP prompt.**

   If you see the following message, you've successfully changed over to the RPM directory:

   ```
   250 CWD command successful.
   ftp>
   ```

7. **Type** mget netscape-comm* **at the FTP prompt.**

   The asterisk is a wildcard, meaning that all filenames that start with netscape-comm are downloaded. You're prompted with a y (yes) or n (no) for each file match found and then you see the following message (or similar):

   ```
   mget netscape-common-4.75-2.i386.rpm?
   ```

   Note: We've designed these steps for you to get the latest version of Netscape available with the latest version of Red Hat. Versions change faster than the seasons in an *open source* world! So don't be alarmed by a slight version change in the file numbers.

8. **Type** y **in response to mget netscape-common-4.75-6.i386.rpm?**

   The download begins and you're prompted when the file download completes.

9. **Type** y **in response to mget netscape-communicator-4.75-6.i386.rpm?**

   You see the following as the next file begins to download:

   ```
   200 PORT command successful.
   150 Opening BINARY mode data connection for 'netscape-
           communicator-4.72-6.i386.rpm' (6049743 bytes).
   ```

10. **Type** bye **at the FTP prompt.**

    A friendly farewell and you're left back at your shell prompt.

At this point, you hopefully have two .rpm files in your home directory: one beginning with netscape-common and one with netscape-communicator. The first file provides the foundation files that Communicator needs in order to run. The second file is the actual Communicator application. To install these programs, follow these steps:

1. **Log in as root**.

2. **Type** rpm -ivvh netscape-common **at a command prompt and press Tab and then Enter.**

   Your screen now scrolls with numerous messages indicating Netscape is installing.

   If you were watching closely, the Tab key actually finished typing the file-name for you. You may have noticed by now that many Linux file names are long and full of strange characters. Pressing Tab searches your current directory for matching filenames. If more than one filename exists with the same starting characters, hit the Tab key twice for a full list of options. This is the command-completion feature built-in to the bash shell, isn't it cool?

3. **Type** rpm -ivvh netscape-common **and press Tab and then Enter.**

   After this command finishes, you've installed Netscape. Check for any error messages that may indicate otherwise.

Test your newly installed browser by clicking the Netscape icon on your GNOME Panel or by choosing Programs➪Internet➪Netscape Communicator.

Configuring Netscape Communicator

Prior to using Netscape Communicator, you'll need to provide some essential configuration information such as your Internet identity and where to find your e-mail server and newsgroup servers. Other options enable you to customize Communicator with preferences such as a home Web site, font sizes, colors, and many other options.

The following steps introduce you to the Preferences dialog box where all the Netscape Communicator configuration parameters are stored:

1. **Start Netscape Communicator by choosing Program➪Internet➪ Netscape Communicator.**

   Netscape should start after a moment. Be patient, Communicator is a large program and it usually takes a few seconds to load from the disk into memory.

Note: The first time you start Communicator after an install you're presented with a license screen. Simply click the Accept button and you aren't bothered by it in the future.

2. **Choose Edit⇨Preferences.**

   The Netscape Preferences window appears, as shown in Figure 8-1.

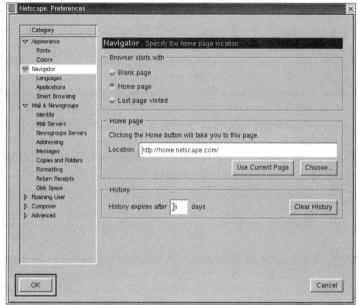

Figure 8-1:
The Netscape Preferences window.

You'll notice that many configuration options are available. Throughout the rest of this chapter, we guide you through configuring a few of the essential settings. Still, we encourage you to explore the many options available along the way.

Netscape Communicator provides an entire menu of help documents. In the upper-right corner of the browser menu is a Help option. Clicking this menu item provides you with several online help options.

In the following list, we describe each of the main categories of the Netscape Preferences window, with a brief description of what you can customize in each category:

✓ **Appearance:** The On Startup launch selection enables you to determine how you want Communicator to start when loaded. If you primarily use Communicator for e-mail, you may want to choose the Messenger Mailbox option. Keep in mind that you can still get to your browser and newsgroups. Selecting your startup preference is a matter of speed and convenience.

The Show Toolbar As selection enables you to determine the cosmetics of your toolbar. Do you like pictures? words? . . . or both!

- **Fonts:** Fonts and Encodings enable you to set your preferred typeface. For desktop resolutions of 1024 x 768 and higher, we recommend jacking up your font sizes immediately (or you'll need a strong magnifying glass).

- **Colors:** Set your text colors and whether you want to override explicit Web page settings. This is an important setting for the colorblind.

✔ **Navigator:** This category enables you to select the behavior of your browser when it's first started. You have the choice to: not show anything, show a specified home Web page (entered into the Location text box), or show the last Web site you visited during your last session. Note that the Location text box also holds the Web site that you are transported to whenever you hit the Home button on the browser.

The History text box enables you to designate how many days you want your browser to remember where you've been. You can click the Clear History button to clear the history manually at any time.

- **Languages:** No, this option doesn't automatically translate the content of a Web page into the preferred language. Rather, some Web page authors provide their Web pages in more than one language. If an option, this merely lets you decide language preference.

- **Applications:** This table is where you designate the application that is to intercept special file types. An example is a `.pdf` file which requires the Adobe Acrobat reader in order to view it. You can specify the application and optional arguments that need to be passed to the program.

- **Smart Browsing:** The *Whats Related* feature of Netscape is a relative newcomer to the Netscape product. It's a drop-down menu from your browser that lists sites that may be related to the currently displayed Web site. You can set characteristics of *Whats Related* here.

✔ **Mail & Newsgroups:** This section of the configuration is where you provide your user identity to the browser, along with how you want your e-mail message to appear (message font characteristics). Much of this information comes from your Internet Service Provider (ISP) when you establish your account.

- **Identity:** Your e-mail identity.

- **Mail Servers:** The Incoming Mail Servers designates the server that stores your e-mail when you aren't online. The Outgoing Mail Server is the server responsible for delivering your e-mail.

- **Newgroups Servers:** Newsgroup servers are like catagorized bulletin boards for e-mail messages. Your ISP generally provides you with a server name, which you can add here.

- **Addressing:** When you address a new e-mail, Netscape searches your local address book and/or a common directory server (if you're on a network and share a common contact directory).

- **Messages:** You can determine how messages are copied and forwarded, including quoting the original message and wrapping text.

- **Copies and Folders:** Enables you to keep copies of sent messages in other folders and/or send a blind carbon copy (BCC) of a message to another e-mail account.

- **Formatting:** Here you determine whether you want your messages composed in plain text or HTML.

- **Return Receipts:** You can demand receipts for your outgoing mail to ensure that it's arriving at the intended destination.

- **Disk Space:** This category provides some options to help you keep your disk tidy. You can limit the size of stored messages and also rotate out old Newsgroup messages to save disk space.

✔ **Roaming User:** This option enables you to retrieve your user profile from anywhere on the Internet. You must have an account on a roaming access server to retrieve this information. This is mostly used by companies with traveling employees requiring a centralized e-mail system.

- **RServer Information:** The Local Directory Access Protocol (LDAP) server address goes here. In short, your e-mail stays on the server rather than being loaded to your local e-mail client (Netscape.) Don't lose too much sleep over this one . . . your company should fill you in on the details if they require you to use LDAP.

- **Item Selection:** This enables you to determine exactly what you want retrieved from your LDAP server — yawwwwwwn!

✔ **Composer:** Netscape Communicator comes with a built-in Web page editor and publisher. This means that you can create your own Web site within Netscape and upload it to a Web server for the entire world to see! You customize Composer in this section.

- **New Page Colors:** Identify various components of your Web page by changing the text colors. You can also set a default background image here.

- **Publish:** Determine publishing options along with the Web server location where your Web creations ultimately reside.

✔ **Advanced:** This category provides options that affect the entire Netscape user environment. Options include not loading images (handy for a slow dialup connection when you're just interested in reading the text) and whether you want to enable Java applets or JavaScript Web pages. Cookies enable the visited Web site to store information on your computer. By storing such items in a cookie as your login ID and preferences, a site such as Amazon.com doesn't need to ask you who you are each time, they just read the cookie information you allowed them to leave during a previous visit.

  • **Cache:** Visiting a Web site entails establishing a network connection with the site and downloading the Web document and included images for viewing on your browser. The browser caches this information on your local hard drive. By doing so, your browser doesn't have to retrieve the same information from the Internet again and again for sites that you frequent. This option enables you to set limits on this local storage space. You can also manually clear your cache here.

  • **Proxies:** If you're part of a local area network (LAN) that has a connection to the Internet, you likely connect to a proxy server. Your System Administrator provides you with this information. You can safely ignore this if you're using a dialup account.

Them Dadgum Browser Plug-Ins

Do you ever get irritated at those Web sites that insist that you download a *plug-in*, or additional piece of software, just to view their site? While annoying if you're just looking for some basic information, these plug-ins can also provide some pretty cool stuff like streaming video and music through your Web browser.

Plug-ins provide *browser capability extensions*, programs that interface with the browser to provide nonstandard features such as sound and video playing. The digital age is still in its infancy, so the industry hasn't yet adopted these multimedia formats as standard. In turn, the developers at Netscape have chosen not to build in support to the Communicator browser. Rather, the plug-in architecture enables software developers to innovate without requiring the supporting browser to know what to do with newly emerging media formats.

Each plug-in may require manual setup steps and not all plug-ins that are available for Netscape are supported by Linux — yet (Apple's QuickTime is one good example). Your Netscape installation includes some plug-ins. To view which plug-ins are installed, choose Help➪About Plug-ins.

The general rule for plug-in installation is to move the required file (usually with a file extension of .so) into the plugin directory, which is located below the Netscape installation (for example, ../.netscape/plugins/*.so).

From the Netscape Preferences dialog box, choose Navigator⇨Applications. The Application file types window appears, as shown in Figure 8-2.

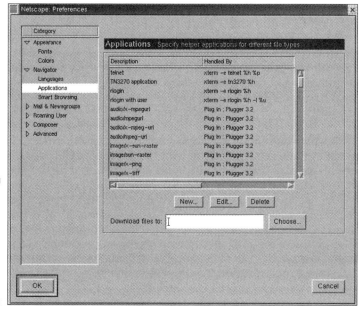

Figure 8-2:
Application
file types in
the
Netscape
Preferences
dialog box.

This window provides you with a simple way to associate a particular file type with a specific program or plug-in. For example, a file with a .rm extension denotes a file in Real Media format that probably contains an audio and/or video presentation. A special plug-in (program) from Real Media is required to play this file for you. This window enables you to match up the file type with the required program.

The difference between a plug-in and an external program is this: a plug-in displays the results in the browser space and an external program runs outside of the browser.

Luckily, Netscape comes preconfigured for many of the common multimedia file types. Any new plug-ins that you're required to download come with instructions for configuring with Linux and Netscape.

Shifting Netscape into Gear

After you finely tune your graphical Internet vehicle, it's time to take it for the road test. In the following sections, we cover some righteous maneuvers with your Netscape browser.

Navigating the Navigator

Netscape Navigator is your viewing window into the wonderful World Wide Web. Its primary purpose is to fetch Web pages on your command, download all the graphics and related files into your computer's memory, and finally render the page for your interactive, viewing pleasure. The default protocol used for fetching Web pages is HTTP (or Hypertext Transport Protocol).

We know what you're thinking: "Doesn't information run around the Internet in little TCP/IP packets? What's up with this HTTP stuff?" Well, *HTTP* is a packaging protocol that describes how data gets boxed for shipment. Does it make more sense to ship your salt shaker collection in one box, or to send each piece one at a time in separate envelopes? Different transport protocols are designed to make efficient use of network resources. Other protocols that ride the TCP/IP freeway include FTP and Telnet. Although more appropriate tools are available for moving files around the Internet, such as FTP, your Netscape browser has the built-in ability to download files (move files to your local computer) straight from the browser window!

When your Web browser first starts up, the home page that you've designated in your Preferences dialog box appears (see the "Configuring Netscape Communicator" section earlier in this chapter).

www.yahoo.com, shown in Figure 8-3, is a popular starting point for many Web users. Any text that is blue and underlined is a hypertext link. Just click any of these links once and your browser sends a request to that site for a peek. If successful, a new Web page is loaded in your browser with more links, images, and digital potpourri.

A Web page usually has many gears backward, but none forward. In other words, a Web page has a pretty good idea about where you've been, but doesn't know where you're going. Your browser is good at leaving popcorn on the cybertrail so that you can find your way back. To be whisked back to the last page you visited, simply click the Back button at the top of the browser.

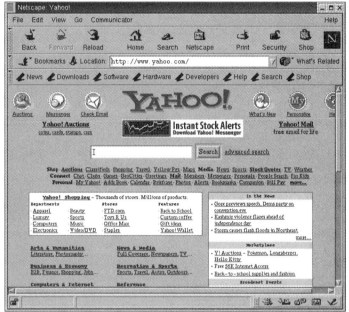

Figure 8-3:
The Yahoo!
home page.

Working the system, e-mail style

In this section, we walk through the process of creating, sending, and reading e-mail with Netscape Communicator. We're assuming you were able to set your e-mail information in the Preferences dialog box.

Start by creating a new e-mail message and sending it to the President of the United States:

1. Choose Communicator⇨Messenger.

The Netscape Mail & Newsgroups window appears, as shown in Figure 8-4.

2. Click the New Msg button.

A Compose window appears, which contains a work area to create your e-mail message.

3. Complete the message, as shown in Figure 8-5.

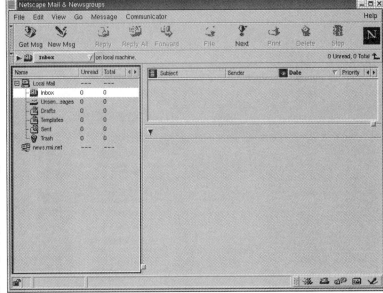

Figure 8-4:
The
Netscape
Mail &
News-
groups
window.

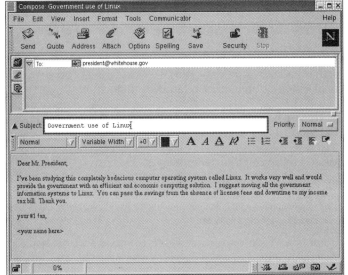

Figure 8-5:
An e-mail
message to
the
President of
the United
States.

4. When you finish typing your message, click the Send button.

Watch for MIBS (Men In Black Suits) to show up at your door and haul you away for interrogation. Just kidding! Actually, this e-mail address gets millions of messages.

Within a few minutes, you'll have mail in your box waiting to be read. No, the President of the United States is not constantly reading and replying to everyone's e-mail. A program called an auto-responder is running on the computer that has responsibility for the President's e-mail. When a message is received, the auto-responder returns a form letter to the e-mail address of the sender. Your message is queued up to eventually be read by the Presidential staff (or so we're told.)

5. **Click the Get Msg button in the Netscape Mail & Newsgroups window.**

   You should have a message waiting for you from the President of the United States.

Many features are available in your mailbox area for composing e-mail and organizing your e-mail. You can create mailing lists, copy mail to more than one recipient, and categorize your sent and received mail into separate folders.

Remembering the good watering holes

Lots of Web sites are out there and you're likely to find some that you want to return to again. You can either write down the addresses for your favorite sites and type the URLs into your browser each time you want to pay a visit, or use the browser's bookmark feature.

We show you how easy it is to create a bookmark and return to your favorite haunts with a couple clicks of the mouse. Try this:

1. **Go to your favorite Web site.**

   A cool Web site appears before you.

2. **Click the Bookmarks icon.**

   A menu appears with options for adding, filing, and editing bookmarks.

3. **Click Add Bookmark.**

   Nothing really exciting happens other than the Bookmark menu disappears and you're back to viewing your Web site. But then. . . .

4. **Click the Bookmark button again.**

Notice that your Web site appears at the bottom of the bookmark list on the menu. All you need to do in order to return to that site later is open this list and click that link. That's all there is to it!

Perusing newsgroups

While e-mail is usually directed at a single individual, you can think of *newsgroups* as public message bulletin boards where people with similar interests come together to discuss their topic. It's also a great place to find technical support.

Choose Communicator⇨Newsgroups and the Netscape Message Center window appears, as shown in Figure 8-6.

Figure 8-6:
The
Netscape
Message
Center.

Right-click the newsgroup server that's highlighted and select Subscribe to Newsgroups. When you added your Newsgroup servers in the Preferences dialog box, you indicated a default news server. As your default server, it's automatically highlighted.

The first time that you select this, you're in for a wait as an index of all the newsgroups downloads to your browser. Tens of thousands of newsgroup titles are out there, so even though it's only downloading the titles, it takes some time. The status bar at the bottom of the dialog box indicates progress.

After all the newsgroup titles have loaded into your browser, you can scroll through the list for topics of interest. To subscribe to a newsgroup, highlight the group name and click the Subscribe button to the right.

Subscribe to the newsgroup `comp.os.linux.announce` to see how this works. Don't worry, by subscribing you aren't flooded with e-mails or announce to the world that you're a member of this group. Rather, subscription is merely telling your browser to remember this group for you.

1. **In the Newsgroup text box, type the name of the newsgroup you want to subscribe to.**

   For example, if you want to subscribe to the Linux announcements newsgroup, type **comp.os.linux.announce**. The group is highlighted.

2. Click the Subscribe button.

A check mark is placed next to the selected newsgroup, as shown in Figure 8-7.

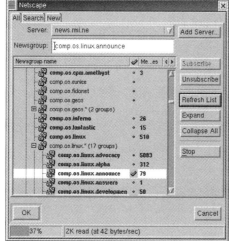

Figure 8-7:
Subscribing
to a
newsgroup
list.

3. Click OK.

You're now back at the Netscape Message Center and see an extra item listed under your news server labeled `comp.os.linux.announce`.

4. Double-click the item for your newsgroup in the Message Center.

The Netscape Mail & Newsgroups window pops up with a message stating that it is loading headers for this group. If it's a busy newsgroup, you may be prompted as to how many of the message headers you want to download.

After the message headers are loaded, you can scroll through the messages and read or contribute to this newsgroup. It's a great education to see what your peers are doing around the world! See Chapter 20 for some good Linux newsgroups.

You need to be aware of the written and unwritten rules for newsgroup etiquette, which vary wildly from group to group. We recommend that you read the FAQ page (Frequently Asked Questions) for the newsgroup and/or lurk for awhile before posting questions and comments. This advice may save you from learning about *flame mail* the hard way! (Flame mail is a term for unfriendly e-mail messages.)

Part III

Getting Up to Speed with Linux

The 5th Wave   By Rich Tennant

Arthur inadvertently replaces his mouse pad with a Ouija board. For the rest of the day, he receives messages from the spectral world.

In this part . . .

In this part of the book, we expand our coverage of Linux beyond what's part and parcel of the operating system to cover its many other facilities and capabilities. These components are critical to making Linux the raging monster of productivity that a well-constructed, properly configured system can represent.

Here, you read about the Linux file system and how to manage its constituent files and directories, as well as control which users or groups are permitted to access these vital system resources. It also includes handy information for navigating GNOME, the GUI of choice for this book. Next, you can read about how to use the Linux command prompt environment known as the shell. Finally, we explore a variety of text editors, emphasizing the easy-to-use vi while monkeying around with various text files.

Chapter 9

Files and Directories

"There is no need to do any housework at all. After the first four years, the dirt doesn't get any worse."

— Quentin Crisp

You can't use a computer without at some point needing to manipulate files and directories. At this point, Linux begins to remind most people of the command-prompt days of MS-DOS. But you'll find a lot of little differences that you have to deal with along the way. Because this is a general Linux tome instead of about one specific distribution, we're going to discuss how to work with files and directories at the command prompt, which rarely changes from distribution to distribution. We get into some fancy stuff near the end.

Comprehending File Types

You find a lot of different file types out there in the Linux world. By types, we're not referring to extensions, such as .exe or .doc. The type issue instead is a reflection of what the file is and how you're meant to use it. In the following sections, we show you how to see what's in your file system, each of the file types that you use in Linux, and how to figure out which type you're looking at.

Listing directory contents

Computer users frequently need to see what files are on their computers and where exactly these files are. The command that you use to do this in the Linux world is `ls`, short for list. If you use this command by itself, all it tells you is what files are in a directory and what directories are in that directory. For example, if you type `ls` at the command prompt in the very base of the directory structure in Red Hat Linux, you see the following:

```
bin   dev   home   lost+found   opt   root   tmp   var
boot  etc   lib    mnt          proc  sbin  usr
```

But this is only the tip of the iceberg for the `ls` command. A bunch of options are available with the `ls` command that you can mix and match to get the results you need. We list the more interesting of these options in Table 9-1.

Table 9-1	ls Options
Option	*Purpose*
`-a`	Displays all files, including those starting with a period.
`-c`	Displays the last time the file was changed.
`--color`	Color codes items by type.
`-l`	Displays a long format file listing.
`-R`	Displays the contents of the directories in this directory.
`-S`	Lists the files by size.
`-t`	Lists the files according to how long ago they were changed.
`-u`	Lists the files according to how long ago they were accessed.

In this table, `-a` and `-l` are by far the most commonly used options. If you're in a brand-new home directory and type `ls`, you see nothing. If you type **ls -a**, you may see:

```
.   ..   .bash_logout   .bash_profile   .bashrc
```

What are the first two entries? The single dot always refers to "right here." It points to the directory that you're currently in. Don't worry if this doesn't make any sense to you at the moment. As you work with other commands and get more familiar with Linux, it will make sense. The two dots refer to the *parent directory*, or the directory one up from where you currently are. For almost all user home directories, the parent is /home. We discuss file system structure in the "Working with the File System" section later in this chapter.

Now, if you type **ls -l** in this directory, you get nothing once again, just:

```
total 0
```

Type one of the most commonly used combinations and you get a lot more information. If you type **ls -la** you get something similar to:

```
total 20
drwx------ 2 dee   dee   4096 Jul 29 07:48 .
drwxr-xr-x 5 root  root  4096 Jul 27 11:57 ..
-rw-r--r-- 1 dee   dee     24 Jul 27 06:50 .bash_logout
-rw-r--r-- 1 dee   dee    230 Jul 27 06:50 .bash_profile
-rw-r--r-- 1 dee   dee    124 Jul 27 06:50 .bashrc
-rw-rw-r-- 1 dee   dee      0 Jul 29 07:48 lsfile
```

You may find some parts of this format easier to understand, at a glance, than others. The first item in each listing (the part with the letters and dashes — for example, the `drwx------` in the first line) is the *permissions* assigned to the item. Briefly, permissions define who can read the file, change it, or run it if it's a program. You can read more about permissions in the "Haggling with Permissions" section later in this chapter. The second item, in this case, 2, is the number of *links* to the item.

A link is a fake file listing that actually points to another file. You use two kinds of links in Linux and Unix:

- ✔ **Soft link:** This link is like a Windows shortcut in that the link points back to the original file, and anything you do to the link happens to the original file. Erase the original file and the link remains, but it becomes unusable. It's broken without the original file.

- ✔ **Hard link:** This link doesn't have a parallel in the Windows world. A hard link isn't just a shortcut; it's another instance of the file itself. The file is only saved in one place, but you can edit either the original or the link and the edit goes through.

The third item (`dee`) is the file's *owner*, and the fourth (`dee`) is the *group*. You can find out more about both of these in the "Haggling with Permissions" section later in this chapter. The fifth item is the file's size in bytes. All directories show up as 4096 bytes. Everything else has its own size. You can tell an empty file from the zero.

The sixth, seventh, and eighth entries are all related to the last time the file was changed: the month (`Jul`), the date (`29`), and the time in 24-hour format (`07:48`). Finally, the ninth item is the actual filename (for example, `bash logout`, in the third row).

Getting information about specific files

You can zoom in and focus on specific files. Of course, you can use the ls command to do this. Typing **ls *filename*** gives you the short listing (where *filename* is the name of the file you're interested in), which isn't all that useful unless you just weren't sure the file was there in the first place. What is more useful is typing **ls -l *filename*** (again designating a specific file for *filename*), which gives you a single line in the same format as the entire directory with the ls -l command.

You're now getting into file types. The very first letter in any long format file listing (ls -l results) tells you what type of file you're dealing with. In Table 9-2, we list the types that you're likely to run into.

Table 9-2		Linux File Types
Label	*Type*	*Description*
-	Regular file	The item is an everyday file, such as a text file or program.
b	Block device	The item is a driver (control program) for a storage medium, such as a hard drive or CD-ROM drive.
c	Character device	The item is a driver (control program) for a piece of hardware that transmits data, such as a modem.
d	Directory	The item is a container for files, also referred to as a folder in some operating systems' lingo.
l	Link	The item is either a hard or soft link.

Why does a directory show up under file types? Linux sees everything as a file. Text files, directories, monitors, hard drives — they're all files to Linux. The file type designation helps the Linux kernel understand how to deal with the file in question.

Linux has commands that can give you something a bit easier to understand than a raw file listing of information. The first of these commands is simply named file, which directly tells you what kind of file you're dealing with. For example, if you typed **file /home,** you would get the following result:

```
/home: directory
```

The file command even traces links for you! You can use it with links in two different ways. If you just use the file command by itself, it tells you about the exact item you gave it. When you use the -L flag with file, it traces a link back to the original and gives you an answer based on the original. So, the query file -L /usr/src/linux actually turns into file /usr/src/linux-2.2.14.

For example, if you type **file /usr/src/linux** you may get:

```
/usr/src/linux: symbolic link to /usr/src/linux-2.2.14
```

Or, you can type **file -L /usr/src/linux** and get:

```
/usr/src/linux: directory
```

Working with the File System

"It was an accident Phyllis."

"Oh, you know, so was Chernobyl."

— From the movie *Quick Change*

You need to know how to move from location to location in the directory structure, how to find out where you are, and how to add and remove things. We suggest logging in to a user account to experiment with what you read about throughout the rest of this chapter. You don't want to delete or move something vital!

Moving through the file system

Linux has two commands that you may find useful for moving around in the file system. The first of these actually lets you see exactly where you are. You may think that you wouldn't need a command like this. Many Linux distributions, however, have the habit of giving you a prompt like the following:

```
[dee@myhost dee]$
```

This prompt tells you that your login name is dee, and that the machine you're on is myhost. The directory you're in, however, is /home/dee, not just dee. Linux uses this format mostly because the directory tree can get pretty huge. A prompt that shows your full location can take up half the line at some points. So, to see exactly where you are, type **pwd**. If you type **pwd** in the directory where this prompt is, you get the following result:

```
/home/dee
```

Now for the actual moving part. You move through the file system with the `cd` command. If you're in the `/home/dee` directory and you want to go to the temporary directory (`/tmp`) because you left a file there, you type **cd /tmp**.

One other thing that you need to be aware of — and that can save you a lot of typing — is that you can type file system locations in two different ways. In the first case, you can type out the whole thing like you've been doing so far. If you're in `/home/dee` and you wanted to switch to the subdirectory files, you can type **cd /home/dee/files**. You have another way to do it though.

If you know where you are and where you want to go relative to where you are, you can use the relative location instead of typing out the whole thing. For example, to switch to the files subdirectory of `/home/dee` from inside `/home/dee`, you can just type **cd files**. The `cd` command understands that you're already in `/home/dee`, so it looks for the `files` directory inside it.

Maybe you're logged in as root and checking up on a few different user directories. You're in `/home/dee` and you want to go to `/home/ralph`. You can either type **cd /home/ralph** or **cd ../ralph.** Remember, the `..` always refers to the directory that contains the one you're currently in. Using `../ralph` tells the `cd` command to back up one directory into `/home`, and then move forward into `ralph`.

Creating files and directories

As you work with your Linux machine, two things that you're probably going to want to do quickly are as follows:

- ✔ **Create your own files:** If you're using the Linux machine for serious work, you're probably going to want to create files for a variety of reasons. You may have a personal journal to keep, or want to make a tip sheet for yourself with the things you find out about Linux during your experimentation.

- ✔ **Create directories:** Eventually those files add up! Directories are there for organizational purposes. Make the most of them.

Making new files

In Linux, you have essentially three ways of creating new files. One is the wonderfully straightforward `touch` command, and we get into the details here. The others are a bit more complex and involve things that you get into as you continue with your explorations, or with this book.

You can create a new, empty file at any time by using the `touch` command. Because the file contains nothing (it just has a name), all you're really doing with this is making an entry in a directory. But this technique does have its uses. You use `touch` in the format `touch filename`, where *filename* is the name of the file you want to create. You can either be inside the directory you want to create the file in, in which case you just type **touch *filename***, or use the techniques we discuss in the previous section. If you're in /home/mike and want to create the file today in your journal subdirectory, then you type **touch journal/today**. Or, if you were in /home/mike/journal and wanted to create the file note in /home/mike, you type **touch ../note**.

When you get to the Permissions section and start experimenting with file permissions, use the touch command to make expendable files that you can mess with without causing yourself problems.

The other methods of creating files depend on what kind of files you want to make. If you want to create a text file, then you can use one of many text editors available for Linux. A *text editor* is a small program that lets you work with raw text with no formatting, like Notepad in Windows. In Chapter 12, we cover text editors that come by default with all Linux distributions.

Finally, the non-text files are items like word processing documents that have a lot of formatting codes, image files like GIFs that are chock full of formatting stuff and have no readable text, and more. You create these files by using the appropriate program for them. To make a word processing file, you use a word processing program such as WordPerfect or StarOffice. Chapters 12 and 20 contain listings of Web sites, some of which offer, or point to places to get, software for Linux. Have fun with them.

Making new directories

As you add more and more files to your home directory and elsewhere, you're going to realize that you need to organize them before you get completely buried and can't find anything quickly. Directories are the perfect tool for filling this need. You create new directories in Linux with the mkdir command. Once again, you can use this in more than one way. If you're in /home/mike and want to create the directory /home/mike/pictures, then you type **mkdir pictures**. If you need to create a temporary directory outside of your home directory with files to share with others, then you type **mkdir /tmp/pictures**.

Moving, renaming, and deleting files and directories

One of the facts of life is that things change. Say you create a file named text one day. Then the next day, you have a pile of text files and need to make a new directory for them. You make the new directory and then move the files into it. Or, say you make a filename too generic you can't tell the difference between text and text5. You need to rename them. Fortunately, Linux has commands to do all of these things easily.

Moving and renaming

You really need to be careful if you're using the root account. Renaming, moving, or deleting system files can wreak total havoc!

You use the same command for both moving and renaming files: mv. To move a file from one location to another, type **mv *original_location new_location,*** where *original_location* is the directory that the file starts in, and *new_location* is where you want to move it to. For example, suppose that you want to move the file /home/mike/text into the directory /home/mike/textfiles. When you're inside /home/mike, type **mv text textfiles**. This is the same as typing mv /home/mike/text /home/mike/textfiles or even mv /home/mike/text /home/mike/textfiles/text. If you make the destination the name of an existing directory, the mv command assumes that you want to put the file into that directory with the same name.

Renaming files is remarkably similar. If you want to rename /home/mike/text to /home/mike/grocery_list, type **mv text grocery_list** from inside /home/mike.

You can even move and rename at the same same time. You can move /home/mike/text into /home/mike/textfiles while renaming it grocery_list all from inside /home/mike by typing **mv text textfiles/grocery_list**.

Getting rid of the junk

A good idea in any operating system is to clean out your files on occasion. If you don't, then you're on the road to having no drive space left, which is definitely no fun. Linux has two different commands for deleting things. One of these is rm (short for remove). If you use this command by itself, it deletes files. For example, if you type **rm ~/test.tif,** the test.tif file may just be deleted without question, or you may get the following:

```
rm: remove 'test.tif'?
```

Type **n** or press Enter to cancel the operation. Otherwise, type **y** to delete the file. Linux contains a number of options, which we list in Table 9-3, that you can use to make this command behave more like the way you want it to.

Table 9-3	Options For rm
Option	*Description*
-d	Removes a directory, even if it's not empty.
-f	Removes items without asking for confirmation.
-i	Asks for confirmation before removing anything.

Option	Description
-r	Continues into subdirectories and removes items there, too.
-v	Prints status information during the removal process.

You can use these options individually or in combinations. If you use the right option, you can use rm to remove a directory as well as a file. For example, if you want to delete /home/mike/textfiles, type **rm -d textfiles** from inside /home/mike. This command removes both the directory and its contents. But it probably prompts you for each item. Although this is often a good idea, you may find it annoying if you have fifteen files in the directory. So type **rm -df textfiles** to ignore all the prompts and just go through with the operation. You'd better be sure, however, that you want to get rid of them!

Suppose that you have a series of subdirectories that you want to get rid of. Maybe you have /home/sally/files, and the files directory has the subdirectories /text, /images, /programs, and more. You can type **rm -r files** in /home/sally to get rid of all of these. Once again, though, you're going to be prompted a lot during this removal process. To eliminate the constant prompting, type **rm -rf files**.

The command rm -rf is perhaps the most dangerous thing you can type on a Linux or Unix system, especially if you're logged in as root. *Be quadruply sure* that you're typing this in the right place if you're logged in as root, and that you really want to get rid of everything in the subdirectories. Many system administrators have typed rm -rf in the root directory by accident only to feel sick as they listen to the drive churn and churn as it deletes everything. You can type Ctrl+C to cancel out of this, but you can't save the already deleted files.

Another way that you can get rid of directories is to use the rmdir command. This program only deletes *empty* directories. A lot of people prefer to use a combination of rm to delete the files, and then rmdir to remove the directories, just to ensure that they aren't making a colossal mess of things. You use rmdir in the format rmdir directory. For example, suppose that you have a temporary directory /tmp/mikesfiles that you want to remove. After typing **rm -r** in that directory for each of the files, type **cd ..** to back up to /tmp (you can't delete a directory if you're currently in it) and then type **rmdir mikesfiles**.

Haggling with Permissions

Take a look at some long format file listings on your machine by typing **ls -l** within a directory. If you find yourself scratching your head, don't worry. The

"Comprehending File Types" section earlier in this chapter gives you a feeling for the first letter on each line, but nine more characters are attached to that item before you get to the next column. This group of nine is the set of *permissions* (also called a *permission set*) for the file or directory. Linux, Unix, and even MacOS use permissions as a way of providing file and directory security by giving you the means to specify exactly who can look at your files, who can change them, and even who can run your programs. You need this when you have a bunch of different users on the same machine, which is networked to the world.

Checking out the triads

Each permission set consists of three sets of triads. Each of the triads has the same basic structure, but controls a different aspect of who can use what. Consider the long format listing for /home/dee in the following code:

```
total 20
drwx------ 2 dee   dee   4096 Jul 29 07:48 .
drwxr-xr-x 5 root  root  4096 Jul 27 11:57 ..
-rw-r--r-- 1 dee   dee     24 Jul 27 06:50 .bash_logout
-rw-r--r-- 1 dee   dee    230 Jul 27 06:50 .bash_profile
-rw-r--r-- 1 dee   dee    124 Jul 27 06:50 .bashrc
-rw-rw-r-- 1 dee   dee      0 Jul 29 07:48 lsfile
```

The very first character in the permission set refers to the type of file; for a directory, the character is shown as a "d", as you see here for the first two items in the preceding list, and files are designated with a dash (-) instead. Each file or directory's permission set is a group of nine characters — that is, the nine characters that follow the first character (for a total of ten). But this group of nine is really three groups of three, as shown in Figure 9-1.

The three triads are read as follows:

✔ The first triad consists of the second, third, and fourth characters in the long format file listing. This triad sets the permissions for the user, or owner of the file (owners are discussed in the "Beware of owners" section later in this chapter).

✔ The second triad consists of the fifth, sixth, and seventh characters in the long format file listing. This triad sets the permissions for the group that is assigned to the file (groups are discussed in the "Hanging out in groups" section later in this chapter).

✔ The third triad consists of the eighth, ninth, and tenth characters in the long format file listing. This triad sets the permissions for other, or everyone who isn't the file's owner or a member of the owning group.

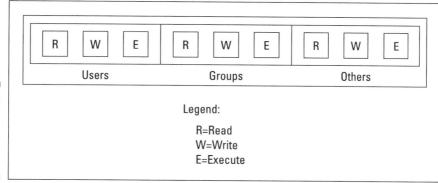

Although each triad is often different from the others, the internal structure of each is made up in the same way. You first focus specifically on how to read one triad before looking at the set of them together. Each triad is comprised of three characters:

✔ The first character is either an r or a dash. The r stands for *read* permission. If r is set, then the triad allows the entity it stands for (user, group, or other) to view the directory or file's contents.

✔ The second character is either a w or a dash. The w stands for *write* permission. If w is set, then the triad allows the entity it stands for to add or edit items to or in this directory or file.

✔ The third character is either an x or a dash. The x stands for *execute* permission. If x is set, then the triad allows the entity it stands for to run programs contained in this directory or to run the particular program in this file.

In all cases, if the dash sits in place of r, w, or x, then the triad doesn't allow the entity the read, write, or execute permission.

The following sections describe owners and groups in more detail.

Beware of owners

You've probably noticed by now that we talk a lot about owners and groups in Linux. Every file and directory has both of these components: a user from the /etc/passwd file that's assigned as its owner and a group from /etc/group assigned as the group well.

Although the everyday user probably doesn't need to change file ownerships too often, root does so on a regular basis. If you add the file comments, for example, into /home/tom while you're on as the superuser, root is going to own that file. The user tom isn't able to do anything with it unless you've set the last triad's permissions to allow the "other" folks (those who aren't the file's owner or in the specified group) to read and write to the file, which is a pretty sloppy way of doing things because the whole idea of permissions is to reduce access, not to give everyone access. Instead, remember to change the file's owner to the user tom. You do this with the chown (change owner) command. For example, by typing **chown tom comments**, root changes the ownership over to tom. Now tom can work with this file and even change its permissions to something he prefers.

Hanging out in groups

Groups are more interesting to work with than owners. You use groups to allow the root user to assign multiple users the ability to share certain file system areas. For example, in many versions of Linux, all users are added to a group called users. Then rather than a long format file listing shown in the "Reading a long format file listing" section earlier in this chapter, you may see the following:

```
total 20
drwx------ 2 dee   users 4096 Jul 29 07:48 .
drwxr-xr-x 5 root  root  4096 Jul 27 11:57 ..
-rw-r--r-- 1 dee   users   24 Jul 27 06:50 .bash_logout
-rw-r--r-- 1 dee   users  230 Jul 27 06:50 .bash_profile
-rw-r--r-- 1 dee   users  124 Jul 27 06:50 .bashrc
-rw-rw-r-- 1 dee   users    0 Jul 29 07:48 lsfile
```

In a distribution like Red Hat Linux, both the user and group are the same by default. This is not always the case, however, as you see from the preceding code listing.

As the root user, you can create new groups or add users to groups in two different ways: directly editing the file that contains group information, or by using special commands. The master file containing the list of existing groups and the group members is /etc/group. When you take a look in this file, you see a bunch of lines that are similar to:

```
dee:x:500:
mary:x:501:
mike:x:502:
```

Each of these lines is in the following format:

```
groupname:x:groupnumber:
```

If you want to create a new group here, go to the end of the file and add a new line (see Chapter 12 for how to use some of the Linux text editors). For example, maybe you're using Red Hat Linux but want a group that has all users in it. You may add:

```
users:x:503:dee,mary,mike
```

Groups can contain other groups, too.

To add someone to an existing group manually, just find the group listed in the file and either add the user's login name after the colon or after the last user. For example, to add tom to the users group created in the previous line of code, edit the file as follows:

```
users:x:503:dee,mary,mike,tom
```

If you want to create a new group without having to edit any files, you can do so using the groupadd command. Use this in the format groupadd groupname, specifying the name of the group that you want to add.

Changing permissions

Permissions and ownerships are assigned to all files during the installation process. From there, every directory and file you create automatically has permissions assigned to it — what these are depends on your distribution. But you may not like the permissions that are already in place. Maybe you want to change them to make your data more secure, or even more accessible. In the listing in the previous section, for example, we don't see the need for everyone on the system to be able to view the contents of lsfile. We can use the chmod (change mode) command to deal with this issue in the format chmod newpermissions filename where *newpermissions* indicates that you want to change the existing permissions for whatever file you specify as *filename*. For example, for lsfile you would type **chmod newpermissions lsfile** at the command prompt.

You can express the *newpermissions* component in two different ways: by the letters or by the numbers, as described in the following sections.

Changing permissions by using letter designations

One method of telling Linux how you want to change a set of permissions is to use letters. You have two groups of characters to use here. The first group consists of:

✔ u for user

✔ g for group

✔ o for other, or everyone

✔ a for all (or u, g, and o has the same effect)

The second group consists of the familiar characters that Linux uses for the permission triad (see the "You and the single triad" section earlier in this chapter): r, w, and x. Next you have the *operators,* which are characters that tell chmod what to do with the permissions relative to the triad you're referring to. These operators are:

- ✔ + to add a permission
- ✔ - to remove a permission
- ✔ = to ensure that a permission is set

Now that you have all the pieces, you can begin putting them together. Start with the example chmod newpermissions lsfile. Your goal here is to allow no users — outside of yourself or your group members — to view the contents of lsfile. From this clue, you know you're referring to the third triad, or the o triad. The permission used to determine whether or not people can view the contents of a file or directory is the r position, and the operator used to take away this permission is the minus (-). So you type **chmod o-r lsfile**. The deed is done: All users in the o (other) group no longer have the ability to view the contents of lsfile. It really is that easy!

You can change multiple triads at the same time in a couple of different ways. For example, if you wanted to change lsfile so that only the owner (dee) can read its contents, then you type **chmod go-r lsfile** to change both the group and other settings simultaneously. Getting even more complex, if you wanted to take away the group members' ability to change the file's contents as well as the group and other's ability to read the file, then you type **chmod go-r,g-w lsfile**.

Permissions by numbers

Another method that Linux users commonly use to change permissions is by using numbers. This format is used all over the place in Linux documentation, from books to courses to manual pages and online references, and so we really thought we should include the info for you here even if it's a bit technical. This method is also really handy if you want to quickly change permissions without having to type all nine characters!

To put it simply, permission numbers allow you to deal with just a raw *base-ten number* — base-ten is our normal number system, where you count from zero to nine, then ten to nineteen, and so on — rather than having to deal with binary bits and bytes (combinations of 0s and 1s).

Look at the following permission set:

```
-rw-rw-r--
```

Ignore the very first item because it tells you what type of file this is; in this case, the dash designates it as a regular file. From there, we have `rw-rw-r--` as the actual permission set. Breaking this into triads, (or sets of three) and you get `rw-` (owner permissions), `rw-` (group permissions), and `r--` (other permissions).

In the following list, the previous line of code is broken into its three triads:

- Triad 1: rw-
- Triad 2: rw-
- Triad 3: r--

In each position in each triad, the important thing to notice is whether a letter or a dash is there. The raw values for each possible item are:

- Every r is worth 4
- Every w is worth 2
- Every x is worth 1
- Every - is worth 0

Each triad keeps its own total. All you need to do is sum the values. So in the case of our example permission set, we have:

Triad	*Conversion to numbers*
`rw-`	$4 + 2 + 0 = 6$
`rw-`	$4 + 2 + 0 = 6$
`r--`	$4 + 0 + 0 = 4$

The numeric permission set is basically set so that the value for the first triad is the first number, the second value is the second number, and the third triad is represented by the third number. The permission set `rw-rw-r--` works out to 664.

If you know exactly what you want to change your permissions to, then you use the format `chmod newpermissions file` with numbers for the permissions. For example, to change `lsfile`'s permission to `rw-------`, you type **chmod 600 lsfile**. This sets the file's permissions from scratch to the new value, which is easier than having to count out six dashes to type **chmod rw—— lsfile**.

Reading a long format file listing

A long format file listing (`ls -l`) is quite easy to read once you get a handle on each of the elements contained within it. We take the following example and go through it — line by line — in the following sections:

```
total 20
drwx------ 2 dee   dee   4096 Jul 29 07:48 .
drwxr-xr-x 5 root  root  4096 Jul 27 11:57 ..
-rw-r--r-- 1 dee   dee     24 Jul 27 06:50 .bash_logout
-rw-r--r-- 1 dee   dee    230 Jul 27 06:50 .bash_profile
-rw-r--r-- 1 dee   dee    124 Jul 27 06:50 .bashrc
-rw-rw-r-- 1 dee   dee      0 Jul 29 07:48 lsfile
```

Line One

```
total 20
```

The first line specifies how many elements are in this listing. Elements include all directories and files.

Line Two

```
drwx------ 2 dee   dee   4096 Jul 29 07:48 .
```

The first letter here is a d, so that immediately tells you that this entry is a directory. Now move to the permissions. Only the first triad has anything turned on here, so the owner (that's dee) is allowed to view the contents of the directory thanks to the r, save files to that directory thanks to the w, and run programs in the directory thanks to the x. No one in the group (including dee), or anyone else, can do any of these things in /home/dee. After this is the number of links to the item, which in this case is 2. Then we have the user that owns this item, dee, and the group that owns this item, also dee. Next is the item size (directories always show as 4096 bytes). Then is the creation or last change date and time. Last is the item name. In this case, it's a period, which stands for the current directory, so the first entry tells you about /home/dee itself.

Line Three

```
drwxr-xr-x 5 root root 4096 Jul 27 11:57 ..
```

Once again, the first letter is a d, so we're looking at a directory. As for the permissions, the first triad refers to the root user, who has all three (rwx) enabled, so root can do anything it wants to do in /home. The second triad is r-x, so anyone in the group (also root in this case) can read the contents of /home and execute programs in there. The third triad is identical to the second, so the same rules apply to everyone else. There are five links to this item, and it is owned by the user root and the group root. After the size and creation/modification date and time comes the name of the item. The `..` stands for the directory above this one, so the second entry tells you about `/home`.

Okay, the root user can do anything he or she wants anywhere. If you're using the structure where every user has his or her own group — Red Hat Linux creates a new group with the same name as the user for every new account, many other distributions have all users assigned to the group `user` — then don't add anyone else except administrator accounts to root's group!

Lines four, five, and six

```
-rw-r--r-- 1 dee   dee    24 Jul 27 06:50 .bash_logout
-rw-r--r-- 1 dee   dee   230 Jul 27 06:50 .bash_profile
-rw-r--r-- 1 dee   dee   124 Jul 27 06:50 .bashrc
```

Now you get to the files, which we recognize by the `-` as the first character. Files are always listed after directories when you use `ls -l`. The permissions for all these items are the same. Their first triad is `rw-`, which means that the owner (dee) can view the file's contents and edit them. The second and third triads for these three are `r--`. Anyone in the dee group can view the contents of these files, and everyone on the entire system can as well. Each has only one link, a different size in bytes, and was created at the same time — in this case, when the account itself was created. The names for these files are `.bash_logout`, `.bash_profile`, and `.bashrc`.

Line seven

```
-rw-rw-r-- 1 dee   dee     0 Jul 29 07:48 lsfile
```

This last item is also a file. You can tell because the first character is a dash. Its first two triads are identical (`rw-`), meaning that the owner (dee) and members of the group (dee) can both view the file's contents and change them. Everyone else, however, can only view the contents because the last triad is `r--`. There is only one link, and this item is owned by the user and group dee. It's empty too, indicated by the file size — `0` bytes. After the creation or last modification date and time, we see the file's name: `lsfile`.

File Managers

Tired of typing stuff at the command prompt? If you prefer, the GUI contains a bunch of *file managers* for you to use. A file manager is a program, such as Windows Explorer, that enables you to dig through and manipulate your files and directories with your mouse instead of at the command prompt. In this section, we take you on a tour of the file managers that, by default, come with popular Linux distributions.

Campaigning with the GNU Midnight Commander

In the GNOME desktop environment, the default file manager is the *GNU Midnight Commander,* also referred to as the GMC. You can find this program in GNOME by clicking the Main Menu button to open the Main Menu, and then clicking the File Manager menu option. Figure 9-2 shows an example of what you can see with the GMC open.

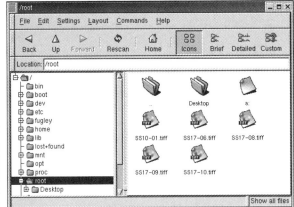

Figure 9-2: The GNU Midnight Commander.

The workings of this file manager should seem familiar compared to those from other operating systems. The GMC has the same two-panel layout and click and drag functionality that you're probably used to.

Browsing your files

Moving through the file system is pretty easy in the GMC. The main thing that you need to keep in mind is that your directories are on the left and your files are on the right. Things that you can do in the GMC are as follows:

- ✔ To open a directory using the left side, locate it in the list and click the plus sign next to it.

- ✔ To open a directory using the right side, locate it in the window and double-click it. Linux automatically displays the files in this directory.

- ✔ To view the files in a directory using the left side, click the directory's folder icon or the name.

- ✔ To view a file's contents or run a program, double-click the item in the listing.

Are you getting too much information about each file or not enough? Experiment with the four buttons on the upper right: Icons, Brief, Detailed, and Custom. Each pulls up a view on the right that gives you a different amount of information on the files and directories there.

Copying and moving files

You can copy and move items using two different methods in the GMC. The first is the usual drag-and-drop method that you're probably familiar with from Windows or MacOS, and the other is using the program's menus. To move a file using the drag-and-drop method, first click the file you want to move in the listing on the right. Then do one of the following:

✔ Drag the file into the folder you want to drop it into in the right pane.

✔ Drag the file into the folder you want to drop it into in the left pane.

You do the same to copy, except you click the item and then hold down the Ctrl key while you drag and drop.

Deleting files and directories

You can't just select something and use the Delete key to get rid of something in the GMC. To delete either a file or a directory from the file system, do the following:

1. **Browse to the file or directory's location.**

   You need the file or directory to appear in the right pane, so you want to click the folder that contains the item.

2. **Select the file or directory.**

   Click the item to highlight its name.

3. **Open the pop-up menu.**

   Right-click over the file and the pop-up menu opens.

4. **Choose Delete in the pop-up menu.**

   Click Delete in the pop-up menu. A dialog box opens asking if you really want to delete the item.

5. **If you're sure, click Yes.**

   If you click Yes, you delete the item. Clicking No leaves it intact.

Viewing and changing permissions

If you've experimented with the different file views, then you already know that only the Custom view shows you a file's permissions. If you try double-clicking those permissions, you see that you can't work with them that way in the GMC. Instead, to change a file or directory's permissions, you need to do the following:

1. **Browse to the file or directory's location.**

   You need the file or directory to appear in the right pane, so click the folder in the left pane that contains the item.

2. **Select the file or directory.**

   Click the item in the right pane to highlight its name.

3. **Right-click the file and choose Properties from the pop-up menu that appears.**

   The Properties dialog box opens with the Statistics tab open.

4. **Click the Permissions tab.**

   The Permissions portion of the Properties dialog box appears, as shown in Figure 9-3.

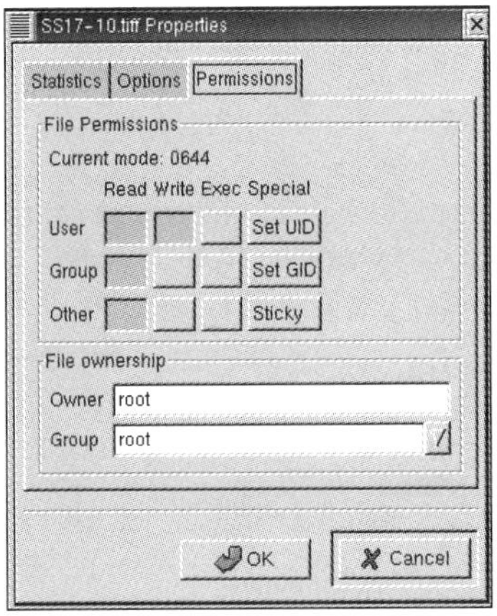

Figure 9-3: The GMC with the Permissions tab open.

5. **Set the new permissions and ownerships.**

   As you can see, the GMC offers you some pretty handy tools for setting the permissions exactly the way you want them without having to remember structure or what numbers go with what letters. You can also change owner and group information here.

   You see three new items in this image:

   Set UID: Use this for programs and scripts. If you want the program or script to pretend it's the file's owner while it's running, then you click this box. Be careful: This is very dangerous if the file's owner is root. In fact, many Linux distributions don't put this into effect for root. It's a major security hole.

   Set GID: This works similar to the way Set UID works, except when the program runs it pretends to belong to the same group that the file does.

Sticky: This has two different functions. In the case of a file, it keeps a current copy of the file always in the swap partition so that it can be loaded faster than usual. Also, a user can't delete a file if he or she doesn't own a file in that directory.

6. Close the dialog box.

When you have everything set the way you want it, click OK to close the dialog box and put the changes into effect.

Chillin' with kfm (KDE File Manager)

In KDE, the default file manager is kfm. You can find this program in KDE in a few different ways. The quickest way is to click the icon at the bottom of the screen that's a picture of a folder with a house on it in the very bottom left of the screen. Another fast method involves clicking the K icon to open the Main Menu button, and then clicking the Home directory menu option. Figure 9-4 shows an example of what you can see with kfm open.

The workings of this file manager should seem familiar compared to those from other operating systems. Although kfm doesn't have a two-panel setup, it does let you click to move from directory to directory, and click and drag to move items within the file system structure.

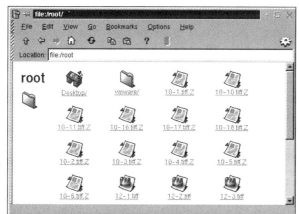

Figure 9-4:
KDE's kfm.

Browsing your files

You're probably used to file managers that let you work in two panes, such as Windows Explorer or maybe even GNOME's GMC. The kfm program uses only a single window. To navigate through the file system, you simply click directories or files to open them. You also have extra buttons available that help you jump around, as shown in Figure 9-4.

Copying files

You may think that it's hard to drag and drop when just clicking an item opens it. You can, however, still use this feature! Just make sure not to click and release the item that you want to move. You have to click it and hold the mouse button down as you drag the item.

For copying and pasting without using drag and drop, do the following:

1. **Right-click the item and choose Copy from the pop-up menu that appears.**

   Your computer copies the item to its memory.

2. **Navigate to where you want to put the copy.**

3. **Right-click in the destination directory and choose Paste from the pop-up menu that appears.**

   Your computer copies the file to this location.

Moving and deleting files

Unfortunately, things aren't always as straightforward as you like them. Moving a file requires a slightly stranger method:

1. **Click the item and drag it an inch or two and then release it.**

   A pop-up menu appears.

2. **Choose Move from the pop-up menu.**

   You get an odd dialog box, as shown in Figure 9-5.

3. **Change the path and/or filename to suit your needs.**

   Leave the part before the colon in place. For example, you may see the following:

   ```
   file:
   ```

4. **Click the Rename button below the text box.**

   You've moved the file.

Fortunately, deleting files and directories is pretty easy in kfm. You just browse to the item you want to delete, right-click it, and choose Delete from the pop-up menu!

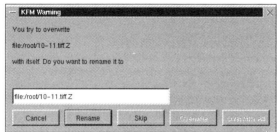

Figure 9-5:
The kfm
Warning
dialog box.

Viewing and changing permissions

You work with permissions in kfm almost exactly the same way you do in the GNU Midnight Commander. If you want to view or modify a file's permissions in this file manager, do the following:

1. **Browse to the file or directory's location.**

2. **Right-click the file or directory and choose Properties from the pop-up menu that appears.**

   The Properties dialog box appears.

3. **Click the Permissions tab.**

   The Permissions tab of the Properties dialog box opens, as shown in Figure 9-6.

4. **Set the new permissions and ownerships.**

   As you can see, the kfm offers you some pretty handy tools for setting the permissions exactly the way you want them without having to remember structure or what numbers go with what letters. You can also change owner and group information here.

5. **Click OK to close the dialog box.**

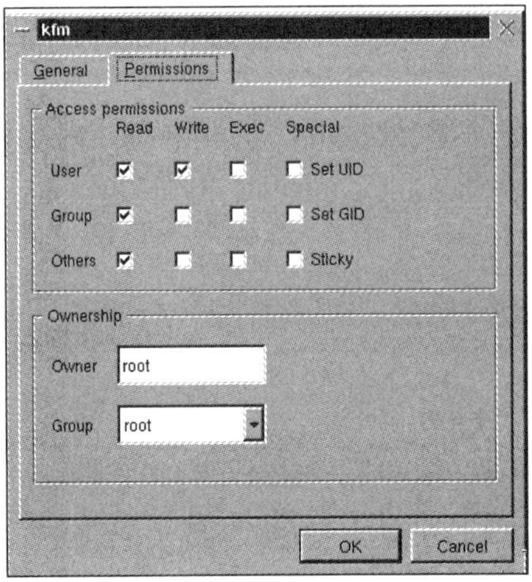

Figure 9-6:
The kfm
Properties
dialog box,
Permissions
tab open.

Wildcards, or Legal Cheating

Working at the command prompt involves a lot of typing. This becomes painfully obvious if you want to deal with a bunch of files and have to type their names one by one. Fortunately, you don't actually have to do this. You have *wildcards* at your disposal.

Wildcards are characters that represent one or more characters. Table 9-4 lists the wildcards that you have available when working with files and directories.

Table 9-4	Wildcards for File Manipulation	
Character	*Name of Character*	*Purpose*
?	Question Mark	Stands for a single missing character.
*	Asterisk	Stands for a group of missing characters.
[]	Square brackets	Allows you to specify a range or group of missing characters.

Suppose, for example, that you have a directory with the following short file listing:

```
afile   cfile   file1file   file2file   fileafile
bfile   file1   file2       file3       filebfile
```

The following list shows you how you can use wildcards to access those files:

- If you type **ls ?file** in this directory, you get the files afile, bfile, cfile.

- If you type **ls file?**, you get file1, file2, and file3.

- If you type **ls file***, you get file1file, file2file, fileafile, file1, file2, file3, and filebfile.

- If you type **ls *file**, you get afile, cfile, file1file, file2file, fileafile, bfile, and filebfile.

- If you type **ls file[1-3]**, you get file1, file2, and file3.

- If you type **ls file[1-3]***, you get file1, file2, file3, file1file, and file2file.

- If you type **ls file[1,a]***, you get file1, file1file, and fileafile.

You may also find filename and command completion useful. The bash shell (the default Linux shell; see Chapter 11) has a feature that finishes a filename for you. If you're working at the command prompt typing a long filename, press the Tab key and bash does the rest. You can also complete commands by pressing the Tab key. You have to type enough letters, however, to make the item unique so nothing else can come up during the completion.

Chapter 10

Gettin' Gooey with the GUIs

In This Chapter

▶ Checking out GNOME

▶ GNOME tips and tricks

▶ Glancing at KDE

*I*n deciding between a command-prompt interface and a GUI, you need to first consider speed. If you plan to compile programs or perform other process-intensive tasks that tend to slow down your machine, running the GUI only is going to add to the speed problem, especially if you don't have a fast computer.

Readability can also be a big issue in choosing between the GUI and the command prompt. If you have a hard time reading text in those small command-prompt windows from within the GUI, you can either make them and their fonts bigger, or you can work directly at the command prompt outside of the GUI. In this case, you may or may not want to actually close the GUI. We cover how you can manipulate all these items in the next section.

The X Window System (or X) opens a world of possibilities that some people find downright overwhelming. In this chapter, we try to narrow it down as much as possible and give you enough information to explore it more deeply, after you're ready. In general, X is a set of applications that work together to provide a graphical interface. Some parts draw the windows, some manage the look and feel, and others handle other aspects of the graphical world for you.

The two biggest GUI contenders for Linux are GNOME and KDE. Because Red Hat Linux 7 comes with this book and GNOME is the default GUI for Red Hat Linux, this chapter mostly covers GNOME. The section "KDE, the Other Windows-like GUI," later in this chapter, includes screen shots and brief coverage of the KDE interface so that you can compare KDE to GNOME.

Checking Out GNOME Basics

GNOME (see Figure 10-1) is the GNU Network Object Model Environment. We know — that doesn't tell you much, does it? It's a full *desktop environment,* which means that it gives you everything you need for the GUI all in one package. You may find it odd to even talk about this if you're used to Windows or MacOS, because for them, it's always been that way. Things are different under Linux. You can stitch together a Frankensteinian mismatch of many different GUI pieces if you want.

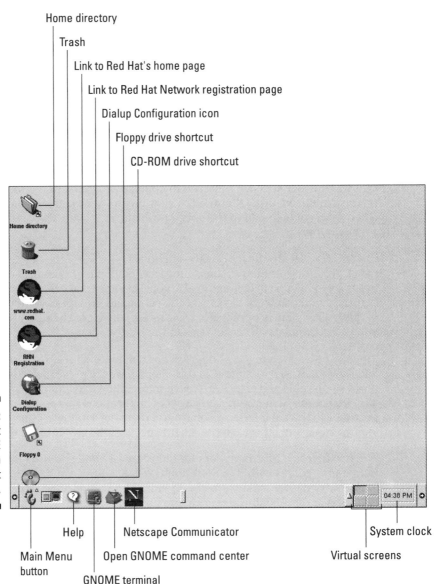

Home directory

Trash

Link to Red Hat's home page

Link to Red Hat Network registration page

Dialup Configuration icon

Floppy drive shortcut

CD-ROM drive shortcut

Figure 10-1:
The default
GNOME
desktop in
Red Hat
Linux.

Help

Main Menu
button

GNOME terminal

Netscape Communicator

Open GNOME command center

System clock

Virtual screens

The main GNOME site is www.gnome.org/.

Many folks find that GNOME has a pretty intuitive layout. Take a tour through the menus and see what's available in this environment. Keep in mind that the tools you have in the menus can depend on what kind of installation you choose to do, so if what you have is different than what you see in descriptions or the figures, don't panic. This desktop environment is essentially broken down into three separate parts: the menus, the Panel at the bottom, and the icons along the left of the background on what's known as the desktop. We take a look at each in the following sections.

The menus

The GNOME menus are all accessible through the button on the lower-left of the Panel that looks like a big footprint, which is called the *Main Menu button.* The Main Menu opens after you click the Main Menu button (duh!) and is shown in Figure 10-2. We talk a bit about the contents of the submenus of the Main Menu in Table 10-1.

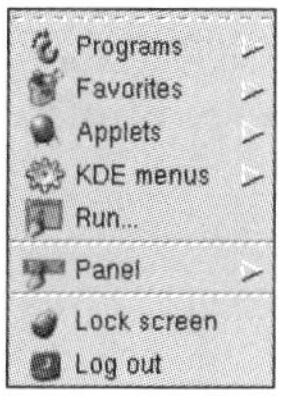

Figure 10-2:
The GNOME
Main Menu.

Table 10-1	GNOME Main Menu Contents
Menu Choice	*What You Find*
Programs	The GNOME and X programs you installed on this system.
Favorites	The contents of your Web browser bookmarks.
Applets	The Java applets — small programs — you installed on this system.
KDE menus	The KDE programs you installed on this system. You see this menu item only if you installed both KDE and GNOME.

(continued)

Table 10-1 *(continued)*

Menu Choice	What You Find
Run	The dialog box that you can use to run a specific program without opening a virtual terminal.
Panel	The tools for manipulating your Panel.
Lock screen	The capability to set your machine so that no one can use your GNOME login without entering your password. This is good if you need to walk away from the computer for a while but don't want to log out of your account, and other people are around.
Log out	The capability to exit the current GNOME session, shut down, or reboot the machine — if you know the root password.

The Programs menu

After you choose the Programs menu from the Main Menu, you get what's shown in Figure 10-3. Depending on what packages you installed on your system, some of these topics may not appear in your GNOME menu. In Table 10-2, we describe what you can find in each of these options.

Figure 10-3:
The GNOME Programs menu.

Table 10-2   GNOME Programs Menu Contents

Menu Choice	What You Find
Applications	A collection of programs that don't fit well into the other headers or groups. Contains an address book, calendar, and more.
Utilities	Small specific-function GNOME and X programs. Contains a calculator, color selector, and font tool.

Menu Choice	What You Find
Development	A collection of GUI-based software development aids.
Games	A collection of games.
Graphics	A variety of graphics programs.
Internet	A variety of Internet tools, such as a GUI Telnet client, Netscape, and more.
Multimedia	A variety of video and sound tools.
Settings	A collection of tools that you can use to configure GNOME and your Linux machine.
System	Tools useful for administrators and users, such as the capability to use the GUI to change your password and take a look at your system logs.
File Manager	The GNU Midnight Commander.
Help System	The Integrated GNOME Help system.

The Applets menu

The Applets menu is accessible from the Applets submenu of the Main Menu. We show you how to add and remove them in the section "Checking Out GNOME Tips and Tricks," later in this chapter. In Table 10-3, we describe what tiny wonders you may find in the Applets menu.

If you're not familiar with Java applets, you can find out more about the Java programming/scripting language at www.java.sun.com/.

Table 10-3	GNOME Applets Menu Contents
Menu Choice	What You Find
Amusements	Games, fortune cookies, and other fun stuff that can reside in your Panel.
Clocks	Clocks to mark the time in various ways and formats.
Monitors	Programs that tell you things about how much load your computer is under and much more.

(continued)

Table 10-3 *(continued)*

Menu Choice	What You Find
Multimedia	Simple sound utilities.
Network	Simple network control and Internet utilities.
Utility	Miscellaneous applets that don't fit easily into the other menus, such as mail-checking utilities and lights to show you what your modem is up to.

The Panel menu

The Panel menu is a submenu of the Main Menu. This menu contains options that enable you to manipulate the icon panel/bar at the bottom of the screen. You can find out how to actually work with this in the section "Checking Out GNOME Tips and Tricks," later in this chapter. For a list of what this menu's items offer, see Table 10-4.

Table 10-4   GNOME Panel Menu Contents

Menu Choice	What You Find
Add to Panel	Applets, menus, and other objects that you can add onto your icon panel.
Create Panel	Options for creating new panels that sit on different parts of the screen.
Remove this Panel	The capability to delete a secondary panel but not the main icon Panel.
Properties	Options for setting this panel's behavior.
Global preferences	Opens the GNOME Control Center to the Panel option to set the baseline behavior of all your panels.
Panel manual	Opens Netscape with Panel-related Help information.
About the Panel	Opens a dialog box with some basic Panel information.
About GNOME	Opens a dialog box with some basic GNOME information.

That's it for the Main Menu's submenus! In the following section, we take a look at the tools available in the Main Menu and how to use them.

Main Menu tools

The Main Menu tools are all fairly simple beasts, available to help new and old Linux users adjust more easily to the GNOME desktop environment.

The Run tool

After you choose the Run option on the Main Menu, the Run Program dialog box appears, as shown in Figure 10-4. To run a program by using this dialog box, do one of the following:

✔ Type the path to the program (including the program) in the text box.

✔ Click the drop-down list button to select a program you already ran by using this dialog box.

✔ Click the Browse button to find and select the program that you want to run.

Figure 10-4:
The GNOME
Run tool.

After you have the program you want, click Run in Terminal if you want the program's output displayed in a virtual terminal; leave this button alone if you want the program to run quietly in the background. Then click the Run button.

The Lock screen tool

After you choose the Lock screen option on the Main Menu as anyone but the root user, your screen fades to black or your screensaver appears — this tool doesn't work for the root user. If anyone moves the mouse or uses your keyboard, a dialog box appears with your login name in it. Access to this GUI session is granted only if your password is entered.

Notice that we say GUI *session* and not machine. Folks who know how to sidestep out of GNOME (something we discuss in the section, "Checking Out GNOME Tips and Tricks," later in this chapter) can change over to a virtual terminal and do whatever they want. So don't think of this as completely securing your machine.

The Log out tool

After you choose the Log out option on the Main Menu, the screen darkens somewhat and the "Really log out?" dialog box opens. To use this box, do the following:

1. **If you want GNOME to remember what items you have open and return you to its current state after you log back in, make sure that you select the Save Current Setup check box.**

2. **Determine whether you want to log out of the machine, shut it off, or reboot it.**

3. **Click Logout, Halt, or Reboot to set the appropriate action or click No if you don't want to do any of these.**

    These options do the following:

    • **Logout:** Exit GNOME and return to the command prompt.

    • **Halt:** Shut the machine down and then off. You must be able to enter the root password to use this option.

    • **Reboot:** Shut the machine down and then bring it back up. You can use this only if you know the root password.

4. **Click Yes to go through with your choice or No if you just changed your mind.**

The Panel

Along the bottom of your GNOME desktop is a long bar with icons on it. This is *the Panel.* Because this bar is neatly divided into sections, take a look at what's in each section from left to right. On the far left of the Panel is the GNOME *Main Menu button* (refer to Figure 10-1), which opens the appropriately named Main Menu.

To the right of this icon is the section where applets show up. You can add small programs to the panel for a variety of reasons. We get into how to do this in the section "Checking Out GNOME Tips and Tricks," later in this chapter.

To use the special character applet, position the cursor where you want to place the character and then click on the character to insert it.

As we continue our journey to the right, we run into the standard set of GNOME tools. You can actually reach all these items through the Main Menu, but they're placed here so that you can find them quickly and easily. Notice the Help icon (refer to Figure 10-1). The next button opens a virtual X terminal, as shown in Figure 10-5, so that you can get a command prompt. Third, and finally, is the GNOME Command Center button. You want to use this one a lot, especially as you're first setting up your system.

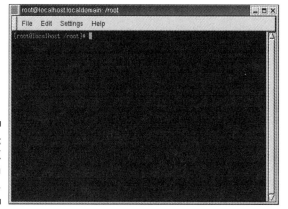

Figure 10-5:
A virtual X
Terminal in
GNOME.

What you see in the next segment to the right depends on what programs you have open. Call this the *status,* or *task,* section of the Panel. Every program you have open has a task dedicated to it in this portion of the Panel. For an example of what you may see, take a look at Figure 10-6.

Figure 10-6:
A sample
collection of
tasks on the
GNOME
Panel.

You can change a program's status three different ways by using these boxes:

- ✔ If the text in the box is shaded so that it's harder to see than the others, as it is in the virtual terminal task box, the program is minimized. You can open the window to work in by clicking the box.

- ✔ If the text in the box isn't shaded but the program's window is hidden by another program, as it is for the GNOME Help Browser box, you can click the task box to bring this program to the front.

- ✔ If the text in the box isn't shaded and the window is the program you're currently using, as it is for the Control Center, you can minimize the program by clicking the box.

In the default GNOME panel setup, the next (and last) item to the right is pretty straightforward. It displays the time and date (refer to Figure 10-1).

See the left-facing arrow at the end of the icon panel's left side and the right-facing arrow at the end of its right side? You can use these to minimize the Panel. Give it a try!

Playing with desktop icons

What you see on your *desktop* (the main GNOME screen) may be very different from distribution to distribution. In the case of Red Hat Linux's setup, a vertical row of icons line the left side of the screen. The first two (refer to Figure 10-1) are GNOME shortcuts that open the GNU Midnight Commander (GMC). The home icon opens the GMC with your home directory's contents displayed, while the trash icon opens ~/.gnome-desktop/Trash. A trash can is a welcome sight to those who accidentally delete files in Linux and find that they can't recover them!

To use the trash can, drag any files you want to delete into it. Later, if you're sure you want to be rid of them, delete them manually from ~/.gnome-desktop/Trash.

The next two icons (refer to Figure 10-1) are the Red Hat-specific ones. The first is a shortcut to a Web page within the Red Hat Web site. The other enables you to register for support. Double-clicking one of these links opens Netscape and takes you to (in order, from top to bottom) the following:

- ✔ Red Hat's main home page, www.redhat.com/. If you want to look at something on the Red Hat site and aren't sure where it is, start here.

- ✔ Red Hat's Network registration tool. Takes down user-support information and what RPM packages you installed so that it can notify you about updates.

Checking Out GNOME Tips and Tricks

"Change is inevitable, except from a vending machine."

— Anonymous

The GNOME desktop environment has an amazing set of features for you to explore, including lots of ways to change the GUI's look and feel. We tried to group the types of changes into related topics for your easy perusal. If you want to get more into the fun of customizing the actual look and feel of GNOME, see Chapter 15. What we cover here is more practical.

Exit stage left

Few things are more frustrating than wanting to get out of a program that you just can't seem to exit. A lot of new Linux users run into just that in GNOME. For whatever the reason, they want to get out of the desktop environment and work straight from the command prompt. You have two ways that you can do this.

These methods of quitting out of GNOME work in almost any GUI combination that you run into in Linux.

The first method involves leaving GNOME without actually leaving GNOME. You can kind of sidestep out of the GUI and go to a command prompt *virtual terminal* — one of the login sessions available in Linux, each of which is tied to a function key — because (and here's the big secret) the GUI is a virtual terminal, too! The function keys F1–F6 take you to virtual terminals where you can log in and do whatever you need to at the command prompt. F7 (or sometimes F8), however, is what returns you to the GUI if you happen to be running one.

Although you can press Alt+F# at the command prompt to move from one virtual terminal to another, you must do something slightly different if you're in the GUI. If you're in GNOME and want to use the virtual terminals, press Ctrl+Alt+F#. You can get back by pressing Alt+F7.

Don't forget about the Logout option in the main GNOME menu. If you don't want to use the GUI again for a while or want to free up the memory and CPU power that the GUI is hogging, choose this option.

If something is wrong and you need to get rid of the GUI in a hurry, press Ctrl+Alt+Backspace. This key combination gets you immediately out of the GUI and stops the programs used to run it, and you end up at a command prompt in one of the virtual terminals.

Press Ctrl+Alt+Backspace only in an emergency. This key combination doesn't *cleanly* stop the programs involved.

How do ya like them applets?

Applets — a collection of mini-programs that do anything from display the time, show system status, or even provide little bits of entertainment — are available out there in the great big world of computer programming. A number of people got it in their heads to write some of these applets specifically for use in the GNOME desktop environment in Linux. So these applets are included with your GNOME installation. Some of these mini-programs are more useful than others. We all need a bit of entertainment in our life, too, though, right?

Adding an applet icon to the Panel

You can have fun sifting through to see what kinds of applets are available to you. Look for them in the main GNOME menu, where you find a submenu called *applets*. Even better, you can quickly and painlessly add them to and remove them from your GNOME Panel as suits your needs. To add an applet to the Panel, do the following:

1. **Right-click any free space on the Panel and choose Applets from the pop-up menu that appears.**

   A submenu appears.

2. **Click to choose the applet you want to add to the Panel.**

   The applet is now on your Panel.

Configuring an applet

After you have an applet running, configuration options may be available that you can play with. Some of these options enable you to change what information is displayed. Others have a variety of look and feel settings, and in general, you can move them around the Panel to where you want them. To check for these and configure those applets that offer this option, do the following:

1. **Right-click the applet and choose Properties from the pop-up menu that appears.**

   The pop-up menu that appears is different from applet to applet. The top portion is always the same, however.

   This action opens a dialog box that's different for every applet.

2. **Configure the applet's behavior.**

   Here is where you get to have some fun. Make changes so that you can see what this applet can do.

3. **Continue playing around until you finish.**

4. **Click Apply to put your changes into effect without closing the dialog box or click OK to put them into effect while closing the dialog box.**

   Your changes go into effect.

The applet pop-up menu items we discuss here (aside from the standards — Properties, Help, and About) include additional things that this applet can do. Clicking these items may do a number of different things: You may open a dialog box with configuration options, open a submenu, or maybe even nothing happens. In the case of a disk space monitoring applet, you can use the menus to change which drive to watch. With some applet menus, the nonstandard options require that you've already done something else before they make any sense.

Ditching an applet

You have room for only so many applets. And if you're like us, you probably don't want to have every bit of free space cluttered up with things. Luckily, you can get rid of the applets you don't want to use. To remove an applet from the Panel, simply right-click the applet you want to remove and choose Remove from Panel from the pop-up menu that appears. With nary a whimper, the applet vanishes from the Panel.

Don't forget the programs

You may be looking at your Panel and wondering why you can put applets on it but can't make any changes to the programs that are on it. After all, a few program icons already appear on the bar by default. The good news is that you can change the programs on the bar! They fit in the same empty spaces that applets do. Unlike with the applets, however, you aren't restricted to putting a program shortcut just on the Panel. You can have one on your desktop, too.

Adding a program to the Panel

If you have a program that you end up using a lot, you can add it to your Panel by doing the following:

1. **Click the Main Menu button and browse to the program that you want to add to the bar.**

   Don't actually open the program. Just point to the menu item with your mouse pointer.

2. **After you select the program in the menu, click it and drag it onto the Panel.**

   An icon for this program now appears on your Panel. It may not be exactly where you tried to place it. In fact, it's probably off to the far right.

After you have your program on the Panel, you can run it just by clicking its icon.

Removing a program from the Panel

If you want to remove one of the programs on the Panel, just right-click the icon that you want to remove and choose Remove From Panel from the pop-up menu that appears. The icon vanishes from the panel. That's it!

Adding a program to the desktop

The Panel has only so much room. Maybe you'd rather have your program shortcuts lined up on the desktop as you do in Windows. To add one of these, do the following:

1. **Click the Main Menu button and choose Programs⇨*Application*, where *Application* is the name of the program that you want to add to the desktop.**

   If you want to add StarOffice to the desktop, for example, choose Programs⇨StarOffice (assuming that you have StarOffice!).

2. **Select the program that you want to add to the desktop.**

   Don't open the program.

3. **Drag the program to the desktop.**

   A little piece of paper graphic follows your mouse pointer until you release the mouse button. After you do so, your new shortcut is added to the desktop.

If you're not happy with where a desktop icon is, click it and then drag it to a new location.

Removing a program from the desktop

To get rid of an icon you have on your desktop, do the following:

1. **Right-click the icon and choose Delete from the pop-up menu that appears.**

   The Delete dialog box opens.

2. **Click Yes to confirm the deletion or No to cancel.**

   If you click Yes, the icon is deleted.

KDE, the Other Windows-like GUI

KDE, as shown in Figure 10-7, is the *K Desktop Environment*. This is the older of the environments that we cover in this book — although not the oldest piece of Linux GUI by any means — and, therefore, is quite stable. Some, however, don't find it as intuitive to navigate as GNOME.

The main KDE Web site is www.kde.org/.

Icon bar

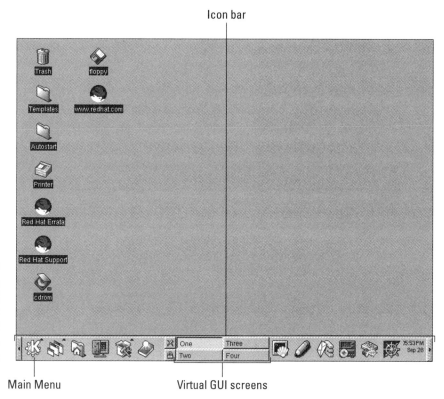

Figure 10-7:
The K
Desktop
Environment
(KDE).

Main Menu   Virtual GUI screens

As you can see from the figure, KDE looks pretty familiar although it's set up a bit differently from GNOME. We suppose that we should say that GNOME is set up differently from KDE, because KDE came first — but only by a bit. An item that should be familiar is the Virtual GUI screen's set of four boxes (numbered 1–4) on the Panel. Almost all GUIs in Linux give you the capability of having multiple GUI screens. Suppose that you have a lot of clutter on your desktop and want to open yet more programs, or maybe you like to have just one thing on the desktop at a time. You can actually have more than one desktop! The boxes for the additional screens are numbered 1 through 4 by default. The highlighted box is the one you're currently in. Figure 10-7 shows that we're in 1 now. If we click 2, we suddenly have a totally new desktop. If you have a bunch of programs in 1, they're still there after you go to 2. You just have the equivalent of four screens in one!

GNOME also gives you the capability of having multiple GUI screens.

One of the biggest functional differences between GNOME and KDE is that, in KDE, anything that you can click on-screen requires only *one* click, not two. If you want to open the Trash can in KDE, for example, you click it just once.

Chapter 11

Breaking Linux Out of Its Shell

* *

In This Chapter

▶ Understanding shell instances

▶ Using redirection and pipes

▶ Working with the bash shell

▶ Customizing the bash environment

* *

"Whom computers would destroy, they must first drive mad."

—Anonymous

*E*veryone needs a place to work. In an office, we may use a nice big desk with lots of drawers and organizers. In school, we have a smaller desk, sometimes with a lifting lid so we can store a few things inside it, and at other times we have just a surface to work on. In this chapter, we discuss the workspace Linux provides and how you can make the most of it.

Playing the Shell Game

You need a place to work on the computer — and we don't mean a desk. In this case we're talking about a place to work within the computer itself. In Linux, this place is where you work is called the *shell*. A shell is not a graphical thing but the sum total of the commands and syntax that you have available to you to do your work.

bash is not a violent act!

The default shell used in Linux is the bash shell. This work environment is based on the original Unix shell, which is called the Bourne shell and is also referred to as sh. bash stands for the *Bourne Again shell*, which is based on the Bourne shell and comes with most Linux distributions. The first time you encounter this shell is when you've finished logging in and get the command prompt. For example, if you're logged in as sue on the machine bartleby in Red Hat Linux 7, your prompt looks like the following:

```
[sue@bartleby sue]#
```

Red Hat Linux 7, which comes on the CDs that accompany this book, uses bash as the default shell, as do many other Linux distributions.

Everything you do from here is determined in some way by the shell's capabilities.

Which login am I in?

One of the most confusing things about Linux shells is that you're constantly moving in and out of them. Each time you log in, you open a *shell instance* — a specific shell with its own settings. This means that if you're logged in two different times on two different virtual terminals, you actually have two shells going. If you change the settings in one of the shells, those settings don't apply to the other! If you make the changes permanent, however, then any new shells you open have the new settings.

If you want your new settings in one login session to apply in your other login session, log out and then log back in. If you have multiple sessions open and want the new settings to apply to everything (including perhaps being in the GUI), you need to leave all of your sessions and re-enter.

The bash Shell at Your Beck and Call

If you understand what a shell really is, you're ready to get down and dirty. (If you don't, you need to refer to the previous section, "Playing the Shell Game.") Each shell has its own way of handling commands and additional sets of tools. In this section, we specifically cover what you can do with the bash shell, starting with working at the command prompt and then getting into bash shell interior decorating.

Command syntax and structure

Many people happily skip through their Linux use without understanding the fundamentals of commands in the bash shell. Note that this approach makes you lose out on some of the cool capabilities available in bash. The more you know about how this shell language works, the more interesting things you can do with it.

The basics of using bash at the command prompt often involve typing a command and any of its flags and values. For example, you enter the **ls -la ~** command to see a long format listing of all files in your home directory, including those that start with a dot — which are typically configuration files and directories.

Detours with redirection

One feature available to you in bash is the ability to add a detour sign in conjunction with a command. One group of such signs is referred to collectively as *redirection*. We specifically stick with redirecting command output here, because this is by far the most common form of detouring. *Output redirection* involves telling a command to send its results to a file instead of to the screen. Typing **ls -la ~** and then pressing Enter produces something like the following:

```
total 20
drwx------ 2 sue   users 4096 Oct 30 07:48 .
drwxr-xr-x 5 root  root  4096 Oct 30 11:57 ..
-rw-r----- 1 sue   users   24 Oct 30 06:50 .bash_logout
-rw-r----- 1 sue   users  230 Oct 30 06:50 .bash_profile
-rw-r----- 1 sue   users  124 Oct 30 06:50 .bashrc
-rw-rw-r-- 1 sue   users    0 Jan  2 07:48  wishlist
```

Want to send this information to a file instead? Enter the **ls -la ~ > listing** command. The > is the detour sign that tells bash to take the data that is otherwise sent to the screen and send it to the file named listing instead.

If you type **ls -la ~ > listing** again, the data is overwritten, meaning that the file's contents are wiped out and replaced with the new output. You can avoid this by using >> as your detour sign, which tells bash to add the command's output to the end of the specified file. So, if you type **ls -la ~ >> listing** in the same directory after making no changes, the contents of listing are now as follows:

```
total 20
drwx------ 2 sue   users 4096 Oct 30 07:48 .
drwxr-xr-x 5 root  root  4096 Oct 30 11:57 ..
-rw-r----- 1 sue   users   24 Oct 30 06:50 .bash_logout
-rw-r----- 1 sue   users  230 Oct 30 06:50 .bash_profile
-rw-r----- 1 sue   users  124 Oct 30 06:50 .bashrc
-rw-rw-r-- 1 sue   users    0 Jan  2  07:48  wishlist
total 20
drwx------ 2 sue   users 4096 Oct 30 07:48 .
drwxr-xr-x 5 root  root  4096 Oct 30 11:57 ..
-rw-r----- 1 sue   users   24 Oct 30 06:50 .bash_logout
-rw-r----- 1 sue   users  230 Oct 30 06:50 .bash_profile
-rw-r----- 1 sue   users  124 Oct 30 06:50 .bashrc
-rw-rw-r-- 1 sue   users    0 Jan  2  07:48  wishlist
```

Just typed a command and now you have to type it again? In bash, you can use the up and down arrow keys to move between previously typed commands. Pressing the up arrow keys once brings the last command you typed to the command prompt. Pressing up again brings the one before that, and so on. If you press down, you'll move backwards through the list. This is great if you just went through a series of long commands and need to redo them. Give it a try!

Laying pipes

Another bash shell feature enables you to connect commands such that the output of one becomes the input for the next. This feature is referred to as a *pipe.* Suppose that you want to look over the details of all files in the /etc directory in long-listing format. If you type **ls -la /etc** to do so, a massive listing appears. A lot of the information scrolls right past you. While you can back up a certain extent by pressing Shift+PageUp, you may not be able to see everything.

You can choose between two different ways to handle this:

- ✔ You can send the data to a file with redirection by typing something like **ls -la /etc > ~/etclisting** (making sure to replace the directory and filename, of course).

- ✔ You can pipe the output to the more command. This command ensures that text doesn't show up more than one screen at a time. It waits until you press the space bar before showing you the next screen's worth of text. Many Linux users find this command very useful.

To pipe the output to more, type **ls -la** *directory_path* **|** **more**, where *directory_ path* is the directory you want to list the contents for. The | symbol (which on the key looks more like two vertical bars stacked on top of each other instead of just one solid line) tells bash that you want to utilize a pipe.

Altering the shell environment

A number of *variables* — words or strings of text that are used in computers to represent a piece of data, such as setting the variable fruit to contain the text apple — contain information about your account and environment settings. The bash shell has a specific set of these variables that it uses regularly and a specific way of dealing with them. In this section, we take a look at what they are and how you can best make use of them.

Variables and environment variables

The first thing that we need to make clear is that the bash shell has two classes of variables: *variables* and *environment variables.* A variable is used in a program and then is gone. Nothing bothers to remember it past that point. An environment variable, used by the shell itself, is pertinent to your working environment in some way, whether it holds your account information, your prompt, or something else.

You can tell the difference between a variable and an environment variable at a glance in bash. Variables may be all lowercase or in upper- and lowercase. An environment variable, however, is always in all uppercase letters.

Common bash environment variables

bash has many environment variables, and you can even create more if you need to. You'll be amazed at the range of items that these variables store. The great thing is that if it's stored in a variable, you can change it to suit your needs! In Table 11-1, we list the environment variables that you're most likely to want to work with.

Table 11-1	Commonly Used bash Environment Variables	
Environment Variable	*Purpose*	*Value*
HISTSIZE	Remembers the number of previously typed commands.	Number of commands
HOME	Sets the location of your home directory.	The path to your home directory
MAILCHECK	Sets how often the bash shell looks to see whether mail has arrived in your mailbox. If mail has arrived, you see a message similar to You have new mail the next time you do something at the command prompt.	Number of seconds to wait between checks
PATH	Sets the directories that bash looks in, and the order to look in them to find a program name that you type at the command prompt.	A series of colon-separated directories
PS1	Sets your command prompt.	A series of the command characters and formatting characters used to form the prompt

Want to see the whole list of environment variables? Type **man bash** and press Enter, and then type **/Internal Field Sep** and press Enter. You see the first line in the section of environment and *shell variables* — a shell variable only exists in a single shell instance, it doesn't persist outside of that — in the bash man pages.

Listing current values

You can see current environment variable settings in two different ways. First, though, you must understand one more thing about how the bash shell handles variables: A variable has one name and its value has another name. For example, we can talk about the prompt environment variable, *PS1*. When we talk about its value, we're talking about *$PS1*.

Now onto how to view variable contents. You can look at them one at a time by using the format echo $variable (inserting appropriate word for variable) — this works for regular and environment variables. For example, to see what the contents of your prompt environment variable look like, type **echo $PS1**. If you're using Red Hat Linux, you see the following:

```
[\u@\h \W]\$
```

See Table 11-2 for the various components available to the bash prompt environment variable. You may want to utilize this information to play around with what your command prompt looks like in one of your user accounts. We tell you how to do this in the next section, "Changing Environment Variables."

Table 11-2	Pieces of the PS1 Puzzle
Component	*Result*
\!	Prints the position of the command in your history list.
\#	Prints the number of commands you've used during the current shell session.
\$	Prints a $ for user accounts or a # for the superuser.
\d	Prints the date in the following format: *day month date.*
\h	Prints the name of the machine you're logged into.
\n	Moves down to the next line.
\s	Prints bash for the bash shell.
\t	Prints XE "\t component" the time in 24-hour format.
\u	Prints your user name.
\w	Prints the lowest current directory level.
\W	Prints the entire current directory.

Type **history** to find out what's in the history list. Then type **!#**, where # is the list location of the command that you want to re-run.

You can also find the settings for all your environment variables at once by typing **env**.

Changing environment variables

You don't have to stick with the original décor of your homey little shell; you can change it. You change the value of an environment variable in the format *variable=value*. For example, the default HISTSIZE setting may be 500. Maybe you want to shrink it so that it only keeps a memory of the last 250 commands. So, you type **HISTSIZE=250**.

Working with non-numbers is a bit trickier. *Static* items — ones that don't change until you manually change them — sometimes need to be enclosed in double quotes (" ") but only for *text strings*. Text strings are collections of letters that you type on the keyboard and this includes the space key. Linux doesn't know whether you're adding another item when you have a space, or whether you're still working on the same one. So, putting the string in quotes — for example, "Joe Blow" — ensures that Linux knows exactly what you're talking about. Things like directories don't count because there aren't any spaces in them, so Linux won't get confused. Take the PATH variable as an example. If you type **echo $PATH**, you get something like the following:

```
/usr/local/bin:/bin:/usr/bin:/usr/X11R6/bin
```

For the path mentioned in the previous line of code, it means that if you type a command (maybe ls), bash first looks for it in /usr/local/bin, then /bin, then /usr/bin, and then /usr/X11R6/bin.

Perhaps you want to add the directory /home/ralph/scripts to the end of the search path. You do this by typing **PATH=$PATH:/home/ralph/scripts**. The $PATH in this case adds to the original contents. Isn't that handy?

So, when do you need quotes? Maybe you want to create a new environment variable that contains a quote you really like (this one's from the movie *Mystery Men*). You type something like the following:

```
QUOTE="We've got a blind date with destiny, and it
looks like she's ordered the lobster."
```

Now, whenever you type echo $QUOTE, you see that text. You don't always use double quotes though. They refer to things that aren't going to change. Some environment variables do, however, change on a regular basis. The most notable of these is the prompt variable PS1. Whether it changes or not depends on what values you put in it. The following raw code shows how bash sees the default prompt:

```
[\u@\h \W]\$
```

As you can see from referring to Table 11-2, this prompt translates to the following:

```
[user@host lowdir]$
```

The `lowdir` entry is the lowest part of the directory you're in. For example, if you're in `/home/jon`, it just prints `jon`. Every time you change directories, this entry changes . . . *if* you've placed it inside single quotes (' '). If you put a prompt entry inside double quotes, then `bash` assumes it doesn't need to pay any more attention to it! Putting it inside single quotes tells `bash` to look at it regularly.

Suppose that you want to change the prompt for your account to look like the following:

```
We've got a blind date with destiny, and it
looks like she's ordered the lobster.
[user@host fulldir]$
```

Yes, that's a lot of text, but some folks like it! How can you do something like that? You simply type the following:

```
PS1='$QUOTE\n[\u@\h \w]\$ '
```

In the preceding line of code, notice the extra space at the end of the prompt before the end quote. You need to add this if you want a space between the $ and the cursor.

If you're going to play around with environment variables, we recommend that you start using the methods that we discuss in this section. After you've decided that you're comfortable with any changes you've made, you can make your changes permanent by opening the `~/.bash_profile` file and adding the same text there. Next time you log in, the changes go into effect.

Chapter 12

Putting the x in Text

*L*ong ago, in a galaxy far, far away, lived an editor named ed. Some were perfectly happy to use this editor for the rest of their lives. Others, however, found ed difficult to use and quickly tired of it. From their frustrations, em was born in London, England. However, the features in em were not enough for some. Another group in Berkeley, California, beefed up em, which resulted in yet another editor — ex.

Still, some people are just never happy. A fellow named Bill Joy in the Berkeley group wanted even more. He especially wanted something that worked well over a slow modem connection (300 bps!), which meant the commands had to be very simple and quick. After several months of laboring through the night, the vi editor was born. That was not the end of the story, though.

From text editors were born word processors, which not only allowed people to input and edit text, but also let them format things with bolds and italics and other fancy stuff that we take for granted today. In this chapter, we take a look at some of the tools that you can use in the text editor and word processing areas.

Getting Prehistoric with vi

People tend to have a love/hate relationship with the vi editor. Some think of vi as a wonderful, efficient, fast-moving tool (often those who know how to use it), while others find it cryptic and confusing. Whether you love it or hate it, you can't get around the fact that if something is wrong with your Linux computer, vi may be the only editor that you have access to. The whole program is small enough to fit on a single floppy disk — a rare thing these days! We suggest that you take the time to get familiar with vi, and then try out other editors and decide which one you like best.

Opening files

Because vi is a text-based text editor, opening a file is pretty straightforward. You just type **vi** *filename* (replacing *filename* with the name of the particular file that you want to see) and the file opens. If the content already exists, then you can see it in the file. Otherwise, you get a blank screen, as shown in Figure 12-1.

Figure 12-1:
The initial
vi screen,
displaying
an empty
file.

Looking for menus? You won't see any. The vi editor has help information, but no menus. Instead, it has *modes*. vi has three basic modes:

  ✔ **Command mode:** vi assumes that everything you type is a vi command.

  ✔ **Insert mode:** vi interprets everything that you type in this mode as text that goes in the file.

  ✔ **ex mode:** You can still use those old ex commands in this mode.

If you have a file open in vi, you can go to the help information by pressing the F1 key. To get out of it, type **:q** and press Enter, which takes you back to vi in command mode.

Entering text

To type text in vi, you need to enter Insert mode. To enter Insert mode, follow these steps:

1. **Press Esc to enter Command mode from any mode you may currently be in.**

   The layout of this screen looks familiar (see Figure 12-1).

2. **Press I to enter Insert mode from Command mode.**

   Notice that the screen changes slightly from mode to mode. Figure 12-2 shows a blank file open in vi while in Insert mode.

Figure 12-2:
The vi
screen in
Insert mode
with an
empty file.

From here, you simply type text until you're finished.

You need to press Enter at the end of each line of text, just as you hit the carriage return on a typewriter. Otherwise, vi doesn't wrap the words properly and actually sees the text as one long line, making it hard for you to use the editing functions.

Editing text

You have a number of ways that you can edit text in the vi editor. You can do it the old-fashioned way by entering Insert mode and manipulating the text using the Delete key, Insert key, and more from your keyboard. However, vi does have some fancier options available. To use any of these options, do the following:

1. **Press Esc to enter Command mode from any mode you may currently be in.**

   The layout of this screen looks familiar (see Figure 12-1).

2. **Use the arrow keys to properly position the cursor for the option to work.**

   See Table 12-1 for an explanation of proper cursor positioning.

3. **Press the key or sequence of keys that executes what you want to do.**

Table 12-1 shows one group of commands that you may want to use.

# indicates the optional ability to include a number so that the command works on more than one line, word, or character. If you don't include a number, vi assumes a 1. Whenever you see an underscore (_), you need to specify a character that the command is to work on.

Table 12-1	Commonly Used vi Editing Commands	
Keystroke(s)	*Initial Cursor Position*	*Result*
a	One space before the place you want to add text.	vi enters Insert mode directly after the cursor's position.
p	Directly where you want the text to appear.	vi copies the buffered text into the document.
#o	Anywhere directly above where you want the new line to appear.	vi adds a blank line or lines below the cursor's position and then enters Insert mode with the cursor within that blank line.
#r_	Directly on top of the (first) character you want to replace.	vi replaces the current character, plus #-1 after it, with the specified character.
#yl	Directly on top of the (first) character you want to copy.	vi copies the specified characters into the buffer.
#yy	Anywhere within the (first) line you want to copy.	vi copies the specified line(s) into the buffer.
u	Anywhere in the file.	vi undoes what you last did.

Keep in mind that, when an option puts you into Insert mode, you need to return to Command mode before you can use editing commands again.

Deleting text

vi has a large collection of commands that are useful for deleting text. You can use the Backspace or Delete keys, of course, but you have a lot of other things that you can do as well. To make use of vi's deletion features, follow these steps:

1. **Press Esc to enter Command mode from any mode you may currently be in.**

    The layout of this screen looks familiar (see Figure 12-1).

2. **Use the arrow keys to properly position the cursor for the option to work.**

    See Table 12-2 for an explanation of proper cursor positioning.

3. **Press the key or sequence of keys that executes what you want to do.**

    Table 12-2 shows one group of commands that you may want to use.

A # indicates that if you include a number, the command works on more than one item.

Table 12-2	Commonly Used vi Deletion Commands	
Keystroke(s)	*Initial Cursor Position*	*Result*
#cc	Anywhere within the (first) line you want to cut.	vi cuts the entire selected line(s).
#dl	Directly on top of the (first) character you want to delete.	vi deletes the specified characters.
#dd	Anywhere within the (first) line you want to delete.	vi deletes the entire selected line(s).
p	Directly where you want the text to appear.	vi copies the buffered text into the document.
#x	Directly on top of the (first) character you want to cut.	vi deletes the specified characters into the buffer.

Don't forget that when an option puts you into Insert mode, you need to return to Command mode before you can use deletion commands again.

Saving files

Just about every text and document editor has at least two different ways of saving a file. The first way involves saving and closing the document. In vi, you accomplish this by doing the following:

1. **Press Esc to enter Command mode from any mode you may currently be in.**

   The layout of this screen looks familiar (see Figure 12-1).

2. **Type** ZZ **to save and close the file.**

   The file closes, and you're now back at the command prompt.

The second method of saving a file involves saving without closing. To save a file and keep working on it in vi, follow these steps:

1. **Press Esc to enter Command mode from any mode you may currently be in.**

   The layout of this screen looks familiar (see Figure 12-1).

2. **Type** : **(a colon) to enter ex mode.**

   The screen changes slightly and now shows a blank file, as shown in Figure 12-3.

Figure 12-3: The vi screen in ex mode with an empty file.

3. **Type** w **and press Enter.**

   The w stands for *write* (or save). You're now back in the file within Command mode.

Want to close the file without saving changes? In the previous step list, follow the first two steps. When you get to Step 3, type **q!** instead of **w.**

Checking Out Other Text-Based Text Editors

As a command prompt Linux user, you have dozens of text editors available to you. We don't want to overwhelm you with choices, so we cover just two more editors that work quite differently from vi, and also from each other. By doing so, we hopefully give you the freedom to choose the editor that works the way that you like to work, rather than leaving you with just one option, which may cause you to spend a lot of time and effort researching others.

Pico

The pico text editor is popular among people who don't want to remember or need a lot of complex editing commands. All they want to do is type in their text and get on with life. For a glance at what an empty file (which you open by typing **pico** *filename*) looks like in pico, see Figure 12-4.

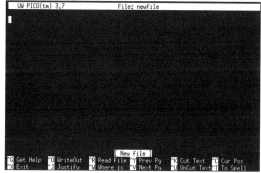

Figure 12-4:
The initial
pico
screen
with an
empty file.

You don't have to worry about modes or memorizing commands with the pico editor. You can plainly see a menu at the bottom of the screen. Wherever you see a carat (^) in the menu, you need to press the Ctrl key to execute the command. So, for example, to save and quit (Exit), type **^X**, or press Ctrl+x (whether you use capital or lowercase letters here doesn't make any difference). In fact, all of the pico commands involve the Ctrl key.

To access the full list of pico commands, press Ctrl+g or F1. To navigate through this list, press Ctrl+v to move down or Ctrl+y to move up. The arrow keys don't work here. Press Ctrl+x after you're finished.

You may not have pico installed by default. Don't worry, you probably have it somewhere in your distribution files. If you're using Red Hat or a related distribution, do the following to install the pico editor (if it's not already there):

1. **Place your Red Hat (or related) CD-ROM in the CD-ROM drive.**

2. **Type** mount /mnt/cdrom **to add the CD-ROM to your file system.**

3. **Type** cd /mnt/cdrom/RedHat/RPMS **to change to the directory containing program packages in Red Hat Package Manager format.**

4. **Type** rpm -ivh pine, **press Tab to complete the filename, and press Enter to install the pine e-mail reader that contains the pico editor.**

   A small line of hash marks (#) appears below the package name as the rpm program installs the package.

5. **Type** cd ~ **to change to your home directory.**

   You can go anywhere you want, really, as long as it's no longer in /mnt/cdrom or anything within that tree of directories.

6. **Type** umount /mnt/cdrom **to remove the CD-ROM from the file system.**

7. **Remove the Red Hat CD-ROM from your CD-ROM drive.**

emacs

Many of its users affectionately refer to the emacs text editor as *bloatware,* because it's bloated with many, many, many features. A lot of people like it because it's capable of such a wide range of functions. As usual, what you choose to use is a matter of what you're comfortable with and what you're trying to accomplish. If you like to try your hand at computer programming, you may very well love the emacs editor. For a glance at what an empty file (which you open by typing **emacs** *filename*) looks like in emacs, see Figure 12-5.

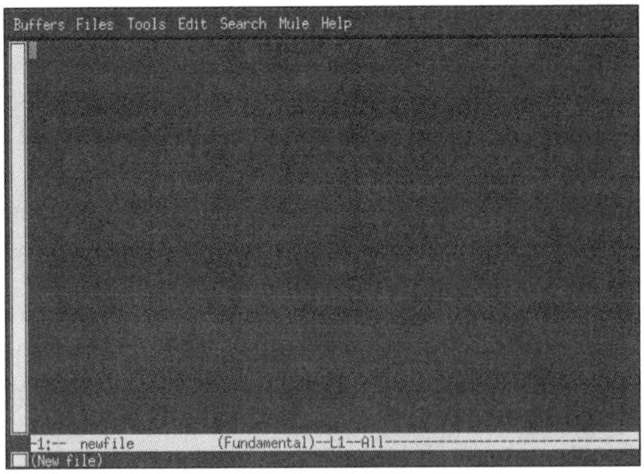

Figure 12-5:
The initial
emacs
screen
displaying
an empty
file.

Accessing the emacs menu

As you can see from Figure 12-5, emacs sports a menu bar at the top of its screen. To use this menu bar, do the following:

1. **Press F10.**

   The menu opens in a new emacs window, splitting your screen in half horizontally, as shown in Figure 12-6.

Your text

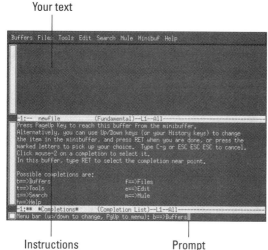

Figure 12-6:
emacs with
the menu
open.

Instructions   Prompt

2. **Use the up and down arrow keys to select the menu option that you want to open.**

   Pressing the up or down arrow keys changes the menu item displayed in the prompt. See Table 12-3 to see what you can expect from each menu.

Table 12-3	Contents of emacs Menus
Menu	*Description*
Buffers	Access to the various screens (your main file, help information, and more) hidden within emacs.
Files	Save files, create new ones, and more.
Tools	Printing, plus a lot of the fancier emacs options, like the ability to read mail or news directly from within emacs.
Edit	Takes you back to your file.
Search	Search for data within your file in many different ways.
Mule	Options for using non-English characters.
Help	A variety of emacs help information.

3. **Press Enter after you've selected your menu choice.**

   The instruction and prompt areas in the screen both change. All the menus display a submenu full of additional options except for the Edit menu, which takes you back to having your text file in the full screen.

Feeling lost? If you press the Esc key enough times, you can get back to your file from the menus at any time. Press it, back up, press it, back up, and continue this until you're back where you want to be.

   4. Use the up and down arrow keys to select the submenu option.

   5. Press Enter to open that option.

   6. Proceed through the menus until you find what you want to do.

As you can see, those menus contain a lot of functions! If you like working with menus, open up an experimental file and muddle your way through them. You're likely to find a number of things that you'll want to use again.

Saving your work

You have a few different ways that you can save your work in emacs. Rather than bewildering you with all the options, we just focus on a single one here. To save your work in emacs, do the following:

   1. Press F10.

   The menu opens in a new emacs window, splitting your screen in half horizontally, as shown in Figure 12-6.

   2. Press f to open the Files submenu.

   The lower portion of the screen changes to display Files options.

   3. Press s to save the file with its current name.

   emacs saves the data and returns to the file in editing mode.

Quitting emacs

You have numerous ways that you can get out of emacs. We cover just one of them here. To exit emacs, do the following:

   1. Press F10.

   The menu opens in a new emacs window, splitting your screen in half horizontally, as shown in Figure 12-6.

   2. Press f to open the Files submenu.

   The lower portion of the screen changes to display Files options.

   3. Press e to exit emacs.

   If you haven't saved the file, you're asked to do so now. If you do want to, press **y**. If not, press **n** and then **y** to confirm. You're now back at the command prompt.

Installing emacs

You very likely don't have emacs installed by default. emacs is a large program and therefore not often installed unless you really want to use it. However, almost all Linux distributions include emacs. If you're using Red Hat or a related distribution, do the following to install the emacs editor (if it's not already there):

1. **Place your Red Hat (or related) CD-ROM in the CD-ROM drive.**

2. **Type** mount /mnt/cdrom **to add the CD-ROM to your file system.**

3. **Type** cd /mnt/cdrom/RedHat/RPMS **to change to the directory containing program packages in Red Hat Package Manager format.**

4. **Type** rpm -ivh emacs-2 **and then press Tab to complete the filename, and then Enter to install part one of the emacs editor.**

   A small line of hash marks (#) appears below the package name as the rpm program installs the package.

5. **Type** rpm -ivh emacs-n **and then press Tab to complete the filename, and then Enter to install part two of the emacs editor.**

   A small line of hash marks (#) appears the same way as before.

6. **Type** cd ~ **to change to your home directory.**

   You can go anywhere you want, really, as long as it's no longer in /mnt/cdrom or anything within that tree of directories.

7. **Type** umount /mnt/cdrom **to remove the CD-ROM from the file system.**

8. **Remove the Red Hat CD-ROM from your CD-ROM drive.**

Going with gnotepad+

You're not just stuck with command prompt-based text editors in Linux. You have lots of options available. In this section, we cover gnotepad+ for those of you who prefer to work in the GUI setting (it comes by default with GNOME).

Remember that if you don't automatically boot into the GUI, you can enter it from the command prompt by typing **startx**.

Starting gnotepad+

To start gnotepad+ from within GNOME, follow these steps:

1. **Click the GNOME Footprint icon to open the main menu.**

2. **Choose Programs➪Applications➪gnotepad+.**

   The program opens, as shown in Figure 12-7.

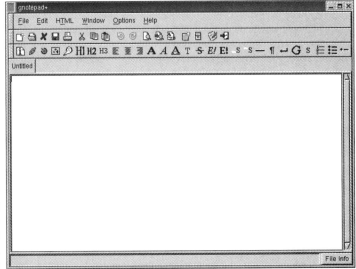

Figure 12-7:
gnotepad+
open with
blank file.

Entering and formatting text

gnotepad+ is strictly a *text editor,* in that you use it to generate raw text, whereas a *word processor* creates marked up text that can only be opened by programs that can read that word processor's file formatting. After referring to Figure 12-7 and reading this, you're probably a bit confused. All those formatting buttons are for creating Web pages. So, if you're into making your own Web pages by hand, this editor just may be for you!

To just enter text, click within the big white space and start typing. That part's easy enough. The confusing part's in the formatting — if you want to create HTML documents. You have two different places to look for formatting functions, as follows:

✔ You can find formatting functions in the menu bar, under the HTML drop-down menu. You can see a large number of features listed here. We're not discussing HTML in this book, so we don't go into them heavily. If you want to learn more about doing Web pages, though, you'd be wise to experiment with these!

✔ You can find HTML formatting functions on the second row of icons (refer to Figure 12-7).

In either case, make sure that you first select the text that you want to format. To select text, do the following:

1. **Click the first character of the text that you want to select and hold the mouse button down!**

   Make sure the vertical line for the cursor's location ends up directly to the left of that character if you want to include it.

2. **Drag the mouse until all the text you want to format is highlighted; continue holding that mouse button down!**

3. **When you've selected everything properly, release the mouse button.**

4. **Click the formatting option that you want to apply, either from the icon bar or from the HTML menu.**

   The formatting is applied to the item.

Saving your work

As usual, you have two choices. You can save your work and keep going, or save it and then exit the program. To just save the file and keep going, do the following:

1. **Click the save button.**

   This button looks like a floppy disk. If you haven't saved this file before, clicking it opens the Save As dialog box, as shown in Figure 12-8.

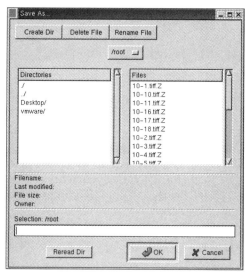

Figure 12-8:
gnotepad+
Save As
dialog box.

2. **Browse through the directories in the left pane until you're within the directory where you want to save the file.**

   Double-click the name of a directory to enter it, or the `..` in the listing to move up a level in the directory tree.

3. **Type the file's name in the Selection text box.**

4. **Click OK to save the file.**

   The dialog box closes.

To close gnotepad+, do the following:

1. **Choose File⇨Exit.**

   If you haven't saved this file since the last time you changed it, the Question dialog box appears, as shown in Figure 12-9.

Figure 12-9:
gnotepad+
Question
dialog box.

2. **If you get the dialog box, click Yes to save your work, or No to abandon it.**

   The program closes.

Word Processors in Linuxland

We want to make sure that you're aware of some of the other options available to you in case you like to explore and check things out. Because we've already covered three different text editors, in this section we briefly discuss word processors, which let you actually format your documents and do a lot of the fancy things that you may already be used to doing in other operating systems.

StarOffice Writer

The StarOffice suite is available at www.staroffice.com/. You can either download this suite or purchase it (plus additional goodies) on CD-ROM. This suite comes with the following components:

Package	Purpose
StarOffice Base	A database program, like Microsoft Access.
StarOffice Calc	A spreadsheet program, like Microsoft Excel.
StarOffice Discussion	A newsgroup reader.
StarOffice Draw	A drawing and image manipulation program.
StarOffice Impress	A presentation building program, like Microsoft PowerPoint.
StarOffice Mail	An e-mail reader, like Eudora.
StarOffice Schedule	A scheduling tool.
StarOffice Writer	A word processing program, like Microsoft Word.

You can get StarOffice for other operating systems too, like Microsoft Windows.

Applixware Words

The Applixware suite is available at www.vistasource.com/products/axware. You can try it out online through the Web site, or purchase it. This suite comes with the following components:

Package	Purpose
Applixware Builder	Enables you to develop your own tools.
Applixware Data	A database program, like Microsoft Access.
Applixware Graphics	A drawing and image manipulation program.
Applixware Mail	An e-mail reader, like Eudora.
Applixware Presents	A presentation building program, like Microsoft PowerPoint.
Applixware Spreadsheets	A spreadsheet program, like Microsoft Excel.
Applixware Words	A word processing program, like Microsoft Word.

Corel WordPerfect

The Corel Office 2000 suite includes WordPerfect 9. Information about this package is available at http://linux.corel.com/. You can purchase this product online or in stores, or use the free WordPerfect 98 that comes with many Linux distributions. This suite comes with the following office components:

Package	Purpose
Corel Presentations 9	A presentation building program, like Microsoft PowerPoint.
CorelCENTRAL 9	A scheduling tool.
Paradox 9	A database program, like Microsoft Access.
Quattro Pro 9	A spreadsheet program, like Microsoft Excel.
WordPerfect 9	A word processing program, like Microsoft Word.

Part IV
Sinking Your Teeth into Linux

The 5th Wave   By Rich Tennant

"This part of the test tells us whether you're personally suited to the job of network administrator."

In this part . . .

This part is where you reach out with Linux beyond the confines of your own computer, to provide access to built-in services and resources, and access other services and resources on a network. We introduce you to Web hosting, FTP, news services, and e-mail, to convince you that your Linux system can function as a serious, snappy service center for any network. In addition, we walk you through the Linux file system — files, directories, and subdirectories — and teach you some practical house-keeping tips.

On the more creative side, you get a crash course on customizing your Linux desktop, complete with color schemes and other themes. You also discover what's required to tweak and tune a Linux system so that you can extract the best performance and capability from your computer. Finally, you explore the basics of system security on a Linux system, including the specifics of monitoring a system's users and their behavior, as well as how to protect yourself from the bad guys.

Chapter 13

Setting Up Your LAN

• •

In This Chapter

▶ Intranets and the Internet

▶ Common types of network services

▶ Laying out your LAN

▶ Sharing network resources

▶ Security on the LAN

• •

*O*ne of the wonderful things about Linux is its capability to function as a single-user system or to integrate with others on a network. The primary reason that we have networks is to share *stuff,* so be glad that you can connect Linux systems together and share resources. The stuff that we can share includes hardware, such as printers, and software, such as databases. And a network makes a great delivery mechanism for messages and data, especially if the information is *big.* You can view movies, play music, and read entire books on your Linux system, but none of these fits on a floppy disk. They're likely to fit on a CD-ROM, but you can also put them on one networked Linux system and access the information from another networked system. Linux can also share data with other non-Linux systems, such as Novell, Microsoft, and Apple systems. In addition, those other operating systems can share their resources with networked Linux systems.

The Two Types of Nets — Intranet and Internet

The primary reason why one would use or setup a network is to share resources. Say, for example, that you have a fancy color printer that you want several people to use. Without a network, each person who wanted to print would need to go to the specific machine that is cabled to the printer, wait his turn, and then print his document. Instead, if you share the color printer on the network, each person can print from his own machine without needing to change systems.

A printer is probably one of the most common types of resources shared. You can also share other hardware such as modems or your broadband access hardware and fax services. In addition to hardware, you can also share software resources. Say, for example, that your company maintains a database of all your clients. If you place the database information on the network, all your employees who need client information can retrieve the information from their desktops. In addition, only one copy of the database contains all the current changes. If you had the database copied on all your users' systems, whenever one made a change to the database information, you'd need to make sure that all the other copies also get the same changes.

Networks come in different sizes and configurations, and several terms describe networks:

- **Local area network (LAN):** Refers to a small geographically contained network.

  You typically find these in small businesses or in homes. LANs usually consist of just a few devices shared on the network and a few computers. A LAN may also represent an entire office building and a couple hundred people or users of the network.

- **Wide area network (WAN):** Usually represents different geographical areas and/or several hundreds to thousands, or even millions, of users.

  A WAN typically consists of many smaller LANs connected to form the WAN. Communication channels, private high-speed cables, broadband, or wireless technologies connect the smaller LANs. Some large WANs use several different technologies to connect their LANs.

> *In case you haven't heard, the Internet is not a superhighway.*
>
> — Bill Washburn, *Internet World Magazine*

The Internet is the largest and probably the most common network that you're familiar with. The Internet encompasses the entire planet and beyond. If the astronauts are orbiting earth in the shuttle or on the International Space Station, they use a network to send and retrieve data with NASA. They also use e-mail to communicate with their families.

Many of the services available on the Internet are also available on a small network. Using your browser to access information on NASA's Web sites, for example, uses a very common Internet service and protocol. Sending e-mail or participating in newsgroups are also common Internet services. But you can also provide these same services on your local network. An *intranet* is a local or private network that provides Internet type services.

In this section, we concentrate on issues surrounding a LAN and Linux. We cover planning and designing your network and use printing as an example of a shared resource. In addition, we also discuss what's involved when your intranet meets the Internet. Bonus Appendix A covers setting up some of the other Internet-type services on your intranet.

Serving up network services

The Internet today is far, far different that what it was in the 1970s. The network services available when the Internet was young, however, are some that we still use today. These include messaging services, which we commonly use today in the form of e-mail. The following sections discuss these services.

In the following examples of Internet services on your intranet, we're referring to Linux systems only. But you can place all these services (and more) on Linux and access them from Linux and non-Linux systems. The opposite is also true — another vendor's operating system may be providing all or some of these services and you can access those with Linux. In summary, Linux *plays well* in a new or existing network.

E-mail services

You can set up Linux to provide e-mail services and interface with other e-mail systems. Doing so enables you to provide an e-mail system on your intranet and to configure the system to interface with external or other e-mail systems. Because e-mail services have been available on the Internet for years, the original interfaces were command-prompt and text oriented.

Figure 13-1 shows an example of a text-based interface to an e-mail system. Figure 13-2 shows an example of a graphical e-mail interface. Most Web browsers provide e-mail support.

Figure 13-1:
E-mail
services
from the
command
prompt.

```
[root@blissranch /root]# mail
Mail version 8.1 6/6/93.  Type ? for help.
"/var/spool/mail/root"; 2 messages 2 unread
>U  1 root@localhost.local  Tue Oct 17 22:38  14/433   "Hello"
 U  2 root@localhost.local  Tue Oct 17 22:39  14/440   "Notice"
& help
     Mail  Commands
t <message list>              type messages
n                             goto and type next message
e <message list>              edit messages
f <message list>              give head lines of messages
d <message list>              delete messages
s <message list> file         append messages to file
u <message list>              undelete messages
R <message list>              reply to message senders
r <message list>              reply to message senders and all recipients
pre <message list>            make messages go back to /usr/spool/mail
m <user list>                 mail to specific users
q                             quit, saving unresolved messages in mbox
x                             quit, do not remove system mailbox
h                             print out active message headers
!                             shell escape
cd [directory]                chdir to directory or home if none given

A <message list> consists of integers, ranges of same, or user names separated
by spaces.  If omitted, Mail uses the last message typed.

A <user list> consists of user names or aliases separated by spaces.
Aliases are defined in .mailrc in your home directory.
&
```

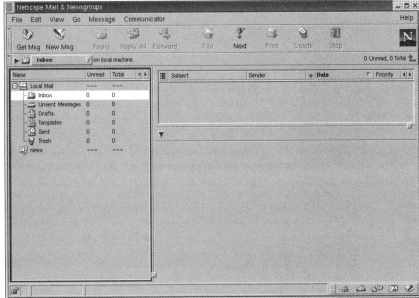

Figure 13-2: E-mail services within a browser.

FTP

FTP (short for *File Transfer Protocol*) provides rapid and efficient transfer of data and files over the Internet. FTP services on the Internet and other networks have been around for years. Sometimes, as you point your browser to a Web site and download an update to a software package, you're actually receiving the file by way of FTP. Fortunately, most browsers today are aware of FTP and automatically support it, making it easier for you to use. But back in the early days of the Internet, you needed to use commands and type stuff at the keyboard. You can still interact with FTP by using a keyboard, but most people prefer to *point and click.* Figure 13-3 shows the command-oriented FTP interface.

```
[root@blissranch /root]# ftp 172.16.3.200
Connected to 172.16.3.200.
220 blissranch FTP server (Version wu-2.6.1(1) Wed Aug 9 05:54:50 EDT 2000) ready.
Name (172.16.3.200:root): mhoag
331 Password required for mhoag.
Password:
230 User mhoag logged in.
Remote system type is UNIX.
Using binary mode to transfer files.
ftp> ?
Commands may be abbreviated.  Commands are:

!               debug           mdir            sendport        site
$               dir             mget            put             size
account         disconnect      mkdir           pwd             status
append          exit            mls             quit            struct
ascii           form            mode            quote           system
bell            get             modtime         recv            sunique
binary          glob            mput            reget           tenex
bye             hash            newer           rstatus         tick
case            help            nmap            rhelp           trace
cd              idle            nlist           rename          type
cdup            image           ntrans          reset           user
chmod           lcd             open            restart         umask
close           ls              prompt          rmdir           verbose
cr              macdef          passive         runique         ?
delete          mdelete         proxy           send
ftp> █
```

Figure 13-3: FTP services from the command prompt.

Figure 13-4 shows a browser FTP interface. In the browser view of FTP, you click directories to navigate up and down the file structure. If you click a file, you're given the options to open it or download and save the file to your system. The text-oriented FTP interface provides the same power by using commands entered at the `ftp>` prompt.

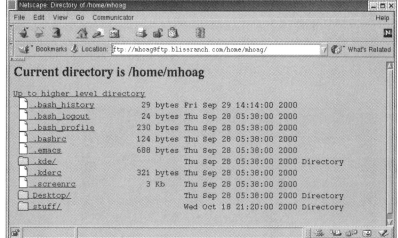

Figure 13-4:
FTP
services
within a
browser.

On your intranet, you can set up Linux to provide FTP services. If you need to transfer files between two Linux systems, FTP is a natural. If you want to download a file, you can use your browser to retrieve the information from another Linux system. In Bonus Appendix A, we cover how to access a Linux FTP server.

Newsgroups

Another veteran Internet service is the *newsgroup* service. Thousands of public newsgroups are accessible on the Internet. You can subscribe to the ones that interest you and participate in an open forum type of environment. Most common browsers have the built-in capability to interact with newsgroups, but you can also use separate newsreader programs.

Linux can provide newsgroup services on your intranet. Imagine that you have a project involving several people who need to work out some ideas. With a news server, you can set up a discussion group for the project team in which they can exchange ideas and comments. Because a discussion group is *threaded,* you can follow a topic's responses and replies, or *thread*, and read and comment on other people's responses.

Telnet

Telnet provides the capability to remotely access and interact with another system. Telnet has been around for some time and is one of the first protocols developed. With Telnet, you can access another system and enter commands at the keyboard, which are executed on the remote system you're attached to. Linux supports the Telnet protocol. You can access a Linux system from another computer and interact with the remote Linux system. In a Telnet session, you can do almost all tasks and run applications that you can perform sitting in front of the Linux system. In the name of security, however, you're not permitted to perform some actions from a remote connection. Figure 13-5 shows an example of a Telnet command interface, or session, from one Linux system to another.

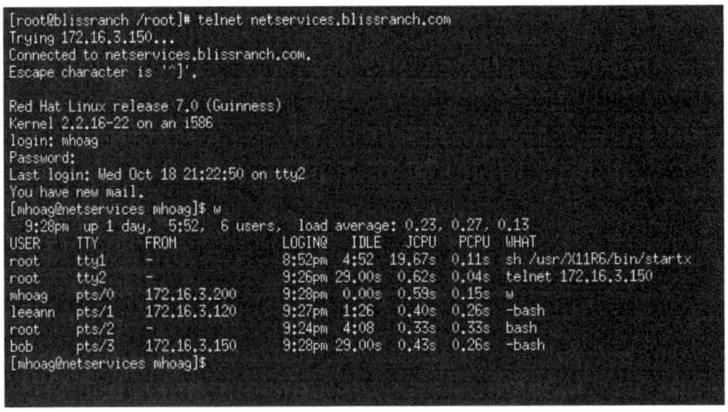

Figure 13-5:
Telnet
session on
one Linux
system
accessing a
remote
Linux
system.

Web services

Probably one of the most common services today is Web services. This service provides a graphical interface to interact with information, and it supports many types of data. You can place a Linux Web server on your local network and provide an Internet service on your intranet. By the way, Linux is one of the most popular operating systems for running a Web server. The best-known Web server software is called Apache, and it runs many major corporations' large intranet *and* Internet Web servers. We discuss Apache in Bonus Appendix A. Figure 13-6 shows the test page from an Apache Web server running on a Linux system.

Distinguishing inside from outside

The concept of *inside* your network refers to services and systems accessing those resources that are physically located on your network. Because everything is local, this usually provides you with fast access to resources and easy access for maintenance. This also provides a level of security. If you keep everything local and don't connect to any other network, you confine any source of problems to your network.

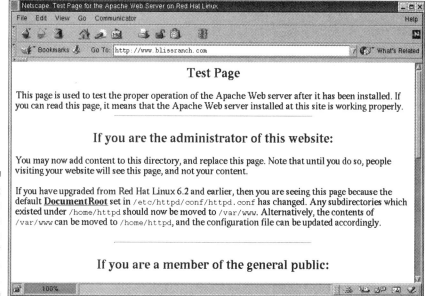

Figure 13-6:
Test page
from the
Apache
Web server
running on
Linux.

Outside your network refers to systems and networks that either aren't under your supervision or are separated physically by some type of *interface device*. Interface devices include components such as routers or WAN connection hardware. If you have two LANs in two different cities connected by a WAN link, you also have the concept that each LAN is *outside* the other.

Another common interface that you may have is between your network (inside) and the Internet (outside). This interface enables users on your intranet to access services on the Internet. That is, the inside can access the outside. You can also set up this interface to enable individuals on the outside (from the Internet) to access resources on the inside (your intranet). This is a very powerful feature. Imagine that you're traveling and you need to get a file from your intranet on one of your Linux systems. From your remote location, you can use the Internet as a transport medium to gain access to your network. In this example, you can view the Internet as an extension of your own network.

You must consider many issues if you interface your network with another network, the first of which is the *communication protocol*. Networks and computers are just like humans: Each has different languages with which to communicate. If two people don't use the same language, they can't understand each other. To solve this problem, one person can switch to the other's language; they can change to another language that both understand; or one can use a translator to convert to the other's language. The same concept applies to networks.

During the development of networks, different languages, or communication protocols, evolved. To support multiple protocols, sometimes the languages are translated to another protocol. The protocol used on the Internet is *Internet Protocol* (IP) and is often referred to as TCP/IP. (TCP stands for *Transmission Control Protocol.*) Linux's *native* language is IP, which makes Linux very easy to communicate with on new or existing IP-based networks. Linux also supports languages used by other operating systems — for example, IPX for Novell systems and AppleTalk for Macintosh systems.

You must also consider how to interface the inside with the outside. Complete solutions are available from vendors whose services may cover a wide range of options. These can include all necessary equipment and software, hardware only, or software only. If you want to use an available local service, you can usually find a solution through your local telephone service provider.

Depending on where you are, you may have other local solutions available to you, which can include solutions that the local television cable system or a local university provides. You may even have a local Internet access solution company or satellite services. In some home-market areas, you can purchase access boxes that work with the local broadband service provider, such as cable modem or DSL, and connect your LAN or home network to the Internet. These devices are discussed in Chapter 7.

After you interface the inside to the outside, you must consider security. How can you protect your systems on the inside from unwanted access from the outside? Besides access concerns, you also need to think about the possibility of viruses or other unwanted programs ending up on your systems. For more details, refer to Chapter 17, in which we cover Linux security issues.

Setting Up Your LAN

After you set up your Linux systems, you need them to *talk* to each other. You also may have a printer attached to one of the Linux systems that you want the other Linux computers capable of printing to the same printer. You're also thinking about adding some other services in the future. In addition, you may need to get your LAN *on* the Internet. You have many factors to consider in building a network, and your initial step is to design and plan it all out first.

There are three kinds of death in this world. There's heart death, there's brain death, and there's being off the network.

— Guy Almes

Planning and designing a LAN

Each device that you want to attach to a network must have a physical interface between the computer's hardware and the *transmission media*. The transmission media is used to carry or transmit the information from one device to another. Copper wire contained in a flexible plastic covering called a *cable* is typically used inside buildings. To transmit information between different geographical locations, wireless technology can be used. Outdoor wireless solutions include microwave and infrared. In addition, wireless can also be used indoors and is a nice option for notebook computers.

For our discussion, our network uses a common transmission media — the typical Ethernet network that you find in most small networks. Ethernet specifies how the information is placed on the transmission media. A common network cable is UTP (unshielded twisted pair). It is rated to carry up to 100 Mbps (megabits per second) and uses a *phone*-type connector (RJ-45). You can purchase these cables with the appropriate connector already attached at most computer supply stores or large home building type stores. Some even carry the cable, connectors, and crimper (the tool to attach a connector to a cable) separately so that you can make your own cables. The supplier may even provide the wiring diagrams for you. If not, you can easily find the correct wiring directions on the Internet.

Cables

Each device that you want to connect must have its own network cable. A single length of cable has a physical limit — 100 meters, or 328 feet. The rating and the quality of the cable have an effect on the maximum distance for each length of cable. Even if the cable is the best, you can't just throw the network cable over and around certain types of electrical devices. The signal travelling down the wire is a small electrical current. External electrical fields can change the current on the wire and scramble the packets of data that zip down the cable. Fluorescent light ballasts, for example, emit a strong electrical field and can alter the signal on a cable passing nearby. As you design the physical layout of your cabling system, keep these types of physical barriers in mind. If you use a certified network wiring company, its workers know all about these types of issues.

Hubs

After you have a cable for each device, you need to connect them. The typical UTP-based Ethernet network is physically arranged in a star. That is, each device connects to a central device. The star doesn't need to be even or straight. As the cables wind their way around physical boundaries, such as walls and ceilings, the star may look like some type of off-world alien or unknown deep-sea creature. The important thing is that all the cables meet at a common point. You plug all the cables into a device called a *hub,* or concentrator. The number of devices a hub can connect ranges from four to 24 or 36. If you have more than 36 devices, you can use more than one hub and connect them so that they function as one big hub. Figure 13-7 shows an example of a hub with network cables attached.

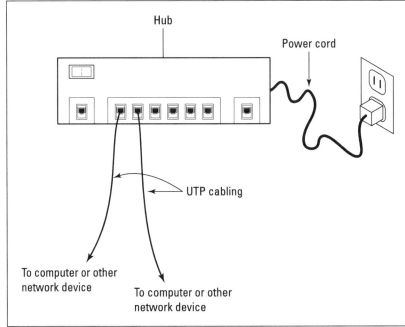

Figure 13-7:
Hub, or
concentra-
tor, with
attached
network
cables.

Company networks often have a wiring closet or room. This is a separate room where all the network cables come together and where the hubs are located. Sometimes, the systems providing network services or servers are in the wiring closet, too. In some networks, *switches* are replacing hubs. Switches are usually more expensive than hubs, but usually their benefits outweigh the cost. If you'd like more information on switches, most switch vendors (for example, Cisco) have good references on their Web sites.

Some newer houses have wiring closets for network cables. These are used for *smart* houses where computers control the house's appliances and electrical devices such as lights. Even if you have an older house without network wiring, choose a central location to place your hub or hubs.

NICs

After you install the cables and place your hubs, you need to plug the cables into the computers. Each device that you want to attach must have some type of network interface, which may be in the form of a *card* that you install in one of the available slots on the system's main board or motherboard. This card is known as a *network interface card* (NIC) and is available from many vendors in various types. Sometimes, the network interface circuitry is part of the computer's motherboard, in which case you can find the connector somewhere on the back of your computer's motherboard where the other connectors are.

If your device doesn't have the capability to install a NIC and/or doesn't have the necessary circuitry built in, you can use an external device between the system and the network cable. You often must use an external device for printers that aren't *network aware*. These printers have no network cable connection and can't accept a NIC card. Hewlett-Packard JetDirect devices are examples of external devices that enable you to connect a printer that itself contains no network hardware to a network. For this situation, the external network device has two connectors. One connects to the printer's connection port, and the other connects to the network. The *intelligence* that makes the printer *networkable* is the external device itself. For more information on these types of devices, refer to a vendor's Web site. Figure 13-8 shows an example of computers and devices attached to the network cable.

Routers

Another planning and design issue that you must consider is how to connect your network to another network. The device that handles this is known as a *router*. The router sends information from one network to another network. You can think of a router as being like the Post Office. The Post Office takes your mail from a mailbox (computer and NIC) to a central location (hub) and from there sends (routes) the mail to its destination. The mail's journey may take it through other Post Offices until it ends up at its final location. The same concept applies to networks connected with routers. Your information travels from network segment to network segment through one or more routers until it reaches its recipient.

Routers come in different forms. A router can be a separate physical device that does only routing and nothing else. These devices are usually more expensive but have several benefits, including security. Because they only route packets of data, the routers themselves contain no data. In addition, most office-grade routers include other features such as firewalls and permissions.

Your Linux system can also act as a router. You can install more than one NIC or interface in your Linux computer. Each network interface is attached to a different network. You can also configure Linux to route different protocols:

- ✔ IP — This is the protocol used on the Internet and in many LANs and WANs
- ✔ IPX — Novell developed this protocol, which can be used on non-Novell operating systems
- ✔ AppleTalk — Apple developed this protocol, which is designed to be used primarily on small Macintosh networks

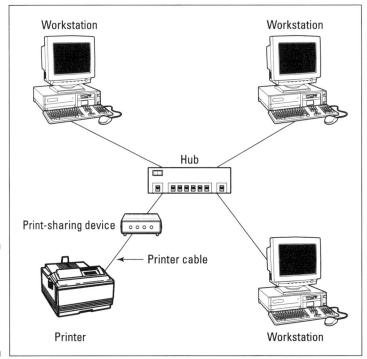

Figure 13-8:
Computers
and devices
attached to
the network
cable.

We address IP routing in the section, "Making Inter and Intra Harmonize," later in this chapter. Figure 13-9 shows an example of networks connected to each other with routers.

Setting up printing services

On any size network, printing is probably one of the most common services provided and requested. In addition, print services can also include faxing to and from the desktop. With a network fax service, the user chooses to fax, not print, from the application on their computer. The information is sent to a fax server, which has access to an interface to the phone system. With some network fax software, incoming faxes can even be directed to the users' desktops or to their e-mail inboxes.

In this section, we step through the process of setting up printing from one Linux system to another Linux computer that has a printer attached. Figure 13-10 shows an example setup. You can set up printing with commands entered at the shell or command prompt. You can also configure the printing environment within X.

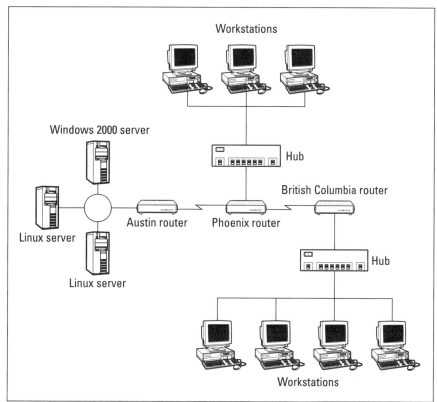

Figure 13-9:
Multiple
networks
connected
with routers.

Printing architecture

If you have several users printing to the same printer, a mechanism to receive and store the print files until the printer is available must be in place. If such a mechanism isn't in place, users can't perform any other activities on their systems until after their print files print. The Linux printing environment provides the capability to store print files temporarily, which is known as *spooling* or *queuing*.

Software known as the *line printer daemon* (lpd) manages the Linux printing service. This is activated automatically after Linux starts if you set up printing. The daemon is responsible for checking to make sure that you configured your environment for printing. The command to send output to a printer is `lpr`.

One of the first tasks the printing management system performs is to make sure that you defined a printer to send your output to. If that checks out, the `print` command output spools to a storage location. This storage location is a directory where the print files are written. The spool directories are located under the `var/spool/lpd` directory. If the spool directory already contains print files or jobs, the last print file added is placed at the end of the line, or queue. After all the print files ahead of yours print, yours is sent to the printer.

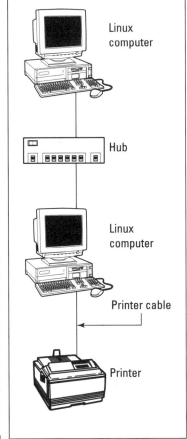

Figure 13-10:
Printing configuration where printer is attached to one Linux computer. The two Linux systems connect to each other on a network.

You can also check the status of your print file in the queue by using the `lpq` command. If you want to configure printing from the command prompt, use the `man` pages to look up the various `print` commands to get started. Bonus Appendix C covers accessing additional information by using `man` pages. As an example, we set up printing by using X.

Configuring printing under X

The primary tool under X to set up printing is the Printer Tool utility. For our example, we set up printing on a Linux system that has a printer attached to the parallel port, as in the following steps:

1. **Click the Main Menu button and choose Programs⇨System⇨Printer Tool.**

2. **To create your printer, click Add.**

3. **In the Add a Printer Entry dialog box, as shown in Figure 13-11, select Local Printer and click OK.**

   A printer is local if it's physically attached to the system where you're setting up printing.

Figure 13-11:
The Add a
Printer Entry
dialog box in
the Print
Tool utility.

   A detection dialog box, labeled Info, appears indicating what parallel ports Linux discovered.

4. **Click OK to close the detection dialog box.**

   If nothing is detected, you need to stop here and check your hardware. Most computers contain at least one parallel printer port. Check to make sure that your system has the correct port and check the BIOS for parallel port settings.

   If Linux detects a printer, the Edit Local Printer Entry dialog box appears, as shown in Figure 13-12. You can change the name of the printer from lp to something that makes sense to you.

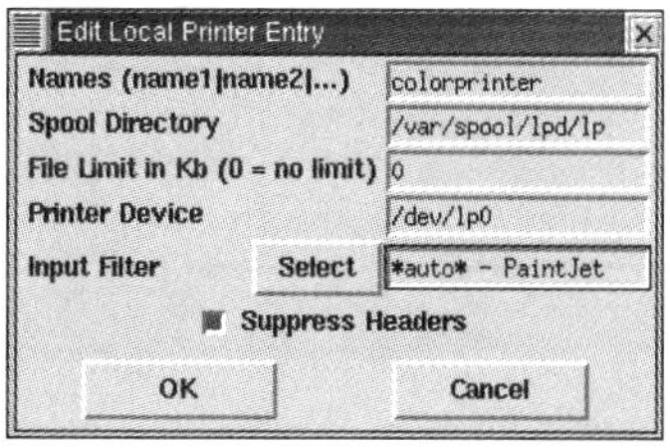

Figure 13-12:
The Edit
Local Printer
Entry dialog
box in the
Print Tool
utility.

5. **Use the Select button to choose your printer from the list of printers and then click OK.**

6. **Click OK to close the Edit Local Printer Entry dialog box.**

   The name that you gave your printer appears in the Print Tool window. The next step is to start the printing services.

7. **Choose Restart lpd from the lpd menu.**

8. **To test your print setup, select your printer and choose either Tests⇨Print ASCII Test Page or Tests⇨Print PostScript Test Page (for PostScript printers) from the Tests menu.**

9. **Click OK in the detection dialog box that appears stating that the Test Page printed.**

The process is almost the same to print from a system to a printer on another Linux computer. Assume that the network is set up and that the Linux systems can communicate with each other. To print on a system *without* the printer attached from to another system's printer, follow these steps:

1. **Click the Main Menu button and choose Programs⇨System⇨Printer Tool.**

2. **To create your printer, click Add.**

3. **In the Add a Printer Entry dialog box (refer to Figure 13-11), select Remote Unix (lpd) Queue and then click OK.**

   A printer is *remote* if it isn't physically attached to the system where you're setting up printing.

4. **In the Edit Remote Unix (lpd) Queue Entry dialog box that appears (see Figure 13-13), type a name for the printer.**

5. **In the Remote Queue field, enter the name of the printer on the remote Linux system.**

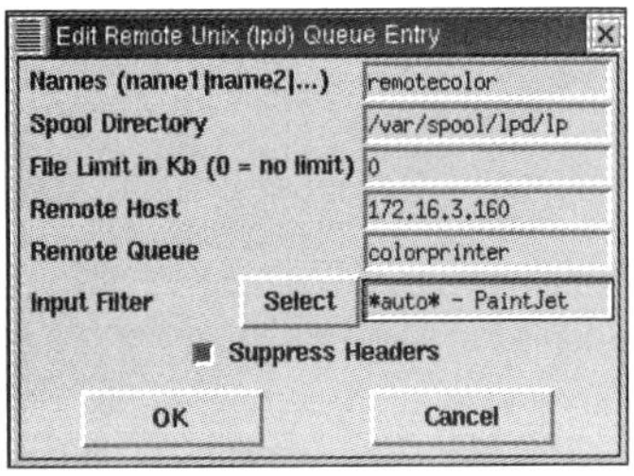

Figure 13-13:
The Edit Remote Unix (lpd) Queue Entry dialog box in the Print Tool utility.

Edit Remote Unix (lpd) Queue Entry	
Names (name1 |name2|...)	remotecolor
Spool Directory	/var/spool/lpd/lp
File Limit in Kb (0 = no limit)	0
Remote Host	172.16.3.160
Remote Queue	colorprinter
Input Filter Select	*auto* - PaintJet
☒ Suppress Headers	
OK	Cancel

6. **In the Remote Host field, enter either the IP number or name of the Linux system where the printer is attached.**

   If you want to use names, you need to have a solution in place to resolve names to IP numbers.

7. **Click the Select button to choose your printer from the list of printers and then click OK.**

8. **Click OK to close the Edit Remote Unix (lpd) Queue Entry dialog box.**

    The name you gave your printer appears in the Print Tool window. The next step is to start the printing services.

9. **Choose Restart lpd from the lpd menu.**

10. **To test your print setup, select your printer and choose either Tests⇨Print ASCII Test Page or Tests⇨Print PostScript Test Page (for PostScript printers) from the Tests menu.**

11. **Click OK in the detection dialog box that appears stating that the Test Page printed.**

Harmony and Security on Your LAN

Networks make sharing information and resources much easier for you. If you need to deliver a file to another individual, you can easily do so on a network. If you don't have a network, however, you may need to use *sneakernet.* Sneakernet is the physical transport of files from one computer to another on a floppy disk or CD-ROM. On occasion, you may still use this method, but you can greatly optimize your information transfer by using a network.

A new problem arises — getting your information from your network to another network. And maybe some of your users need to access a Web server on another network. To solve this latter problem, you need to connect two or more networks through some type of interface. This interface is typically a router (see the section, "Routers," earlier in this chapter) or *gateway,* another term for a router address sometimes used in network setup dialog boxes, to route information and requests from one network to another. In addition, after you open your front door to another network, you introduce security and integrity concerns. In this section, we only touch on each of these topics — we could write entire books about each.

Making inter and intra harmonize

IP routing refers to moving data between two IP networks, which you can accomplish by using dedicated routers — and also by using a Linux system. The only difference between the two methods is that a Linux IP router requires two (or more) NIC cards in place. You attach one NIC card to one network and a second NIC card to the other network. Both segments are using IP, but they're different IP networks. To enable IP forwarding, you edit your `/etc/sysconfig/network` file and add the entry for enabling IP forwarding. Figure 13-14 shows an example of the `network` file with the IP forwarding entry in the last line.

Figure 13-14:
The
/etc/sys
config/
network
file with IP
forwarding
enabled.

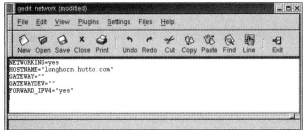

To apply the setting, restart your network services. At a command prompt, navigate to the /etc/rc.d/init.d directory and enter **./network restart**.

You need to set a default gateway on the other Linux systems on each network, which tells the systems how to get to the network on the other side of the router. This is set in the /etc/sysconfig/network file with the GATEWAY and GATEWAYDEV entries. Figure 13-15 shows an example of a network file containing the gateway entries.

To apply the settings, navigate to the /etc/rc.d/init.d directory. At a command prompt, type **./network restart**.

Figure 13-15:
The
/etc/sys
config/
network
file with
gateway
entries
included.

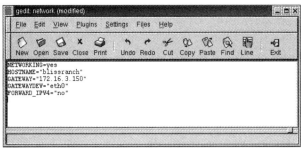

If you want to interface your network with the Internet, you have several solutions available. As a company, you may already have a solution in place and need to contact the appropriate parties to get the necessary IP-related information. If you have no existing Internet-access solution, you need to investigate solutions in your local area, which may be available through your local telephone service provider, cable company, or satellite services. To interface with most commercial service providers, you sometimes must purchase their equipment or certain types of equipment.

For home or small office use, you may be able to use DSL, cable modem, or satellite services. For these, you need to have the hardware to interface with the provider's transmission media. You can configure Linux to work with these types of services. This is a growing and changing field, so you need to do some searching on the Internet for solutions or suggestions.

Securing your LANs

If you attached your network to another network, you've opened a potential *hole* (or *holes*) for unauthorized access. This is where a firewall comes into play. A *firewall* is a device that sits between your network and the other side. This can be a dedicated hardware device or software running on a machine. You can configure Linux as a simple firewall without any add-ons. If you want more substantial protection, however, investigate the various firewall products/packages available.

You can set up a Linux system between your network and the other network to help reduce unauthorized access from the outside. This Linux system has two network interfaces: one attached to your network and the second attached to the other network. This other network can be your access to the Internet or another network in your organization.

To restrict access from the outside, configure the Linux system as a *Network Address Translation* (NAT) router. NAT translates the IP numbers on one side to an IP number that's compliant with the other side's IP numbers. On Linux, this is known as *IP Masquerading* but also just as NAT. To set up NAT correctly, you need to use IP numbers on your network that are in the private IP address ranges. Unfortunately, we can't go into any further detail because of the scope of this book. You can, however, check out the following for a good reference guide that starts you down the NAT path:

```
http://mirrors.indyramp.com/ipmasq
```

Linux has been remarkably resistant to viruses. You can bet, however, that somebody out there is working on a Linux virus or two. You can keep track of virus problems by subscribing to notification services (some of which are provided by anti-virus software vendors). You may also want to visit www.sans.org and investigate the SANS (System Administration, Networking, and Security) Institute. It's dedicated to virus and security issues on a variety of operating systems.

Finally, one last comment about security: To configure your IP numbers, routing off or on, gateway, and printing all require superuser or root privileges. After you configure and enable the features, these standard user accounts can use the services.

Chapter 14

Checking Out the Linux File System

In This Chapter

▶ Discovering the root directory and subdirectories

▶ Discerning partitions from directories

▶ Adding removable media to the file system

▶ Caring for your file system

▶ Adding a new hard drive

I have an existential map. It has "You are here" written all over it.

— Steven Wright

*O*ne of the most frustrating things about learning a new operating system is figuring out where it keeps files. Instead of keeping all the important system files in a single directory, like the C:\WINDOWS directory in Microsoft Windows, Linux follows the lead of its Unix cousins and spreads things out a bit more. Although the setups involve different methods, they're both logical. They also both require that you understand where to look.

Another issue that you come across is adding new *media* — hard drives, floppy disks, CD-ROM's, Zip disks, and more — onto the existing file system. In this chapter, we focus on how the file system is organized and other handy things, such as how to access data on a floppy disk.

Introducing the Linux File System

Picture your hard drive. Maybe you have Linux all by itself on there, or maybe it's sharing it with another operating system such as Microsoft Windows. All the hard drive space that you allocated for Linux during the installation process is your Linux *file system*. Because you're running your

own Linux machine, you must be familiar with how it's put together —
especially the sections that are dangerous to mess with!

Walking through the layout

As you probably already noticed, the Linux file system is deeply layered. It
consists of lots of directories and subdirectories. Most of the internal information in an operating system such as Microsoft Windows is hidden away in
the Windows directory. In Linux, however, this information is scattered around
a bit wider and for good reason: Lots of files are involved! But after you come
to understand it, you see that Linux maintains a logical order to where it
keeps things.

Meet the root directory

Everything in the Linux file system is relative to the root directory, which is
referred to as /. The *root directory* is the file-system base, a doorway into all
of your files. The root directory contains a mostly predictable set of subdirectories. Each distribution varies slightly, but certain standards exist to
which they all conform. The standards keep us all sane.

Rather than flood you with everything at once, we start by talking about just
the items that are directly off of root. Table 14-1 lists the standards and some
of the more common extras. An asterisk (*) at the end of a description indicates
that you shouldn't mess with this directory unless you have a specific reason
to, because it contains files that are very important to the functioning of your
system.

Table 14-1	Standard / Contents in Linux
Directory	*Contains*
/bin	The commands that everyone needs to use at any time.*
/boot	The information that boots the machine, including your kernel (which we discuss in Chapters 4 and 15).*
/dev	The device drivers for all the hardware that your system needs to interface with.*
/etc	The configuration files that your system and many of its software packages use.*
/home	The home directories for each of your users.
/lib	The code that many programs, and the kernel, use.*
/mnt	The spot where you add temporary media, such as floppy disks and CD-ROMs.

Directory	Contains
/opt	The location that many people decide to use for installing new software packages, such as word processors and office suites.
/root	The superuser's (root user's) home directory.
/sbin	The commands the system administrator needs access to.*
/tmp	The place where everyone and everything stores temporary files.
/usr	The programs that machines can actually share between them.
/var	The data that changes frequently, such as log files and your mail.

Some of these directories have some equally important subdirectories, so we're going to dig a bit deeper now.

Meet the /etc subdirectories

Although the exact subdirectories that exist in /etc can change from distribution to distribution, the following two are fairly standard:

- ✔ The /etc/X11 directory contains configuration details for the X Window System (X), which runs your Graphical User Interface (GUI). See Chapter 10 for more on the GUI.

- ✔ The /etc/opt directory contains configuration files for the programs in the /opt directory, if you decide to use it.

Meet the /mnt subdirectories

You may or may not have any subdirectories in /mnt by default. Typically, however, you at least have the following:

- ✔ The /mnt/floppy directory for adding a floppy disk to your file system.
- ✔ The /mnt/cdrom directory for adding a CD-ROM to your file system.

In the "Adding Media to Your File System" section later in this chapter, we show you how to actually add these items.

Meet the /usr subdirectories

The /usr directory is often referred to as its own miniature file-system hierarchy. It has a lot of important or interesting subdirectories, as shown in Table 14-2. An asterisk at the end of a description indicates that you need to leave that directory alone unless you have good reason to mess with it — *after* you gain a lot of experience with Linux and know exactly what changes you need to make — so that you don't accidentally alter something your system needs to function correctly. An important thing to remember about this segment of the file system is that many Linux users often use /usr to store programs that can be shared with other machines.

Table 14-2	Standard /usr Subdirectories
Subdirectory	*Contents*
/usr/X11R6	The actual files that run the X Window System.*
/usr/bin	The commands that aren't essential for users but are useful.*
/usr/games	The games that you install on your system, except for those that you can choose to place in /opt.
/usr/include	The C programming language needs these files for the system and its programs.*
/usr/lib	The code used by many of the programs in this /usr subhierarchy.*
/usr/local	The programs and other items that you want to keep locally, even if you're sharing everything else in /usr.
/usr/sbin	The commands that aren't essential for administrators but are useful.*
/usr/share	The information that you can use on any Linux machine, even if it's running incredibly different hardware from what this one is running.*
/usr/src	The source code that you use to build the programs on your system.

Partitions Versus Directories

One very important thing that you must understand about the Linux file system is that it may not all be on one single hard drive or hard-drive partition. If you've dealt with this point during the installation, you probably already know it. But maybe you sidestepped this issue by using one of the install classes that does things for you automatically.

What really confuses people later, however, is that partitions and directories tend to blend together. In the Microsoft Windows world, if you use separate hard drives or partitions, you have a specific letter designation for each one.

The primary hard drive is C:, the next is D:, and so on. Under Linux, each of these drives and partitions quietly blends in.

If you partitioned your hard drives on your own, you know that you needed to specify a *mount point* — which is like an empty spot in a puzzle, where the outside partition or media can be plugged into the rest of the file system — for each partition. In the case of a hard drive partition, the mount point isn't in the /mnt part of the file system. It's actually an item in the root directory — maybe /boot or / or /usr. You literally attach permanent items, such as hard drives and partitions, right into the file system and can't tell the difference. Linux doesn't want to know or care about the difference. It just wants to do its thing. But don't worry — you do have reliable designations that are related to where in the scheme of hardware you can find your drive. See Table 14-3 for a breakdown of popular designations.

Table 14-3	Common Drive Designations
Designation	*Description*
/dev/cdrom	CD-ROM drive
/dev/fd0	Floppy drive #1
/dev/fd1	Floppy drive #2
/dev/hda	First IDE hard drive
/dev/hda1	First IDE hard drive, first primary or extended partition
/dev/hda2	First IDE hard drive, second primary or extended partition
/dev/hdb	Second IDE hard drive
/dev/hdb1	Second IDE hard drive, first primary or extended partition
/dev/hdb2	Second IDE hard drive, second primary or extended partition
/dev/sda	First SCSI hard drive
/dev/sda1	First SCSI hard drive, first primary or extended partition

You probably see a pattern by now. A hard drive has a three-letter designation:

✔ An IDE drive's designation starts with /dev/hd; the first drive of this type is a, the second b, and so on. The third IDE drive looks like this: /dev/hdc.

✔ A SCSI drive's designation starts with /dev/sd; the first drive of this type is also a, the second b, and so on. The third SCSI drive looks like this: /dev/sdc.

The number that follows the three-letter designation represents your partitions. We cover partitioning your hard drive in Chapters 2 and 3.

In Figure 14-1, we break down this concept, hopefully making it a bit more accessible. In this case, the user created three partitions for Linux. The first IDE drive is a single partition, allocated for the root partition. The second IDE drive is broken into two partitions. The first was given /usr, and the second /var.

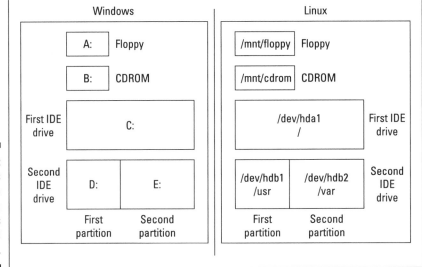

Figure 14-1: Linux versus Windows in handling partitions and hard drives.

If you move around the file system, you can't tell which of these directories is on which drive. The prompt, for example, doesn't change depending on which drive each directory is on; it just doesn't matter as far as the commands you use to move around.

Adding Media to Your File System

The items in /mnt, such as /mnt/floppy and /mnt/cdrom, are *temporary media*: disks that you must add to the file system if you want to work with them and then remove after you're done. Although this may sometimes be done automatically — some distributions have tools in the GUI that automatically mount a CD-ROM after you close the drive — you often must do it manually. But you can pretty easily do it if you know how.

Adding media temporarily

Rarely do you want to keep removable media (floppy disks, CD-ROMs, even Zip disks) always in the drive. Even if you did, you probably don't always want the same disk, so you need a way to tell Linux that you attached the disk and where. You can do so by using the mount command at the command prompt or in a command prompt window in the GUI by doing the following:

1. **Make note of whether you're trying to access a floppy or a CD-ROM.**

   The newest Linux distributions have a handy feature that automatically mounts a CD-ROM after you place it in the drive — if you're in the GUI. Although not all distributions have this feature, the one that we include with this book does.

2. **If it's a floppy, type** ls /mnt/floppy; **if it's a CD-ROM, type** ls /mnt/cdrom.

   If the directory doesn't exist, you need to create it. Use the mkdir command as follows: mkdir /mnt/location (specifying the location).

3. **If it's a floppy, make note of the operating system that the disk comes from.**

   Table 14-4 shows what operating system corresponds to what type label.

4. **Put the command together in the following format:** mount -t type /dev/device /mnt/location.

   You need to replace italicized words with specific information. To mount a floppy disk that you put together under Windows 98, for example, type **mount -t vfat /dev/fd0 /mnt/floppy**.

Table 14-4	File System Types That Your Floppy Disk Can Contain
Type	*Description*
ext2	Linux
msdos	Windows 3.11 or earlier
vfat	Windows 95 or later

If you're mounting a CD-ROM, always use the command as follows: mount -t iso9660 /dev/cdrom /mnt/cdrom (unless for some reason the distribution hasn't made the shortcut from the exact CD-ROM driver to /mnt/cdrom). You may be able to use just mount /mnt/cdrom in some distributions. For a Linux floppy, you can skip the type stuff and just try mount /mnt/floppy or mount /dev/fd0 /mnt/floppy.

To remove the item later, type umount /mnt/location.

Do *not* remove a floppy disk without correctly unmounting it, or you may wind up with missing data! Although you don't need to worry about data with CD-ROMs, you often can't remove the disk until you unmount it. And you can't unmount an item if you're already in it, so make sure that you're not anywhere in its directories before you do so.

If you've got both Windows and Linux set up on your computer and can boot from either operating system (a *dual-boot setup*), you can mount your Windows partition while you're in Linux! This is a great way to transfer files back and forth if you need to.

Formatting disks

A floppy disk often comes as a blank slate or formatted for Windows or Macintosh use. If the disk is a blank slate, no computer can use it for anything. No computer running any operating system can store data on a totally blank floppy disk. A disk must have a file system on it to store information within that file system's format. That's what formatting a disk is all about: building a file system. You can either format a disk from the command prompt or use a GUI tool to do it. We cover both here in case you're not using GNOME.

Formatting at the command prompt

To format a floppy at the command prompt so that Linux can recognize it as a Linux disk, follow these steps:

1. **Place the floppy in the disk drive.**

2. **Type** mke2fs /dev/fd0.

   Technical information about the information being written to the disk scrolls past. After the light on the floppy drive turns off, you can either eject the disk or mount it onto the file system and use it.

After you format the floppy, you can mount it, as we discuss in the section "Adding media temporarily," earlier in this chapter.

Formatting in GNOME

To format a floppy in GNOME so that Linux can recognize it as a Linux disk, follow these steps:

1. **On the icon bar, click the Footprint icon to open the main menu.**

2. **Click Programs⇨Utilities⇨gfloppy.**

   The Format a Floppy dialog box opens, as shown in Figure 14-2.

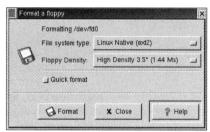

Figure 14-2:
The gfloppy
disk
formatting
tool in
GNOME.

3. **Place the floppy in the floppy drive.**

4. **Make sure that the File system type drop-down list box is set to Linux Native (ext2) (refer to Figure 14-2).**

5. **Make sure that the Floppy Density drop-down list box is set to High Density 3.5" (1.44MBs) (refer to Figure 14-2).**

6. **If you aren't sure whether the disk is error free, make sure that the Quick format check box is unchecked.**

   Unchecking this box makes the formatting take significantly longer. It may take a minute or so to finish.

7. **Click the Format button to format the disk.**

   The Format Progress dialog box opens with a progress bar. After this line fills in, the format is complete. Then the Floppy Formatted Successfully dialog box opens.

8. **Click OK to close the Floppy Formatted Successfully dialog box.**

   Both this dialog box and the Format Progress dialog box close. Now the Format Another Floppy dialog box opens.

9. **Click No if you're done; click Yes if you want to format another floppy, and start the process all over again.**

   If you click No, the Floppy dialog box closes along with the Format Another Floppy dialog box.

Care and Feeding of Your File System

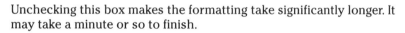

Regardless of what operating system you're using, you need to keep your file system healthy and happy. Everything that you need to operate the machine and do your work (or play) on it exists in that file system. Keep it in good shape and it's sure to treat you well in return. Fortunately, Linux does some of this automatically for you.

Checking the file system

Whenever you shut down your machine, you can use the -f option to skip the file system check after the machine comes back up. Even if you do this every time, Linux only enables you to get away with it a set number of times before it decides to take over and do a check anyway. However, we recommend *not* always using -f. Checking the file system costs you an extra minute or so in boot time, although it can save you panicked hours of trying to revive a damaged machine later.

You can also manually check file systems by using the e2fsck command as follows:

1. **Type** df **to see whether the item that you want to check is mounted.**

   The df command lists the currently mounted partitions and media, as well as some statistics about them. You may, for example, see what's shown in Figure 14-3.

```
[root@localhost /root]# df
Filesystem          1k-blocks     Used Available Use% Mounted on
/dev/hda5            4040000   1029792   2804980  27% /
/dev/hda2              23333      2480     19649  12% /boot
/dev/hdb             654848    654848         0 100% /mnt/cdrom
[root@localhost /root]#
```

2. **If the item is mounted and not vital for using the system, type** umount *mount point* **(specifying a particular mount point) to remove it from the file system.**

   If you want to manually check a portion of the file system that's vital for the running of your Linux machine (/, /bin, and so on), you must boot with rescue disks so that you can unmount these directories to check them. (Rescue disks are special boot disks that you use in emergencies, such as when your system isn't booting correctly; see Chapter 5 for more information.) This is a huge pain! Luckily, Linux actually checks these directories while it's booting so that you don't need to do so manually.

3. **Type** e2fsck /dev/*device* **(specifying a particular device) to run the check.**

   This can take a while. Table 14-5 shows a few options that you may be interested in adding. If you decide to use an option, use the format e2fsck options /dev/device (specifying any options and a particular device).

4. **Type** mount /dev/*device mount point* **(specifying a particular device and mount point) to put the partition back in the file system if you want or need to do so.**

Table 14-5	Commonly Used Options for e2fsck
Option	*Purpose*
-f	Convinces e2fsck to check the file system even if it tells you that the file system's already been checked and declared clean.
-n	Answers "no" to all questions regarding whether things should be fixed or not.
-p	Repairs the file system without asking any questions at all; subsequently, you can't see what's been done.
-y	Answers "yes" to all questions regarding whether things should be fixed or not.

Segmenting the problem areas

Even if you've already installed Linux at this point, some people often reinstall several times before they're really happy with the setup. One smart thing that you can do is place parts of the file system that change frequently onto their own partitions. The segments of concern traditionally are /var and /tmp at the very least. These portions of the file system can change many times — every day, every hour, or more often on some machines. If changes occur this much, something's more likely to go wrong with the disk media.

Isolating these directories onto partitions minimizes the damage these changes can inflict on the rest of the file system. If /tmp is on its own partition and disk damage occurs from wear and tear due to /tmp's constantly changing contents, this problem can affect other files only within /tmp. If /tmp is in with the root partition and something goes wrong with /tmp, however, another segment of the file system may later try to use that part of the hard drive. If you placed a critical file there, you can suddenly have quite a serious problem.

Leaving spare room

One of the most insidious problems that all computer users run into from time to time is a lack of disk space. The scope of this problem really depends on a number of things. The primary issue is that, if your root partition becomes 99 or 100 percent full, you're going to need to use emergency rescue techniques to boot the machine and clean it out. That's no fun, is it?

In the beginning, you're probably not in danger of filling the drives, unless you barely had enough room to install Linux in the first place. Over time, you're probably going to forget about watching the drives for remaining space. Even experienced administrators run into this problem, so certainly you're forgiven if you do it as well! Save yourself the worry and make sure that you know how to get regular updates about how full all of your partitions are. To access the drive updates, follow these steps:

1. **Log into the account that you tend to use the most.**

2. **Type** vi .bash_profile **to open your main login settings file.**

   The file opens in the vi editor.

3. **Type** G **to jump to the end of the file.**

   The cursor is now on the last line.

4. **Type** o **to open a new line after the line your cursor rests on and to enter** vi**'s Insert mode.**

5. **Type** df -h.

   You really only need the df command by itself; the -h option refers to human-readable, making the amount of space used and available easier for you to read.

6. **Press Esc to return to** vi**'s Command mode.**

7. **Type** ZZ **to save and close the file.**

   Next time that you log into this account and from then on, you get a list of the space available and used on all mounted media.

Sharing Files By Using NFS

If you install multiple Linux computers on a network, you may want to share a partition or section of the file system between two or more of them. You can share the /usr hierarchy (see the section, "Meet the /usr subdirectories," earlier in this chapter) among multiple Linux machines. An even more popular item to share is the /home hierarchy, which enables you to access the same files in your user directories regardless of which Linux machine you're logged into. A lot of steps are involved in making this work, so we break it down into tasks.

All these instructions assume that the users on each machine have the same usernames. If Bob uses the username bob on the primary, pferd on another, and blue on a third, you need to adjust his settings so that his home directory always points to /home/bob, even if his account's something else. To do so, see the section, "Changing the home directory," later in this chapter.

Creating a shared directory

You first need to set up the directory that's going to contain every machine's home directories. You may want to make this its own partition, or even a separate hard drive, depending on how many users you actually have and how much space you expect them to use. To set up this directory, follow these steps:

1. **Choose which Linux machine you want to host the central** /home **directory.**

2. **Log into that machine as root.**

3. **Open the file** /etc/exports **in your preferred text editor.**

   This is the Network File System (NFS) central configuration file. By default, it's empty.

4. **Type** /home   networkaddress(rw,root_squash).

   This line ensures that the /home directory and all its subdirectories are sharable between all the computers in your *networkaddress*. If the outside computers access this share, they can both read and write to their directories. We're not, however, letting root access its home directly remotely. Really, we don't need to — the root home directory is /root, not /home!

   The format of *networkaddress* is important here. In Chapter 7, we show you how to set up your Internet connection, and in Chapter 13, we show you how to set up your Local Area Network (LAN). Refer to these chapters if you need to brush up on this information because you need a basic grasp of it. The *networkaddress* entry can be any one of the following:

   • A single full IP address. (You can have a copy of this line for each individual machine if you want, rather than merging them into one line.)

   • A single machine's full name and domain information in the format *host.domain.extension.*

   • All machines in a domain in the format **.domain.extension.*

   • The entire network IP information in the format *network/netmask.*

   Inside the parentheses, we set the rules for access. In this case, the rw refers to read-write access so that people can both look at information in this directory and save their own files to it. The root_squash means that root can't use this shared directory. Although you can remove this item, you're often best off leaving it alone. The root account has a lot of high-level permissions and you want to limit its capability to move from one machine to another as much as possible.

5. **Save and exit the file.**

6. **Reboot the machine.**

   You have other ways to accomplish this same thing, but beginners — as do some lazy advanced users — often find just rebooting easiest. Doing so loads all the configuration changes that you just made.

Preparing to replace /home on your secondary machines

You can't just go ahead and mount the NFS export — the share we show you how to create in the previous subsection — onto the other machines. You must set up these secondary machines to use them, which is especially important because they all already have their own /home directory structure! If you've been using these machines for a while, you may have important files in those /home directories. To get the machines ready to host centralized /home information, follow these steps on each secondary machine in turn:

1. **Log in as root.**

2. **Make sure that no one but root is logged in at the moment.**

   Unless you allow people to remotely access the machine, you don't need to worry about this.

3. **Type** mv /home /home-old.

   This action actually moves the entire contents of /home into a new directory, /home-old. Still, don't allow anyone to log in as anything but root. Your users have no /home directories to use!

If people are waiting to use the computers, go through this entire process on each secondary machine so tht people can use the other computers while you're working on one.

Permanently mounting our remote /home

In the preceding sections, we tell you how to determine which machine hosts the central /home directory for all your user accounts, how to then set this machine up so that your other Linux machines can access this directory using NFS, and finally how to adjust the secondary machines so that their /home directories don't conflict with the new one. Here, we tell the secondary machines where to find the central /home directory.

Each Linux machine has a central file that it uses to tell it what to mount onto the file system at boot time. This file also contains any shortcuts that may be on your system for typing things such as mount /mnt/cdrom instead of mount -t iso9660 /dev/cdrom /mnt/cdrom. It's here that you can tell your machine to automatically mount the remote /home directory. To accomplish this, follow these steps on each secondary machine in turn:

1. **Log in as root.**

   No one but root should be logged in. Users have no home directories!

2. **Open the file** /etc/fstab **in your favorite text editor.**

   This file may look something like what you see in Figure 14-4. Don't let it intimidate you! At the same time, don't change anything unless you really understand what it does.

Figure 14-4: Example of an /etc/ fstab file.

3. **Open a new blank line at the end of the file.**

4. **Add the new line in the following format:**

   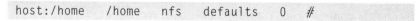
   ```
   host:/home    /home    nfs    defaults    0    #
   ```

   This line tells Linux to use NFS to go to the machine *host* (name or IP address) and mount *host*'s /home directory as this machine's /home directory with the same settings that all the other drives have. The # represents where in the mount order to mount the drive. Look in the last column for the largest number and use one bigger. In Figure 14-4, for example, the largest number on the right is 2. You would use a 3 for # in this case.

5. **Save and exit the file.**

6. **Type** shutdown -rf now **to immediately reboot the machine.**

   Handle the boot process as you always do, making sure that you boot into Linux.

7. **Log into the machine as a regular user.**

   The user's home directory now contains what it did on the primary machine!

8. **Copy your files over from** /home-old/user.

   If you move /home, you take its permission structure with it, which means that users can get into /home-old/user to get their other files. Make sure that you tell them about this. If you give people a deadline, you can later remove /home-old.

Changing the home directory

Everyone's account must point to the correct home directory. Suppose, for example, that the user bob has the user account pferd on one machine and blue on another. To fix it so that he can use his centralized home directory on the secondary machines, follow these steps on each secondary machine in turn:

1. **Log in as root.**

2. **Type** usermod -d /home/primaryaccount localaccount.

   So on the computer where Bob's account is pferd, type **usermod -d /home/bob pferd**.

Adding a New Hard Drive

One day, you may need to add a hard drive to your Linux system. This requires that you install the drive — a daunting task by itself! — and then partition it, format it, and mount it. We walk through how to do all of this specifically in the context of adding a new drive — to soothe your jangled nerves.

Partitioning your drive

Although many third-party partitioning programs are out there, only one comes with every Linux distribution: fdisk. A lot of people find it pretty scary, but don't worry; you get through it with our help. To partition your hard drive after you physically install it, follow these steps:

1. **Determine what partitions you want on the drive.**

   This may seem like a straightforward issue. But we're talking here about a system where Linux is already installed. If it wasn't installed, you just partition and add the drive during the installation process. So what did you add this drive for? Are you moving a directory over to it? Are you creating a whole new hierarchy or subhierarchy? Take a look at the drive's size and break it up on paper before you continue.

2. **Log in to the machine that you installed the drive in as root.**

3. **Determine what device the drive is.**

   If this is your second IDE hard drive, for example, the device is
   /dev/hdb. (See Table 14-3.)

4. **Type** fdisk /dev/device **to start the** fdisk **program.**

   The following text appears on-screen:

   ```
   Command (m for help):
   ```

5. **Type** n **and press Enter to tell** fdisk **that you want to add a new
   partition.**

   The following text appears on-screen:

   ```
   Command action
   l        logical (5 or over)
   p        primary partition (1-4)
   ```

6. **Type either** l **or** p **and press Enter to proceed.**

   Because users often want to create only one or two partitions on a new
   drive, we're assuming that you want to create only two. In this case, you
   can have two primary partitions, so you don't need to go the extended
   and logical route. Type **p**. You now see the following:

   ```
   Partition number (1-4):
   ```

7. **Type** 1 **and press Enter.**

   This is the first partition you're creating on the brand new drive. If it's
   your second or third time through, use the appropriate number. You
   now see something similar to the following:

   ```
   First cylinder (1-45102, default 1):
   ```

8. **Press Enter to start the new partition at the beginning of the new drive.**

   You now see the following:

   ```
   Using default value 1
   Last cylinder or +size or +sizeM or +sizeK
   (1-45102, default 45102):
   ```

9. **If you want to use the entire drive for this partition, press Enter; otherwise, type** +sizeM **to tell** fdisk **how many MBs to make this partition
   and press Enter.**

   The *size* is how many MBs to make the drive. So if you want to divide the
   example drive in half, type **+22551**. Notice the lack of the M here. Just
   halving the cylinder count is easiest in this case. If you want to make the
   partition 500MB, type **+500M**.

   After you press Enter, you create the partition.

10. **If you want to create another partition, repeat Steps 4–8; otherwise,
    you're finished.**

Formatting your new partition

After you create a partition, you must format it so that you can place Linux files on it. Type **mke2fs /dev/*device*** to format the partition. In this case, the *device* entry refers to the new partition. If you just added a third IDE hard drive and are formatting its first partition, type **mke2fs /dev/hdc1**.

Doing so formats the drive. This formatting process can take much longer than formatting a simple floppy disk, so you may want something else to do while you're waiting.

If you're setting up a new hard drive, a smart idea is to check it for bad sectors, too. Type **mke2fs -c /dev/*device*** if you want to do so.

Mounting your new partition

After you install, partition, and format the drive, you can set up to permanently mount the new partition onto the file system each time that you boot the machine. To accomplish this, follow these steps:

1. **Log in as root.**

2. **Open the file /etc/fstab in your favorite text editor.**

   This file may look similar to Figure 14-4.

   Don't change anything unless you really understand what it does.

3. **Open a new blank line at the end of the file.**

4. **Add a new line for each of the partitions in the format:**

   ```
   /dev/device    mountpoint    ext2    defaults    0    #
   ```

   To determine which device you're dealing with, refer to Table 14-3.

   You need also to decide where this drive fits in the file system hierarchy. The # represents where in the mount order to mount the drive. Look in the last column for the largest number and use one bigger. In Figure 14-4, for example, the largest number on the right is 2, so in this case, use a 3 for #.

5. **Save and exit the file.**

6. **Create the mount point by typing** mkdir mountpoint.

   The *mountpoint* must exist so that you can attach something to it.

7. **Type** shutdown -rf now **to immediately reboot the machine.**

   Handle the boot process as you always do, making sure that you boot into Linux.

Chapter 15

Customizing Your System

. . . .

. . . .

Either this wallpaper goes or I do.

— Oscar Wilde

*H*ere's a topic some people really get into. If you like to fiddle with your computer so that it's set up just the way you like it, then this chapter is for you. Think of your computer like a car. The desktop is the exterior. We tell you how to repaint, reupholster, replace the hubcaps and tires, and even add racing stripes if you want. We also take some time to get under the hood a bit and look at what you can do to get the engine tuned just right.

Playing with Themes

You may be familiar with the ability to install desktop themes under Microsoft Windows. A *theme* in the desktop world refers to color schemes, images, and sounds applied to all portions of the desktop — window borders, fonts, icons, sound effects, and more — as part of a single, centralized entity. Many people are happy to find out that themes are available in the Linux world as well.

Setting your theme

Most Linux distributions install with a collection of themes already assembled. In Red Hat Linux (the distribution that comes with this book), you can tour the available themes in GNOME and choose one by following these steps:

1. **On the main icon panel, click the Toolbox icon to open the GNOME Control Center.**

2. **On the right side of the Control Center, click the + next to Desktop to access the Desktop menu, and then click Theme Selector.**

   The Theme Selector opens on the right side in the Control Center, as shown in Figure 15-1.

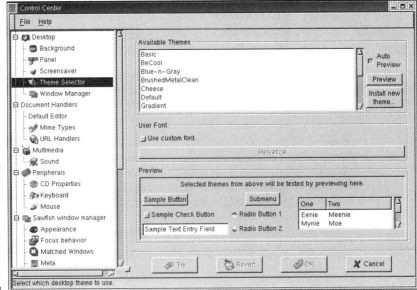

Figure 15-1: The Theme Selector, within the GNOME Control Center.

3. **Under Available Themes, select the Auto Preview check box.**

   This option means that whenever you click a theme name that you're interested in, the items in the Preview pane change to display a sample of what the theme looks like.

4. **Click the theme that you want to sample.**

   Look in the Preview pane toward the bottom of the window. Its contents change to represent what the various components of your screen look like if you use this theme. Notice how the window in Figure 15-2 is different from the window in Figure 15-1.

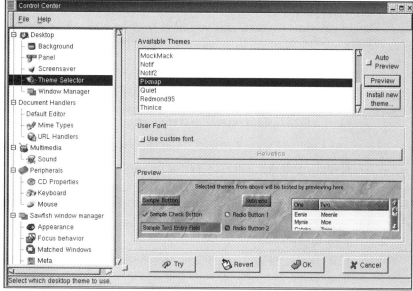

Figure 15-2:
The Preview
section
changes to
reflect what
a theme
looks like.

5. **Continue previewing themes until you find one that you really like.**

   You're still not committing at this point, so don't worry.

6. **Under the Preview pane, click the Try button to see how this theme looks when you apply it to your desktop.**

   This process may take some time, depending on the speed of your computer. The changes you see may be minor, or your desktop may look incredibly different.

7. **If you don't like the theme you're trying out, click Revert and return to Step 5; otherwise, click OK.**

   If you click Revert, the desktop changes back to its current theme setting, which is probably Default. Clicking OK sets GNOME to remember the theme that you've chosen and closes the Theme Selector.

8. **Choose File⇨Exit to close the Control Center.**

Altering a theme

You don't have to leave a theme exactly the way it is. You can choose a theme that you mostly like and then change it into one that you really like. Because this is a pretty long and involved process, we break it down into several easy tasks.

Choosing themes you want to change

Before you can alter a theme, you have to choose the one that you want to change. To accomplish this, follow these steps:

1. **On the icon panel, click the Toolbox icon to open the GNOME Control Center.**

2. **On the right side of the Control Center, click the + next to Desktop to access the Desktop menu and then click Theme Selector.**

    The Control Center opens the Theme Selector (see Figure 15-1).

3. **Under Available Themes, select the Auto Preview check box.**

    This option ensures that you will see a sample of what a selected Theme will look like.

4. **Browse the themes until you find the one that you want to base your new theme on.**

    Note the name of the theme and what aspects you'd like to change. Be as detailed as possible. You need this information in the next section.

5. **Choose File⇨Exit to close the Control Center.**

Copying themes to your home directory

You don't have to log in as root to alter existing themes — any user can do this — which is why we recommend that you make a *copy* to change and experiment with rather than mess with the original theme directory. If you alter the original, you aren't able to change it back if something goes wrong. And, if another person uses the original theme, they may be annoyed when they get your altered version instead. For information on selecting a theme to alter, see the previous section.

To copy an original theme to your home directory, follow these steps:

1. **On the main icon panel, click the Footprint icon to open the main GNOME menu.**

2. **Choose Programs⇨File Manager to open the GNU Midnight Commander (GMC).**

    The File Manager opens.

3. **Navigate to the** /usr/share/themes **directory.**

    If you're not using Red Hat Linux, the theme data may be elsewhere. Try typing **slocate theme | more** at the command prompt to get a screen-by-screen listing of directories and filenames with the word theme in them.

4. **Right-click the folder containing the theme you want to change.**

   The GMC file manipulation pop-up menu opens.

5. **Choose Copy in the pop-up menu.**

   The Copy dialog box opens.

6. **Either type the destination path in the Destination text box or click the Browse button to navigate to the place where you want to copy this theme.**

7. **Click OK to copy the folder to its new location.**

   You now have a personal copy of the theme that you want to change stored in your own home directory. After doing this, you have to figure out which files to alter in order to get the look you want.

Choosing theme parts you want to change

GNOME has a default look and feel. All these items are defaults in both a collective and individual sense. When you use a theme, each piece of this personalized look and feel — icon, background color, and image — is stored in a separate file and overrides the defaults. Anything that isn't prescribed in the theme stays with the default setting. This is why you'll see more images and files associated with some themes than with others.

To decide which parts of a theme you want to change (for information on copying themes to alter, see the previous section, "Copying themes to your home directory"), follow these steps:

1. **Navigate to the location of a copied theme file.**

   For example, if you copied the Pixmap theme to /home/fluff, then use the GMC to go to /home, then /home/fluff.

2. **Open the directory where the copy of the theme resides.**

   This directory likely contains very little, such as a file or two and another directory or two.

3. **Double-click the gtk subdirectory.**

   gtk refers to the GNOME desktop environment. Each theme is designed for a particular environment. The gtk subdirectory is shown in Figure 15-3. Note files that end in .png or .xpm (both of these are file extensions for picture files). In Pixmap's case, it's .png.

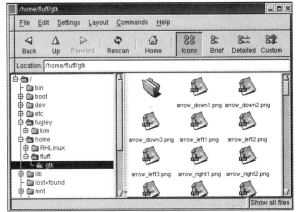

Figure 15-3:
The
contents of
the Pixmap
theme's gtk
subdirectory.

4. **Choose Commands⇨Run Command to open the Enter command to run dialog box.**

   This dialog box is shown in Figure 15-4.

Figure 15-4:
The
contents of
the GMC's
Enter
Command
to Run
dialog box.

5. **Type** ee *png **in the text box (or** ee *xpm**); then click OK.**

   The Electric Eyes program opens, as shown in Figure 15-5. It lists image files contained in this particular theme. Some of the image files are icons or pointers, and others are backgrounds or colors for window borders.

6. **Take a look through the item list and write down those that you may want to change.**

   Don't proceed to the next step until you finish.

   You may find it helpful to have the Control Center open to your chosen theme so that you can easily put each image into context.

7. **Click the Exit This Program button to close Electric Eyes.**

   You find this button on the far left on the button bar at the top of the Electric Eyes window.

Figure 15-5:
The Electric
Eyes
program
displays
image files
in the
Pixmap
theme.

Now that you've identified the files associated with the changes you want to make, it's time to get down to business and make your new theme.

Making changes to an existing theme

Here's where we get to the fun stuff. While some people like to make their own themes from scratch, most start by taking one that already exists and altering it to suit their own tastes.

To make changes to an existing theme (see the previous sections for choosing a theme that you want to alter), follow these steps:

1. **On the main icon bar, click the Footprint icon to open the main GNOME menu and then choose Programs⇨Graphics⇨The GIMP to open the GIMP image manipulation program.**

   If you didn't install graphics packages initially, you may not have this program installed. It should be on your distribution CD-ROM. If you've never run the GNU Image Manipulation Program (GIMP) in this account before, then you have to go through some setup steps. If you've already done these, then skip to Step 8.

   For those who haven't run the GIMP before, you first see the welcome screen shown in Figure 15-6.

2. **Click Continue to proceed through the setup routine.**

   The next screen that you see provides explanation of the files the installer is going to create in your home directory. If you're interested, click different files and folders to find out more about them.

3. **Click Continue to proceed to the installation itself.**

   You're not installing the GIMP program here — it's already installed; otherwise, you couldn't have run it in the first place. This installation is setting up all the files and folders that you saw in the previous step, literally just copying them into place. When the installation is complete, you see the log screen that lists what the installer did.

Figure 15-6:
The GIMP
installer
Welcome
screen.

4. **Look through the log if you choose to do so and then click Continue to proceed to the configuration phase.**

   The GIMP Performance Tuning screen appears.

5. **Change existing values if you want or click Continue to proceed.**

   Most people probably don't care to change the items here. The next screen is for setting GIMP Monitor Resolution (see Figure 15-7).

6. **Click the Get Resolution from X-Server check box so that you don't have to manually fill in information.**

   This is a nice cheat provided by the GNOME folks. Using this setting means that even if you change from one resolution to another, the GIMP always knows what you're using. Otherwise, you'd have to set it manually.

7. **Click Continue to finish the setup and finally open the GIMP.**

   You encounter one or more dialog boxes while the GIMP opens. The main menu is shown in Figure 15-8.

Figure 15-7:
The GIMP
Monitor
Resolution
screen.

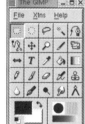

Figure 15-8:
The GIMP
main menu.

8. Choose File➪Open to open the Load Image dialog box.

This dialog box is shown in Figure 15-9.

9. Browse to ~/theme/gtk to display your chosen theme's files in the Files listing on the right.

In our example, it is the /home/fluff/gtk directory.

10. Click the file that you want to alter.

If you aren't sure which file you want, click a filename and then click the Generate Preview button to see a small version of what it looks like.

11. Click OK to open this file.

The file opens in its own window. If you can't find it, look on the icon bar for its icon, which has the filename on it.

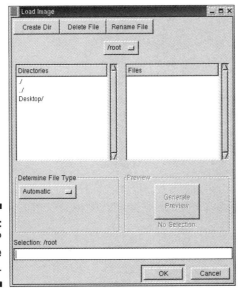

Figure 15-9:
The GIMP
Load Image
dialog box.

12. **Change this picture.**

    The GIMP is quite a complex image editor. To access its many features, ignore the icon buttons for now. Right-click the image to open the GIMP main pop-up menu and experiment from there.

    If you find the GIMP too frustrating, use a different image editor. You can even use one on another operating system as long as it can handle the image file format (indicated by the following file extensions: .png, .xpm, and so on).

13. **Save the changes by right-clicking the image to open the main pop-up menu, and then choosing File⊳Save.**

    You can also save changes by pressing Ctrl+S if the image is currently selected.

14. **Return to Step 8 for the next file that you want to change.**

    We recommend testing each file one at a time rather than making your changes all at the same time.

    After you've changed all the files that you want to change, proceed to Step 15.

15. **Change your new theme's name to differantiate it from the original.**

    Use the GMC or the command prompt, whichever you prefer.

Now that you've got the theme you really want to see on your desktop, it's time to tell GNOME to use it.

Telling GNOME to use a personalized theme

GNOME is not psychic. It needs to know that it should use a particular theme, and if you've created your own by altering an existing theme, then GNOME needs to know where to find it. (For more on how to create your own theme, see the previous sections in this chapter.)

To tell GNOME about your new theme, follow these steps:

1. **On the main icon bar, click the Toolbox icon to open the GNOME Control Center.**

2. **On the right side of the Control Center, click the + next to Desktop to access the Desktop menu and then click Theme Selector.**

   The Control Center opens the Theme Selector (refer to Figure 15-1).

3. **In the Available Themes area, click Install New Theme to tell GNOME about your altered theme.**

   The Select a Theme to Install dialog box opens, as shown in Figure 15-10.

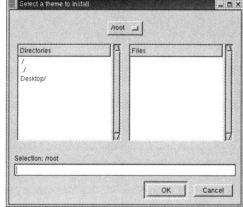

Figure 15-10:
The Theme Selector's Select a theme to install dialog box.

4. **Browse to the directory containing the altered theme.**

5. **Click OK to add the theme to the personalized theme listing.**

   The Control Center reappears. Your theme is now listed in alphabetical order with the others.

6. **Click your personalized theme in the listing.**

   The Preview pane gives you an idea of what it looks like.

7. **Click Try to apply your theme to your desktop.**

8. **If you're happy with your new theme and want to keep it, click OK; otherwise, click Revert and return to editing the theme.**

Checking Out Other Shells

Other shells are available in Linux. We recommend two in particular that you can try out if you're the type to experiment: `tcsh` and `pdksh`. Remember that a *shell* is your working environment. When you change the shell, you change certain things about how it works. Your prompt changes slightly. You have to do your shell scripts a bit differently. So, if you're not into experimenting with these things or are just not ready yet, don't change your shell (for now).

Meeting the enhanced C shell

The enhanced C shell (`tcsh`) is a newer version of the older C shell, just like `bash` is a newer version of the old Bourne shell. If you've done a lot of C programming and are comfortable working in that kind of format, then this shell may be for you. Although `tcsh` has a number of commands that you're probably already familiar with, it also has additional commands and environment variables that are unique to the C shell and its children and some that are unique to `tcsh` itself.

If you're interested in finding out more about this shell, type **man tcsh** at the command prompt. It may take you some time to read through, but keep plugging at it.

Meeting the Public Domain Korn shell

The Public Domain Korn shell is based on the Korn shell, which is a child from the two original shells, Bourne and C. We use `pdksh` in Linux instead of `ksh` because of licensing issues. People who write a lot of shell scripts particularly love this shell, which has a lot of interesting script debugging features. You find a lot of commands that you're probably familiar with in this shell, but you find a lot of confusion too.

If you're interested in finding out more about `pdksh`, type **man pdksh** at the command prompt. Shell `man` pages aren't the easiest thing to read, but you'll work your way through if you stick with it.

`pdksh` isn't always installed by default. The Red Hat Package Managers (RPMs) includes `pdksh` in its own package on the Red Hat distribution CD-ROMs if you want to install it (and comes with most other distributions).

Changing your shell

Has someone been going on and on to you about how one shell is cooler than another? Or, maybe you're an inquisitive type and feel pretty comfortable in the default bash shell and are ready to see what else is available to you. You can change your current shell at any time using the chsh command.

Before you change shells, however, you need to know which ones are installed on your system. So, type **chsh -l** to take a look. For example, you may see the following result:

```
/bin/bash2
/bin/bash
/bin/sh
/bin/ash
/bin/bsh
/bin/tcsh
/bin/csh
```

If you don't see the shell you want to use, then you need to install it on your system. How you do so depends on the distribution that you use, but most distributions come with a nice collection of shells. You can have as many installed as you want, but you can only use a single shell at a time.

When you're ready to change your shell, type **chsh -s /path/shell**. For example, type **chsh -s /bin/tcsh** to change to the C shell.

Constructing Your Own Kernel

You've been happily using Linux, minding your own business, and then one day, you futilely try to get a software package working that simply won't cooperate. You get a distinctive error message, so you ask fellow Linux folks what you can do. What do they say in their attempt to be helpful? "Oh, just recompile the kernel." Uh huh. "Why don't I just disassemble and reassemble my car while I'm at it?" may be your initial response. Believe it or not, this process really isn't as painful as it sounds. Be brave and read on.

Deciding when to rebuild

Actually, the reason to rebuild your kernel is often not as drastic as trying to solve error messages. We can think of many and varied reasons to rebuild a kernel. The following items are the most common of these reasons:

✔ You need to add support for a new device or devices and don't want to mess with individual device drivers.

✔ You want to go through the experience of rebuilding the kernel, just to find out more about it.

✔ You've heard that rebuilding the kernel makes it smaller and faster. That's mostly right. Some feel it doesn't really change the speed all that much. But if you're low on memory or want to check it out for yourself, go for it! A lot of unnecessary stuff is in there to make sure that the default kernel works with everything. For example, the default kernel contains support for many devices you don't have and provides support for services that you don't need. Fortunately, you can remove these items.

Rebuilding the kernel

Some folks find rebuilding an existing kernel easier than getting a new one. The processes are quite different. In a way, you're about to get an introduction to compiling software. Don't worry! This is a basic step-by-step kind of introduction. We're also hoping to help you feel more comfortable later when you run into something besides the kernel that you have to compile.

Introducing the tools

Because recompiling the kernel involves programming tools, you need to make sure you have all the necessary tools installed before starting. Otherwise, you may have to stop partway through and hunt down yet one more thing to install. In general, you need the following:

✔ **The GNU C compiler, which may be included as either** gcc **or** egcs: This program is what's used to take C programming language code and compile it (or change it) into a raw computer langauge that the computer can run.

✔ **The source code for the kernel:** This package name is probably something similar to kernel-source or Linux. It may also include the version number of the kernel. You also need the kernel *header* files (these files contain code additions), which may be packaged separately.

✔ **The GNU C libraries:** Many C programs look to a bunch of files in order to reuse code during the compilation process. The kernel source code is no exception. These library collections are likely labeled either libc or glibc.

✔ **Additional C compilation tools:** These may or may not be bundled together for your distribution, but they should all be included in the package. Look to the Linux distribution's documentation or Web site to find out what items you need to compile C programs if they are not in a recognizable package.

Checking for and installing the tools in Red Hat Linux

In this section, we walk you through how to check for the programming tools under Red Hat and its children. You need these same tools no matter what distribution you're using — unless they have some other method of rebuilding kernels that we're not aware of — so pay attention to the package names even though different distributions probably don't use RPMs.

To ensure you have all the necessary tools installed in Red Hat Linux, follow these steps:

1. **Log in as root.**

2. **Type** rpm -q kernel-headers glibc-devel binutils cpp gcc ncurses ncurses-devel make kernel-source **at the command prompt and then press Enter.**

   The combination `rpm -q` tells the RPM tool that you want to check whether particular packages are installed. What you see after entering the command is a list of all the package names that must be installed in order for you to build a new kernel. If you didn't go out of your way to install the programming utilities, you get output similar to the following:

   ```
   package kernel-headers is not installed
   package glibc-devel is not installed
   package binutils is not installed
   package cpp is not installed
   package gcc is not installed
   ncurses-5.1-1
   package ncurses-devel is not installed
   package make is not installed
   package kernel-source is not installed
   ```

3. **Place the Red Hat CD-ROM in the CD-ROM drive.**

4. **Type** mount /mnt/cdrom **and press Enter.**

   The Red Hat CD-ROM is mounted onto the file system.

5. **Type** cd /mnt/cdrom/RedHat/RPMS **and press Enter.**

   You change to the Red Hat packages directory.

6. **Make a note of which packages were not installed, in the exact order that we list them in Step 2.**

   RPM manages package *dependencies*, meaning that it watches out that you aren't installing things that require absent programs to work properly. If you install the missing items in the order that we've listed them in Step 2, then you won't run into dependency problems.

7. **For each package that you need to install, type** rpm -ivh *packagename* **and then press Tab to complete the package name.**

8. **Press Enter to install the package.**

The only item these instructions don't work for is `gcc`, the GNU C Compiler is discussed in the "Introducing the tools." section earlier in this chapter. Type **ls gcc*** to see which version you have of this package and then make sure to type **rpm -ivh gcc-#** before pressing Tab. The # is the first part of the version number.

Creating the old configuration file

An amazing number of options are available when you configure a Linux kernel. Rather than being forced to configure your new kernel from scratch, you have the option of building an old configuration file first. Later, when you open the configuration program, you can then modify what you already had rather than starting from the very beginning. Otherwise, you have to set every configuration option, which can get pretty tedious and confusing.

To build this old configuration file, do the following:

1. **Log in as root.**

You need to be in the superuser account to have access to everything.

2. **Type** cd /usr/src **and press Enter.**

This directory contains the *source code* (raw material) directories for one or more programs.

3. **Type** ls **and press Enter.**

You should see at least one directory named `linux`. In Red Hat Linux, you see something similar to what's shown in Figure 15-11, as an `ls -l` listing.

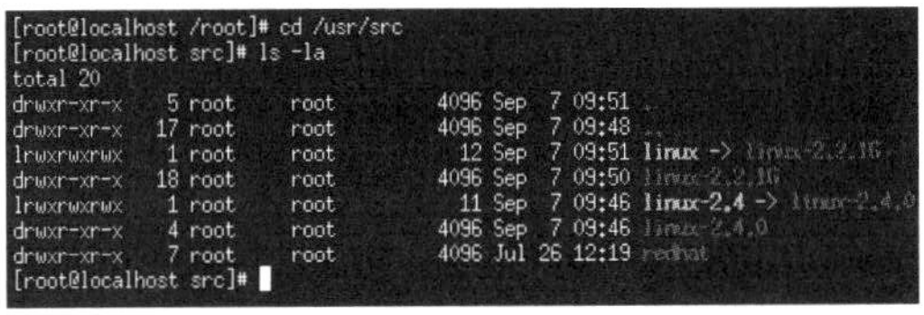

Figure 15-11:
Long format
file listing
of /usr/src
in Red Hat
Linux.

```
[root@localhost /root]# cd /usr/src
[root@localhost src]# ls -la
total 20
drwxr-xr-x    5 root    root     4096 Sep  7 09:51 .
drwxr-xr-x   17 root    root     4096 Sep  7 09:48 ..
lrwxrwxrwx    1 root    root       12 Sep  7 09:51 linux -> linux-2.2.16
drwxr-xr-x   18 root    root     4096 Sep  7 09:50 linux-2.2.16
lrwxrwxrwx    1 root    root       11 Sep  7 09:46 linux-2.4 -> linux-2.4.0
drwxr-xr-x    4 root    root     4096 Sep  7 09:46 linux-2.4.0
drwxr-xr-x    7 root    root     4096 Jul 26 12:19 redhat
[root@localhost src]#
```

4. **Determine which directory you need.**

In all likelihood, you need either `/usr/src/linux` or `/usr/src/linux-version`.

5. **Type** cd *directory* **to change to the directory you chose in Step 4.**

6. **Type** make oldconfig **to build the old configuration file.**

All the information scrolls across your screen as well as being stored in a file. Often, you even see instructions on what you need to do next!

After the old configuration file is in place, you can actually start configuring the new kernel. The next section addresses how to accomplish this.

Configuring your kernel

The Linux kernel comes with three different tools that you can use to configure a new version. We highly recommend that you build a default configuration file to start from, as we recommend in the previous section. Otherwise, you have to do everything from scratch.

To configure your new kernel using the GUI version of the configuration tool, follow these steps:

1. **Type** startx **if you aren't already in the GUI.**

   The nicest kernel configuration tool is a GUI tool.

2. **Click the Terminal icon to open a virtual terminal, if you don't have access to a command prompt.**

   If you're not placed in the /usr/src/linux or equivalent directory again, use the cd command to change back into that directory first.

3. **Type** make xconfig **to open the configuration tool.**

   The program shown in Figure 15-12 opens. If you can't use the GUI for some reason, type **make menuconfig** instead. This gives you a command-prompt version of the tool that is slightly different from the point-and-click tool that we show you here, but the command-prompt version is also menu-driven. You won't be able to use a mouse, but you can use the arrow keys to choose the menu that you want and then press Enter to open a menu, and so on.

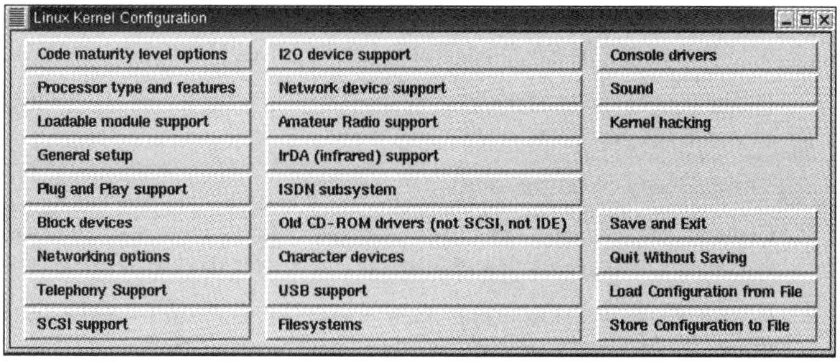

Figure 15-12: The GUI kernel configuration tool.

Linux Kernel Configuration		
Code maturity level options	I2O device support	Console drivers
Processor type and features	Network device support	Sound
Loadable module support	Amateur Radio support	Kernel hacking
General setup	IrDA (infrared) support	
Plug and Play support	ISDN subsystem	
Block devices	Old CD-ROM drivers (not SCSI, not IDE)	Save and Exit
Networking options	Character devices	Quit Without Saving
Telephony Support	USB support	Load Configuration from File
SCSI support	Filesystems	Store Configuration to File

4. **Choose a category that you want to alter and click it.**

   This is where things get confusing! We highly recommend that you go through each category and see what's there. Don't worry though, we walk you through one. Almost everyone wants to do this one! Click the Old CD-ROM drivers (not SCSI, not IDE) button to open the dialog box shown in Figure 15-13. Clicking any category opens a new dialog box similar to this.

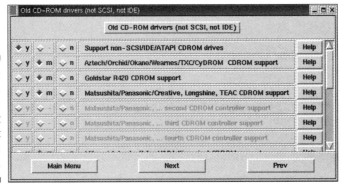

Figure 15-13:
The tool's
Old CD-ROM
drivers (not
SCSI, not
IDE) dialog
box.

5. **If you want to completely deactivate this category, click the n diamond in the first line if it contains the word support.**

   The first line of many categories sets whether support is included for these items at all. In the case of old CD-ROM drivers, unless you have an ancient CD-ROM drive (from before perhaps 1993), you have no reason to keep these items in the kernel. They're just weighing it down. Click *n* for this one.

   Disabling a category causes all its options to become unavailable.

6. **If you don't often need this category but may need it sometime, then click the m diamond (assuming it's available) if the line contains the word *support*.**

   The Linux kernel isn't all in one piece. There's one big central piece that's the kernel itself and then there are lots of little pieces called modules. The kernel picks up and drops modules as it needs them. Anything that you don't use often (maybe a floppy drive driver) should be in a module to reduce the size of your kernel the rest of the time.

7. **If the item is disabled (n is selected) but you need it, click the y diamond to turn it on.**

   The options become available to alter.

8. **Choose one by one whether you want each item in the main kernel (y), in a module (m), or disabled (n). Click the appropriate diamond.**

   Not all items let you make them modules, so don't be surprised when you run into ones that don't give you the m option.

   Aren't sure what an item does? Click the Help button. It pulls up information about the item so that you can make an educated decision.

9. **After you finish with a category, click the Main Menu button to close the dialog box.**

10. **After you finish configuring the kernel, click the Save and Exit buttons to proceed.**

    The Kernel build instructions dialog box opens. This contains the same information that you get in the following section, "Building your new kernel."

11. **Click OK to close the dialog box.**

You've just finished the hardest part! You may want to exit the GUI for now to make your code building go faster.

Building your new kernel

Building a brand-new kernel sounds like a daunting process. Fortunately, it's not all that difficult when you get right down to it. After everything is in place and have taken the time to change the kernel configuration to match your needs, it's time to let the computer do the rest of the dirty work. (Start at the "Rebuilding the kernel" section earlier in this chapter and proceed down to this one if you want to make completely sure your kernel is set up the way you want it.)

To have the computer compile your new kernel, follow these steps:

1. **Type** make dep **to have the compilation software set things up for you.**

   This may take a few minutes. Have something else available to do, or browse through this book while you wait.

2. **Type** make bzImage **to build the main kernel.**

   Depending on how fast or slow your machine is, you may want to go off and have lunch or something while you're waiting. This step can take 15 to 30 minutes, or longer. The amount of time depends on how fast your computer is, how much memory it has, and how much functionality you left in the main kernel.

3. **Type** make modules **to build the pieces the kernel picks up and drops.**

   This process can take quite a while. It depends on how many items you set as modular as opposed to turning them off or putting them in the central kernel.

4. **Type** make modules_install **to put the modules where the kernel can find them.**

   This is a pretty quick process. You see a series of lines starting with Installing modules and then it's done.

5. **If your Linux machine is booting from a SCSI hard drive, then type** uname -r **to see which kernel version you're using, and then type** mkinitrd /boot/initrd-*version version* **and press Enter.**

   This process creates a special version of the kernel used only when you boot the machine. You need it to make sure that Linux can use your SCSI drive when it's booting.

6. **Type** make clean **and press Enter to get rid of the temporary files your computer created while building the kernel.**

You now have your very own custom kernel! Linux doesn't know about it yet, though.

Moving the kernel into place

When Linux builds a new kernel for you (see the previous section for more information), it places the main file in a temporary location. You have to manually put the kernel in its new home. There are a number of reasons for this. The main reason is that the programs doing the building don't know whether you want this kernel to replace an old one, what you want to name it, or a number of other issues that are critical to not messing up your system. Remember, the kernel is Linux itself!

Do the following to put your kernel into place:

1. **Type** cp /boot/vmlinuz /boot/vmlinuz.old **to make a backup copy of the kernel you're using right now.**

   Never delete the old kernel before you test the new one!

2. **Type** locate bzImage **and press Enter.**

   Not all distributions put the new kernel image in the same place. This command makes sure that you aren't lost in the next step!

3. **Type** cd /usr/src/linux/arch/i386/boot **or the equivalent that matches where your new kernel was placed.**

   Change the directories as necessary. You may need to change the linux part to linux-version, for example.

4. **Type** cp bzImage /boot/vmlinuz **to replace the old kernel.**

   This is why we backed up the old kernel in Step 1.

5. **Type** cd /usr/src/linux **to change back to the main source directory.**

6. **Type** cp System.map /boot **to copy the new map file into the boot directory or partition.**

Now all of the kernel files are properly in place! Next, you have to tell Linux how to find them.

Telling Linux about the kernel

Linux needs to be able to find the kernel at boot time. You have to be careful at this point because you can't be 100 percent sure that this new kernel — the one that we show you how to build in the previous sections — is going to work! So, we tell Linux about the new one, but leave ourselves with the option of using the old one if we need it. To do so, follow these steps:

1. **Type** cp /etc/lilo.conf /etc/lilo.conf.backup **to create a backup of your boot loader's configuration file.**

2. **Type** vi /etc/lilo.conf **to open the LILO configuration file.**

   This file contains something like the following:

   ```
   boot=/dev/hda
   map=/boot/map
   install=/boot/boot.b
   prompt
   timeout=50
   message=/boot/message
   linear
   default=linux

   image=/boot/vmlinuz-2.2.16-17
          label=linux
          read-only
          root=/dev/hda1
   ```

3. **Press** i **to enter the** vi **Insert mode.**

4. **Cursor down to the line above the line containing the word** *image.*

5. **Add the following section:**

   ```
   image=/boot/vmlinuz
          label=linux
          read-only
          root=/dev/hda1
   ```

   Make sure that the root line is the same as it is in your file's other root line. For example, in Step 2, the root line is:

   ```
          root=/dev/hda1
   ```

   This matches what we have in this step's root line.

6. **Edit the original label statement (such as in Step 2) so that it ends up as the following:**

   ```
          label=linux-old
   ```

   The second half of the file now looks similar to the following:

   ```
   image=/boot/vmlinuz
          label=linux
          read-only
          root=/dev/hda1

          image=/boot/vmlinuz-2.2.16-17
          label=linux-old
          read-only
          root=/dev/hda1
   ```

7. **Press Esc to return to the** vi **Command mode.**

8. **Type** ZZ **and press Enter to save and close the file.**

9. **Type** /etc/lilo -v **and press Enter to rerun LILO so that it loads the new options.**

That's it! Finally. All you have to do is test and see if your new kernel boots okay.

Testing your new kernel

To test your new kernel, all you need to do is reboot! When you get the LILO prompt, type **linux** to try out the new kernel. If for some reason the machine doesn't boot properly, reboot and type **linux-old** at the boot prompt to boot into the safe old kernel. You can then go through the whole kernel creation process again and get the new one working correctly.

If your new kernel doesn't work, the following are just a couple things that you can do:

✔ Return to the"Configuring your kernel" section and go through the configuration again. You may have disabled features that are vital to your system's ability to work properly.

Can't figure out which features you added and removed, and which ones were there before? Reboot under the linux-old kernel, and follow the instructions in the section "Creating the old configuration file." Then, follow the instructions in "Configuring your kernel" just long enough to allow you to browse through and see how this one's different from the new one.

✔ See Chapter 19 for additional advice on troubleshooting your Linux problems.

Chapter 16

Tuning and Optimizing Linux

* *

In This Chapter

▶ Exploring swapping

▶ Looking at disk efficiency

▶ Discovering tools to watch the action

▶ Thinking about busy servers

* *

A great feature of Linux on a single-user computer is that Linux doesn't really need much tuning and optimizing. Keeping an eye on your resource usage to ensure all is running smoothly and efficiently, however, is a good idea. When Linux is set up to perform specific tasks, such as to function as a Web server or e-mail server, you may need to do some tuning so these services perform well on Linux. At the end of this chapter, we take a look at some of these specialized situations, but first you can take a look at some things to watch for on your ordinary everyday Linux system.

> *In theory, there is no difference between theory and practice. But, in practice, there is.*
>
> — Jan L.A. van de Snepscheut

Managing Memory and Disk Space

Linux is very flexible and can run on a wide variety of hardware systems. Two performance-related areas that can vary quite a bit are speed and storage-space features. If you're running Linux on a new fast system, then hardware constraints may not be an issue. If you're running Linux on an older computer system, however, then hardware may impact how well Linux runs.

> *Computers in the future may weigh no more than 1.5 tons.*
>
> — Popular Mechanics, 1949

Linux, like other operating systems, can't have *too much* memory. On the other hand, insufficient memory is one area that can affect Linux performance. In this section, we cover how Linux handles things when physical memory is low.

Another area that impacts performance is your storage system. We're talking about hard drives, not boxes and closets. Again, the newer the better, and if you have a few extra dollars, we recommend SCSI over IDE. Most non-server Linux systems use IDE drives so we cover tuning techniques for IDE-based systems as well. You can find hardware details about IDE and SCSI in Chapter 2.

Finally, another area affecting performance is the CPU. The type, speed, and number of processors all have a role. The fastest and newest are usually the best. But a lot of folks stick Linux on older computers that don't run other operating systems well (or at all). If the CPU is too old and slow, you may not like the performance. However, we've been quite pleased with Linux running the X Window System (which we mostly just call X for short) and several applications on half the hardware as other popular Intel-based operating systems!

Getting creative with swap space

Linux automatically uses all the memory you have in your system. On Intel platforms, Linux can address all the available space permitted by a 32-bit operating system, and 32 bits gives you a maximum of 4GB of memory. You probably don't need more than 4GB of memory, if anywhere near that, but Linux's performance really degrades when available memory is insufficient. In this section, we show you how Linux handles things when physical memory or RAM (Random Access Memory) is low.

Linux can run on very small amounts of memory if not much is needed beyond the command prompt, on a basic single-user system, or a workstation on a small network. Like most other operating systems, however, Linux performs better when more physical memory is available. You need to have at least 16MB of memory for a personal-use machine. If you're anticipating running a lot of services and/or heavy usage (for example, a Web server), you need to increase the memory.

Memory isn't the only thing that benefits resource-intensive processes; you need to also consider the speed of the processor.

To increase the amount of available memory for applications, Linux uses a process called *disk paging* in which a specified amount of disk space is set aside as *swap space*. When Linux requires more physical memory than what's available, it *swaps* out, or exchanges, pages of memory holding inactive contents to the swap space. This makes more physical memory available to the process that needs it. Sometimes, this feature is called *virtual memory,* or virtual RAM. The applications running have no idea this is going on and they *think* they have lots of physical memory. The ability to swap memory contents to and from the hard drive also enables the support of more simultaneous users on the same system.

A nice advantage of this virtual memory system is the ability to share these memory pages between applications. For example, if you're running the vi editor and you open up another vi session, you have only one copy of the vi code in memory. (For more about the vi editor, see Chapter 12.) You're therefore able to run the same program more than once in the same amount of physical memory where, if all the programs had to have their own space, it wouldn't fit.

If you really want to improve performance, you have to add more physical RAM.

Calculating how much swap space you need

You can calculate the amount of virtual memory your system can work with by adding the amount of physical memory to the amount of swap space. When determining the amount of swap space to create, you must have at least 16MB total virtual memory and, out of this, 4MB physical RAM is the bare minimum.

You can make the size of a swap area pretty much any size you want — as long as the size of your swap area plus physical memory doesn't exceed 4GB. But, if you configure an individual swap space larger than 128MB, you waste disk space because Linux only uses 128MB no matter how big the swap space is. If you need more than 128MB, you can have more than one swap area. In fact, you can have up to 16 separate swap areas per Linux system, which means that you can have as much as 16 times 128MB — 2GB — of swap space!

You should never need to set your total swap area greater than three times the amount of physical RAM. If you're performing a lot of intensive graphics under X, though, you may need more swap space. Remember, your mileage may vary.

Avoiding swap files

Linux supports implementation of swap space in two forms:

 ✔ **A swap partition:** A disk partition specified as type Linux swap (ID=82).With a swap partition, you reserve an area of the disk only for swapping and the disk blocks are contiguous.

 ✔ **A swap file:** A file placed somewhere in your Linux file system.With a swap file, the contents of the file may be distributed across non-contiguous blocks, which negatively affects access performance.

Swap partitions are more efficient to use than swap files and, therefore, the preferred method. With a swap partition, you create a partition on the disk that is only used for swapping. A dedicated swap partition is more efficient because the memory pages can be stored and retrieved quickly from contiguous disk blocks. Disk blocks are *chunks* of disk space, and access by the drive hardware is much faster if data can be stored on contiguous blocks of disk space. In contrast, a swap file may be located on non-contiguous disk blocks. If data is sprinkled over non-contiguous disk blocks, the drive must work harder to locate and find the contents of the swapped memory pages. For best performance, use swap partitions.

Because of the increased use of storage space (slower to access than physical memory), the overall performance of your system also drops when it's doing a lot of swapping. When physical memory is too low and/or your swap space is too small, your drive systems begin to thrash about. So much time is spent moving memory contents back and forth from the drive that nothing else is happening, and the drive's lights are going wild. Now is the time to bite the bullet and add more physical memory. Swap space is no substitute for physical memory!

Why do you pay a price for using swap space over adding more physical RAM? Well, remember that your disks are primarily mechanical devices. Information is read from and written to a set of spinning circular platters stacked inside the external shell of the hard drive like a multiple-layer cake. The filling between each layer is air and floating above each surface of these platters are heads. The heads perform the changes (magic) to the platters' surfaces to represent your data. Whenever data is read from or written to the disk, as it is when swap space is used, the head for the appropriate platter must physically move to the spot *over* the designated location. This moving back and forth over the surfaces of the disk can only go so fast and is considerably slower than the transmission of electrical signals through your system's circuitry. Even with the current fast hard drives and disk subsystems available today, mechanical operations are still slower than electrical currents. What helps on newer hard drives is the presence of multiple heads above each platter surface so switching between heads on the same track is considerably faster than moving the heads to another track. Obviously, on an older system, the negative impact of older disk architecture may be more significant.

Knowing where to put your swap partition

Another issue to consider is where on the disk you should place the swap partition. Older hard drives have the same number of sectors on each track. Newer drives that use *ZBR* (*z*one *b*it *r*ecording) have more sectors on the outer or longer tracks than on the inner shorter tracks. Because the disk spins at a constant *rpm* (revolution per minute) speed, you get better performance on the outer tracks of drives using ZBR. On ZBR drives, try to place the partition as close to the outer edge as possible (meaning one of the first partitions on your drive). For older drives, placing the swap partition in the middle of the drive leads to faster access.

Spreading swap space across multiple drives

You can spread your swap space across different drives (if you have multiple drives, of course). This methodology may help to improve performance, especially on older hardware and IDE-based systems. Instead of tying up one channel only for swapping, you can spread the load across different drives on different channels. You may want to also consider setting aside one disk channel for swapping and leaving the other for file system access.

The most efficient use of swap space is to use partitions on drives that aren't occupied with a lot of other disk-intensive tasks, and to spread swap space across multiple fast drives with multiple drive heads.

Creating a swap partition

Linux comes equipped with tools to manage your disk partitions. In this section, we walk you through creating a swap partition using cfdisk.

Your first step is to define a partition dedicated to swap. In our example, we have a system with two hard drives. The first drive, /dev/hda, already has a swap partition on it. We're creating another partition for swap space on the second drive, /dev/hdc. To do so, follow these steps:

1. **Type** cfdisk /def/*hard_drive* **at a command prompt and press Enter, where** *hard_drive* **is the designation of the hard drive you want to create a swap partition (such as hdc in Figure 16-1).**

   The initial screen displays the current partitions on the second drive. Figure 16-1 shows the partitions on a typical hard drive. The drive has one partition (hdc1), which is 32MB in size, and a Linux partition (ext2) that's labeled /boot. The drive also has about 1.3GB of free space. You have to have or create free space available on your hard drive to be able to create a swap partition.

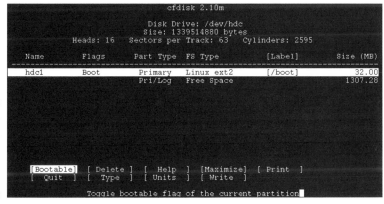

Figure 16-1: cfdisk showing the partitions on a hard drive.

2. **Use the up and down arrow keys on the keyboard so the selection area is on the Free Space entry.**

When you have Free Space selected, the options at the bottom of the screen change. Use the right and left arrow keys to move the selection at the bottom of the screen to select New, as shown in Figure 16-2.

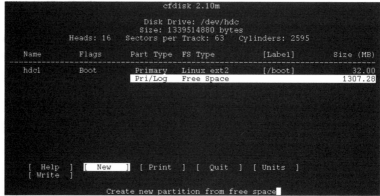

Figure 16-2: cfdisk options after selecting Free Space.

Press Enter to change the options for partition type, which are shown in Figure 16-3. For this example, you're creating a primary partition.

3. **Use the right and left arrow keys to select Primary and press Enter.**

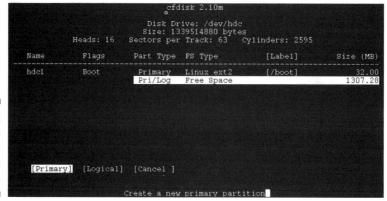

Figure 16-3: cfdisk's partition type options.

The option changes with a Size field so that you can enter the size (in megabytes) of the partition.

4. **Type the size that you want into the Size field and press Enter.**

On the next screen, you can choose to place the partition at the beginning or end of the free disk space.

5. **Choose Beginning (see Figure 16-4) and press Enter.**

   Now you need to change the partition type from Linux to swap.

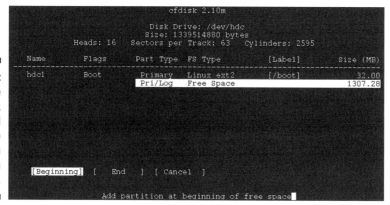

Figure 16-4:
The
cfdisk
command
showing the
partition
location
options.

6. **Use the right and left arrow keys to move the selection to the Type option and press Enter.**

   The screen displays three columns of file types (more than can fit on one screen).

7. **Press any key (the space bar, for example) to bring up the remaining options.**

8. **At the Enter file system type prompt, type** 82 **for Linux swap and press Enter.**

   Notice that the file type for your new partition shows that it's a Linux swap, as for hdc3 in Figure 16-5. Although you've created the partition, the Linux system isn't aware of it yet.

9. **Use the right and left arrow keys to select the Write option and press Enter.**

10. **To actually write the changes, type** yes **at the confirmation prompt and then press Enter.**

    If you do not do this, then nothing on your hard drive is changed.

11. **After the message** Writing partition table to disk **clears, you can choose Quit to exit the application.**

12. **After the partition changes are written to disk, reboot your system if instructed to do so.**

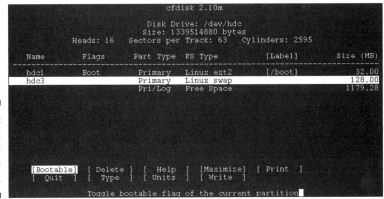

Figure 16-5:
cfdisk
showing the
Write
options.

Even though you've created a swap partition, it isn't ready to participate as swap space. So you need to prepare the swap partition with the mkswap command. At a command prompt, type **mkswap** and the full filename (including pathname) of the new swap partition. We recommend that you add the -c option to mkswap to check for any bad disk blocks while it's creating the swap partition architecture. For this example, enter the following:

```
mkswap -c /dev/hdc3
```

Your next task is to activate the new swap partition so that you can use it. To do so, use the swapon command and specify the full filename of the new swap partition. For this example, enter the following:

```
swapon /dev/hdc3
```

If you want the new swap partition available when you restart the system, you need to edit your /etc/fstab file as follows: Add a line at the end of your /etc/fstab file that contains the same information as your other swap entry. On this new line, change the partition number to reflect your new swap partition. In Figure 16-6, this number is /dev/hdc3.

Directory structures and disk fragmentation

Where you place the file system directories affects the overall performance and efficiency of Linux. If you place all the files on one partition, the drive's system may be over-tasked when servicing the reads and writes. Also, if everything is on one partition, how do you handle ballooning directories that can quickly use up all the available disk space?

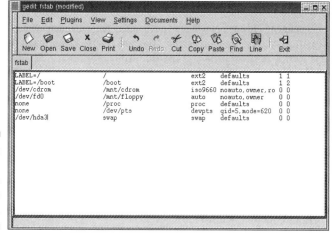

```
gedit fstab (modified)                                    _ □ X

 File   Edit   Plugins   View   Settings   Documents   Help

  ♢      ♤     ♧    x    ♢        ↶    ↷    ✂    ♤     ♧    ♤    ♤     ◁
 New   Open  Save Close Print   Undo  Redo  Cut  Copy Paste Find  Line    Exit

 fstab

LABEL=/                  /                  ext2     defaults       1 1
LABEL=/boot              /boot              ext2     defaults       1 2
/dev/cdrom               /mnt/cdrom         iso9660  noauto,owner,ro 0 0
/dev/fd0                 /mnt/floppy        auto     noauto,owner   0 0
none                     /proc              proc     defaults       0 0
none                     /dev/pts           devpts   gid=5,mode=620 0 0
/dev/hda3|               swap               swap     defaults       0 0
```

Figure 16-6:
The /etc/
fstab file
showing the
added line.

Spreading directory structures across different hard drives

One technique that you can use to improve performance and to help growing directories is to spread the directory structure over multiple drives. We suggest placing primarily read-only files on one drive and placing read/write files on another physical drive, which enables the operating system to alternately read and write across different storage devices. Files that are primarily read-only include the Linux binaries such as /bin, /usr/bin, and /usr/lib. Read/write files include /home, /tmp, and /var. If you use these techniques on newer systems with enhanced IDE features, you may not see much performance gain.

If you're using an IDE system, spread the files over the master drives on the primary and secondary channels rather than placing all the files on a single channel's master and slave drives. This reduces the contention on one channel and spreads the load across both channels. If you have a CD-ROM drive that isn't that peppy, however, you may do better by leaving both hard drives on the same channel and placing the slow CD-ROM on its own separate channel.

You can look at the lifetime of files to get another view on the number of partitions and what is on them. Temporary files are on one partition and other, longer life files are on another partition. Long-life files are those that include the Linux operating system: /bin, /sbin, /usr/sbin, /usr/bin, and any other files in directories that store applications but not data. The directories holding more transient files include /var/spool/lpd, /var/spool/news, and /tmp. Also, be sure to consider the files in /home and their average lifetime (if you can determine one!). You may find it better to place /home on a separate partition. We suggest placing /var on one partition, /home on another, and / (root directory) on a separate partition. In addition, your directories can only grow as far as the partition boundary and aren't able to run your other directories out of town.

Disk fragmentation

Because the size of a file rarely fits exactly into the number of disk blocks allocated for it, you may have to store the rest of the file somewhere else on the partition. The total area the file occupies, therefore, is over non-contiguous blocks that hinder performance because the drive's heads may have to move more to get all the pieces of the file. The features of the Linux native file system (ext2, ID=83) are designed to reduce fragmentation. One technique ext2 performs is to set aside eight contiguous blocks at the end of a file in anticipation of the file's growth. On average, a Linux system suffers 2–5 percent fragmentation, which isn't significant.

Using msdos (FAT16, ID=1) as a partition type for your Linux system introduces file fragmentation. If your Linux system is coexisting with another operating system that uses FAT16, FAT32, or NTFS, create separate partitions for Linux and use ext2 for Linux.

Tracking Memory and Disk Space

Linux comes with a set of utilities for observing memory and disk space usage. Some are command prompt (shell) driven and others are available under X. Here we uncover a few of these and show you what they do.

What's in the memory

To look at the state of your memory (your Linux memory, that is), you can execute the free command at a command prompt. free reports values in 1024-byte memory blocks. Figure 16-7 shows sample results of the free command.

Figure 16-7:
Results of
the free
command.

```
[root@localhost /root]# free
             total       used       free     shared    buffers     cached
Mem:        127820     114632      13188      47564      35916      45036
-/+ buffers/cache:      33680      94140
Swap:        72252        820      71432
[root@localhost /root]#
```

You can see in Figure 16-7 that the output of the free command displays information in columns and rows. In the following list, we describe the columns that you see in Figure 16-7:

✔ **Total:** The amount of physical memory; it's slightly less because the bit of memory used by the kernel is subtracted.

✔ **Used:** Represents the amount of physical memory currently occupied.

- **Free:** Indicates the amount of available physical memory and is simply the value of the Total column minus the value of the Used column.

- **Shared:** The amount of physical memory holding code shared between multiple applications or processes.

- **Buffers:** The amount of memory used by the kernel buffer cache. The kernel buffer cache is used to speed up disk operations by allowing the reads and writes to be handled directly from memory rather than bothering the CPU. Applications can reclaim this memory if needed.

- **Cached:** Indicates how much memory the file caching is using. *File caching* holds file contents in memory to provide quick access to files. Information stored in memory can be retrieved faster than pulling it off the hard disk. Notice that, in Figure 16-7, most of the physical memory is used. That isn't bad, however, because file caching used some of it.

The vertical rows in Figure 16-7 are described in the following list, starting with the second row (the first is just the column heads for the columns described in the previous list):

- **Mem:** The second row (Mem:) displays memory values and the headings indicate the type of memory. When an application needs more memory, it can reclaim the memory used for cache and buffers.

- **-/+ buffers/cache:** This line indicates the actual state of the physical memory. In Figure 16-7, notice the big differences in the used and free values on the Mem: and -/+ buffers/cache: rows.

- **Swap:** The last row in Figure 16-7 (Swap:) indicates the state of the virtual memory. In Figure 16-7, the first value is the amount of physical memory plus the amount of swap space. The swap space may be reported as slightly less than what you specified. This is because each swap area maintains a map of how each page in the swap area is being used. This map takes up a few blocks of the swap area and is usually only a few kilobytes per swap area. The second entry (used) shows the amount of swap space in use and the last entry (free) displays the amount of swap space available. In Figure 16-7, we have plenty of swap space available!

Keeping track of who's doing what in memory

To find out what's going on in the system's memory, you can execute the top command at a shell prompt (see Figure 16-8). Most of the entries that top displays are self-explanatory. With top, you also have some switches you can use such as setting the refresh rate. Use the Linux documentation, such as the man pages, to assist you with delving into top in more detail.

ON THE CD

We cover the `man` pages and other help resources in Bonus Appendix C, which you can find in PDF form on CD3.

```
 6:09pm  up  2:13,  2 users,  load average: 0.13, 0.07, 0.04
51 processes: 49 sleeping, 2 running, 0 zombie, 0 stopped
CPU states:  3.9% user,  1.9% system,  0.0% nice, 94.0% idle
Mem:   127820K av,  116848K used,   10972K free,   49836K shrd,   35916K buff
Swap:   72252K av,     820K used,   71432K free                   46632K cached

  PID USER     PRI  NI  SIZE  RSS SHARE STAT %CPU %MEM   TIME COMMAND
 1535 root      13   0  8948 8948  3120 R    4.7  7.0   0:14 X
 1714 root       8   0  1016 1016   812 R    0.9  0.7   0:00 top
 1702 root       3   0  4076 4076  3244 S    0.1  3.1   0:00 gnome-terminal
    1 root       0   0   528  528   456 S    0.0  0.4   0:04 init
    2 root       0   0     0    0     0 SW   0.0  0.0   0:00 kflushd
    3 root       0   0     0    0     0 SW   0.0  0.0   0:00 kupdate
    4 root       0   0     0    0     0 SW   0.0  0.0   0:00 kpiod
    5 root       0   0     0    0     0 SW   0.0  0.0   0:00 kswapd
    6 root     -20 -20     0    0     0 SW<  0.0  0.0   0:00 mdrecoveryd
   61 root       0   0     0    0     0 SW   0.0  0.0   0:00 khubd
  275 root       0   0   536  536   436 S    0.0  0.4   0:00 syslogd
  285 root       0   0   756  752   348 S    0.0  0.5   0:00 klogd
  300 rpc        0   0   504  504   416 S    0.0  0.3   0:00 portmap
  316 root       0   0     0    0     0 SW   0.0  0.0   0:00 lockd
  317 root       0   0     0    0     0 SW   0.0  0.0   0:00 rpciod
  327 rpcuser    0   0   712  712   592 S    0.0  0.5   0:00 rpc.statd
  342 root       0   0   424  420   360 S    0.0  0.3   0:00 apmd
```

Figure 16-8:
Results of the `top` command.

GNOME also provides utilities to display memory usage. To view your memory usage information in GNOME, follow these steps:

1. **Click the Main Menu button and choose Programs⇨System⇨System Monitor.**

   The GNOME System Monitor appears. This is essentially a graphical twist to the `top` utility that we describe at the beginning of this section. At the top of the Processes (all) window, you see colored bars representing the current memory state.

2. **Select the Memory Usage (resident) tab at the top of the window to see the processes occupying memory displayed in a map-like format.**

   Figure 16-9 shows sample results of the System Monitor.

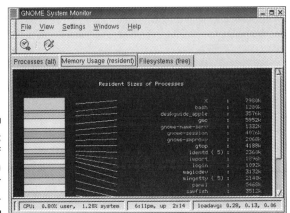

Figure 16-9:
Results of the System Monitor application.

Another tool that you can use to display overall memory and swap usage is System Info. To access System Info in GNOME, follow these steps.

1. **Click the Main Menu button and choose Programs⇨System⇨System Info.**

   The GNOME System Info window appears.

2. **Click the Detailed Information button at the top of the window and then the Memory Information tab to view memory information (see Figure 16-10).**

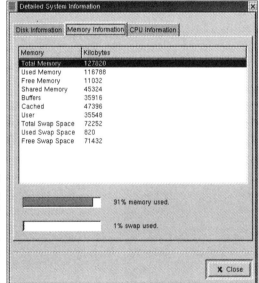

Figure 16-10:
The Memory Information tab of the System Info application.

Keeping an eye on disk space

Uh-oh! "How much disk space do I have left?" or "Where has all the disk space gone?" are typical exclamations from computer users — not just Linux users. Before you install that big graphic program or decide to store a lot of user files, you need to know how much hard drive space you have available. Linux provides several tools to discover how much drive space you have available and how much you've already used.

One of these tools is the command prompt utility df. This utility reports the disk space usage. Because the output of df may be difficult to interpret, try using the h option. The h option means to display information in *human-readable* format. To show your display space in readable format, use df -h.

Figure 16-11 shows an example of the results you get using the df command with the -h option. The information displayed includes the size of the partition, the amount of space used, the amount of available space, and the percentage of space used.

Figure 16-11:
Results of
the df
command
with the -h
option.

```
[root@blissranch /home]# df -h
Filesystem          Size Used Avail Use% Mounted on
/dev/hdc2           1.9G 1.2G 739M  61% /
[root@blissranch /home]#
```

Figure 16-11: Results of the df command with the -h option.

Another command, du, shows the amount of space individual files use. The disk usage, or du, command defaults to the display of visible files and directories at the location where you execute the command. Using the du command with the -ach options shows you all (a) files at the directory location where you execute the command and a total at the end of the display (c) in human-readable form (h), as shown in Figure 16-12.

```
4.0k    ./.mc/history
4.0k    ./.mc/Tree
16k     ./.mc
4.0k    ./.Xauthority
0       ./.gnome-desktop/Home directory
4.0k    ./.gnome-desktop/Trash
4.0k    ./.gnome-desktop/RH.com
4.0k    ./.gnome-desktop/rhn_register.desktop
4.0k    ./.gnome-desktop/rp3-config.desktop
0       ./.gnome-desktop/fd0
20k     ./.gnome-desktop
0       ./.ICEauthority
12k     ./.swp
4.0k    ./.bash_history
8.0k    ./.gnp/apprc
4.0k    ./.gnp/appgtkrc
4.0k    ./.gnp/sessionrc
4.0k    ./.gnp/recentrc
24k     ./.gnp
0       ./fugley2
4.0k    ./testtext
420k    .
420k    total
[root@localhost RHLinux]#
```

Figure 16-12: Results of the du command with the -ach options.

The GNOME interface has a couple of tools available. GNOME DiskFree displays hard drive space usage in a dashboard interface.

To view your drive usage information, click the Main Menu button and choose Programs⇨System⇨GNOME DiskFree. The GDiskFree window appears and the *dashboard* panel displays the amount of disk space currently in use. If you have more than one hard drive in your system, a separate panel appears for each drive. For example, Figure 16-13 shows two hard drives.

Figure 16-13:
Results of
the GNOME
DiskFree
application.

You can also use System Info to display disk space statistics. To access
System Info, click the Main Menu button and choose Programs⇨System⇨
System Info. The GNOME System Info appears. To see the disk information,
click the Disk Information tab, as shown in Figure 16-14.

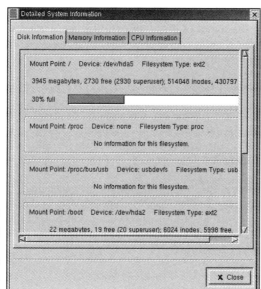

Figure 16-14:
Checking
out your disk
info.

Tweaking to Handle Busy Linux Servers

If you're going to use Linux as a Web, e-mail, or FTP server for a large organization's intranet or on a server accessible from the Internet, you must consider performance issues. For these types of servers, you need plenty of
physical memory and the fastest storage systems and other hardware you
can find.

If Linux is performing a lot of CPU-intensive tasks, such as rendering graphics, then multiple processors may help speed up these tasks. Linux supports SMP (symmetrical multiple processors) and automatically installs the appropriate kernel elements for SMP support.

To help disk-intensive services, such as reading and writing lots of data, SCSI is better suited for these tasks than IDE. You can add more physical drives to a SCSI system than you can with IDE. IDE supports up to four physical drives per computer but SCSI supports up to seven drives on one SCSI interface channel. In addition, you can have more than one SCSI interface channel per computer and therefore can handle more than seven drives. Also, the architecture of SCSI permits faster access to stored data and faster writing of information. For more details on SCSI and IDE hardware, see Chapter 2.

If you're considering RAID 5 (Redundant Array of Inexpensive Disks) on Linux, the vast majority of solutions are SCSI based. RAID 5 provides hardware fault tolerance in the event of disk failure and is a common hardware solution on mission-critical servers. Refer to the following Web site for information about RAID 5 and Linux.

```
www.redhat.com/support/docs/tips/raid/RAID-INDEX.html
```

To reduce disk swapping, make sure you have plenty of physical memory so that you need only a little swap space. You can monitor the amount of swap space with the `free` command, which we cover in the "What's in the memory" section earlier in this chapter.

Separating tasks across multiple servers helps memory usage by dedicating the Linux system's resources to one task, such as serving up Web pages, instead of splitting its resources among different services. Dedicate separate Linux systems for your Web servers and use others for e-mail, FTP, and so on.

Chapter 17

Security

I am Inspector Clouseau and I am on official police business.

— Inspector Clouseau

Security. Here's a buzzword that you can't escape. Anywhere that you read about the Internet, you see reports of break-ins, new viruses, and dire warnings about the security of our systems. In some ways, this hype is necessary to keep everyone on their toes. The biggest problems you get with security — whether it's in your home, at work, or on a computer somewhere — happen when you get lax.

You wouldn't leave the front door of your house open when you went to work, would you? How about leaving it shut and locked but with a few nice big windows open? The problem is that many people do this every day with their computers and they don't even know it! So, we take a look at where your open doors and windows are and what you can do to secure them.

Implementing User and Administrator Security

Every user's actions affect your overall system security. If your family or officemates need access to your Linux machine, then take the time to sit down and explain the facts of secure life to them. They can then take this information and apply it to the other computers they use, because these issues aren't specific just to Linux.

Daily tasks for users

Fortunately, you, and the users you're letting onto your machine, can do a number of things to contribute to your machine's security.

Choosing passwords

The first line of defense from intruders is the entire collection of passwords on your system. If even one of the accounts has a weak password, then you may be in for some trouble. When choosing passwords, follow these rules:

- ✔ Don't use any part of your name.
- ✔ Don't use the names of friends, loved ones, or pets.
- ✔ Don't use birthdays, anniversaries, or other easily guessed dates.
- ✔ Don't use dictionary words.
- ✔ Don't keep your password written down near your computer, unless it's buried in something else, such as writing it into an address.
- ✔ Don't tell anyone your password. If someone needs to access specific files, give the person an account and set up permissions and groups properly so they can do so.
- ✔ Do use a mix of lowercase letters, capital letters, and numbers.
- ✔ Do use acronyms made from sentences, such as having the password "McniT" to stand for "My cat's name is Tabby."

Every person on your system needs to follow these rules, including you! Consider keeping a sheet of paper with the rules on it to keep next to the machine.

We can't stress this enough: *Never* give out your password. Make sure that the people on your machine understand this. You can always find alternative methods to accomplish a task without giving out your password.

Getting new software

All users can download and install new software. Of course, the program(s) they install are limited to the user's own permissions. The thing to be careful of here — with any operating system — is that you don't get a version of a program that's been tampered with, or is even an all-out fake trying to trick folks into installing it.

Give your users a list of Web sites that you trust, such as the ones listed in this book, and tell them that if they aren't sure whether or not they can trust a particular Web site, they need to ask you for your opinion. This means, of course, that you need to look around and decide what sites you trust and what sites you don't.

Daily tasks for the administrator

If users need to be careful, then the administrator of a Linux machine (or any machine) needs to be doubly watchful. As the person in charge, it's your job to make sure that this computer stays intruder-free. Aside from making sure that you do all of the same things a user would do for both your user account(s) and the superuser (root) account, you must do one additional thing, no matter what Linux distribution you're running, and that's keeping up to date with security problems.

Every operating system has security issues. You can't escape them. The people that manage to avoid break-in problems are those who stay informed and apply fixes when they appear. Almost all Linux distributions offer the ability to find out about and grab fixes. If the instructions aren't in their documentation, then they'll be on the distributors' Web sites.

In the case of Red Hat Linux, write to the e-mail address `redhat-watch-list-req@redhat.com` with the word *subscribe* as the subject and nothing in the body. This adds you to the Red Hat Watch mailing list. You'll receive announcements whenever a new security problem is uncovered with a Linux or Red Hat package, including instructions on how to fix the problem.

When you get one of these warnings from Red Hat, keep the following in mind:

- ✔ **Are you using this program?** You potentially can receive warnings about everything that comes with the distribution. You can determine whether or not the warning pertains to you in a number of ways, depending on the distribution and package. A quick way of telling if you're using a program is to type **man program**. If the package is installed, then the help for it comes up; the help information isn't installed unless the program is.

- ✔ **Are you using the same version of the program that you're being warned about?** You may be using an older or newer version. You have to read the warning message carefully to see what range of versions it covers. If it doesn't mention one, then assume that the warning applies to you too (just to be safe).

Plugging the Holes and Fixing the Leaks

Although you can't plug some holes until you find them — such as the items pointed out in security notifications — others come prepackaged. The natural thing to wonder when reading about a known security hole in the shrink-wrapped version of a Linux distribution is why this is, if they're known holes, they're not plugged up in the first place. Good question. The answer is that the people building the Linux distributions don't know exactly what you, in particular, want to do. They do their best to meet the security needs of an average user, which isn't exactly right for everyone. But rest easy, because this issue's a lot easier to deal with than you may think.

Understanding network dangers

It's important that you don't have any network services running that you don't intend to use. To understand why, you first need to comprehend a bit about how these services work. Every network service listens to an assigned place leading to the outside world. For example, if you're running a Web server, then it's listening to *port* 80. Think of a port as an apartment number. Whenever a person wants to look at one of your Web pages, they point their browser toward your Web server, which is typically named something like `www.mywebserver.org`. This is the street that you live on. Along with a name, this server also has an IP address, which is something like 192.168.15.65. This is the street address assigned to your apartment building. The apartment building is full of doors leading to various network services. Apartment 80 always leads to the Web server — unless you set yours up differently. Don't do that unless you want people to have a hard time getting to it.

You can see which port corresponds to which network service in the file `/etc/services`.

It's possible to have a certain amount of security protecting each port, just like an apartment door. You may have just a bit of security, like a normal key lock. Or, you may have a deadbolt, a combination lock, and other gizmos protecting the point of entry. Here is where the metaphor begins to break down, though. You're not likely to decide that a particular apartment can't have anyone going in or out. With a computer's network services, however, this is a very important thing to consider. If you're not going to run an FTP server, for example, then having ports 20 and 21 functioning just provides more doors for potential intruders to attack through.

Plugging network holes

Linux manages incoming connections in two different ways. The first involves individual programs. You can control these using the tools that we describe in the next section. The second method of managing incoming connections, however, involves a central program that watches on many ports. This program then answers the door when a network client — maybe an FTP client — comes knocking and starts up the program that handles the service.

The program that handles these centralized network services is the *superdaemon*. (You can refer to Bonus Appendix A on the CD for a discussion concerning daemons — we do just a quick review here.) A daemon is a program that runs in the background and typically handles network services. The superdaemon is the daemon that starts and stops a bunch of other daemons. This program is `inetd`.

If you're using Red Hat Linux 7 (which is on the CDs that were included with this book), then you're in luck. They're no longer using `inetd`, so you can skip to the next section. If you're not using this version of Red Hat or Red Hat at all, then we have a quick test to see whether you need to tighten up your networking or not.

To conduct this test and plug any holes, follow these steps:

1. **Type** man inetd.

   If you see the `inetd` man page, then continue with the remaining steps.

   If you don't see the `inetd` man page, then that's it. You're done with the test and using the more secure superdaemon, so you don't need to plug holes.

2. **Open** /etc/inetd.conf **in your favorite text editor.**

   This is the superdaemon configuration file. Each distribution has a slightly different setup, so our instructions are going to direct you on how to navigate the file and find what you may want to turn on or off.

3. **Move down through the file, looking for any line that doesn't start with a #.**

   The hash mark, or #, denotes a *comment* in this file and many others. Linux ignores any text on a line after the #. So, if there's no #, Linux is going to use the text on the line.

4. **Determine whether you need this service or not.**

   This part sounds a bit trickier than it really is. Many of these have distinctive names like `telnet` or `ftp`. The thing to remember is that you're not dealing with accessing other machines from this one when you edit this file. You're dealing with how people can access this machine. So, if you don't want someone to be able to FTP into this machine, you don't want the ftp service line active. Table 17-1 shows a list of services that you may want to shut off.

5. If you're not going to use this service, add a # at the beginning of the line.

This comments out the service so that Linux ignores it.

6. When you're done commenting out the services you don't need, save and exit the file.

7. Restart inetd (the superdaemon) according to the best practices for your particular distribution.

Doing this enables inetd to load the new configuration.

Table 17-1	Network Services Run by the Superdaemon That You May Not Want
Service Name	*Purpose*
finger	An old service that allows you to have what is basically a text Web page that includes any information that you want.
ftp	Enables users to use an FTP client to log in to their personal accounts — or one they've broken into — and download or upload files.
pop	The Post Office Protocol (POP) mail service enables people to use a POP client like Eudora or Microsoft Outlook to check their mail on this machine. You have no reason to do this unless this machine is a mail server, which it likely isn't.
talk	You may see many versions of this one, such as ntalk and dtalk, which are all similar to talk and use the same considerations as for talk. This program enables users to form a two-way real-time discussion connection, kind of like a DCC chat in IRC. talk is rarely used today, however, because programs such as IRC have more features.
telnet	Enables users to use a Telnet client to log in to their personal accounts — or one they've broken into — from another machine.

Plugging software holes

When someone's already in your system — whether they're allowed to be there or not — you have additional security concerns to keep in mind. One of these involves what software you have on the machine. Each piece of software is a potential security hole, believe it or not. If someone can get a program to crash in just the right way, they can get greater access to your system than they should. This is a very bad thing!

You can do two things to close software holes. One of these is to remove all programs that you don't need. (We discuss the other in the section, "Daily tasks for the administrator," earlier in this chapter.) You can always add them later if necessary. How exactly you do this depends on the package management scheme your distribution runs. The following works at the command prompt on Red Hat, and all other distributions that use RPM.

To remove all programs that you don't need, follow these steps:

1. **Type** rpm -qa | more **to see every package you have installed, a screen at a time.**

   The list displayed is probably a bit daunting! We suggest that you don't try to review and delete them all at once. Do a group of packages, and maybe come back the next day and do another. The start of the list may look like the following:

   ```
   filesystem-2.0.7-1
   glibc-2.1.91-18
   termcap-11.0.1-3
   ```

   You can also use one of the GUI package managers. In Red Hat, it's GnoRPM.

2. **In another virtual console, type** rpm -qi *packagename* **for the package that you want to investigate, without the version number.**

   Detailed information about this package is displayed. For example, see Figure 17-1 to see the data on glibc-2.1.91-18. We got this information by typing **rpm -qi glibc**.

```
ash-0.2-26
at-3.1.8-12
--More--
[1]+  Stopped                    rpm -qa | more
[root@localhost /root]# rpm -qi glibc
Name        : glibc              Relocations: (not relocateable)
Version     : 2.1.92             Vendor: Red Hat, Inc.
Release     : 14                 Build Date: Wed 30 Aug 2000 04:19:26 P
M CDT
Install date: Tue 26 Sep 2000 09:49:31 AM CDT    Build Host: porky.devel.redhat.
com
Group       : System Environment/Libraries   Source RPM: glibc-2.1.92-14.src.rpm
Size        : 40186297           License: LGPL
Packager    : Red Hat, Inc. <http://bugzilla.redhat.com/bugzilla>
Summary     : The GNU libc libraries.
Description :
The glibc package contains standard libraries which are used by
multiple programs on the system. In order to save disk space and
memory, as well as to make upgrading easier, common system code is
kept in one place and shared between programs. This particular package
contains the most important sets of shared libraries: the standard C
library and the standard math library. Without these two libraries, a
Linux system will not function.  The glibc package also contains
national language (locale) support and timezone databases.
[root@localhost /root]#
```

Figure 17-1:
Information
about the
RPM
glibc.

3. **Read the package information and determine whether or not you need this program.**

   We know, sometimes this is easier said than done. You may want to do several passes through the list. Get rid of the obviously unnecessary programs first. After that, go through again when you understand the system better and get rid of some more. Remember that you can put programs back if it turns out that you need them.

4. **If you don't want or need this package, type** rpm -e *packagename* **to get rid of it, where you designate the package name without the version number.**

   Although you probably don't want to get rid of glibc (which is required to help some programs run), we'll stick with this example. Type **rpm -e glibc** to get rid of that package.

   If you get an error message that tells you that this package is required to satisfy *dependencies,* this means that other packages use this one to function. You have to decide if you want to get rid of all the packages that need this one first.

We know, this is a pretty involved process. You get to know quite a lot about your system along the way, however, and the more you know, the better off you are.

Being Ever Vigilant

One last security issue that you may want to configure concerns *log files.* Your network programs, kernel, and other programs all run log files, which contain records of what's been happening on your system. You may be amazed at just how much information gets put in them! They're mostly in /var/log; take a look sometime. It's frightening.

Fortunately, tools are available that can help us mere mortals sift through the wheat looking for the chaff of bugs and intruders. The one we focus on here is the Simple WATCHer, or SWATCH. This tool is written in the Perl programming language, which is popular for building many items used on the Web.

Getting SWATCH

SWATCH may or may not come with your Linux distribution. It doesn't come with Red Hat by default, for example. So, to get SWATCH, follow these steps:

1. **Enter the GUI.**

2. **Open your favorite Linux Web browser.**

   By default, this is usually Netscape.

3. **Go to** `www.engr.ucsb.edu/~eta/swatch/`.

   This is the SWATCH home page.

4. **Click one of the download options for the latest version.**

   Netscape opens the Save As dialog box.

5. **Navigate to where you want to place the file and click OK.**

   The file downloads. It comes in a `.tar` version, but it isn't zipped.

6. **In a virtual console, type** tar -xvf *filename* **to unpack the file, where filename is the name of the file you want to unpack.**

You've now downloaded the code you need for SWATCH and unpackaged it so that you can work with it. Now, you need to install the program itself.

Installing SWATCH

After you've downloaded the SWATCH file and unpacked its contents, follow these steps to install it on your system:

1. **Make sure you're logged in as root; if you're not, type** su **and enter the root password when you're prompted.**

   Isn't that a neat trick? Now you have root privileges. Remember when you're done doing root stuff to type **exit** to return to your normal account.

2. **Use the** cd **command to move into the directory created when you unpacked the SWATCH file.**

   You're now in the SWATCH main directory.

3. Type man perl **to ensure that you have the Perl programming materials installed on your system.**

4. **If you get an error, install Perl using the techniques required by your distribution.**

   With Red Hat, this requires that you mount the Red Hat CD-ROM and install the perl package as root.

5. **Within this SWATCH directory, type** perl Makefile.PL.

   The installer begins asking some questions. For example, it may say that you don't have the Time::Hires 1.12 module — a Perl time-calculation handling module — installed and ask if you want it. Always answer y when asked if you want to install a module.

6. **You're asked if you're ready to begin manual configuration. Answer no.**

   This tells the program to do the configuration itself. This process can take a few minutes as information scrolls down your screen, so be patient. The installer checks for Perl modules it needs, compiles code, and runs tests. Letting the automatic version run is much better than having to do it by hand!

   It's best to make sure that you're connected to the Internet when you run this configuration tool. If you need any modules, the configuration program grabs them itself.

   When you get back to the command prompt, you're ready to proceed to configuring SWATCH for your needs.

Configuring SWATCH

This is where the real artistry comes in. You have to put a lot of time into setting up what log file aspects SWATCH needs to keep an eye on for you, but it's worth it in the end. We're going to recommend that you use another handy tool in order to decide the kinds of things you want to watch for and then use that information to configure SWATCH. This first tool is the GNOME System Log Viewer, which we discuss in the next section.

After you use the GNOME System Log Viewer to gather the information you need, see the section titled "Translating System Log Viewer data into useful SWATCH entries" to build your SWATCH configuration file.

Getting data from the System Log Viewer

GNOME offers the System Log Viewer for your convenience. Although no one can watch their logs twenty-four hours a day/seven days a week, you really need to become familiar with what shows up in them on a regular basis. You can't pick out the unusual items unless you recognize them as unusual.

To use the System Log Viewer, do the following:

1. **Log in as root.**

   This gives you access to the most log files.

2. **Type** startx **to enter GNOME, if you're not already in there.**

   This is a GUI tool so you have to be in the GUI.

3. **From the main toolbar, click the Footprint icon.**

   The main GNOME menu opens.

4. **Choose Programs⇨System⇨System log monitor.**

   The System Log Viewer opens, as shown in Figure 17-2.

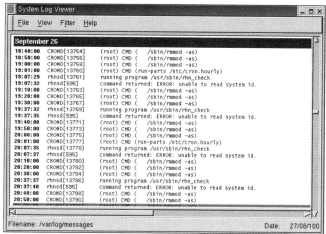

Figure 17-2:
A sample
GNOME
System Log
Viewer.

5. **Scroll through this viewer's contents and examine normal system operation.**

   Give yourself a few weeks to really get used to this.

6. **If you want to know more about an entry, click it and then click View⇨Zoom to see if the System Log Viewer can give you additional information.**

   An example Zoom view dialog box is shown in Figure 17-3.

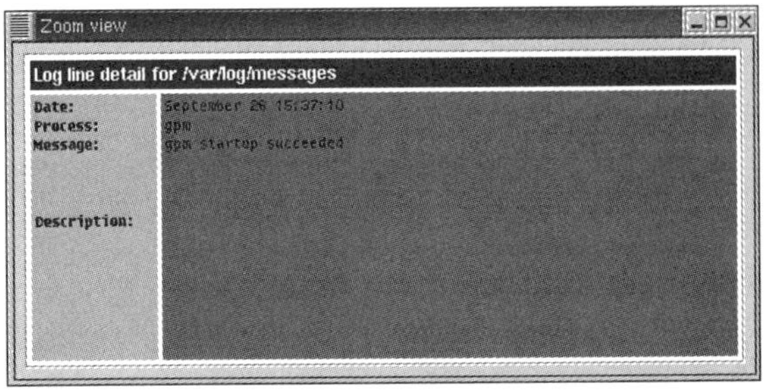

Figure 17-3:
A sample
GNOME
System Log
Viewer
Zoom view
dialog box.

Translating System Log Viewer data into useful SWATCH entries

Eventually you may find something that you're worried about in your log entries — from both the System Log Viewer and manually glancing through many of the files in the /var/log directory. Or, maybe you just want to practice, so you'll know exactly how to keep an eye out for later. To build a useful SWATCH entry so that you can put this tool to work, follow these steps:

1. **Make sure that you're logged in as root, or use** su **to attain root privileges.**

   You need this level of authority to access everything.

2. **Open** ~/.swatchrc **in your favorite text editor.**

   This is an empty file initially.

3. **Begin all SWATCH entries with either the word ignore or watchfor.**

   Think of this as training a watchdog. Certain things are below the program's notice, so start the line with **ignore**. Others are important to keep an eye out for, so start the line with **watchfor**. This second item is what you use for most of your entries.

4. **Add a space and then a forward slash (/).**

   This starts the section that contains the text that SWATCH needs to watch for.

5. **Type the text that you want SWATCH to keep an eye out for.**

6. **Add another forward slash.**

   This closes the text to watch for section.

7. **Press Enter and then Tab.**

   You're getting ready now to tell SWATCH what to do when it finds what you specified.

8. Choose the actions that you want SWATCH to take.

Table 17-2 outlines the most popular actions that you have available to you. You can use as many actions as you want, but you can have only one per line; otherwise, SWATCH isn't able to use the information properly.

Table 17-2	SWATCH Actions	
Action	*Result*	*Values*
bell	Repeats the line containing the text on your console and then makes a noise to get your attention.	Number of times to make the noise.
echo	Sends a copy of this line on your console, with one or more modifications to get your attention.	One or more of the following specifications: black, blink, blue, bold, cyan, green, inverse, magenta, normal, red, underscore, white, yellow.
exec	Run a command.	The command to run.
mail	Send mail to the specified people containing the lines with the matching text.	E-mail address.

9. If you want to add any more, return to Step 3 and repeat.

10. After you finish, save and exit the file.

Want to see some premade `.swatchrc` files? Look in the directory containing the unpacked SWATCH package where you find a subdirectory called `examples`. Enter this directory and you find example files already in place. You may even want to use one.

Running SWATCH

When you have all your swatch configurations in place, you need to run SWATCH so that it can do its job. Believe it or not, this part is really easy. Just enter the directory containing the unpacked SWATCH package and type **./swatch &**. That's it! The program starts running. It's pretty uninteresting in and of itself because it just sits there while it's keeping an eye on your log files. The & symbol has the program run in the background so you can still use your virtual console's command prompt.

The SWATCH program keeps running until you reboot.

Part V
The Part of Tens

The 5th Wave — By Rich Tennant

"Bill Gates dreams...
*Yes, he sleeps with his glasses on.

JUSTICE DEPT.

"THAT'S RIGHT, MS. BINGAMAN, HE'S COLLECTING A ROYALTY FROM EVERYONE ON EARTH, AND THERE'S NOTHING WE CAN DO ABOUT IT."

In this part . . .

*W*e cover answers to the questions most frequently asked about Linux, explain some key Linux troubleshooting tips and tricks, and show you where the good Linux stuff lives online and in print so that you can continue to educate yourself on this fascinating computing environment. We only hope you enjoy reading this part of the book as much as we enjoyed writing it!

Chapter 18

Ten Questions Most Frequently Asked

*P*art of the Linux mindset is an incredibly strong "do it yourself" attitude. Nevertheless, you may occasionally try doing things yourself and get stuck despite your best efforts. Never fear, help is near! In this chapter, we answer some of the most commonly asked questions about Linux that may help you get unstuck. If you're looking for help on specific troubleshooting issues, turn to Chapters 19 and 20 in which we tackle and point to a plethora of resources that you can consult when it's time to cry Help!

What Is Linux, Anyway?

For the truly uninitiated, Linux is a curious and puzzling phenomenon. The best answer to the question that launches this section is this: Linux is an operating system that you can download for free. Linux also belongs to a vast community of developers working in concert and is no single company's proprietary possession. That's why anybody and everybody — from home-based hobbyists to software professionals — can access the source code for Linux and make changes to that code.

Everything about Linux is out in the open and freely available to anyone who's interested, explaining why Linux is known as an *open source* operating system and called free software. This also explains why companies such as Red Hat, SuSE, Caldera, and many others, can sell and distribute Linux on CD-ROM or across the Internet, and why even those companies must keep the Linux code they offer open for public inspection, comment, and changes.

Linux is an open source version of Unix that started as the brainchild of Linus Torvalds in 1991. At that time, Torvalds was a student at the University of Helsinki, and he began his work by targeting the Intel 80386 PC processor (today, Linux runs on most Intel processors and is one of the most widely ported operating systems for PCs in general). Torvalds sought to create a new version of Unix, so he enlisted the help of a group of programmers to create a new operating system that he named Linux.

Since that time, Linux has grown and evolved substantially. A large cadre of volunteer software developers work on the Linux kernel and use the Internet to share information, coordinate activities, and decide what changes become permanent parts of Linux. Over time, this project has become self-sustaining and self-regulating, to the point where developers manage the responsibility for parts of Linux. If somebody decides they want to leave the project, other developers step in to take over the responsibilities vacated by their departure.

The result is the powerful, robust, and full-featured operating system known as Linux that continues to change and grow, and that is widely available around the world today, on CDs, and over the Internet.

Is Linux Ready for Business Use?

The answer to this question is a resounding yes, if recent marketplace trends and statistics are any indication. Today, Linux is the fastest-growing operating system for servers, and it's making major headway on the desktop. Unlike proprietary operating systems, you can install and upgrade Linux for free. Low cost makes Linux attractive to small businesses that don't have big IT budgets but who must nevertheless use computers as part of their day-to-day activities.

Cost isn't the main factor that makes Linux attractive to business, though. Companies of any size find Linux attractive due to its stability and reliability. Linux can run for months — even years! — without having to be restarted or rebooted. Also, because the source code for Linux is open to the public, bugs get fixed quickly and easily without having to wait for a vendor's next software release cycle to roll around. Linux also runs on just about any kind of computer, including older, outdated PCs, and thereby offers businesses a way to keep their hardware investments working alongside newer, more capable machines.

Linux's flexibility helps to explain why major IT vendors — including IBM, Netscape, Oracle, and Sun — have understood and embraced the benefits of Linux in-house, and why they support Linux-based solutions for their customers. It also helps to explain why major corporations — including Burlington Coat Factory, Sony Electronics, Sallie Mae, and Mercedes-Benz, among many others — have made Linux an important part of their IT infrastructure. The same also goes for a multitude of educational and research institutions around the world, where Unix has long been a key component of their IT infrastructures.

Whether your organization is concerned about cost, reliability, usability, or simply wants to be in good company with other, like-minded organizations, Linux has a role to play in the business world.

Who Distributes Linux?

The short answer to this question — nearly everybody! — is neither precise nor terribly satisfying. So we've provided the names and URLs of the top 14 Linux distribution sites in Table 19-1.

Table 19-1	Where to Find Linux Distributions
Distributor	*Web Site*
Best Linux	www.linux.com/getlinux/pages/bestlinux/
Caldera/OpenLinux	www.linux.com/getlinux/pages/openlinux/
Corel	www.linux.com/getlinux/pages/corel/
Debian	www.linux.com/getlinux/pages/debian/
LuteLinux	www.linux.com/getlinux/pages/lute/

(continued)

Table 19-1 *(continued)*

Distributor	Web Site
Mandrake Linux	`www.linux.com/getlinux/pages/mandrake/`
MkLinux	`www.linux.com/getlinux/pages/mklinux/`
Red Hat	`www.linux.com/getlinux/pages/redhat/`
Slackware	`www.linux.com/getlinux/pages/slackware/`
Stampede	`www.linux.com/getlinux/pages/stampede/`
Storm Linux	`www.linux.com/getlinux/pages/storm/`
SuSE	`www.linux.com/getlinux/pages/suse/`
TurboLinux	`www.turbolinux.com/downloads/`
Yellow Dog Linux	`www.linux.com/getlinux/pages/ydl/`

Note: We point you to the distribution pages at `www.linux.com` rather than the vendor's pages whenever possible because `www.linux.com` is a wonderful clearinghouse for all kinds of Linux information, including an even more comprehensive list of distributions than the one we provide here (in case 14 aren't enough!). Please, check it out!

What Comes with Linux?

Linux is more than just an operating system — it's an entire server and desktop environment, replete with tons of add-ons, GUI tools and interfaces, supplementary programs, and much more. Following is a short list of what ships with Red Hat Linux 7.0 (the version on the CDs included with this book). Although the details vary from distribution to distribution, this hopefully gives you a pretty good idea of what to expect in any version of Linux you download or buy on CD:

- ✔ **File Services:** NFS, Samba
- ✔ **Graphics programs:** GIMP 1.2 (image manipulation, retouching, and paint capabilities)
- ✔ **Mail server software:** SendMail, POP, and IMAP servers
- ✔ **Multimedia tools:** viewers for JPEG, GIF, PNG, TIFF, MPEG, AVI, and QuickTime video

- **Programming tools:** C, C++, FORTRAN, Pascal, assembler, BASIC, perl, python, Tcl/TK, LISP, Scheme, plus a debugger and a memory debugging library
- **Publishing tools:** TeX, LaTeX, groff, plus PostScript, PDF, and DVI viewers
- **X Windows system:** Xfree86 version 4.0.1

Now how much would you pay? Open source means that the price stays the same: Free (if you download the distribution) to reasonable (if you buy a CD).

Can Linux Run with Other Operating Systems?

This question addresses the common need for a computer's ability to boot to two or more operating systems. We're happy to report that the answer to the question that heads this section is of course it can!

The most common operating systems that users want to run on the same machine as Linux are Windows 98, Windows NT, and Windows 2000. In all three cases, the basic approach is the same: Install the other operating system first, make sure it works, then install Linux and make some simple changes to the LILO boot file. Most distribution sites provide detailed instructions on how to do this. For example, the Red Hat Linux FAQs, which cover installation and other general questions, deal directly with these issues. To read all the details, please visit the following Web page:

```
www.redhat.com/support/docs/faqs/rhl_general_faq/FAQ-4.html
```

If you want to run three or more operating systems on a single PC, we recommend that you look into management software designed for that purpose. Most boot management programs that ship with operating systems can handle two operating systems (more, if they're all from the same vendor), but if you want to do some serious mixing and matching, we recommend that you buy a more serious tool to do the job right. Today's best picks in this narrow but crucial product space are as follows:

- **PowerQuest's Partition Magic:** www.powerquest.com
- **Paragon Software's Partition Manager:** www.paragon-gmbh.com/n_pm.htm

Will Linux Work on a Laptop?

Making Linux work on a laptop is a trying, and sometimes chancy, proposition. Even the distribution vendors' technical support Web pages and FAQs shy away from this topic. Instead, nearly everybody points to a single, spectacular resource on the subject: the *Linux Laptop Pages*. If you're aiming to install Linux on a laptop, we suggest that you visit these pages before you even THINK about starting the install process. You can visit this outstanding Web site at `www.cs.utexas.edu/users/kharker/linux-laptop/`. It's a veritable treasure trove of information. Be sure to put it on your hit list!

How Do I Keep Linux Up to Date?

The short answer is: through constant attention and effort. A longer answer to this question requires us to remind you that the answer to most real questions in life is: That depends. What it depends on in this case is the mechanism, or mechanisms, that your distribution site may support. Most such operations post updates and notices to a Web page, assuming that users check the page regularly and take appropriate action when new stuff appears. Other such operations may operate mailing lists for update or new release notification, or they may post such notifications to an appropriate Linux newsgroup.

The thing is, you're going to have to poke around your distribution site to learn how it posts upgrades and where to get them. For Red Hat Linux (the poster child for this book), visit their official update page at `www.redhat.com/errata` to grab the latest and greatest updates. For new releases, you have to poke further around their site on a release-by-release basis. Red Hat also operates a mailing list called `redhat-announce-list` to publicize updates, which you can check at `www.redhat.com/mailing-lists/redhat-announce-list/`.

Arrgh! I Forgot My Root Password — What Do I Do?

Just as money is the root of all evil, the root account holds the keys to the administrative kingdom on any Linux machine. That's why losing or forgetting the password that goes with that account is a real bummer! Fortunately, you don't need to blow the installation away and reinstall to fix this problem.

The following recipe may not work on all versions of Linux. If you try it and it doesn't work for your version, check out the FAQs at your distribution site, or contact your distribution organization's technical support staff. If this happens to you, please accept our sympathy (and apologies).

To insert a new root password, follow these steps:

1. **When the system produces the** `boot:` **prompt that precedes a Linux boot-up, type** linux single **at a command prompt and press Enter.**

2. **At the next prompt, type** passwd root.

   This prompts you for a new root password.

3. **Type in a new password and write it down somewhere safe.**

4. **Now, you can type** shutdown -r now **to shutdown the system immediately.**

   When you restart, you're hopefully able to use your new root password.

This is too easy and makes a strong case for controlling physical access to your Linux machines — especially servers. The frightening part is that *anybody* who can get to the keyboard of a Linux machine can do this and take over root user privileges on that machine. Take steps to keep this from happening to you!

What's the Right Response to the Linux Boot Prompt?

When you start up a Linux machine (especially if that machine runs no other operating systems), you're presented with a prompt that looks like this: `LILO boot::`.

The machine happily waits forever for you to respond at this prompt, and it doesn't continue booting until you tell it what to do next. For normal Linux booting to commence, all you have to do is press the Enter key. After a while (anywhere from 20 seconds to 10 minutes, depending on what kind of PC you've got and what services you're running), you get a login prompt. At that point, you're able to type in an account name and its password and get to work.

Be careful when typing passwords, because they're case-sensitive and must match their definitions exactly.

Don't let the boot prompt slow you down — remember, press the Enter key!

My Screen Goes Blank! What Can I Do?

The first thing that you must do is relax and take a deep breath. Things are running normally, even if you don't like what *normal* means. Fortunately, this situation — which usually reflects a *screen blanker* kicking in or Advanced Power Management (APM) turning off your PC's monitor — is easy to fix.

If you're running a screen saver program, you may want to turn it off. In text mode, the Linux kernel automatically turns on a screen saver unless you enter the following command at the command prompt:

```
Setterm -powersave off -blank 0
```

On the other hand, if you notice that your hard disks and other drives have spun down, APM may be kicking in and disabling your monitor. You can disable APM by logging in to your system as root, typing **ntsysv** at the command prompt, and deselecting APM when the utility opens. When you exit the utility, reboot the system, because APM runs deep in the kernel and can't turn off without a restart.

Of course, if you're running some kind of third-party screen saver program, all you need to do is turn it off or lengthen its blank-out interval. Because we don't know which one you're using, we can't tell you how to change its behavior. We resort to an old standby to tell you what to do: *RTFM* (*R*ead *T*he *F*abulous *M*anual, or help file, or whatever). Good luck!

Chapter 19

Ten Lovely Troubleshooting Tips

*T*roubleshooting is like reading a mystery novel. You have some facts, symptoms, and details, but you don't know who did it. You have to take what information you have, work with it, look at the different possibilities, and then narrow down the possibilities to a single suspect. Then you need to test your theory and prove that your suspect is the actual guilty party.

> *Once you eliminate the impossible, whatever remains, no matter how improbable, must be the truth.*
>
> — Sherlock Holmes (by Sir Arthur Conan Doyle, 1859-1930)

Troubleshooting problems in Linux (or any operating system) can encompass many hardware and software issues. Whether the operating system or the hardware or a service is giving you headaches, the following are some basic troubleshooting techniques that you can start with:

✔ Write down any and all symptoms that the system is experiencing, including what actions you can and can't do. Jot down any information you may see in error messages.

✔ Take a look at the Linux log files. You can find most of these in the /var/log directory.

✔ Compare your problem system with a working system. Sometimes comparing configuration files and settings may reveal the problem or narrow down the possibilities.

✔ Check to make sure all the hardware is connected properly and powered on. Verify that all cables and connections are attached properly and are set at the correct specifications.

✔ Remove any hardware that you've recently changed or added before the problem started and check if the problem disappears. If it does, then you can probably suspect the hardware is the culprit.

✔ Stop unnecessary services and applications that aren't related to the problem at hand. You may easily figure out what's happening if other services and applications aren't getting in the way.

✔ Check whether the problem is reproducible or not. Does the same sequence of events produce the problem? For example, suppose that when you go to print to the color printer, nothing happens. If *every* time you attempt to print, nothing happens, then the problem is reproducible. If, instead, sometimes your information is printed, and other times it isn't, the problem pattern is not the same and is not reproducible. Unfortunately, problems that are non-reproducible are often more difficult to resolve because no set pattern of events re-create the problem.

After you've come up with a solution, take a few moments to document the situation. Note the symptoms of the problem, the cause of the problem, and the solution you implemented. The next time you encounter the same problem, you're able to call upon your notes for a solution instead of reinventing the wheel.

> *Each problem that I solved became a rule, which served afterwards to solve other problems.*
>
> — Rene Descartes (1596-1650), "Discours de la Methods"

If you don't have any problems to troubleshoot (yet), document your environment *before* you do have a problem. You may want to print some of this information, because a future problem may prevent you from accessing your files.

In this chapter, we cover some tips to start with when you encounter a problem with Linux.

> *We all agree that your theory is crazy, but is it crazy enough?*
>
> — Niels Bohr (1885-1962)

Managing Installation Woes

Installing Linux on new hardware can often go without any bumps or bruises. But, even with the latest and greatest hardware, you may still come across some hurdles. If you're having trouble installing Linux and the computer has a functioning operating system already installed, you may be able to use that operating system to document the hardware settings.

Before you install Linux, document your machine's hardware components and settings. This information includes:

- Configuration settings for your various interface cards.

- Interrupts, I/O ports, DMA, and base memory settings.

- Information that you find in the BIOS (Basic Input/Output System), including the drive specifications attached to your IDE channels or SCSI bus.

- The size of your drives, whether they're master or slave for IDE, or the ID numbers if the system is using SCSI. Your system may have both IDE and SCSI, so document both areas.

- Information about your CD-ROM drive and where it's attached. If your system has hardware interface cards and these devices have settings in the BIOS, document that information also.

An area that can give you headaches when installing Linux is video. So many different types of video cards, settings, and monitors are available that if you don't have the right combo, you may not have acceptable resolution and/or color desktop settings. Prior to installing Linux, record the following:

- Your video card/interface brand, model number, memory, and resolution capabilities. Linux can attempt to probe the video card for you, but if it doesn't gather the correct information, the settings may not be appropriate for your hardware.

- Your monitor brand, model, and resolution capabilities. If your monitor isn't on the list of monitors compatible with Linux, determine the monitor or monitors it is equivalent to and use those for your settings.

If your system has the video imbedded in the circuitry of the system or motherboard, be sure to determine the video compatibility. On some imbedded video circuitry, we've seen video probe report configuration information that doesn't match the actual capabilities. In some cases, this difference may be enough to reduce the video to 16 colors and 640 x 480 resolution.

You need to be cautious of hardware labels that include the term *Win* (as in Windows). These components, such as *Winmodem*, are designed for Windows operating systems. Instead of containing all the configuration and software on the hardware, these components are designed to use the Windows operating system to handle some of the load. Only a very slight chance exists that you may be able to find a Linux driver for *Win* hardware. If you do find one, copy it to a floppy *before* installing Linux. If you can't find a driver and you need a modem, put down a little cash and get a real modem.

The default installation mode for some distributions, such as Red Hat, is graphical. Some graphical installations try to determine all of your hardware for you and, if at some point in the installation phase incorrect configuration parameters are applied, your Linux system may be nonfunctional or incomplete when you try to reboot after installation.

If you're having trouble installing Linux in graphical mode, try using text mode (or interface), which doesn't require you to enter command codes but presents the options in text menus that you highlight with the arrow keys and select with the Enter key. The text installation mode usually presents you with more options than the graphical installation mode, so you're able to change the probed settings to match your hardware configuration settings.

If you're still having installation problems, try skipping some of the hardware components at installation time. For example, bypass the network interface card, sound card, and so on. If your installation is successful without these components, then you have a pretty good idea which hardware component or components are giving you problems. You can always go back and add the supporting software pieces for the hardware at a later time.

> *When ideas fail, words come in very handy.*
>
> — Goethe (1749-1832)

If you're encountering problems installing a software package or application, make sure you've read the installation and/or readme notes. Some software packages depend on the existence of other software components. The installation notes include these requirements and often indicate where you can locate and/or download the additional software components.

When you're installing Linux or applications, pay attention to disk space. If you encounter a disk full error when installing, you need to change the size of the partition or move existing directories and files to other partitions.

Conquering Configuration Problems

When configuring your Linux machine, you may encounter problems with the /etc/lilo.conf file. This file indicates the operating system or systems that your system can boot to and some Linux startup settings. Linux is capable of booting from any of your hard drives — not just the master IDE drive on the primary IDE channel. Consider the following when this file gives you trouble:

- ✔ If you've altered or added hard drives, you may need to change the boot line in the /etc/lilo.conf file.

- ✔ If you haven't made hardware changes, check to make sure that your lilo.conf file is referring to the correct location of the Linux image.

- ✔ If the location under the /boot directory or the device for the root entry is incorrect, your system isn't able to boot to Linux. In this situation, your rescue or emergency disk is helpful. See Chapter 5 for instructions on how to create a rescue disk.

- ✔ If you're working with a multiboot operating system environment, check that your /etc/lilo.conf file contains entry stanzas for each of your operating systems. Each operating system or Linux installation needs to be in a separate stanza.

- ✔ If your file contains entries to switch to a higher resolution display but you're having boot problems, try reducing the video setting to simple VGA.

When you modify the /etc/lilo.conf file, don't forget to run LILO at a command prompt. If you forget to do this, your changes to /etc/lilo.conf aren't applied and your system startup doesn't change.

Before you change configuration settings, look for the current environment settings in the /proc directory. Here you find files that contain information about the current hardware and configuration settings. For example, take a look at the following files in the /proc directory:

- ✔ interrupts — lists used/detected interrupts in use

- ✔ cpuinfo — indicates CPU vendor, model, speed, and other CPU features

- ✔ ioports — lists used/detected IO port values in use

- ✔ modules — lists the loaded modules

- ✔ meminfo — reports the amount of the physical memory, swap area(s), free memory, and other memory-related values

- ✔ partitions — displays the partitions and information for each storage device

- ✔ mounts — indicates the volumes currently mounted and their file system type and status

Linux allows you to use spaces and other characters in filenames that you may or may not be able to use in other operating systems. Some Linux applications may *stumble,* however, when they encounter file or directory names containing spaces. Usually, a safe bet is to stick with alphanumeric characters and avoid spaces and odd characters, such as question marks, exclamations points, and so on.

Perfecting Printing

Most Linux distributions include a printer configuration tool called printtool. This utility enables you to select the printer type, the name of the printer device, and its location. From this information, printtool creates the /etc/printcap file, which contains the print configuration information. The syntax of the /etc/printcap file is *strict* and if you aren't familiar with the syntax, /etc/printcap can be confusing. If you're having trouble printing from one system, check out the /etc/printcap file of a working system.

If you were able to print earlier to your network printer, haven't made any changes, and can't print now, try using the ping utility to see if you can access the printer. You may want to use the Internet Protocol (IP) number of the printer rather than its Domain Name System (DNS) name, so as not to complicate matters with a possible DNS error if a DNS problem exists.

If you can reach the printer by its IP number, check to make sure lpd is running. If this isn't running on the system hosting the printer and/or the system trying to access the printer, the file won't print. You can use the printtool utility to restart the application or lpc from the command prompt.

If lpd is running and the /etc/printcap file isn't at fault, you can contact the network printer by its IP number; take a look at the print queue and see if your print files are *stuck* in the print queue. Use the lpq command to assist in this process. In Chapter 13, we cover these various printer utilities. You can use the line printer control program, lpc, to disable or enable printers and queues, reorder print jobs in the queue, start and stop print services, and other tasks. The man page for lpc is a good starting point for using lpc.

Nipping Network Troubles in the Bud

If you aren't able to configure your network card on your system, verify the hardware settings for your card. Linux is pretty good at detecting most common network cards from different vendors, including older models. This isn't always true, however, during the installation process. You may need to specify the network card driver and settings after the system is installed and is up and running.

When you're experiencing network problems, consider the following points:

- ✔ If you run `ifconfig` (one of the best tools for determining your network card configuration) and only see the output for `lo` (loopback), Linux isn't using your network card.

- ✔ If you see an entry for `eth0` for Ethernet systems, this is a pretty good indication that Linux recognizes your network card.

- ✔ If your network card is recognized but you can't do anything on your network, make sure you have a valid IP number and subnet mask for your network.

- ✔ If you're using Dynamic Host Configuration Protocol (DHCP) and `ifconfig` shows the IP address for `eth0` as `0.0.0.0`, your system didn't get an IP number and, therefore, can't communicate.

- ✔ If you need to use your system before addressing the DHCP issue, manually enter a valid, non-conflicting IP number and subnet mask for your network. If you can then access the network, you need to look at either the DHCP server and its settings or why your system is unable to obtain an address.

- ✔ If your system has the proper configuration settings, use the `ping` application to try pinging other systems on your network. You may want to use the IP numbers of the other systems instead of their DNS names. If another problem with name resolution is lurking and you use DNS names, you may complicate your troubleshooting.

- ✔ If your system *can* access other systems on your network but can*not* access the Internet or another network, make sure the system has a gateway IP address specified. The gateway, or router address, tells your system where to go when it encounters a reference to an IP address outside your network.

- ✔ If you have the gateway IP number set but can't get to the *outside,* make sure you can `ping` the gateway address. If you can't `ping` the gateway number, then you aren't able to go outside your network.

The IP configuration and/or related applications files on your system can also potentially cause problems if they become corrupted. To check, type **ping localhost** at a command prompt.

If this command fails, the problem is probably one of the IP component files. To correct this, you need to replace the files with a known good copy from another source. If you can `ping` your machine's IP number but not another machine, then you may have an incorrect or misconfigured network card driver.

Making Maintenance Work for You

One of the best maintenance processes is to properly shut down or restart the Linux system. If you just turn the power off, you don't allow the operating system to save or close any open files, update log files, and so on. Most distributions have a shutdown or restart application in the X Window System. Also, most support the same processes through command-prompt entries. The following shows a few examples:

```
shutdown -h now
shutdown -r now
reboot
CTRL+ALT+DEL key sequence
```

In Chapter 5, we discuss the importance of following proper shutdown procedures.

Finally, make sure to update your system. If you installed Linux five years ago, the kernel probably isn't current. Most distributions contain update packages or Web site information for getting updates.

Backing Up to Move Forward with Confidence

The hardware in your Linux systems *will* fail! Unfortunately, you have no way of knowing *when*. If you're using older hard drives or you've been running your Linux system on the same hardware for the last five years, don't be surprised if a hard drive fails, or the power supply fails, or some other hardware piece falls by the wayside. Thus, we recommend that you place a current copy of your critical information and/or files on removable media and store these files in a safe place.

Linux has always provided a mechanism to back up files to tape and then restore the information. The *interface,* however, isn't all that intuitive and is setup and initiated at the command prompt. You may want to investigate other backup programs that provide a friendlier interface and more options. You can get information about *Amanda*, a common backup program, at `www.amanda.org`.

After you back up your files onto tape or other removable media, make sure you store the backup at a location other than where the Linux systems reside. A major cause of data loss isn't necessarily due to human error but from events such as earthquakes, floods, and so on. If you keep the backup tapes in the same room or vicinity as the Linux systems, the backups may also suffer the same natural disaster damage as your Linux computers — leaving you stuck with no backup at all.

For online fault tolerance of your storage system, Linux supports RAID (*R*edundant *A*rray of *I*nexpensive *D*isks). Most RAID systems use SCSI storage architecture. You can get more information about Linux and RAID with your distribution's HOWTO files and other sources available on the Internet.

Stopping Scripting Screw-ups

A script contains a series of commands collected to perform some task (usually repeatedly) that saves you from typing all the commands at a prompt one line at a time. If you're having trouble with a script, consider the following:

- ✔ Make sure spelling or syntax errors aren't causing the problems. Remember, most things in Linux are case sensitive, so a simple slip of the Shift key may make an entire script nonfunctional.

- ✔ If your script contains several sections to perform different tasks, try commenting out all lines except for one task. If the script then works for the task specified, then uncomment out one line at a time and run the script between each edit. When you encounter your first error, you probably have a good idea on what line the error occurred and where to make the appropriate correction.

- ✔ Start simple when you're writing a script from scratch. Make sure the script works before you start doing *fancy* stuff. If your recent addition causes the script to fail, then you know where the problem resides.

- ✔ Verify the content of any variables your script may be dependent on. Use the echo statement in the script to display the contents of the variables you're using. You may need to use the echo command at several places in your script so that you can watch what's happening to the value of the variables.

For more information about scripts, see Bonus Appendix D on CD3. For more on variables, see Chapter 11.

Saving System Security

One of the most important security things that you must remember is: DO NOT LOG IN AS ROOT. If you need to perform a task that needs this type of permission and you're already logged in using your account, use the su command to temporarily gain access as root. When you complete doing the task that requires the root account, use exit to go back to the current user account.

The following are other considerations that you need to keep in mind regarding security:

- ✔ Make sure that your user accounts require passwords.
- ✔ Utilize file system security to restrict access to specific files or directories.
- ✔ Put a firewall between your network and the *outside* if your network is interfacing another network over which you don't have control. You can find many good references on the Internet for configuring Linux as a firewall.
- ✔ Use the w command to determine who is actually attached to your system and what resources they're using. Here you may find unwanted users, or notice that an account has been logged in for an unusually long period of time.
- ✔ Be aware of security holes in Linux (or any operating system). You can usually find good documentation and discussions regarding security issues in some of the larger online Linux forums.
- ✔ Check out the SANS (*S*ystem *A*dministration, *N*etworking, and *S*ecurity) Institute, which maintains information about most operating systems and potential areas where security can be compromised. Go to www.sans.org and take a look at their Web site. You can also add yourself to an e-mail list that sends out weekly security summary reports.
- ✔ Go to www.bastille-linux.org for information about a current Linux project that's striving to identify and *fix* Linux so that it's an even more secure operating system.

Tuning In to Performance Problems

The amount of physical memory and swap space you're using may affect performance. If you have a fast CPU and lots of disk space but very little memory, your system may suffer. Make sure you have sufficient physical memory to handle the services.

If your Linux system is starting to use more swap space, your disk systems may begin to *thrash*. Thrashing occurs when your machine can accomplish nothing else but moving innards around on the hard drive.

Take a look at your boot scripts and make sure you aren't loading unused services when you start up the Linux system. You can typically find boot scripts in subdirectories below the /etc/rc.d directory.

The top command is a good utility for observing the Linux system's memory usage, CPU info, and which applications are using the most resources. Other useful utilities include free, which displays the amount of free and used memory, and df, which reports disk space usage. See Bonus Appendix D for more information on monitoring system resources.

Improving Internet Access

To improve your Internet access, you can look at several things that don't involve Linux. Check your local area for broadband or high-speed services. Linux works with many common broadband systems, such as cable modems and digital satellites. Because a lot of these technologies are recent or evolving, probably your best source for more information is the Internet.

A Linux solution that can help improve your access is to set up a *caching proxy server,* which caches or stores in memory Web pages you've visited and, in most cases, also stores a copy on the local hard drive. This allows faster display of the Web page because pulling the file from memory is a lot faster than accessing the same file again on the Internet.

One caching proxy server to investigate and possibly use is *Squid.* The *Apache Web server* can also be used as a caching proxy server.

I have not failed. I've just found 10,000 ways that won't work.

— Thomas Alva Edison (1847-1931)

Chapter 20

Ten Superior Sources of Linux Information

*L*inux isn't just an online phenomenon itself (in fact, it's one of the few major league operating systems that you can download from the Internet for free); it's also the stuff of which Internet infrastructure is made. For that reason, it comes as no surprise that more good information about Linux is available online than you could ever encompass, even with an extra lifetime or two. That's why we had such a hard time coming up with the ten best Linux resources for this chapter. That's also why we cheated — the last section is a grab bag that contains more good Internet stuff than we could cover in the first nine entries!

The Best Ever Linux Resource

It's funny that we had trouble picking only ten Linux resources; if we had to pick only *one*, www.linux.com is it, the ideal general starting place for any Linux-related investigation. This site is a treasure trove and includes a great search engine, plus a broad range of useful Linux information, downloads, pointers, and documentation. For example, when we went looking for sources of Linux distributions for Chapter 18, we quickly figured out that it was easier to go through www.linux.com to get to all of the key sites than to visit each vendor or organization, one at a time!

Keeping the Bad Guys at Bay

Although plenty of security-related sites and information are available on the Web, we were hard-pressed to find a site that approached this important topic from a Linux point of view. Then we came across the Linux Security homepage at http://stjohnchico.org/~jtmurphy/.

This is the only all-Linux security site we've found online, but that doesn't mean it's lacking in any way. Here, you'll find lots of information about Linux-specific security matters, with pointers to Linux information on all the good general security sites online. Exhaustive, exhausting, and worthwhile!

The Kernel's at Linux Headquarters

Linux headquarters operates a kernel-focused (or should we say, obsessed?) Web site at www.linuxhq.com/. In addition to providing pointers to information, downloads, patches, CHANGES files, and more, for two versions of the Linux stable kernel (what ordinary mortals use) and one version of the developer's kernel (what hackers and demigods use), this site also has pointers to all kinds of additional information. This includes a great list of Linux distributions, information about kernel programming, Linux vendors, and a whole lot more. If you want to open the hood on Linux and start rooting around, this is a great site to add to your toolbox.

Everything Linux

How can you go astray at a site named "Everything Linux"? Easy — you may not exactly go astray, but you'll find enough interesting stuff to distract you from your task at hand that you may find yourself looking blearily up at the clock at 3 a.m. and asking yourself "Where did the time go?" This site is accessible in two flavors, with or without HTML frames:

With frames: `www.eunuchs.org/linux/frames.html`

Unframed: www.eunuchs.org/linux/noframes.shtml

Here, you'll find news, reviews, and opinions about Linux topics, along with pointers to most of the good Linux stuff on the Web (including, not coincidentally, all the other stuff that appears in this chapter).

Who GNU Linux?

`GNULinux.com`, another great general-purpose Linux Web site, has a great news corner, all kinds of online forums, information aimed specifically at newbies (new users), a superb collection of help guides and product reviews, and a wonderful collection of Linux miscellany. Stop here for some of the best information about how to work Linux for video and sound, manage your Internet configuration, and dual- or multiboot your Linux system with all the major operating systems, and some interesting minor ones, too! Visit the home page at `www.gnulinux.com/`.

Lifelong Learning Includes Linux

`Learnlots.com` is a source for online tutorials of all kinds, but its Linux tutorials make it particularly worth a visit for readers of this book. You'll find a plethora of tip-top Linux tutorials at `www.learnlots.com/linux.cfm`. Linux tutorials available here cover everything from the operating system itself to the many add-on tools and subsystems that so many distributions include (and so many users use, of course).

Peerless Linux Publications Online

As with everything else about Linux, there's no shortage of online newsletters, magazines, and other periodical sources of information. Here's our short list of the best ones, purely for your perusal:

- ✔ *The Linux Gazette*: A monthly online Linux-focused publication that's also part of the Linux Documentation Project (LDP), this magazine includes lots of timely, useful information, and a plethora of pointers to other Linux information online.

    ```
    www.linuxgazette.com/
    ```

- ✔ *Linux Journal*: Another monthly Linux publication that's available in print as well as online. Published by SSC, this magazine includes information about Linux distributions, product reviews, industry news, and other cool stuff.

    ```
    www2.linuxjournal.com/
    ```

- ✔ *LinuxWorld*: A monthly Linux-focused publication from IDG that focuses more on industry news, activities, and product reviews than the others, in the form of a more mainstream "trade rag." Still worth reading, though!

    ```
    www.linuxworld.com/
    ```

- ✔ For another handful of interesting online Linux publications, check the list of Linux publications at:

    ```
    www.wildcard.demon.co.uk/nodes/Linux+Publications.html
    ```

Supporting Linux Online

Linuxcare is a professional, for-profit organization devoted to Linux training, technical support, and information sharing. If you need serious professional Linux help, you need LinuxCare. In addition to for-a-fee information and services, you find plenty of free white papers and other good stuff on this site. Visit this excellent outfit at `www.linuxcare.com/`.

Slashdot: The Crème de la Nerd

The subtitle for this Web site, "News for Nerds," says it all; Slashdot is a Web site for Linux bigots by Linux bigots about deeply technical subjects of all kinds, some more related to Linux than others, but all weirdly fascinating. All your authors insisted that this site be included in our list, and none of them can explain why. If you come up with a good, inarguable reason — please, tell us what it is (our e-mail addresses are listed in the author bios in the front matter of this book)! Visit the Slashdot site at `http://slashdot.org/`.

More Tips Off the Linux Berg

We've had the devil's own time closing in on only *ten* top Linux resources online. That's why we cheated and turned this last one into a grab bag of additional Web sites, newsgroups, and even some information about updating Red Hat Linux (otherwise, we'd be neglecting our book's poster child — Red Hat Linux 7 — after all).

Web sites

The following are Web sites that didn't quite fit into any of the other sections in this chapter, but their rich and useful content merits special attention. Be sure to visit these sites while exploring Linux information online:

- ✔ `www.linuxdoc.org`: The Linux Documentation Project is a great bookmark for your browser. You'll find yourself returning often when trying to find specific answers, or even just to browse for topics of interest. The LDP contains several types of documentation, including full-length books, HOWTO documents, FAQs, and much, much more.

- ✔ `http://support.redhat.com`: This is Red Hat's support forum where you'll find a wealth of Linux support information, albeit with a strong Red Hat flavor. In addition to errata and update information on specific versions of Red Hat, you'll also find tutorials to help you configure additional services on your Red Hat Linux computer.

- ✔ `http://freshmeat.net`: Do you ever feel left out while your cronies yak about the newest Linux software or latest version releases? Now you can keep up with a healthy daily serving of bug fixes, new software releases, announcements, commentary, and a comprehensive index of all known Linux software. Freshmeat is a staple for the *release early, release often* hackers so prevalent in the open source community.

Newsgroups

Newsgroups are online discussion groups in which people read and post messages to one another on specific topics. The Internet currently hosts over 80,000 newsgroups, with more being introduced daily.

Deja.com's Usenet Discussion Service (`www.deja.com/usenet`) is the largest discussion archive on the Internet. You can search and browse Usenet (newsgroup) discussions and other public online forums with a single simple search. This is a great place to start looking for technical support or information or to locate discussion groups that reflect your interests.

See if you can pick out the newsgroup from the following list that appeals broadly to Linux lovers everywhere, but that has nothing to do with Linux *per se* (Hint: "Thank ya. Thank ya vurry much!").

- `comp.os.linux.advocacy`: Updates you on what kinds of products and services are new and interesting.

- `comp.os.linux.hardware`: Keeps you informed on what's going on with Linux hardware and computers.

- `comp.os.linux.misc`: Lets you know what's happening with all kinds of miscellaneous Linux topics.

- `comp.os.linux.networking`: Tells you what's going on in the wonderful world of Linux networking.

- `alt.elvis.sighting`: Keeps you up-to-date on the current and past activities of that hunka burnin' love.

Keeping Your System Up-to-date

Red Hat Linux 7 includes a utility called the Update Agent that enables you to install new packages as they become available, directly from Red Hat. It also enables you to refresh installed software with the latest enhancements and bug fixes. To run the Update Agent, click the Footprint icon in GNOME and choose Programs⇨System⇨Update Agent.

When you register your Red Hat installation at `www.redhat.com/now`, you're issued a username and password that you must use to configure the Update Agent.

Part VI
Appendixes

The 5th Wave   By Rich Tennant

"Sure, at first it sounded great — an intuitive network adapter that helps people write memos by finishing their thoughts for them."

In this part . . .

The Appendixes in this part are multifarious and magnificent. In Appendix A, you find a comprehensive list of Linux commands, with explanations and syntax details. Appendix B provides a glossary to help explain and defuse all the items of techno-babble that we were unable to avoid throughout the rest of the book. To close out this show, Appendix C details the contents of the CD-ROMs that accompany this book.

These appendixes are like the instructions that come with a Christmas present for your kids (or yourself, who knows . . .): you don't always have to read them, but they're handy to have around should you ever need 'em! Just remember, when it comes to a Linux system of your very own, "some assembly is required!" Have fun!

Appendix A

Common Linux Commands

C omputing novices often marvel at the keyboard dance that the Linux expert typically performs. The expert does know about modern technological advances such as the mouse and graphical interface but these keyboard musicians prefer the home keys and know that they can get some serious work done during the latency that normally occurs while reaching for the pointing device. This takes some proficiency in typing and also requires some familiarity with the variety of levers in the GNU toolbox.

We've divided this appendix into two sections. We categorize a slew of commands to help you zero in on the right tool for the job in the first section. And in the second section, we provide an alphabetic reference of the previously categorized commands.

So read on . . . and dazzle your friends with your command-prompt finesse. When they ask you how and where you figured out all those commands, just smile and mumble something about the voices in your head . . . and of course, keep this section dog-eared and within reach of your computer.

Command Cliques

You can categorize commands into *function groups*. Often, you need reference to a command to perform a specific operation and an alphabetic list or search of all commands may be tedious and time consuming. By grouping commands, you may be introduced to a similar command to perform the operation that you need.

Archiving/compression

Although disk space isn't as much of a premium as it once was, bandwidth and backup media still are. Subsequently, this group provides a potpourri of tools for compacting and organizing data for storage.

```
ar, bzip2, compress, cpio, dump, gunzip, gzexe, gzip,
        restore, tar, uncompress, unzip, zcat, zcmp, zip
```

bash built-in commands

A few of the commands appear to have a phantom existence. In other words, if you search through your search $PATH, they likely don't appear anywhere in your file system. Remember that, as you type commands at the prompt, you're communicating with a program that's written to understand certain keywords. These keywords or commands, included in the following list, are actually built in to the shell program.

```
alias, bg, cd, export, fg, history, jobs, logout, set,
        source, test, umask, unalias, unset
```

Note that if you use a shell other than bash, these bash commands may not be available.

```
apropos, man, manpath, whatis, whereis, which
```

Locating details about command-prompt options of a command is a never-ending pursuit. The man page system provides some helpful guides at your fingertips for rapidly finding this detailed information.

Communication

As a system administrator, you find these utilities useful for providing infor-mation about your users and communicating with them.

```
finger, wall, write
```

Files/file system

File organization

Boxing, packing, sorting, shipping . . . we're always shuffling files around on our system. File organization commands provide tools for moving files and file system units around.

```
cp, dd, dir, ln, mkdir, mv, pwd, rename, rm, rmdir, shred
```

File attributes

Files are a lot like candy bars. The wrapper provides information about the ingredients, size, package date, and so on — all descriptive of the tasty nugget inside. (Perhaps the wrapper is even child proofed.) Files keep all this wrapper information in an *inode.* Along with the capability to change file inode information, these commands also can return information about the actual content of the file.

```
chage, chattr, chgrp, chmod, chown, file, stat, sum, touch,
        wc
```

File filters

A file filter enables you to dump in one file and output a processed result. To sort the contents of the password file alphabetically, for example, you can type the command `sort /etc/passwd`. Listed here are a few of the tools available for mulching data into something meaningful.

```
cmp, colrm, column, comm, csplit, cut, iff, diff3, expand,
        fmt, fold, join, look, merge, paste, rev, sort,
        split, strings, tac, tr, unexpand, uniq, uuencode,
        uudecode
```

File locators

Where, oh, where can my file be? These commands help you locate files in Linux's monster tree-structure file system.

```
find, locate, updatedb
```

File utilities that deserve their own category

Although some may argue that these are *just commands,* others can argue that the ceiling of the Sistine Chapel is *just a painting.* Although these commands sport short names, nothing's simple or powerless about them. These are industrial-strength data-manipulation tools. You need just a few minutes to get the basics but a lifetime to master the tools. If you manage the ability to wrangle these beauties, you achieve respected geek status.

```
convert, gawk, grep, sed
```

File Viewers

File browsing is a favorite pastime of many a system user. These tools provide a variety of utilities for viewing the contents of readable files of all sizes. Unlike using a full-screen editor, you cannot damage the contents of a file with these as they're read-only tools.

```
cat, head, less, more, tail
```

Miscellaneous file commands

These file commands don't seem to fit into any other category.

```
basename, dircolors, hexdump, newer, nl, od, patch, test, xxd
```

Wholesale file system commands

Commands that provide information or perform action on the entire file system, from creation, to tuning, to repair and recovery. Some of these commands return information only while others also provide you with surgical instruments for the serious file-system hacker.

```
badblocks, debugfs, dumpe2fs, e2fsck, e2label, fdformat,
        fsck, mkfs, df, du, ls, lsattr, mount, quota,
        quotacheck, quotaon, resize2fs, sync, tune2fs,
        umount
```

Miscellaneous

The leftovers — we can't classify these commands anywhere else.

```
cal, clear, dc, echo, eject, expr, oclock, openvt, resize,
        script, tee, toe, unbuffer
```

mtools

The mtools suite of utilities provides a nice way to transfer information to your Microsoft friends. Although Linux has native support for Microsoft Windows/DOS file systems, your Microsoft cohorts don't have access to

Linux (ext2) file systems. To keep everyone happy, just utilize the preformatted MS-DOS diskettes with the mtools commands and keep everyone exchanging files.

```
mcat, mcd, mcopy, mdel, mdeltree, mdir, mdu, mformat, mlabel,
        mmd, mmount, mmove
```

Printing

The printing system is the combination of programs that handle the routing of data from you to the printer. These commands enable you to add, verify, and remove print jobs from the queue.

```
cancel, lp, lpq, lpr, lprm, lpstat, lptest, pr
```

System control

These commands provide system-wide information and control. Many commands can be run by normal users of the system to obtain system information; however, those commands that actively change the configuration of the system need to run while you're logged in as root.

Kernel module handling

You may sometimes need to add kernel support for an additional device (software or hardware). If this need arises, you have limited choices: You can either rebuild the kernel or install a loadable kernel module. Although rebuilding a kernel doesn't exactly require a Ph.D. in nuclear science, consider it a time-consuming nuisance that's best to avoid. The following commands enable you to include the kernel support you need while the system is running.

```
depmod, insmod, lsmod, modprobe, rmmod
```

Processes

Most of your system activity requires processes. Even when your system appears idle, a dozen or so processes are running in the background. These commands enable you to check under the hood to make sure that everything that needs to be running is running and you're not overheating or overtaxing resources.

```
at, atq, batch, crontab, env, fuser, kill, killall, nice,
        pidof, pkill, ps, pstree, renice, sleep, top,
        usleep, watch
```

System action commands

System action commands provide tools for controlling your host. Rather than getting or setting information your host may need, these commands incite your system to action.

```
dhcpcp, halt, kbdrate, logger, mesg, mkbootdisk, poweroff,
        reboot, sash, setleds, setterm, shutdown, stty,
        tset, tzselect
```

System information

System information command tools are for setting and/or checking your host configuration. These are a few *doctor* tools for probing and prodding your system for vital statistics. The command `uptime`, for example, tells you how long your system's been running since last time you booted it.

```
arch, date, ddate, fgconsole, free, hostid, hostname, hdparm,
       hwclock, ifconfig, kernelversion, netstat
       printenv, route, runlevel, tty, uname, uptime,
       vmstat
```

Users/groups

Who are the people in your neighborhood and what are they doing? These commands enable you to change user profiles and provide specific information about your system users.

```
checkalias, chfn, chsh, faillog, gpasswd, groups, id, last,
        lastlog, listalias, mkpasswd, mktemp, newalias,
        newaliases, newgrp, passwd, su, users, uuidgen, w,
        who, whoami
```

Linux Command Reference, Alphabetic Style

Each command in the following list provides the command name, a short description, and, in many cases, an example of usage if the syntax is ambiguous. Please keep in mind that this is *not* a comprehensive listing of available commands nor does it provide you *all* the usage options available. To determine detailed usage of a particular command, view the man or info page . . . but you already knew that, right?

Note: Some commands are for system administration and may require you to log in with a full root environment.

A

alias (alias [-p] [*name*...]): Provide information about the aliases currently defined as well as the command for assigning shell aliases.

apropos (apropos keyword...): Find man pages containing a keyword in the description field. Returns the same information as the man -k command.

ar (ar [*options*] [*membername*] *archive files*...): GNU archive program that enables you to create, modify, and extract files in an archive (a single file that contains many other files).

arch (arch): Display the CPU architecture. Results may be i386, i486, i586, alpha, sparc, arm, m68k, mips, and ppc. The arch command is the same as the uname -m command.

at (at [*options*] *TIME*; at -c job [job...]): Queue jobs for later execution. You can specify an absolute time in the future to execute one or more commands or specify a relative time to the current time or a time in the future to execute your jobs.

atq (atq [*options*]): Examine jobs queued for later execution with the at command.

B

badblocks (badblocks [*options*] *device block-counts*): Search a disk partition for disk locations that are physically incapable of reliably storing data.

basename (basename *name* [*suffix*]): Strip leading or trailing information from a fully qualified pathname. In other words, basename just returns the actual file name rather than the full pathname.

batch (batch [*options*]): Execute jobs when load level permits. For busy hosts, this enables you to submit your job in a kindly manner, simply asking the host to process your request when it's a little less burdened.

bg ([CTRL]-Z; bg): (bash built-in) Submit a suspended job that the shell is performing into the background.

bzip2 (bzip2 [*options*] [*filenames*...]): Compression utility, newer and more efficient than gzip, that uses the Burrows-Wheeler block-sorting text-compression algorithm and Huffman coding.

C

cal (cal [*options*] [*month* [*year*]]): Display a calendar to the screen. By default, it displays the current month's calendar, but a few command-prompt options provide you with a rich set of calendar options.

cancel (cancel [*options*] *request-id*): Cancel a print job for a system using the LPRng printer suite. This works similar to the lprm command and uses the same options.

cat (cat [*file...*]): Concatenate files to stdout. In simpler terms, this displays the contents of a file, or any other standard input, to the standard output device.

cd (cd; cd /*directory...*): (bash built-in) Enables you to travel throughout your file system hierarchy. Changes the current working directory.

chage (chage [options] user): The System Administrator uses this to change user password expiration parameters. You can change the number of days between required password changes for the user.

chattr (chattr *files...*): Alter the behavior of files by changing default attributes on an ext2 file system. Note that some of these attribute changes are not supported until the release of the ext3 file system.

checkalias (checkalias *alias, alias, ...*): Check for a currently defined alias. *Note:* This refers to e-mail aliases, not shell aliasing.

chfn (chfn [*options*]): Enables the user to change the personal information in the /etc/passwd field that the finger utility reports from. Four fields are prompted for: Name, Office, Office Phone, and Home Phone.

chgrp (chgrp [*options*] *group file...*): The System Administrator uses this to change the primary group ownership of a file.

chmod chmod [*options*] *mode file...*): The owner of a file, or root user, can use this to change the permissions of a file. The utility accepts the symbolic mode or octal mode for permission assignment. All levels of permission, (**R**ead **W**rite e**X**ecute), may be set for User (owner), **G**roup, and/or **O**ther.

chown (chown [*options*] *file...*): Command to change file and/or group ownership of a file. Only the root user may change ownership of a file.

chsh (chsh [*options*]): Change the default login shell for a user account. The /etc/passwd file is updated with the selected shell.

clear (clear): Clear the terminal screen, if possible.

cmp (cmp [*options*] *file1 file2* [*skip1* [*skip2*]]): Compare the content of two files. If files are identical, the command returns nothing. If a difference exists, however, cmp exits and reports the line and byte number where the first difference occurred.

colrm (colrm [*startcol* [*endcol*]]): Remove text columns from standard input. Each character in the input line is considered a separate column.

column (column [*options*] [*file...*]): Filter used to create columnar lists from input. Lists can be filled row first or column first.

comm (comm [*options*] *file1 file2*): Compare two sorted files line by line. Matching lines are indented while nonmatches are staggered in the left margin, indicating a difference in the line.

compress (compress [*options*] [*name...*]): Reduce the size of the named files utilizing compression. If successful, the file(s) is compressed and renamed with a .Z extension.

convert (convert [*options*]): Powerful command-prompt utility that converts an image type from one format to another.

cp (cp [*options*] *source dest*): Copy files and directories.

cpio (cpio [*options*]): Copy files to and from archives. Inode information is kept intact with each archived file.

crontab (crontab *file*-u *user*; crontab [*option*] *user*): Program to maintain process schedule lists for recurring processes. Normally, the System Administrators use this command, although individual users can also maintain their own process schedule table.

csplit (csplit [*options*] *file pattern...*): Split one file into multiple files. Use line numbers or string matches to determine separation point(s) of original file content.

cut (cut [*options*] [*file...*]): Extract sections from each line of a file or standard input.

D

date (date [*options*]): Display or set the system date and time.

dc (dc): Reverse-polish desk calculator that provides unlimited precision arithmetic. The on-line version of those calculators that have an *enter* key rather than an *equals* key.

dd (dd [*options*]): The disk duplicator is used as a low-level copy utility that can duplicate entire devices without regard to the contents. It can also perform EBCDIC to ASCII conversion.

ddate (ddate [+*format*] [*date*]): Converts Gregorian dates to Discordian dates. You know . . . like the number 23?

debugfs (debugfs [*options*]): The do-it-yourself ext2 file system surgery kit, for when fsck just isn't enough to repair your file system.

depmod (depmod [*options*]): Create a dependency list to ensure that the command modprobe can load the kernel modules in the correct order. Some loadable modules require supporting modules to be loaded prior.

df (df [*options*]): Display used and available disk space for all currently mounted file system volumes.

dhcpcd (dhcpcd): Gather assigned TCP/IP information from a network DHCP server and configure the local network interface.

diff (diff [*options*] *from-file to-file*): Compare the contents of two files and display lines that are different.

diff3 (diff3 [*options*] *mine older yours*): Compare the contents of *three* files and display lines that are different.

dir (dir): List files in a directory. Slightly less cryptic than the ls command for those trying to break the DOS habit.

dircolors (dircolors [*options*]): Set or display the filename colors for ls output. Color may be set to recognize file extension or type.

du (du [*options*] *directory*): Report the number of disk blocks each file is consuming. Command-prompt option provides report in *bytes* as well.

dump (dump [*options*] *directory*): Utility used to back up an ext2 volume. Provides for nine levels of incremental backup and can divide the backup content across multiple media.

dumpe2fs (dumpe2fs *device*): Display detailed information about an ext2 volume.

E

e2fsck (e2fsck [*options*] *device*): Check and optionally repair a damaged ext2 volume.

e2label (e2label device [*new-label*]): Display or change the label on an ext2 volume.

echo (echo [*options*]): Display a line of text to standard output.

eject (eject [*options*]): Command-prompt instruction to open the CD-ROM drive caddy or eject the media in a ZIP or JAZ device.

env (env [*options*]): Run a program in a modified environment. Create and assign environment variables for one execution of a command.

expand (expand [*options*] [*file...*]): Convert tabs to spaces in a file or standard input and write to standard output.

export (export variable-name): (bash built-in) Designate that all subshells and subshell processes receive a copy of the variable automatically.

expr (expr *expression...*): Evaluate comparison or mathematical expressions. Prints the result of the expression to standard output.

F

faillog (faillog [*options*]): Set login failure configuration and reports on user login failure. Only reports unsuccessful logins.

fdformat (fdformat [*options*] *device*): Perform a low-level format on a floppy disk.

fg (fg [*job or process*]): (bash built-in) Internal shell function to bring a background process into the foreground.

fgconsole (fgconsole): Display number of active virtual consoles.

file (file [*options*] *file...*): Perform several tests to determine file type. Handy for verifying that a file is ASCII before it appears on-screen.

find (find [*path...*] [*expression*]): Search all branches of a given point in the file system hierarchy for files matching a provided regular expression.

finger (`finger` `[options]` `[user]` `[user@host...]`)**:** Utility for finding registration information about a user, such as login name, real name, terminal name, phone number, login status, and so on.

fmt (`fmt` `[options]` `[file...]`)**:** Simple text processor used to globally format text. Can perform functions such as remove multiple spaces between words.

fold (`fold` `[options]` `[file...]`)**:** Wrap each input line to a specified width. Handy for changing the margins in text documents.

free (`free` `[options]`)**:** Display amount of free and used memory in the system. Reports both physical and swap memory.

fsck (`fsck` `[options]` `filesys` `[...]`)**:** Check and repair a file system.

fuser (`fuser` `[options]` `filename...` `[options]` `filename...`)**:** Display the process IDs (PIDs) of processes using the specified file(s). Find out what program is holding a particular file in an *open* state.

G

gawk (`gawk` `[options]` `[-f` `program-file]` `text-file`**: GNU** `awk`)**:** More than just a command, `awk` is a complete language named after its developers: *A*ho, *W*einberger, and *K*ernighan.

gpasswd (`gpasswd` `[options]` `group`)**:** Set group password if shadow passwords are enabled.

grep (`grep` `[options]` `pattern` `[files...]`)**:** Search files named in command-line or standard input for lines containing a given regular expression or pattern.

groups (`groups` `[options]`)**:** Display the groups that a user is a member of.

gunzip (`gunzip` `file`)**:** Decompress files compressed by using `gzip`.

gzexe (`gzexe` `[name...]`)**:** Create compressed, executable files that automatically run when decompressed.

gzip (`gzip` `[options]` `[name...]`)**:** Compression utility that reduces the size of files. Each compressed file assumes a `.gz` extension. (Uses LZ77 coding.)

H

halt (/sbin/halt [*options*]**):** Perform an expeditious, yet systematic system shutdown.

hdparm (hdparm [*options*] [*device*]**):** Tune the IDE controller to take advantage of performance options that may be available with the disk drive hardware.

head (head [*options*] [*file*...]**):** Display the first *n* lines of a file or standard input to standard output. Default is 10 lines.

hexdump (hexdump [*options*] *file*...**):** Output files in ASCII, decimal, hexadecimal, or octal format.

history (history**):** (bash built-in) Display the current bash shell history.

hostid (hostid [*options*]**):** Display the numeric ID of the host in hexadecimal format.

hostname (hostname [*options*] *dnsdomainname***):** Display or set the hostname. Used by networking programs to identify the machine.

hwclock (hwclock**):** Query and set the hardware clock

I

id (id [*options*] [*username*]**):** Display effective UIDs and GIDs for the current user.

ifconfig (ifconfig [*interface*]**):** Display the status of the current network configuration or configure the network interface.

insmod (insmod [*options*]**):** Install loadable kernel module. References the /etc/modules.conf file if it exists.

J

jobs (jobs**):** (bash built-in) Display background processes (jobs) of the current shell session.

join (join [*options*] *file1 file2***):** Join adjacent lines of two files. Each identical *join field* is written to standard output.

K

kbdrate (kbdrate [*options*]): Set the keyboard repeat rate and delay time (the length of time you need to hold the key for it to repeat.)

kernelversion (kernelversion): Display the *major* and *minor* version of kernel.

kill (kill [*options*] *pid*): Send a signal to a process. Default is the TERM signal that is a request to the process to remove itself and release resources.

killall (killall [*options*]): Send a signal to a process by name. All processes bearing the same name get napalmed.

L

last (last [*options*]): Display a listing of users who have logged in since the last time the /var/log/wtmp file was created.

lastlog (lastlog [*options*]): Examine login history of system users. Formats and prints the contents of the /var/log/lastlog file.

less (less [*options*] [*filename*]): File viewer with more features than more. That's right: less is faster, provides backward paging, and works with a wide variety of terminals.

listalias (listalias [*options*]): List user and system aliases; primarily used for e-mail. Do not confuse these aliases with bash aliases.

ln (ln [*options*] *source* [*dest*]): Create a link to a specified target. Soft and hard links can be created to point to the same file.

locate (locate [*options*] *pattern*...): Search a pre-built system file database to find files quickly.

logger (logger [*options*] [*message*...]): Make a request to the syslogd daemon to post an entry to the system logs.

logout (logout): (bash built-in) Exit from a current login shell.

look (look [*options*] *string* [*file*]): Perform a binary search to display lines beginning with a given string.

lp (lp [*options*] [*file...*]): Send print request to LPRng print service.

lpq (lpq [*options*]): Examine the print spool queue.

lpr (lpr [*options*]): Spool print job for device queueing by the printer daemon.

lprm (lprm [*options*]): Remove a print job from the queue.

lpstat (lpstat): Display information about the LP print service.

ls (ls [*options*]): List information about the files in a directory.

lsattr (lsattr [*options*]): List file attributes of an ext2 volume.

lsmod (lsmod): Display information about currently loaded kernel modules.

M

man (man [*options*]): Format and display the on-line manual pages. The man command uses the PAGER environment variable to determine method for viewing results.

manpath (manpath): Display a user's search path for man page files.

mcat (mcat): Write raw data to a floppy disk.

mcd (mcd [*msdosdirectory*]): Change MS-DOS directory on floppy disk.

mcopy (mcopy [*options*] *sourcefile targetfile*): Copy files on an MS-DOS formatted floppy disk to and from Linux without manually mounting the floppy device.

mdel (mdel [*-v*] *msdosfile* [*msdosfiles...*]): Delete a file on an MS-DOS formatted disk.

mdeltree (mdeltree [-v] msdosdirectory [msdosdirectories...]): Delete entire MS-DOS tree structure.

mdir (mdir [*options*] *msdosdirectory*): Display the contents of an MS-DOS directory on floppy disk.

mdu (mdu): Display the space occupied by an MS-DOS directory.

merge (merge [*options*] *file1 file2 file3*): A three-way file merge that combines separate changes from two files into an original.

mesg (mesg [n] [y]): Control write access to your terminal so that pesky co-workers can't needlessly *spam* you with the write command.

mformat (mformat [*options*] *drive:*): Add an MS-DOS file system to a floppy disk.

mkbootdisk (mkbootdisk): Create a self-contained boot floppy for a running system. Includes all needed files and drivers to emergency boot your system.

mkdir (mkdir [*options*] *dir...*): Create a new directory.

mkfs (mkfs [*options*] *filesys* [*blocks*]): Create a Linux ext2 volume on a predefined disk partition.

mkpasswd (passwd [*options*] *file*): Generate a new password. Handy for creating cryptic passwords for users reluctant to select strong passwords of their own.

mktemp (mktemp [*options*] *template*): Create a unique filename for temporary work.

mlabel (mlabel [*options*] *drive:* [*new_label*]): Create an MS-DOS volume label on a formatted disk.

mmd (mmd [*options*] *msdosdirectory* [*msdosdirectories...*]): Create an MS-DOS subdirectory on a formatted disk.

mmount (mmount *msdosdrive* [*mountargs*]): Mount an MS-DOS formatted device.

mmove (mmove [*options*] *sourcefile targetfile*): Move or rename an MS-DOS file on a formatted disk.

modinfo (modinfo [*options*] *module-file*): Display specific information about a kernel module such as author, filename, and description.

modprobe (modprobe [*options*] *modul*): Load kernel modules in correct order, satisfying dependencies along the way.

more (more [*options*] [*filename...*]): Pager to view text files and standard output a page at a time. You see less using more than if you use less.

mount (mount *filesys*): Mount a file system of any supported type in the current file system hierarchy.

mpartition (mpartition): Create an MS-DOS partition.

mv (mv [*options*] *source dest*): Rename or move file(s) or directories.

N

netstat (netstat [*options*]): Display network connections, routing tables, interface status, and other network statistics.

newalias (newalias [*option*]): Install new elm aliases for user and/or system. elm, unrelated to the bash shell alias command, is a Mail User Agent.

newaliases (newaliases): Rebuild the e-mail aliases database from the /etc/aliases file. This is not related to the bash shell alias command.

newer (newer [*options*] *file1 file2*): Compare file modification times.

newgrp (newgrp [*group*]): Change a user's effective GID to a new group.

nice (nice [*options*]): System Administrator command that executes a program with modified scheduling priority.

nl (nl [*options*] [*file...*]): Generates a file or standard input listing with line numbers added to each line.

nslookup (nslookup [*options*]): Query Internet domain name servers. You can use this command in interactive and noninteractive mode.

O

oclock (oclock): Simple clock that runs on an X desktop.

od (od [*options*] [*file...*]): Display the contents of files in octal and other formats.

openvt (openvt [*options*] - *command_line*): Start a shell and optionally execute a command, with options, on the next free Virtual Terminal.

P

passwd (passwd [*name*]): Utility that enables users to change their own passwords or that enables the System Administrator to change any password.

paste (paste [*options*] [*files...*]): Glue corresponding lines of files together to standard output. Default *tab* character is used to delimit fields.

patch (patch [*options*] [*origfile* [*patchfile*]]): Modify a file by applying just the differences from the original. You can create patch files with the diff command.

pgrep (pgrep [*options*]): Look up a process ID (PID) based on a name or other process attributes.

pidof (pidof [*options*] *program...*): Find PID of running program.

ping (ping [*options*]): Command that sends packets to network hosts and verifies that network hosts are available.

pkill (pkill [*options*]): Send a signal to a process based on name or other process attributes.

poweroff (poweroff [*options*]): Systematic shutdown of the system. halt, reboot, and shutdown all perform the same function.

pr (pr [*options*] [*file...*]): Another text-formatting tool to paginate or columnate files for printing.

printenv (printenv [*variable*]): Display the current shell environment.

ps (ps [*options*]): Display a snapshot of currently running processes.

pstree (pstree [*options*]): Display hierarchy of system processes, which provides a nice visual of process lineage.

pwd (pwd): Print Working Directory — display the pathname of the current directory.

Q

quota (quota [*options*]): Display disk usage and limits. System Administrator may impose limits on the amount of disk space available to users.

quotacheck (`quotacheck [options]`): Scan file system for disk usage, either by user or group.

quotaon (`quotaon [options] filesys`): Switch file system quota on and off.

R

rcp (`rcp quota [options] file1 file2; rcp quota [options] file... directory`): Remote File Copy — copy files between hosts.

rdate (`rdate [options] host...`): Retrieve date and time from a network host. Use `rdate` to synchronize host times throughout a network.

reboot (`reboot`): Restart the system by performing an orderly shutdown and subsequent boot.

rename (`rename from-file to-file`): Rename files. Handy for performing multiple filename changes.

renice (`renice priority [options]`): Change priority of running process. Process can be set from –20 (greatest CPU timeslice) to +19.

resize (`resize [options]`): Shell command that alters xterm window size.

resize2fs (`resize2fs [options] device [new-size]`): Utility that resizes an `ext2` file system volume.

restore (`restore [options]`): Restore files archived with `dump`.

rev (`rev [file]`): Reverse the order of characters in every line of a file or standard input.

rm (`rm [options] file...; rm [options] directory...`): Remove (delete) file(s) and/or directories.

rmdir (`rmdir [options] dir...`): Delete empty directories.

rmmod (`rmmod [option] module...`): Unload a kernel module, providing that no modules are currently in use or dependent loaded.

route (`route [options]`): Display or set the kernel IP routing table.

rpm (`rpm [options]`): Red Hat Package Manager. Primarily installs and updates software packages.

runlevel (`runlevel`): Display current and previous system `runlevel`.

S

sash (`sash [options]`): Standalone shell with built-in commands. Useful for system recovery if shared libraries aren't available.

script (`script [-a] [file]`): Record everything printed on your terminal.

sdiff (`sdiff -o outfile [options] from-file to-file`): Find differences between two files and merge them interactively.

sed (`sed [options] command [file...]`): Stream Editor. Perform powerful text transformation on an input stream and send the results to standard output.

set (`set varName ?value?`): (`bash` built-in) Set shell variables.

setleds (`setleds [options]`): Display and set the keyboard `leds` of the current terminal.

setterm (`setterm [options]`): Set terminal attributes.

shred (`shred [options] file...`): Delete a file securely, overwriting the file contents on disk prior to deletion.

shutdown (`shutdown [options]`): Perform an orderly and secure shutdown of the system while providing user notification.

sleep (`sleep number[options]`): Pause for a specified amount of time. `sleep` delays the start of a process.

sort (`sort [options] [file...]`): Sort lines of text files.

source (`source filename`): (`bash` built-in) Read and execute commands in the current shell environment.

split (`split [options] [infile [outfile-prefix]]`): Split a file into multiple files based on byte count or lines.

stat (`stat [filenames...]`): Display all inode contents of a file.

strings (`strings [options] [file...]`): Display the strings of printable characters in files. Useful for noodling information from executable or other binary files.

stty (`stty [setting...]`): Display or change terminal line characteristics.

su (su [*options*] [*user* [*arg...*]]): Switch User (*not* SuperUser). Used to change the effective UID to a different user.

sum (sum [*options*] [*file...*]): Count and display the checksum and blocks in a file.

sync (sync [*options*]): Force a flush of file system buffers to disk and update the superblock.

T

tac (tac [*options*] [*file...*]): Concatenate and print files in reverse order.

tail (tail [*options*] [*file...*]): Display the last *n* lines of a file. Default number of lines is 10 but you can change it.

tar (tar [*options*] *file...*): Tape archive utility. Store and extract files from an archive known as a *tarfile* or *tarball*.

tee (tee [*options*] [*file...*]): Split output in two directions. You can, for example, use tee to write output to the screen *and* to a file.

test (test [*expression*]): Check file types and compare values. Returns an exit status of true or false.

toe (toe [*options*] *file...*): Provides information about the preconfigured terminal types that can be used.

top (top [*options*]): Display a continually updated status of CPU processes. Sorted with the most CPU intensive processes at the *top*.

touch (touch [*options*] *file...*): Change file timestamps to current. If file doesn't exist, it is created with a 0-byte count.

tr (tr [*options*] *string*): Filter for translating, editing, and/or deleting characters from a standard input stream.

tset (tset [*options*] [*-m mapping*] [*terminal*]): Determine the type of terminal in use and initialize the terminal accordingly.

tty (tty [*options*]): Display the filename for the terminal connected to standard output.

tune2fs (`tune2fs [options] device`): Adjust tunable file system parameters on an `ext2` volume.

tzselect (`tzselect [options] feature device`): Utility that selects a time zone.

U

umask (`umask [options]`): (`bash` built-in) This setting is subtracted from full permissions to determine the security of newly created files.

umount (`umount [options]`): Detach file systems from the file hierarchy.

unalias (`unalias [-a] [name...]`): (`bash` built-in) Release the current definition for a particular shell alias.

uname (`uname [options]`): Display system information.

unbuffer (`unbuffer program [args]`): Immediately displays output for processes that are normally buffered. Buffered processes don't display anything until an entire page is created in memory.

uncompress (`uncompress [options] [file...]`): Decompress files compressed with Lempel-Ziv encoding.

unexpand (`unexpand [options] [file...]`): Convert spaces to tabs in a file or standard input.

uniq (`uniq [options] [input [output]]`): Discard duplicate lines from standard input or a sorted file.

unset (`unset [options] [name...]`): (`bash` built-in) Release an assigned shell variable.

unzip (`unzip [options] filename[.zip]`): List, test, and extract compressed files in ZIP format commonly used to compress files on an MS-DOS system.

updatedb (`updatedb [options]`): Update the database `locate` uses to find files in the file-system hierarchy.

uptime (`uptime`): Display how long the system has been running since the last system boot.

users (users): Display the currently logged-in users of the host.

usleep (usleep [*microseconds*]): Pause for a specified amount of time in microseconds. Delay the start of a process.

uudecode (uudecode [*options*] [*file...*]): Decode a file created by the uuencode command.

uuencode (uuencode [*options*] *infile remotefile*): Encode a binary file to ASCII and output to standard output or a file.

uuidgen (uuidgen [*options*]): Generate a new, universally unique identifier (UUID).

V

vmstat (vmstat [*options*] [*delay* [*count*]]): Display information about processes, memory, and CPU activity.

W

w (w [*options*] [*user*]): Display information about the users currently logged in to the host and their controlling processes.

wall (wall [*file*]): Send a message to every logged-in user's terminal.

watch (watch [*options*]): Execute a program periodically, displaying the first screen of output each time run.

wc (wc [*options*] [*file...*]): Display the number of bytes, words, and lines in files.

whatis (whatis *keyword...*): Searches the man page files for complete word matches.

whereis (whereis [*options*] *filename...*): Locate binary, source, and man page files for a command.

which (which *progname...*): Display full path of a command location.

who (who [*options*]): Display who's logged in.

whoami (whoami**):** Display currently effective User ID (UID) of the user logged into the terminal.

write (write *user* [*ttyname*]**):** Send a message to another currently logged-in user by copying lines from your terminal to theirs.

Z

zcat (zcat [*options*] [*file...*]**):** Compress or expand files from standard input and write to standard output.

zcmp (zcmp [*cmp-options*] *file* [*file*]**):** Compare compressed files.

zip (zip [*options*] [*zipfile list*]**):** Package and compress files. Create files compatible with PKZIP, commonly used for MS-DOS compression.

Appendix B

Glossary

• •

ADSL (Asymmetrical Digital Subscriber Line): A high-speed communications technology that uses regular telephone lines. ADSL supports data transfer rates of 1.5 Mbps.

Apache Web server: A powerful, widely used Web server that is highly configurable and easily customized. The source code is freely available and distributed with an unrestrictive license. The server runs on several platforms, including Windows 9*x*/ME and Window NT/2000, Netware 5.x, and most versions of Unix.

applet: A small program that runs independent of an operating system, but can be executed from within a variety of applications.

`bash`: The default shell used in Linux. `bash` stands for *Bourne Again shell* — the Bourne shell, or sh, is the original Unix shell. The `bash` shell is a highly configurable user interface.

BIOS (Basic Input/Output System): A chip on your computer's motherboard that stores information about your hardware. The BIOS is read and tested at boot time to ensure that the hardware is working properly.

bloatware: *See* emacs.

browser: Also called a Web browser. A program used to access and request HTML documents for display on a monitor screen. Netscape Navigator is an example of a browser.

browser war: Competition between two software companies for dominance in the Web browser marketplace. The term is commonly used to refer to the battle between Microsoft and Netscape Communications regarding Internet Explorer and Netscape Communicator (a suite that contains Navigator), respectively.

cable modem: A device that provides for high-speed Internet access using cable television cables.

caching proxy server: A proxy server that stores, either in memory or on a hard drive, Internet objects (for example, Web pages) you've visited. The next time you access the page, it's pulled from the server's cache, which is faster than pulling up the page from the Internet.

command prompt: The line on a display screen where you enter commands in text mode.

configuration file: A simple text file that can be viewed and altered with your favorite editor. An executable file reads commands from the configuration file and acts upon those directives. *See* executable file.

controller: An interface device that orchestrates the transfer of information between a CPU and a peripheral device, such as a disk drive, CD-ROM drive, or monitor.

copyleft software: Software that can be altered and freely redistributed with no restrictions to the next user to also copy and redistribute it, or use it in any way they choose.

desktop environment: The on-screen representation of the Linux, or other, operating system in which you can change the background color and image, icons, and so on.

device driver: A small software program that interfaces between a computer's operating system and a peripheral device, such as a network interface card or modem.

DHCP (Dynamic Host Configuration Protocol): A protocol that assigns IP addresses automatically to computers and devices on a network.

directory: A folder that contains files and subdirectories, creating a hierarchical and organized system for file storage and retrieval.

display manager: A graphical mode program that appears after a Linux computer boots and validates a username and password. The display manager offers many customization options.

distribution: One of many packaged variations of the Linux operating system, such as Red Hat or Caldera.

DMA (Direct Memory Access): Special hardware technology that speeds up the transfer of data by bypassing a computer's CPU when accessing RAM.

DNS (Domain Name System): The Internet protocol that resolves hostnames into IP addresses.

domain: Also called zone. A group of computers and other devices on a network that are administered from the same security database and share the same part of an IP address.

dynamic IP address: An IP address that is assigned by DHCP. *See also* static IP address.

emacs (Editing MACroS): A real-time display text editor, referred to as bloatware.

e-mail: Short for *electronic mail*. A general term for messaging systems used on many types of networks, from LANs to the Internet. Popular e-mail software programs include Netscape Messenger, Microsoft Outlook and Outlook Express, and Eudora.

environment variable: A global text string set by a Linux shell, such as bash, that holds information about your account, prompt, and so on, that can be changed and accessed by other running programs. An environment variable, in bash, is always in all capital letters.

Ethernet: A networking protocol that is the basis of the IEEE (Institute of Electrical and Electronics Engineers) 802.3 specification. It supports data transfer rates of 10 Mbps, but newer versions, such as Fast Ethernet and Gigabit Ethernet, support 100 to 1000 Mbps, respectively. Ethernet is the most popular type of networking technology in use today.

executable file: A binary file that runs compiled commands when launched. An executable file often reads the contents of a configuration file as part of its process. *See* configuration file.

fdisk: A utility that enables you to view and make changes to your hard drive's partitions.

FHS (Filesystem Hierarchy Standard): A specification primarily used by developers that defines a standard arrangement of many of the files and directories common to Linux distributions.

FIPS (First nondestructive Interactive Partition Splitting program): A free, nondestructive disk partition modification program used in Linux.

file manager: A GUI program, such as Windows Explorer, that lets you browse through and manipulate files and directories.

file system: In Linux, the hierarchical arrangement of files and directories.

FTP (File Transfer Protocol): A TCP/IP-based protocol used on networks, including the Internet, to transfer files.

gateway: A networking device that translates information between two dissimilar network architectures or data formats. A gateway is commonly used in e-mail systems for the exchange of messages.

getty: A text-mode program that appears after a Linux computer boots and validates a username and password. The getty, unlike its graphical counterpart the display manager, allows few customization options.

GMC (GNU Midnight Commander): The default file manager in the GNOME desktop environment.

GNOME (GNU Network Object Model Environment): A GUI desktop environment in Linux, similar to KDE in function.

GNU: (Pronounced "ga-new.") It means *Gnu's Not Unix.* GNU mainly refers to the Unix-like operating system tools that arose from Richard Stallman's free software project effort (in cooperation with the Free Software Foundation). When combined with the kernel that Linus Torvalds developed, the complete operating system *Linux* was born.

GPL (General Public License): A unique and innovative software license that protects software users under copyright law to use, alter, and distribute the software in any way they choose. GPL also stands for Guaranteed Public for Life. *See* copyleft software.

GUI (Graphical User Interface): (Pronounced "gooey.") An alternative to a command prompt driver interface, a GUI enables users to access programs, run commands, change configuration settings, and more, by using a mouse to point and click graphical or menu items rather than issuing commands from a command prompt.

gFTP client: An FTP client in Linux. gFTP offers a visual representation of the local file system and a remote file system, and a point and click file transfer interface.

Gnotepad+: (Pronounced "ga-notepad.") A popular GUI-based text editor.

group: A collection of two or more users on a network. A group offers system administrators an easy method of assigning or restricting rights to several users at a time.

hardware: The tangible parts of a computer: case, hard drive, CPU, adapter cards, keyboard, monitor, and so on.

host: A computer on a network that stores data that is accessed by users on the network. A host on a TCP/IP network must have a unique IP address.

HTTP (HyperText Transfer Protocol): The protocol that serves as the base for Internet communications, defining how messages are formatted and transmitted and how Web servers and browsers should respond to requests.

hub: A multiport networking device that connects LAN segments. A passive hub simply passes information from one segment to another. An active hub regenerates the signal between segments to help ensure delivery of the data.

Internet: Another term for the World Wide Web. The Internet is a worldwide conglomeration of connected mainframes, Web servers, and individual computers that use common protocols, such as TCP/IP and FTP, to share and transfer data. A common element of the Internet is a Web page, which is primarily an HTML document available for viewing by any user on the Internet.

interrupt: A signal to the CPU that a peripheral device has performed an event and is requesting attention. Each type of hardware is assigned its own interrupt number for identification. The CPU addresses each interrupt separately and passes the request on to the appropriate device.

I/O (Input/Output) port: A location in a computer's memory where devices temporarily store data to be picked up by the processor.

IP (Internet Protocol) address: Also called an IP number. A 32-bit numeric address that uniquely identifies computers or devices on a TCP/IP network.

IP (Internet Protocol) routing: The process of moving data between two IP networks.

ISDN (Integrated Services Digital Network): A digital communications technology that offers increments of 64-Kbps connections, most often used by small office/home office users to connect to WANs.

ISP (Internet Service Provider): A company that provides Internet access and other Internet-related services, such as IP address leasing, for a fee.

KDE (K Desktop Environment): An alternative GUI desktop environment in Linux, similar in function to GNOME.

kernel: The core of the Linux operating system. The kernel is the interface between the system's hardware and software.

kfm (KDE file manager): The default file manager in the KDE desktop environment.

LAN (local area network) : A group of computers and devices that are attached by network cabling and use a common set of protocols to share information.

LILO (LInux LOader): The program that executes a Linux kernel at boot time. If the computer has more than one operating system installed, `LILO` enables the user to boot to any of the operating systems.

link: Two kinds of links are used in Linux and Unix — soft and hard. A soft link is like a shortcut that points to the original file and any changes you make to the link are made to the original file. Erase the original file and the link remains, but it becomes unusable. It's broken without the original file. A hard link isn't just a shortcut; it's another instance of the file itself. The original file is only saved in one place, but you can edit the hard link and the edits appear in the original file as well.

Linux: An Open Source operating system, built around the Unix framework, that is now widely used as a Web server in many companies and organizations. Linux is multi-platform, interoperable with many existing networking protocols, highly configurable, stable, and free, among many other praiseworthy traits.

LinuxConf: A configuration and activation utility that allows you to change many Linux system settings, such as user and group accounts, network configuration, and LILO settings, and activate system tools such as printtool, modemtool, and kernelcfg.

loadable module: A small program that is called from within an operating system to provide a service or function that isn't a part of the operating system.

log file: A file, usually a text file, that contains a list of actions that have occurred. Network programs, the kernel, and many other programs write to log files.

login prompt: The command prompt area or GUI text box in which a username and password are entered to log into a system.

loopback interface: A phantom network interface that allows your computer to listen to itself and use network programs without having a physical network device.

lpd: The *l*ine *p*rinter *d*aemon; Linux printing service manager.

Mac OS: The GUI-based, Macintosh operating system.

man pages: A comprehensive, online help system in Linux.

MBR (Master Boot Record): A small program that runs when a computer is turned on and determines which partition to boot from. The MBR is stored in the first sector of a hard drive.

Microsoft Windows: The dominant GUI operating system in the world today.

modem (MOdulator/DEModulator): A communications device that changes digital signals from a computer to analog signals, transmits the data to another modem, which translates the analog signals back to digital for the receiving computer.

motherboard: In a computer, the main circuit board into which all components (video card, RAM, CPU, controller cards, and so on) plug to operate together.

mount point: In Linux, a disk partition.

Netscape Navigator: The Web browser that's part of the Netscape Communicator suite.

newsgroup: One of thousands of online discussion groups on the Internet in which participants post and read messages and share information on a particular topic of interest.

NIC (network interface card): An adapter card in a computer that has one or more ports to which a network cable attaches. The NIC is the hardware interface that enables the computer to communicate on a network.

Open Source software: Software that can be altered and redistributed without a fee and few restrictions.

operating system: The basic program on a computer that runs the main system and hardware. Every computer must have an operating system to work.

owner: The user who created a file or directory.

parent directory: The two dots near the top of a directory display that refer to the parent directory, or the directory one level up from where you are now. In Linux, for almost all user home directories, the parent is /home.

partition: The basic physical unit of a hard drive or other form of mass storage.

permissions: Rights assigned to users and/or groups to access files or directories.

pico: A text editor used in Linux that's based on the Pine mail system composer.

PID (process ID): A non-negative identification number for running programs.

ping: A command that searches for an IP address on a network to determine whether that computer or device is available. The ping command is frequently used to check connections on the Internet.

pipe: A bash shell feature that enables commands to be connected together such that the output of one becomes the input for the next.

plug-in: A small program or module that works within an application to offer a service or function that wasn't originally part of the application. Web browsers, such as Netscape Navigator, use many plug-ins that provide multimedia functions.

Post Office Protocol (POP) server: A server, most often under the control of an Internet Service Provider, that enables dial-up access to the Internet.

queuing: The process of storing files (usually print files) temporarily until they're ready to be accessed. Also called spooling.

Red Hat Linux: A popular version of the Linux operating system.

redirection: In bash, the use of a detour sign in conjunction with a command. Redirecting command output, for example, involves the use of a symbol in a command to send the results to a file instead of to the screen. The ls -la ~ > listing command sends the results of the ls -la command to the file listing rather than to the screen.

root directory: The parent directory of all other directories in Linux and Unix. The root directory is represented in the file system tree structure by a / (forward slash).

root user: The administrator account in Linux. The root user has all rights within the system. Also called superuser.

router: A networking device that connects networks with different physical media and uses a routing table to determine the destination of data packets. A router also chooses the best route between any two hosts, reducing network traffic.

RPM (Red Hat Package Manager): An open packaging system distributed under the GPL that developers use to package source code for end users, and assists end users in the installation and upgrading of their Linux files. RPM is available in Red Hat Linux and Linux distributions and Unix systems.

sector: The smallest physical unit on a disk.

shell: The user interface for Linux and Unix. A shell may be command prompt driven or menu driven.

shell scripting: The process of creating a list of commands in a text file that can be run with a single command. Scripting saves the user the time of typing the same group of commands repeatedly at a command prompt.

SMTP (Simple Mail Transport Protocol): A TCP/IP protocol used to transfer e-mail across a network, including the Internet.

sneakernet: A method of data sharing that involves copying data from one computer to a floppy disk and carrying (walking) that floppy to another computer for data retrieval.

software: A general term for programs or applications that can be electronically stored and run on computers. Software is most often tested and packaged before distribution to end users.

source code: The human-readable text that represents the instructions that we want to communicate to the computer. Source code must be compiled, or translated, into native binary language to make it computer-readable.

spooling: *See* queuing.

static IP address: An IP address that's manually assigned to a computer or device. *See also* dynamic IP address.

superuser: *See* root user.

SWATCH (Simple WATCHer): Security software that monitors and filters information written to log files and carries out a specified action when it detects a pre-determined pattern in the log.

symlink: Short for *sym*bolic *links*. Marker files or shortcuts in Linux that point to files containing script instructions.

tarball file: Similar to WinZip or PKZip files, an archive file created with the Unix tar utility that contains one or more compressed files. The files can be extracted and decompressed back to their original form. Archive files are commonly used to shrink files temporarily for faster transfer between remote computers and via the Internet.

TCP/IP (Transport Control Protocol/Internet Protocol): A popular communications protocol suite that supports data transfer between hosts in networks, such as the Internet.

Telnet: A terminal emulation program used on networks to connect to a remote computer and enter and process commands as if the user were working directly on the remote computer.

Tux: The formal name of the mascot penguin that represents Linux.

Unix: A less-than-user-friendly but powerful network operating system that supports a multi-user, multitasking environment. Unix was one of the first network operating systems introduced and became the foundation for the Internet.

user: A person who uses a computer.

vi: A popular text-based text editor. Documents are edited in vi in one of three modes — command, insert, and ex.

Web site: A group of Web pages, either in a simple or complex arrangement, for a particular individual, company, or organization on the Internet. A Web site always contains at least a home page.

WYSIWYG (What You See Is What You Get): (Pronounced whiz-ee-wig.) A term that describes software that provides the user with an on-screen representation of the expected printed output.

WAN (wide area network): An internetwork that connects multiple LANs, usually over a large geographical area. WAN links are often provided by third parties as part of the public telephone system, or more expensively in the form of leased lines or satellites. The Internet is currently the largest WAN in the world.

Winmodem: A software-based communications technology that consists of a telephone cable interface and relies mainly on your computer's operating system to function. Linux generally doesn't support Winmodems.

xdm (X display manager): The display manager that runs under the X Window System. *See also* display manager.

X Window System: A Linux GUI that's invoked from a command prompt with the startx command.

Appendix C

About the CD-ROMs

* *

*T*he CD-ROMs included with this book contain the full distribution of Red Hat Linux 7, along with the companion programs listed in this appendix, and much more!

The CD-ROMs include the following:

- ✔ **Red Hat Linux 7:** A complete copy of the latest and greatest version of Red Hat Linux, for your computing pleasure.

- ✔ **RPM 4.0 (Red Hat Package Manager):** Red Hat's newest software distribution and installation management environment, wherein Linux updates and new facilities are packaged for easy installation on your Linux machine.

- ✔ **KDE (the K Desktop Environment)** and **GNOME** (GNU Network Object Model Environment): The two leading graphical user interfaces for Linux — you can pick the one you like best!

- ✔ **Netscape Communicator 4.75:** The best of breed Web browser for your Linux machine is just waiting for your surfing pleasure.

- ✔ **Samba 2.0.7:** The best way to integrate Linux servers with Windows users, Samba lets your Linux machine masquerade as a Windows NT Server so that Windows users can grab files and print documents hassle-free.

- ✔ **Apache Webserver 1.3.12:** The world's most popular (or at least, most frequently used) Web server software.

- ✔ **Bonus content:** Four bonus appendixes and an HTML links page including hyperlinks to all of the URLs in the book!

System Requirements

Make sure that your computer meets the following minimum system requirements. If your computer doesn't match up to most of these requirements, you may have problems using the contents of the CD.

- ✔ A PC with an Intel-compatible 486 or faster processor.

- ✔ MS-DOS 6.02 or Microsoft Windows 3.1 or later is convenient to help you set up your system, but you can install from a Linux bootable floppy without needing DOS or Windows, if you prefer.

- ✔ At least 8MB of total RAM installed on your computer. For best performance, we recommend at least 32MB of RAM or more. (Linux can handle as much RAM as you can fit into a typical PC and more is almost always better than less.)

- ✔ At least 800MB (the barest minimum) up to 2GB of hard drive space available, if you want to install all the software from this CD. (You need less space if you don't install every program, but you'll want to go ahead and make 2GB of space available to give yourself the most options.)

- ✔ A CD-ROM drive — double-speed (2x) or faster (the faster the CD-ROM drive, the faster your installation experience).

- ✔ Just about any VGA monitor will do, but you'll want one that's capable of displaying at least 256 colors or grayscale.

- ✔ A keyboard and a mouse, so you'll have a way to communicate with your Linux system and tell it what to do!

- ✔ A 3.5" floppy drive, so that you can create an emergency boot disk for your Linux system (and though we hope you never need one, you'll thank your lucky stars you've got one, if you ever do). With this tool in your PC, you can also use it to boot from a floppy should you ever need to do that as well.

- ✔ A PDF viewer so that you can read the bonus appendixes we've included on CD3. Luckily, xpdf is installed by default with the Workstation installation of Red Hat Linux 7 (which we show you how to set up in Chapters 2 and 3) and opens automatically when you double-click a PDF file.

- ✔ Optional: A modem with a speed of at least 14,400 bps; here again, the faster your Internet connection, the less time it will take to update your installation to the most recent versions. Your authors use cable modems or DSL for their Internet connections and like the increased speed very much when it comes to dealing with the many and varied sources of Linux software and updates online.

If you need more information on PC basics, check out *PCs For Dummies,* 6th Edition, by Dan Gookin (published by IDG Books Worldwide).

Using the CD

You can take either of two basic approaches to using the Red Hat Linux installation CDs. We cover each of these in separate step-by-step lists. Here's where we tell you how to pick which set of instructions you'll want to follow. The two ways to use these CDs are as follows:

- ✔ If you can boot from your CD drive (and this probably means you've got a newer PC, probably with a Pentium processor or better), follow the instructions in the section, "Booting from the CD."

- ✔ If you can't boot from your CD drive, for whatever reasons, follow the instructions in the section, "Booting from a Linux Floppy." This means that you boot from a Linux boot floppy, with CD1 that came with this book already inserted into your CD drive (to create a Linux boot floppy to enable this approach, please check out the instructions in Chapter 2). The floppy disk handles the very beginning of the process and then turns the rest of the installation over to the CD.

Booting from the CD

To install the items from the CD to your hard drive, follow these steps:

1. **Insert the CD into your computer's CD-ROM drive.**

2. **Reboot your PC.** (As long as your PC is configured to boot from the CD, this starts the Linux installation process for you automatically.)

3. **Congratulations!** The Linux installation process is now underway. For the rest of the gory details on this fascinating task, please consult Chapter 3.

Booting from a Linux floppy

To install the items from the CD to your hard drive with a boot disk (we show you how to make one in Chapter 2), follow these steps:

1. **Insert the CD into your computer's CD-ROM drive, and insert a bootable Linux floppy into your computer's floppy drive — see the instructions for creating a bootable Linux floppy in Chapter 2.**

2. **Reboot your PC.** (This starts the Linux installation process for you automatically.)

3. **Congratulations!** The Linux installation process is now underway. For the rest of the gory details on this fascinating task, please consult Chapter 3.

And some people say that installing Linux is hard! What could be easier than this? On the other hand, if all you want to do is investigate the contents of the Linux installation CDs (CD1 and CD2, to be exact), simply insert them into your machine's CD player (one at a time, please — you won't like what happens if you try to read all three at once, trust us!). After that, you can browse through each CD's contents, which we describe in the "What You'll Find" section later in this appendix.

Checking out the bonus content

To check out the bonus appendixes, mount CD3 in Red Hat Linux (typing **mount cdrom** at a GNOME virtual terminal and then pressing Enter should do the trick in Red Hat Linux 7) if it isn't already mounted. Next, open the GNOME File Manager (by clicking the Main Menu button and then choosing Programs⇨File Manager) and then navigate to the /linux_for_dummies directory on CD3 and double-click the icon representing the bonus appendix you wish to view. xpdf then opens the file and you can use the navigation buttons at the bottom of the xpdf window to check out the chapter (click the arrow buttons to flip pages).

For the links page, simply navigate to the file (in the same folder as the PDF appendixes mentioned in the preceding paragraph) using the GNOME File Manager and double-click the file to automatically open it in Netscape Navigator.

What You'll Find

Here's a summary of the software on the CDs arranged by directory organization. If you use Windows, the CD interfaces help you navigate the CDs easily; you'll only be able to surf the CD in a meaningful way if you've already got Linux installed.

You probably won't need to spend much time using CD1 after you've installed Linux on your machine. That's because Linux copies everything you need from that CD onto your machine during the installation process. You may need to access CD2 at some point or another, should you decide to install any of the supplementary software that it contains.

About CD1

The contents of CD1 pretty much consists of Red Hat Linux 7, plus certain key software distributions that are installed automatically or that you can opt to install should you choose to do so during the installation process. This CD doesn't contain a whole lot more, beyond some useful install utilities and a handy-dandy README file from Red Hat that explains precisely what you'll find. The directory structure looks like the following (except lacking our handy annotations, of course):

```
/mnt/redhat
    |----> RedHat              -- current Linux release
    |      |----> RPMS          -- binary packages, incl:
    |      |                        OS, GUIs, Apache, etc.
    |      |----> base          -- info on 7 release
    |                               used by install process
    |----> images              -- boot & ramdisk images
    |----> dosutils            -- DOS install utilities
    |----> COPYING             -- copyright information
    |----> README              -- general read me file
    |----> RPM-GPG-KEY         -- GPG sigs for Red Hat pkgs
```

Outside of the RedHat/RPMS directory, access to the dosutils, the README file, and the GPG signature for the Red Hat software (in the RPM-GPG-KEY directory), you probably won't need to access much else on this CD (and the install program handles most of that for you on your behalf).

About CD2

CD2 consists mainly of Red Hat Linux 7, additional RPMs, and source packages. You're either prompted to install these during the installation process or can choose to install them after. CD2 also includes a README file from Red Hat that explains precisely what you find on the CD. The directory structure looks like the following (except lacking our handy annotations, of course):

```
/mnt/redhat
    |----> RedHat
    |      |----> RPMS          -- addtl binary pkgs, incl:
    |      |                        games, tools, & utilities
    |      |----> instimage     -- NFS installer tree
    |
    |----> SRPMS               -- source pkgs, incl:
    |                               RPM pkgs for 3rd-party
    |                               tools & utilities
    |----> preview             -- alpha & beta pkgs
    |                               (source & binary) for
    |                               adventurous users only
    |----> COPYING             -- copyright info
    |----> README              -- CD 2 read me file
    |----> RPM-GPG-KEY         -- GPG sigs for Red Hat pkgs
```

Outside of the RedHat/RPMS directory, the SRPMS directory, and the GPG signature for the Red Hat software (in the RPM-GPG-KEY directory), you probably won't need to access much else on this CD (and the Red Hat Package Manager program handles most of that for you on your behalf).

Both packages include GPG signatures because the installer can check the contents of files it tries to install against the stored signatures to make sure that the files haven't been changed (and the assumption is that all changes would be for the worse, such as Trojan horses or viruses) because they were written to the CD. Thus, signatures provide a way to make sure everything is safe and wholesome for your computer!

About CD3

CD3 contains documentation files for Red Hat Linux 7. These include "The Official Red Hat Linux Getting Started Guide," "The Official Red Hat Linux Installation Guide," and "The Official Red Hat Linux Reference Guide." In addition, you'll find many FAQs and HOWTOs that help you learn more about or offer step-by-step instructions for using your Linux system, and a README file from Red Hat themselves describing the contents of the CD (that README is just named "README" whereas the one for this book is named "IDGB_README"). You can install the guides on your computer's hard drive or view them on the CD. Either way, keep them handy — you'll probably refer to them time and again!

In the /linux_for_dummies directory on CD3, you'll also find a README file including the text from this appendix and four bonus appendixes (named BonusAppA.pdf through BonusAppD.pdf) and a links page to all the URLs in this book (named links.html).

If You've Got Problems (Of the CD Kind)

We tried our best to locate programs that work on most computers with the minimum system requirements, as did Red Hat for its operating system. Alas, your computer may differ, and some programs may not work properly for some reason.

The two likeliest problems are that you don't have enough memory (RAM) for the programs you want to use or that you have other programs running that are affecting the installation or running of a program. If you get error messages like Not enough memory or Setup cannot continue, try one or more of the following methods and then try using the software again:

- ✔ **Turn off any anti virus software that you have on your computer.** Installers sometimes mimic virus activity and may make your computer incorrectly believe that a virus is infecting it.

- ✔ **Close all running programs.** The more programs you're running, the less memory is available to other programs. Installers also typically update files and programs; if you keep other programs running, installation may not work properly.

✔ **In Linux, close your GUI environment and run demos or installations directly from a shell.** The interface itself can tie up system memory or even conflict with certain kinds of interactive demos. Use the command prompt to browse files on the CD and launch installers or demos.

✔ **Have your local computer store add more RAM to your computer.** This is, admittedly, a drastic and somewhat expensive step. If you have a modern PC with less than 32MB of RAM, however, adding more memory can really help the speed of your computer and enable more programs to run at the same time.

If you still have trouble installing the items from the CD, please call the IDG Books Worldwide Customer Service phone number: 800-762-2974 (outside the U.S.: 317-572-3993).

Index

• *E* •

• Q •

• R •

• S •

• *X* •

Notes

Notes

Notes

Notes

IDG Books Worldwide, Inc.
Linux source code mail-in coupon

In an attempt to provide you with CDs packed with greater amounts of accompanying software, we're offering the source code (which usually comes packaged with the Linux operating system) via mail. This offer is valid for a period of 1 year from the date of purchase of this book. After you mail in the coupon below with a dated cash-register receipt and a money order for **$8.95** for orders within the U.S. or **$12.95** for orders outside the U.S., you will receive the corresponding source code on CD-ROM.

Return this coupon, with original receipt and money order (U.S. funds only), to the address listed below. Please make sure that you list the Part #_____ on your check or money order so that we can ensure that you receive the correct CD. Please allow 4–6 weeks for delivery.

Name _____

Company _____

Address _____

City _____ **State** _____ **Postal Code** _____

Country _____

E-mail _____ **Telephone** _____

Detach and return this coupon to:
Media Development Department
IDG Books Worldwide, Inc.
Part #_____ Fulfillment
10475 Crosspoint Blvd.
Indianapolis, IN 46256

IDG BOOKS WORLDWIDE ®

GNU GENERAL PUBLIC LICENSE

Version 2, June 1991
Copyright © 1989, 1991 Free Software Foundation, Inc.
59 Temple Place - Suite 330, Boston, MA 02111-1307, USA

Preamble

The licenses for most software are designed to take away your freedom to share and change it. By contrast, the GNU General Public License is intended to guarantee your freedom to share and change free software — to make sure the software is free for all its users. This General Public License applies to most of the Free Software Foundation's software and to any other program whose authors commit to using it. (Some other Free Software Foundation software is covered by the GNU Library General Public License instead.) You can apply it to your programs, too.

When we speak of free software, we are referring to freedom, not price. Our General Public Licenses are designed to make sure that you have the freedom to distribute copies of free software (and charge for this service if you wish), that you receive source code or can get it if you want it, that you can change the software or use pieces of it in new free programs; and that you know you can do these things.

To protect your rights, we need to make restrictions that forbid anyone to deny you these rights or to ask you to surrender the rights. These restrictions translate to certain responsibilities for you if you distribute copies of the software, or if you modify it.

For example, if you distribute copies of such a program, whether gratis or for a fee, you must give the recipients all the rights that you have. You must make sure that they, too, receive or can get the source code. And you must show them these terms so they know their rights.

We protect your rights with two steps: (1) copyright the software, and (2) offer you this license which gives you legal permission to copy, distribute and/or modify the software.

Also, for each author's protection and ours, we want to make certain that everyone understands that there is no warranty for this free software. If the software is modified by someone else and passed on, we want its recipients to know that what they have is not the original, so that any problems introduced by others will not reflect on the original authors' reputations.

Finally, any free program is threatened constantly by software patents. We wish to avoid the danger that redistributors of a free program will individually obtain patent licenses, in effect making the program proprietary. To prevent this, we have made it clear that any patent must be licensed for everyone's free use or not licensed at all.

The precise terms and conditions for copying, distribution and modification follow.

TERMS AND CONDITIONS FOR COPYING, DISTRIBUTION AND MODIFICATION

0. This License applies to any program or other work which contains a notice placed by the copyright holder saying it may be distributed under the terms of this General Public License. The "Program", below, refers to any such program or work, and a "work based on the Program" means either the Program or any derivative work under copyright law: that is to say, a work containing the Program or a portion of it, either verbatim or with modifications and/or translated into another language. (Hereinafter, translation is included without limitation in the term "modification".) Each licensee is addressed as "you".

   Activities other than copying, distribution and modification are not covered by this License; they are outside its scope. The act of running the Program is not restricted, and the output from the Program is covered only if its contents constitute a work based on the Program (independent of having been made by running the Program). Whether that is true depends on what the Program does.

1. You may copy and distribute verbatim copies of the Program's source code as you receive it, in any medium, provided that you conspicuously and appropriately publish on each copy an appropriate copyright notice and disclaimer of warranty; keep intact all the notices that refer to this License and to the absence of any warranty; and give any other recipients of the Program a copy of this License along with the Program.

   You may charge a fee for the physical act of transferring a copy, and you may at your option offer warranty protection in exchange for a fee.

2. You may modify your copy or copies of the Program or any portion of it, thus forming a work based on the Program, and copy and distribute such modifications or work under the terms of Section 1 above, provided that you also meet all of these conditions:

   a) You must cause the modified files to carry prominent notices stating that you changed the files and the date of any change.

   b) You must cause any work that you distribute or publish, that in whole or in part contains or is derived from the Program or any part thereof, to be licensed as a whole at no charge to all third parties under the terms of this License.

   c) If the modified program normally reads commands interactively when run, you must cause it, when started running for such interactive use in the most ordinary way, to print or display an announcement including an appropriate copyright notice and a notice that there is no warranty (or else, saying that you provide a warranty) and that users may redistribute the program under these conditions, and telling the user how to view a copy of this License. (Exception: if the Program itself is interactive but does not normally print such an announcement, your work based on the Program is not required to print an announcement.)

   These requirements apply to the modified work as a whole. If identifiable sections of that work are not derived from the Program, and can be reasonably considered independent and separate works in themselves, then this License, and its terms, do not apply to those sections when you distribute them as separate works. But when you distribute the same sections as part of a whole which is a work based on the Program, the distribution of the whole must be on the terms of this License, whose permissions for other licensees extend to the entire whole, and thus to each and every part regardless of who wrote it.

Thus, it is not the intent of this section to claim rights or contest your rights to work written entirely by you; rather, the intent is to exercise the right to control the distribution of derivative or collective works based on the Program. In addition, mere aggregation of another work not based on the Program with the Program (or with a work based on the Program) on a volume of a storage or distribution medium does not bring the other work under the scope of this License.

3. You may copy and distribute the Program (or a work based on it, under Section 2) in object code or executable form under the terms of Sections 1 and 2 above provided that you also do one of the following:

   a) Accompany it with the complete corresponding machine-readable source code, which must be distributed under the terms of Sections 1 and 2 above on a medium customarily used for software interchange; or,

   b) Accompany it with a written offer, valid for at least three years, to give any third party, for a charge no more than your cost of physically performing source distribution, a complete machine-readable copy of the corresponding source code, to be distributed under the terms of Sections 1 and 2 above on a medium customarily used for software interchange; or,

   c) Accompany it with the information you received as to the offer to distribute corresponding source code. (This alternative is allowed only for noncommercial distribution and only if you received the program in object code or executable form with such an offer, in accord with Subsection b above.)

The source code for a work means the preferred form of the work for making modifications to it. For an executable work, complete source code means all the source code for all modules it contains, plus any associated interface definition files, plus the scripts used to control compilation and installation of the executable. However, as a special exception, the source code distributed need not include anything that is normally distributed (in either source or binary form) with the major components (compiler, kernel, and so on) of the operating system on which the executable runs, unless that component itself accompanies the executable.

If distribution of executable or object code is made by offering access to copy from a designated place, then offering equivalent access to copy the source code from the same place counts as distribution of the source code, even though third parties are not compelled to copy the source along with the object code.

4. You may not copy, modify, sublicense, or distribute the Program except as expressly provided under this License. Any attempt otherwise to copy, modify, sublicense or distribute the Program is void, and will automatically terminate your rights under this License. However, parties who have received copies, or rights, from you under this License will not have their licenses terminated so long as such parties remain in full compliance.

5. You are not required to accept this License, since you have not signed it. However, nothing else grants you permission to modify or distribute the Program or its derivative works. These actions are prohibited by law if you do not accept this License. Therefore, by modifying or distributing the Program (or any work based on the Program), you indicate your acceptance of this License to do so, and all its terms and conditions for copying, distributing or modifying the Program or works based on it.

6. Each time you redistribute the Program (or any work based on the Program), the recipient automatically receives a license from the original licensor to copy, distribute or modify the Program subject to these terms and conditions. You may not impose any further restrictions on the recipients' exercise of the rights granted herein. You are not responsible for enforcing compliance by third parties to this License.

7. If, as a consequence of a court judgment or allegation of patent infringement or for any other reason (not limited to patent issues), conditions are imposed on you (whether by court order, agreement or otherwise) that contradict the conditions of this License, they do not excuse you from the conditions of this License. If you cannot distribute so as to satisfy simultaneously your obligations under this License and any other pertinent obligations, then as a consequence you may not distribute the Program at all. For example, if a patent license would not permit royalty-free redistribution of the Program by all those who receive copies directly or indirectly through you, then the only way you could satisfy both it and this License would be to refrain entirely from distribution of the Program.

    If any portion of this section is held invalid or unenforceable under any particular circumstance, the balance of the section is intended to apply and the section as a whole is intended to apply in other circumstances.

    It is not the purpose of this section to induce you to infringe any patents or other property right claims or to contest validity of any such claims; this section has the sole purpose of protecting the integrity of the free software distribution system, which is implemented by public license practices. Many people have made generous contributions to the wide range of software distributed through that system in reliance on consistent application of that system; it is up to the author/donor to decide if he or she is willing to distribute software through any other system and a licensee cannot impose that choice.

    This section is intended to make thoroughly clear what is believed to be a consequence of the rest of this License.

8. If the distribution and/or use of the Program is restricted in certain countries either by patents or by copyrighted interfaces, the original copyright holder who places the Program under this License may add an explicit geographical distribution limitation excluding those countries, so that distribution is permitted only in or among countries not thus excluded. In such case, this License incorporates the limitation as if written in the body of this License.

9. The Free Software Foundation may publish revised and/or new versions of the General Public License from time to time. Such new versions will be similar in spirit to the present version, but may differ in detail to address new problems or concerns.

    Each version is given a distinguishing version number. If the Program specifies a version number of this License which applies to it and "any later version", you have the option of following the terms and conditions either of that version or of any later version published by the Free Software Foundation. If the Program does not specify a version number of this License, you may choose any version ever published by the Free Software Foundation.

10. If you wish to incorporate parts of the Program into other free programs whose distribution conditions are different, write to the author to ask for permission. For software which is copyrighted by the Free Software Foundation, write to the Free Software Foundation; we sometimes make exceptions for this. Our decision will be guided by the two goals of preserving the free status of all derivatives of our free software and of promoting the sharing and reuse of software generally.

Installation Instructions

To install the items from the CD to your hard drive, follow these steps:

1. **Insert CD1 into your computer's CD-ROM drive.**

2. **Reboot your PC.** (As long as your PC is configured to boot from the CD, this starts the Linux installation process for you automatically.)

3. **Congratulations!** The Linux installation process is now underway. For the rest of the gory details on this fascinating task, please consult Chapter 3.

To install the items from the CD to your hard drive with a boot disk (we show you how to make one in Chapter 2), follow these steps:

1. **Insert CD1 into your computer's CD-ROM drive, and insert a bootable Linux floppy into your computer's floppy drive — see the instructions for creating a bootable Linux floppy in Chapter 2.**

2. **Reboot your PC.** (This starts the Linux installation process for you automatically.)

3. **Congratulations!** The Linux installation process is now underway. For the rest of the gory details on this fascinating task, please consult Chapter 3.

For more information, see the "About the CD-ROMs" appendix (Appendix C to be exact).

Limited Warranty

IDG Books Worldwide, Inc. (hereafter IDGB) warrants that the Software and Software Media are free from defects in materials and workmanship under normal use for a period of sixty (60) days from the date of purchase of this Book. If IDGB receives notification within the warranty period of defects in materials or workmanship, IDGB will replace the defective Software Media.

IDGB AND THE AUTHOR OF THE BOOK DISCLAIM ALL OTHER WARRANTIES, EXPRESS OR IMPLIED, INCLUDING WITHOUT LIMITATION IMPLIED WARRANTIES OF MERCHANTABILITY AND FITNESS FOR A PARTICULAR PURPOSE, WITH RESPECT TO THE SOFTWARE, THE PROGRAMS, THE SOURCE CODE CONTAINED THEREIN, AND/OR THE TECHNIQUES DESCRIBED IN THIS BOOK. IDGB DOES NOT WARRANT THAT THE FUNCTIONS CONTAINED IN THE SOFTWARE WILL MEET YOUR REQUIREMENTS OR THAT THE OPERATION OF THE SOFTWARE WILL BE ERROR FREE.

This limited warranty gives you specific legal rights, and you may have other rights that vary from jurisdiction to jurisdiction.

Dummies Books™
Bestsellers on Every Topic!

GENERAL INTEREST TITLES

BUSINESS & PERSONAL FINANCE

Accounting For Dummies®	John A. Tracy, CPA	0-7645-5014-4	$19.99 US/$27.99 CAN
Business Plans For Dummies®	Paul Tiffany, Ph.D. & Steven D. Peterson, Ph.D.	1-56884-868-4	$19.99 US/$27.99 CAN
Business Writing For Dummies®	Sheryl Lindsell-Roberts	0-7645-5134-5	$16.99 US/$27.99 CAN
Consulting For Dummies®	Bob Nelson & Peter Economy	0-7645-5034-9	$19.99 US/$27.99 CAN
Customer Service For Dummies®, 2nd Edition	Karen Leland & Keith Bailey	0-7645-5209-0	$19.99 US/$27.99 CAN
Franchising For Dummies®	Dave Thomas & Michael Seid	0-7645-5160-4	$19.99 US/$27.99 CAN
Getting Results For Dummies®	Mark H. McCormack	0-7645-5205-8	$19.99 US/$27.99 CAN
Home Buying For Dummies®	Eric Tyson, MBA & Ray Brown	1-56884-385-2	$16.99 US/$24.99 CAN
House Selling For Dummies®	Eric Tyson, MBA & Ray Brown	0-7645-5038-1	$16.99 US/$24.99 CAN
Human Resources Kit For Dummies®	Max Messmer	0-7645-5131-0	$19.99 US/$27.99 CAN
Investing For Dummies®, 2nd Edition	Eric Tyson, MBA	0-7645-5162-0	$19.99 US/$27.99 CAN
Law For Dummies®	John Ventura	1-56884-860-9	$19.99 US/$27.99 CAN
Leadership For Dummies®	Marshall Loeb & Steven Kindel	0-7645-5176-0	$19.99 US/$27.99 CAN
Managing For Dummies®	Bob Nelson & Peter Economy	1-56884-858-7	$19.99 US/$27.99 CAN
Marketing For Dummies®	Alexander Hiam	1-56884-699-1	$19.99 US/$27.99 CAN
Mutual Funds For Dummies®, 2nd Edition	Eric Tyson, MBA	0-7645-5112-4	$19.99 US/$27.99 CAN
Negotiating For Dummies®	Michael C. Donaldson & Mimi Donaldson	1-56884-867-6	$19.99 US/$27.99 CAN
Personal Finance For Dummies®, 3rd Edition	Eric Tyson, MBA	0-7645-5231-7	$19.99 US/$27.99 CAN
Personal Finance For Dummies® For Canadians, 2nd Edition	Eric Tyson, MBA & Tony Martin	0-7645-5123-X	$19.99 US/$27.99 CAN
Public Speaking For Dummies®	Malcolm Kushner	0-7645-5159-0	$16.99 US/$24.99 CAN
Sales Closing For Dummies®	Tom Hopkins	0-7645-5063-2	$14.99 US/$21.99 CAN
Sales Prospecting For Dummies®	Tom Hopkins	0-7645-5066-7	$14.99 US/$21.99 CAN
Selling For Dummies®	Tom Hopkins	1-56884-389-5	$16.99 US/$24.99 CAN
Small Business For Dummies®	Eric Tyson, MBA & Jim Schell	0-7645-5094-2	$19.99 US/$27.99 CAN
Small Business Kit For Dummies®	Richard D. Harroch	0-7645-5093-4	$24.99 US/$34.99 CAN
Taxes 2001 For Dummies®	Eric Tyson & David J. Silverman	0-7645-5306-2	$15.99 US/$23.99 CAN
Time Management For Dummies®, 2nd Edition	Jeffrey J. Mayer	0-7645-5145-0	$19.99 US/$27.99 CAN
Writing Business Letters For Dummies®	Sheryl Lindsell-Roberts	0-7645-5207-4	$16.99 US/$24.99 CAN

TECHNOLOGY TITLES

INTERNET/ONLINE

America Online® For Dummies®, 6th Edition	John Kaufeld	0-7645-0670-6	$19.99 US/$27.99 CAN
Banking Online Dummies®	Paul Murphy	0-7645-0458-4	$24.99 US/$34.99 CAN
eBay™ For Dummies®, 2nd Edition	Marcia Collier, Roland Woerner, & Stephanie Becker	0-7645-0761-3	$19.99 US/$27.99 CAN
E-Mail For Dummies®, 2nd Edition	John R. Levine, Carol Baroudi, & Arnold Reinhold	0-7645-0131-3	$24.99 US/$34.99 CAN
Genealogy Online For Dummies®, 2nd Edition	Matthew L. Helm & April Leah Helm	0-7645-0543-2	$24.99 US/$34.99 CAN
Internet Directory For Dummies®, 3rd Edition	Brad Hill	0-7645-0558-2	$24.99 US/$34.99 CAN
Internet Auctions For Dummies®	Greg Holden	0-7645-0578-9	$24.99 US/$34.99 CAN
Internet Explorer 5.5 For Windows® For Dummies®	Doug Lowe	0-7645-0738-9	$19.99 US/$28.99 CAN
Researching Online For Dummies®, 2nd Edition	Mary Ellen Bates & Reva Basch	0-7645-0546-7	$24.99 US/$34.99 CAN
Job Searching Online For Dummies®	Pam Dixon	0-7645-0673-0	$24.99 US/$34.99 CAN
Investing Online For Dummies®, 3rd Edition	Kathleen Sindell, Ph.D.	0-7645-0725-7	$24.99 US/$34.99 CAN
Travel Planning Online For Dummies®, 2nd Edition	Noah Vadnai	0-7645-0438-X	$24.99 US/$34.99 CAN
Internet Searching For Dummies®	Brad Hill	0-7645-0478-9	$24.99 US/$34.99 CAN
Yahoo!® For Dummies®, 2nd Edition	Brad Hill	0-7645-0762-1	$19.99 US/$27.99 CAN
The Internet For Dummies®, 7th Edition	John R. Levine, Carol Baroudi, & Arnold Reinhold	0-7645-0674-9	$19.99 US/$27.99 CAN

OPERATING SYSTEMS

DOS For Dummies®, 3rd Edition	Dan Gookin	0-7645-0361-8	$19.99 US/$27.99 CAN
GNOME For Linux® For Dummies®	David B. Busch	0-7645-0650-1	$24.99 US/$37.99 CAN
LINUX® For Dummies®, 2nd Edition	John Hall, Craig Witherspoon, & Coletta Witherspoon	0-7645-0421-5	$24.99 US/$34.99 CAN
Mac® OS 9 For Dummies®	Bob LeVitus	0-7645-0652-8	$19.99 US/$28.99 CAN
Red Hat® Linux® For Dummies®	Jon "maddog" Hall, Paul Sery	0-7645-0663-3	$24.99 US/$37.99 CAN
Small Business Windows® 98 For Dummies®	Stephen Nelson	0-7645-0425-8	$24.99 US/$34.99 CAN
UNIX® For Dummies®, 4th Edition	John R. Levine & Margaret Levine Young	0-7645-0419-3	$19.99 US/$27.99 CAN
Windows® 95 For Dummies®, 2nd Edition	Andy Rathbone	0-7645-0180-1	$19.99 US/$27.99 CAN
Windows® 98 For Dummies®	Andy Rathbone	0-7645-0261-1	$19.99 US/$27.99 CAN
Windows® 2000 For Dummies®	Andy Rathbone	0-7645-0641-2	$19.99 US/$27.99 CAN
Windows® 2000 Server For Dummies®	Ed Tittel	0-7645-0341-3	$24.99 US/$37.99 CAN
Windows® ME Millennium Edition For Dummies®	Andy Rathbone	0-7645-0735-4	$19.99 US/$27.99 CAN

Dummies Books™
Bestsellers on Every Topic!

GENERAL INTEREST TITLES

FOOD & BEVERAGE/ENTERTAINING

Title	Author	ISBN	Price
rtending For Dummies®	Ray Foley	0-7645-5051-9	$14.99 US/$21.99 CAN
oking For Dummies®, 2nd Edition	Bryan Miller & Marie Rama	0-7645-5250-3	$19.99 US/$27.99 CAN
tertaining For Dummies®	Suzanne Williamson with Linda Smith	0-7645-5027-6	$19.99 US/$27.99 CAN
ourmet Cooking For Dummies®	Charlie Trotter	0-7645-5029-2	$19.99 US/$27.99 CAN
rilling For Dummies®	Marie Rama & John Mariani	0-7645-5076-4	$19.99 US/$27.99 CAN
alian Cooking For Dummies®	Cesare Casella & Jack Bishop	0-7645-5098-5	$19.99 US/$27.99 CAN
exican Cooking For Dummies®	Mary Sue Miliken & Susan Feniger	0-7645-5169-8	$19.99 US/$27.99 CAN
uick & Healthy Cooking For Dummies®	Lynn Fischer	0-7645-5214-7	$19.99 US/$27.99 CAN
ine For Dummies®, 2nd Edition	Ed McCarthy & Mary Ewing-Mulligan	0-7645-5114-0	$19.99 US/$27.99 CAN
inese Cooking For Dummies®	Martin Yan	0-7645-5247-3	$19.99 US/$27.99 CAN
iquette For Dummies®	Sue Fox	0-7645-5170-1	$19.99 US/$27.99 CAN

SPORTS

aseball For Dummies®, 2nd Edition	Joe Morgan with Richard Lally	0-7645-5234-1	$19.99 US/$27.99 CAN
olf For Dummies®, 2nd Edition	Gary McCord	0-7645-5146-9	$19.99 US/$27.99 CAN
y Fishing For Dummies®	Peter Kaminsky	0-7645-5073-X	$19.99 US/$27.99 CAN
otball For Dummies®	Howie Long with John Czarnecki	0-7645-5054-3	$19.99 US/$27.99 CAN
ockey For Dummies®	John Davidson with John Steinbreder	0-7645-5045-4	$19.99 US/$27.99 CAN
ASCAR For Dummies®	Mark Martin	0-7645-5219-8	$19.99 US/$27.99 CAN
ennis For Dummies®	Patrick McEnroe with Peter Bodo	0-7645-5087-X	$19.99 US/$27.99 CAN
occer For Dummies®	U.S. Soccer Federation & Michael Lewiss	0-7645-5229-5	$19.99 US/$27.99 CAN

HOME & GARDEN

nnuals For Dummies®	Bill Marken & NGA	0-7645-5056-X	$16.99 US/$24.99 CAN
ontainer Gardening For Dummies®	Bill Marken & NGA	0-7645-5057-8	$16.99 US/$24.99 CAN
ecks & Patios For Dummies®	Robert J. Beckstrom & NGA	0-7645-5075-6	$16.99 US/$24.99 CAN
owering Bulbs For Dummies®	Judy Glattstein & NGA	0-7645-5103-5	$16.99 US/$24.99 CAN
ardening For Dummies®, 2nd Edition	Michael MacCaskey & NGA	0-7645-5130-2	$16.99 US/$24.99 CAN
erb Gardening For Dummies®	NGA	0-7645-5200-7	$16.99 US/$24.99 CAN
ome Improvement For Dummies®	Gene & Katie Hamilton & the Editors of HouseNet, Inc.	0-7645-5005-5	$19.99 US/$26.99 CAN
ouseplants For Dummies®	Larry Hodgson & NGA	0-7645-5102-7	$16.99 US/$24.99 CAN
ainting and Wallpapering For Dummies®	Gene Hamilton	0-7645-5150-7	$16.99 US/$24.99 CAN
erennials For Dummies®	Marcia Tatroe & NGA	0-7645-5030-6	$16.99 US/$24.99 CAN
oses For Dummies®, 2nd Edition	Lance Walheim	0-7645-5202-3	$16.99 US/$24.99 CAN
ees and Shrubs For Dummies®	Ann Whitman & NGA	0-7645-5203-1	$16.99 US/$24.99 CAN
egetable Gardening For Dummies®	Charlie Nardozzi & NGA	0-7645-5129-9	$16.99 US/$24.99 CAN
ome Cooking For Dummies®	Patricia Hart McMillan & Katharine Kaye McMillan	0-7645-5107-8	$19.99 US/$27.99 CAN

TECHNOLOGY TITLES

WEB DESIGN & PUBLISHING

ctive Server Pages For Dummies®, 2nd Edition	Bill Hatfield	0-7645-0603-X	$24.99 US/$37.99 CAN
old Fusion 4 For Dummies®	Alexis Gutzman	0-7645-0604-8	$24.99 US/$37.99 CAN
reating Web Pages For Dummies®, 5th Edition	Bud Smith & Arthur Bebak	0-7645-0733-8	$24.99 US/$34.99 CAN
reamweaver™ 3 For Dummies®	Janine Warner & Paul Vachier	0-7645-0669-2	$24.99 US/$34.99 CAN
ontPage® 2000 For Dummies®	Asha Dornfest	0-7645-0423-1	$24.99 US/$34.99 CAN
TML 4 For Dummies®, 3rd Edition	Ed Tittel & Natanya Dits	0-7645-0572-6	$24.99 US/$34.99 CAN
va™ For Dummies®, 3rd Edition	Aaron E. Walsh	0-7645-0417-7	$24.99 US/$34.99 CAN
ageMill™ 2 For Dummies®	Deke McClelland & John San Filippo	0-7645-0028-7	$24.99 US/$34.99 CAN
ML™ For Dummies®	Ed Tittel	0-7645-0692-7	$24.99 US/$37.99 CAN
vascript For Dummies®, 3rd Edition	Emily Vander Veer	0-7645-0633-1	$24.99 US/$37.99 CAN

DESKTOP PUBLISHING GRAPHICS/MULTIMEDIA

dobe® In Design™ For Dummies®	Deke McClelland	0-7645-0599-8	$19.99 US/$27.99 CAN
orelDRAW™ 9 For Dummies®	Deke McClelland	0-7645-0523-8	$19.99 US/$27.99 CAN
esktop Publishing and Design For Dummies®	Roger C. Parker	1-5685-4234-1	$19.99 US/$27.99 CAN
igital Photography For Dummies®, 3rd Edition	Julie Adair King	0-7645-0646-3	$24.99 US/$37.99 CAN
icrosoft® Publisher 98 For Dummies®	Jim McCarter	0-7645-0395-2	$19.99 US/$27.99 CAN
isio 2000 For Dummies®	Debbie Walkowski	0-7645-0635-8	$19.99 US/$27.99 CAN
icrosoft® Publisher 2000 For Dummies®	Jim McCarter	0-7645-0525-4	$19.99 US/$27.99 CAN
indows® Movie Maker For Dummies®	Keith Underdahl	0-7645-0749-1	$19.99 US/$27.99 CAN

Dummies Books™
Bestsellers on Every Topic!

GENERAL INTEREST TITLES

EDUCATION & TEST PREPARATION

The ACT For Dummies®	Suzee Vlk	1-56884-387-9	$14.99 US/$21.99 CAN
College Financial Aid For Dummies®	Dr. Herm Davis & Joyce Lain Kennedy	0-7645-5049-7	$19.99 US/$27.99 CAN
College Planning For Dummies®, 2nd Edition	Pat Ordovensky	0-7645-5048-9	$19.99 US/$27.99 CAN
Everyday Math For Dummies®	Charles Seiter, Ph.D.	1-56884-248-1	$14.99 US/$21.99 CAN
The GMAT® For Dummies®, 3rd Edition	Suzee Vlk	0-7645-5082-9	$16.99 US/$24.99 CAN
The GRE® For Dummies®, 3rd Edition	Suzee Vlk	0-7645-5083-7	$16.99 US/$24.99 CAN
Politics For Dummies®	Ann DeLaney	1-56884-381-X	$19.99 US/$27.99 CAN
The SAT I For Dummies®, 3rd Edition	Suzee Vlk	0-7645-5044-6	$14.99 US/$21.99 CAN

AUTOMOTIVE

Auto Repair For Dummies®	Deanna Sclar	0-7645-5089-6	$19.99 US/$27.99 CAN
Buying A Car For Dummies®	Deanna Sclar	0-7645-5091-8	$16.99 US/$24.99 CAN

LIFESTYLE/SELF-HELP

Dating For Dummies®	Dr. Joy Browne	0-7645-5072-1	$19.99 US/$27.99 CAN
Making Marriage Work For Dummies®	Steven Simring, M.D. & Sue Klavans Simring, D.S.W	0-7645-5173-6	$19.99 US/$27.99 CAN
Parenting For Dummies®	Sandra H. Gookin	1-56884-383-6	$16.99 US/$24.99 CAN
Success For Dummies®	Zig Ziglar	0-7645-5061-6	$19.99 US/$27.99 CAN
Weddings For Dummies®	Marcy Blum & Laura Fisher Kaiser	0-7645-5055-1	$19.99 US/$27.99 CAN

TECHNOLOGY TITLES

SUITES

Microsoft® Office 2000 For Windows® For Dummies®	Wallace Wang & Roger C. Parker	0-7645-0452-5	$19.99 US/$27.99 CAN
Microsoft® Office 2000 For Windows® For Dummies® Quick Reference	Doug Lowe & Bjoern Hartsfvang	0-7645-0453-3	$12.99 US/$17.99 CAN
Microsoft® Office 97 For Windows® For Dummies®	Wallace Wang & Roger C. Parker	0-7645-0050-3	$19.99 US/$27.99 CAN
Microsoft® Office 97 For Windows® For Dummies® Quick Reference	Doug Lowe	0-7645-0062-7	$12.99 US/$17.99 CAN
Microsoft® Office 98 For Macs® For Dummies®	Tom Negrino	0-7645-0229-8	$19.99 US/$27.99 CAN
Microsoft® Office X For Macs For Dummies®	Tom Negrino	0-7645-0702-8	$19.95 US/$27.99 CAN

WORD PROCESSING

Word 2000 For Windows® For Dummies® Quick Reference	Peter Weverka	0-7645-0449-5	$12.99 US/$19.99 CAN
Corel® WordPerfect® 8 For Windows® For Dummies®	Margaret Levine Young, David Kay & Jordan Young	0-7645-0186-0	$19.99 US/$27.99 CAN
Word 2000 For Windows® For Dummies®	Dan Gookin	0-7645-0448-7	$19.99 US/$27.99 CAN
Word For Windows® 95 For Dummies®	Dan Gookin	1-56884-932-X	$19.99 US/$27.99 CAN
Word 97 For Windows® For Dummies®	Dan Gookin	0-7645-0052-X	$19.99 US/$27.99 CAN
WordPerfect® 9 For Windows® For Dummies®	Margaret Levine Young	0-7645-0427-4	$19.99 US/$27.99 CAN
WordPerfect® 7 For Windows® 95 For Dummies®	Margaret Levine Young & David Kay	1-56884-949-4	$19.99 US/$27.99 CAN

SPREADSHEET/FINANCE/PROJECT MANAGEMENT

Excel For Windows® 95 For Dummies®	Greg Harvey	1-56884-930-3	$19.99 US/$27.99 CAN
Excel 2000 For Windows® For Dummies®	Greg Harvey	0-7645-0446-0	$19.99 US/$27.99 CAN
Excel 2000 For Windows® For Dummies® Quick Reference	John Walkenbach	0-7645-0447-9	$12.99 US/$17.99 CAN
Microsoft® Money 99 For Dummies®	Peter Weverka	0-7645-0433-9	$19.99 US/$27.99 CAN
Microsoft® Project 98 For Dummies®	Martin Doucette	0-7645-0321-9	$24.99 US/$34.99 CAN
Microsoft® Project 2000 For Dummies®	Martin Doucette	0-7645-0517-3	$24.99 US/$37.99 CAN
Microsoft® Money 2000 For Dummies®	Peter Weverka	0-7645-0579-3	$19.99 US/$27.99 CAN
MORE Excel 97 For Windows® For Dummies®	Greg Harvey	0-7645-0138-0	$22.99 US/$32.99 CAN
Quicken® 2000 For Dummies®	Stephen L . Nelson	0-7645-0607-2	$19.99 US/$27.99 CAN
Quicken® 2001 For Dummies®	Stephen L . Nelson	0-7645-0759-1	$19.99 US/$27.99 CAN
Quickbooks® 2000 For Dummies®	Stephen L . Nelson	0-7645-0665-x	$19.99 US/$27.99 CAN

Dummies Books™
Bestsellers on Every Topic!

GENERAL INTEREST TITLES

CAREERS

Cover Letters For Dummies®, 2nd Edition	Joyce Lain Kennedy	0-7645-5224-4	$12.99 US/$17.99 CAN
Cool Careers For Dummies®	Marty Nemko, Paul Edwards, & Sarah Edwards	0-7645-5095-0	$16.99 US/$24.99 CAN
Job Hunting For Dummies®, 2nd Edition	Max Messmer	0-7645-5163-9	$19.99 US/$26.99 CAN
Job Interviews For Dummies®, 2nd Edition	Joyce Lain Kennedy	0-7645-5225-2	$12.99 US/$17.99 CAN
Resumes For Dummies®, 2nd Edition	Joyce Lain Kennedy	0-7645-5113-2	$12.99 US/$17.99 CAN

FITNESS

Fitness Walking For Dummies®	Liz Neporent	0-7645-5192-2	$19.99 US/$27.99 CAN
Fitness For Dummies®, 2nd Edition	Suzanne Schlosberg & Liz Neporent	0-7645-5167-1	$19.99 US/$27.99 CAN
Nutrition For Dummies®, 2nd Edition	Carol Ann Rinzler	0-7645-5180-9	$19.99 US/$27.99 CAN
Running For Dummies®	Florence "Flo-Jo" Griffith Joyner & John Hanc	0-7645-5096-9	$19.99 US/$27.99 CAN

FOREIGN LANGUAGE

Spanish For Dummies®	Susana Wald	0-7645-5194-9	$24.99 US/$34.99 CAN
French For Dummies®	Dodi-Kartrin Schmidt & Michelle W. Willams	0-7645-5193-0	$24.99 US/$34.99 CAN

TECHNOLOGY TITLES

DATABASE

Access 2000 For Windows® For Dummies®	John Kaufeld	0-7645-0444-4	$19.99 US/$27.99 CAN
Access 97 For Windows® For Dummies®	John Kaufeld	0-7645-0048-1	$19.99 US/$27.99 CAN
Access 2000 For Windows For Dummies® Quick Reference	Alison Barrons	0-7645-0445-2	$12.99 US/$17.99 CAN
Approach® 97 For Windows® For Dummies®	Deborah S. Ray & Eric J. Ray	0-7645-0001-5	$19.99 US/$27.99 CAN
Crystal Reports 8 For Dummies®	Douglas J. Wolf	0-7645-0642-0	$24.99 US/$34.99 CAN
Data Warehousing For Dummies®	Alan R. Simon	0-7645-0170-4	$24.99 US/$34.99 CAN
FileMaker® Pro 4 For Dummies®	Tom Maremaa	0-7645-0210-7	$19.99 US/$27.99 CAN

NETWORKING/GROUPWARE

ATM For Dummies®	Cathy Gadecki & Christine Heckart	0-7645-0065-1	$24.99 US/$34.99 CAN
Client/Server Computing For Dummies®, 3rd Edition	Doug Lowe	0-7645-0476-2	$24.99 US/$34.99 CAN
DSL For Dummies®, 2nd Edition	David Angell	0-7645-0715-X	$24.99 US/$35.99 CAN
Lotus Notes® Release 4 For Dummies®	Stephen Londergan & Pat Freeland	1-56884-934-6	$19.99 US/$27.99 CAN
Microsoft® Outlook® 98 For Windows® For Dummies®	Bill Dyszel	0-7645-0393-6	$19.99 US/$28.99 CAN
Microsoft® Outlook® 2000 For Windows® For Dummies®	Bill Dyszel	0-7645-0471-1	$19.99 US/$27.99 CAN
Migrating to Windows® 2000 For Dummies®	Leonard Sterns	0-7645-0459-2	$24.99 US/$37.99 CAN
Networking For Dummies®, 4th Edition	Doug Lowe	0-7645-0498-3	$19.99 US/$27.99 CAN
Networking Home PCs For Dummies®	Kathy Ivens	0-7645-0491-6	$24.99 US/$35.99 CAN
Upgrading & Fixing Networks For Dummies®, 2nd Edition	Bill Camarda	0-7645-0542-4	$29.99 US/$42.99 CAN
TCP/IP For Dummies®, 4th Edition	Candace Leiden & Marshall Wilensky	0-7645-0726-5	$24.99 US/$35.99 CAN
Windows NT® Networking For Dummies®	Ed Tittel, Mary Madden, & Earl Follis	0-7645-0015-5	$24.99 US/$34.99 CAN

PROGRAMMING

Active Server Pages For Dummies®, 2nd Edition	Bill Hatfield	0-7645-0065-1	$24.99 US/$34.99 CAN
Beginning Programming For Dummies®	Wally Wang	0-7645-0596-0	$19.99 US/$29.99 CAN
C++ For Dummies® Quick Reference, 2nd Edition	Namir Shammas	0-7645-0390-1	$14.99 US/$21.99 CAN
Java™ Programming For Dummies®, 3rd Edition	David & Donald Koosis	0-7645-0388-X	$29.99 US/$42.99 CAN
JBuilder™ For Dummies®	Barry A. Burd	0-7645-0567-X	$24.99 US/$34.99 CAN
VBA For Dummies®, 2nd Edition	Steve Cummings	0-7645-0078-3	$24.99 US/$37.99 CAN
Windows® 2000 Programming For Dummies®	Richard Simon	0-7645-0469-X	$24.99 US/$37.99 CAN
XML For Dummies®, 2nd Edition	Ed Tittel	0-7645-0692-7	$24.99 US/$37.99 CAN

Dummies Books™
Bestsellers on Every Topic!

GENERAL INTEREST TITLES

THE ARTS

Art For Dummies®	Thomas Hoving	0-7645-5104-3	$24.99 US/$34.99 CAN
Blues For Dummies®	Lonnie Brooks, Cub Koda, & Wayne Baker Brooks	0-7645-5080-2	$24.99 US/$34.99 CAN
Classical Music For Dummies®	David Pogue & Scott Speck	0-7645-5009-8	$24.99 US/$34.99 CAN
Guitar For Dummies®	Mark Phillips & Jon Chappell of Cherry Lane Music	0-7645-5106-X	$24.99 US/$34.99 CAN
Jazz For Dummies®	Dirk Sutro	0-7645-5081-0	$24.99 US/$34.99 CAN
Opera For Dummies®	David Pogue & Scott Speck	0-7645-5010-1	$24.99 US/$34.99 CAN
Piano For Dummies®	Blake Neely of Cherry Lane Music	0-7645-5105-1	$24.99 US/$34.99 CAN
Shakespeare For Dummies®	John Doyle & Ray Lischner	0-7645-5135-3	$19.99 US/$27.99 CAN

HEALTH

Allergies and Asthma For Dummies®	William Berger, M.D.	0-7645-5218-X	$19.99 US/$27.99 CAN
Alternative Medicine For Dummies®	James Dillard, M.D., D.C., C.A.C., & Terra Ziporyn, Ph.D.	0-7645-5109-4	$19.99 US/$27.99 CAN
Beauty Secrets For Dummies®	Stephanie Seymour	0-7645-5078-0	$19.99 US/$27.99 CAN
Diabetes For Dummies®	Alan L. Rubin, M.D.	0-7645-5154-X	$19.99 US/$27.99 CAN
Dieting For Dummies®	The American Dietetic Society with Jane Kirby, R.D.	0-7645-5126-4	$19.99 US/$27.99 CAN
Family Health For Dummies®	Charles Inlander & Karla Morales	0-7645-5121-3	$19.99 US/$27.99 CAN
First Aid For Dummies®	Charles B. Inlander & The People's Medical Society	0-7645-5213-9	$19.99 US/$27.99 CAN
Fitness For Dummies®, 2nd Edition	Suzanne Schlosberg & Liz Neporent, M.A.	0-7645-5167-1	$19.99 US/$27.99 CAN
Healing Foods For Dummies®	Molly Siple, M.S. R.D.	0-7645-5198-1	$19.99 US/$27.99 CAN
Healthy Aging For Dummies®	Walter Bortz, M.D.	0-7645-5233-3	$19.99 US/$27.99 CAN
Men's Health For Dummies®	Charles Inlander	0-7645-5120-5	$19.99 US/$27.99 CAN
Nutrition For Dummies®, 2nd Edition	Carol Ann Rinzler	0-7645-5180-9	$19.99 US/$27.99 CAN
Pregnancy For Dummies®	Joanne Stone, M.D., Keith Eddleman, M.D., & Mary Murray	0-7645-5074-8	$19.99 US/$27.99 CAN
Sex For Dummies®	Dr. Ruth K. Westheimer	1-56884-384-4	$16.99 US/$24.99 CAN
Stress Management For Dummies®	Allen Elkin, Ph.D.	0-7645-5144-2	$19.99 US/$27.99 CAN
The Healthy Heart For Dummies®	James M. Ripple, M.D.	0-7645-5166-3	$19.99 US/$27.99 CAN
Weight Training For Dummies®	Liz Neporent, M.A. & Suzanne Schlosberg	0-7645-5036-5	$19.99 US/$27.99 CAN
Women's Health For Dummies®	Pamela Maraldo, Ph.D., R.N., & The People's Medical Society	0-7645-5119-1	$19.99 US/$27.99 CAN

TECHNOLOGY TITLES

MACINTOSH

Macs® For Dummies®, 7th Edition	David Pogue	0-7645-0703-6	$19.99 US/$27.99 CAN
The iBook™ For Dummies®	David Pogue	0-7645-0647-1	$19.99 US/$27.99 CAN
The iMac For Dummies®, 2nd Edition	David Pogue	0-7645-0648-X	$19.99 US/$27.99 CAN
The iMac For Dummies® Quick Reference	Jennifer Watson	0-7645-0718-4	$12.99 US/$19.99 CAN

PC/GENERAL COMPUTING

Building A PC For Dummies®, 2nd Edition	Mark Chambers	0-7645-0571-8	$24.99 US/$34.99 CAN
Buying a Computer For Dummies®	Dan Gookin	0-7645-0632-3	$19.99 US/$27.99 CAN
Illustrated Computer Dictionary For Dummies®, 4th Edition	Dan Gookin & Sandra Hardin Gookin	0-7645-0732-X	$19.99 US/$27.99 CAN
Palm Computing® For Dummies®	Bill Dyszel	0-7645-0581-5	$24.99 US/$34.99 CAN
PCs For Dummies®, 7th Edition	Dan Gookin	0-7645-0594-7	$19.99 US/$27.99 CAN
Small Business Computing For Dummies®	Brian Underdahl	0-7645-0287-5	$24.99 US/$34.99 CAN
Smart Homes For Dummies®	Danny Briere	0-7645-0527-0	$19.99 US/$27.99 CAN
Upgrading & Fixing PCs For Dummies®, 5th Edition	Andy Rathbone	0-7645-0719-2	$19.99 US/$27.99 CAN
Handspring Visor For Dummies®	Joe Hubko	0-7645-0724-9	$19.99 US/$27.99 CAN

YOUR ONLINE RESOURCE

WWW.DUMMIES.COM

Discover Dummies Online!

The Dummies Web Site is your fun and friendly online resource for the latest information about *For Dummies®* books and your favorite topics. The Web site is the place to communicate with us, exchange ideas with other *For Dummies* readers, chat with authors, and have fun!

Ten Fun and Useful Things You Can Do at www.dummies.com

1. Win free *For Dummies* books and more!
2. Register your book and be entered in a prize drawing.
3. Meet your favorite authors through the IDG Books Worldwide Author Chat Series.
4. Exchange helpful information with other *For Dummies* readers.
5. Discover other great *For Dummies* books you must have!
6. Purchase Dummieswear® exclusively from our Web site.
7. Buy *For Dummies* books online.
8. Talk to us. Make comments, ask questions, get answers!
9. Download free software.
10. Find additional useful resources from authors.

Link directly to these ten fun and useful things at
http://www.dummies.com/10useful

SURF THE NET

WWW.DUMMIES.COM

For other technology titles from IDG Books Worldwide, go to
www.idgbooks.com

Not on the Web yet? It's easy to get started with *Dummies 101®: The Internet For Windows® 98* or *The Internet For Dummies®* at local retailers everywhere.

IDG BOOKS WORLDWIDE

Find other *For Dummies* books on these topics:
Business • Career • Databases • Food & Beverage • Games • Gardening • Graphics • Hardware
Health & Fitness • Internet and the World Wide Web • Networking • Office Suites
Operating Systems • Personal Finance • Pets • Programming • Recreation • Sports
Spreadsheets • Teacher Resources • Test Prep • Word Processing

IDG BOOKS WORLDWIDE
BOOK REGISTRATION

We want to hear from you!

Visit **http://my2cents.dummies.com** to register this book and tell us how you liked it!

- ✔ Get entered in our monthly prize giveaway.

- ✔ Give us feedback about this book — tell us what you like best, what you like least, or maybe what you'd like to ask the author and us to change!

- ✔ Let us know any other *For Dummies®* topics that interest you.

Your feedback helps us determine what books to publish, tells us what coverage to add as we revise our books, and lets us know whether we're meeting your needs as a *For Dummies* reader. You're our most valuable resource, and what you have to say is important to us!

Not on the Web yet? It's easy to get started with *Dummies 101®: The Internet For Windows® 98* or *The Internet For Dummies®* at local retailers everywhere.

Or let us know what you think by sending us a letter at the following address:

For Dummies Book Registration
Dummies Press
10475 Crosspoint Blvd.
Indianapolis, IN 46256

**BESTSELLING
BOOK SERIES**